New Spirits of Capitalism?

New Spirits of Capitalism?

Crises, Justifications, and Dynamics

Edited by
Paul du Gay and Glenn Morgan

OXFORD
UNIVERSITY PRESS

OXFORD

UNIVERSITY PRESS

Great Clarendon Street, Oxford OX2 6DP
United Kingdom

Oxford University Press is a department of the University of Oxford.
It furthers the University's objective of excellence in research, scholarship,
and education by publishing worldwide.

British Library Cataloguing in Publication Data
Data available

Library of Congress Cataloging in Publication Data
Data available

ISBN 978-0-19-959534-1

Preface

This book began life when the two editors, Paul du Gay and Glenn Morgan, worked together at Warwick Business School (WBS). The publication of Boltanski and Chiapello's book *The New Spirit of Capitalism* clearly offered the possibility to link the distinctive interests characteristic of WBS at the time across a number of dimensions, that is, cultural theories of social reproduction and change, the evolution of work organization, the nature of management in the public and private sectors, as well as the analysis of new forms of capitalism. The book's range, depth of theoretical insight, and empirical detail offered plenty for 'critical' social scientists inside and outside business schools to engage with, not least in the context of the unfolding of the financial crisis. Therefore, following a number of preliminary meetings, the editors decided to organize a small workshop focusing on the explanatory power and reach of the New Spirits thesis, and its capacity to speak to and elucidate the contemporary crisis of financialized capitalism. The event was co-funded by WBS and the ESRC Centre for Research on Social and Cultural Change (CRESC) based at the University of Manchester and the Open University and of which Paul du Gay was a member. We would like to thank both organizations for their support. We would also like to thank all the participants for their contributions, and in particular Luc Boltanski and Eve Chiapello for accepting our invitation to the workshop and taking part in an open and constructive way, even when their book was subjected to heavy criticism. Following the workshop, the editors decided to develop this book drawing in part on papers presented at the original workshop but also commissioning new papers. We would like to thank all the authors for their cooperation in this process, and to express our gratitude to David Musson and Emma Booth at Oxford University Press for encouraging us in this endeavour and helping us to bring it to fruition. Our overall aim was not only to provide both a balanced critique and overview of *New Spirit* (a decade or more after its original publication in French) but also to show how it could be deployed in a variety of empirical studies to develop new insights into the functioning and regulation of capitalism in the contemporary era. We hope the book will encourage others to continue to address and develop the crucial issues which *The New Spirit of Capitalism* elucidated.

Paul du Gay
Copenhagen Business School
Glenn Morgan
Cardiff Business School

May 2012

Contents

Contents

List of Contributors

Luc Boltanski is Professor at the École des Hautes Études en Sciences Sociales, Paris, and along with Luc Thevenot, one of the main founders of the Groupe de Sociologie Politique et Morale which building on Bourdieu has developed its own distinctive identity as the source of a new form of 'pragmatist' social theory which is gaining worldwide influence. This approach has become known in the English-speaking world through *The New Spirit of Capitalism* published first in French in 1999, and the book with Thevenot entitled *On Justification* (first translated in 2005). More recently, Boltanski's *On Critique* has been translated into English (Polity Press, 2010). Boltanski has written many articles and books on a diverse range of subjects; others translated into English include *The Making of Class: Cadres in French Society* (Cambridge University Press, 1987) and *Distant Suffering: Morality, Media and Politics* (Cambridge University Press, 1999).

Eve Chiapello is Professor at the HEC School of Management, Paris, France. She teaches Economic Sociology, Organization Theory, Qualitative Research Methods, and Social Studies of Management Instruments. She has published the following books: *Artistes versus Managers* (Paris: Métailié, 1998) and *Le Nouvel Esprit du Capitalisme* (Paris: Gallimard, 1999, with Luc Boltanski), translated to English (*The New Spirit of Capitalism*, Verso, 2005). She has also published several articles in *Accounting, Organizations and Society*, *Sociologie du travail*, *Critical Perspectives on Accounting*, *Discourse and Society*, *European Journal of Social Theory*, etc.

Paul du Gay is Globaliseringsprofessor in the Department of Organization (IOA) at Copenhagen Business School (CBS). His work is located in the sociology of organizational life and cultural studies. His publications include, *Consumption and Identity at Work*, *In Praise of Bureaucracy*, and *Organizing Identity*. He is currently writing a monograph for Routledge entitled *For State Service: Office as a Vocation*, and editing *The Oxford Handbook of Sociology, Social Theory, and Organization Studies: Contemporary Currents* (with Paul Adler, Glenn Morgan, and Mike Reed). At CBS, he directs the Velux research programme 'What Makes Organization?', and co-directs the 'Business in Society Public–Private Platform'.

Susanne Ekman is Assistant Professor at Department of Organization, Copenhagen Business School. Her research area is in the field of management, knowledge work, professional ethos, and late modernity. Susanne's work is mainly ethnographic. Recent work relevant for this volume includes the book *Authority and Autonomy: Paradoxes in Modern Knowledge Work* (Palgrave Macmillan, 2012).

List of Contributors

Isabelle Huault is Professor of Organization Studies at Paris Dauphine University. She is Head of the DRM Management Research Centre (UMR CNRS 7088). Her research interests lie in the sociology of financial markets, neo-institutionalism, and critical studies with a focus on the social studies of finance and the social construction of markets and organizations.

Peer Hull Kristensen is Professor in the Department of Business and Politics at Copenhagen Business School. He was Chair of the European Group on Organization Studies (EGOS) from 2001 to 2003. His research examines the inter-relationship between firms and institutions, particularly in relationship to labour markets, skills, teamwork, and training. Recent books include *Nordic Capitalisms and Globalization: New Forms of Economic Organization and Welfare Institutions* (Oxford University Press, 2011, edited with K. Lilja) and *Local Players in Global Games: The Strategic Constitution of a Multinational Corporation* (Oxford University Press, 2005, with Jonathan Zeitlin).

Glenn Morgan is Professor of International Management at Cardiff Business School, Cardiff University. His research focuses on different forms of capitalism, the impact of globalization and neo-liberalism, and the changing nature of firms and organizations. From 2005 to 2008, he was Editor-in-Chief of the journal *Organization: The Critical Journal of Theory, Organization and Society*. Recent edited books include *Capitalism and Capitalisms in the 21st Century* (Oxford University Press, 2012, edited with R. Whitley) and *The Oxford Handbook of Comparative Institutional Analysis* (Oxford University Press, 2010, edited with J. L. Campbell, C. Crouch, O. K. Pedersen, and R. Whitley).

Silke Ötsch is Assistant Professor at the Department of Sociology of the University of Innsbruck. She also worked as Project Coordinator at the Department of Sociology and as Researcher and Lecturer at the Faculty of Architecture at the University of Innsbruck. She holds a doctorate in architectural theory from the Bauhaus-University Weimar and studied in Weimar and Paris. She is active in taxation and financial market regulation for Attac and other networks. Her main field of research is financialization, sociology of the profession of the architect, offshore economy, international taxation, regulation, and civil society.

Martin Parker is Professor of Organization and Culture at the University of Leicester School of Management, after a brief sojourn at Warwick Business School. He is Editor-in-Chief of the journal *Organization: The Critical Journal of Theory, Organization and Society*. His current writing is mostly concerned with culture and representation, as well as forms of alternative organization. His latest book is *Alternative Organization: Outlaws, Crime and Culture* (Routledge, 2012).

Pier Paolo Pasqualoni is a Lecturer at the Institute of Educational Science, University of Innsbruck, Austria, specializing in civil society and social movements, conflict transformation and group dynamics, identity and diversity, migration, and higher education research. He also teaches at the Free University of Bolzano (Italy) and at Ramkhamhaeng University (Bangkok, Thailand).

Hélène Rainelli-Weiss is Professor of Finance at the Sorbonne Graduate Business School. Her research interests are in the sociology of financial markets, behavioural finance, and the epistemology of finance. She received her MBA from the Lyons Management

School (France), her MSc in Finance from the University of Lancaster (UK), and her PhD in management sciences from the University of Rennes (France).

Alan Scott is Professor in the School of Behavioural, Cognitive and Social Science, University of New England, NSW, Australia. His research is in the areas of political and organizational sociology, and social theory. Recent work relevant to the theme of this volume includes *State Transformation or Regime Shift?* (co-authored with Paul du Gay), *Sociologica* (2/2010), *Capitalism as Culture* (and as *Kultur*), and 'Weber-Simmel-Hirschman', *Journal of Classical Sociology* (2012). He is also co-editor of the *Wiley-Blackwell Companion to Political Sociology* (2012).

Kathia Serrano-Velarde is Assistant Professor for Sociology of Organization and Culture at Heidelberg University. Her research focuses on the transformation processes in European education and research. She wrote her award winning Ph.D. (Humboldt Universität zu Berlin) on the emergence of a German market for quality assurance agencies. From 2007 to 2008, she worked as postdoctoral fellow at the Centre de Sociologie des Organisations in Paris before joining the Max Weber Institute of Sociology at Heidelberg.

Nigel Thrift has been Vice-Chancellor of the University of Warwick since July 2006. He is one of the world's leading human geographers and social scientists. He is a Fellow of the British Academy. His current research spans a broad range of interests, including international finance, cities and political life, non-representational theory, affective politics, and the history of time.

Hugh Willmott is Research Professor in Organization Studies, Cardiff Business School, and a Visiting Professor at the University of Technology, Sydney. He has previously held professorial appointments at the UMIST (now Manchester Business School) and Cambridge and visiting appointments at the Universities of Lund, Uppsala and Innsbruck. He co-founded the International Labor Process Conference and the International Critical Management Studies Conference. He has contributed to leading management and social science journals and has published numerous books. Full details can be found on his homepage: https://sites.google.com/site/hughwillmottshomepage

List of Tables

1

Understanding Capitalism: Crises, Legitimacy, and Change Through the Prism of *The New Spirit of Capitalism*

Paul du Gay and Glenn Morgan

Introduction

Published in France in 1999 (and then in English in 2005 with a new preface), *The New Spirit of Capitalism* (NSC) immediately became something of a publishing sensation in France (and later in the United Kingdom and the United States), enjoying a scope and scale of public commentary rarely enjoyed by social science texts, especially ones weighing in at 843 densely argued pages. It received considerable attention in the French media, for example, sparking debate not simply about the meaning, significance, and effects of contemporary mutations in economic and organizational life, but becoming a reference point in political discussions about the future of the welfare state and the possibilities both of collective action in a 'networked' world, and of reconciling the interests of social justice with the 'laws of the markets' (Leca and Naccache, 2006). Such a reception is not as surprising as it might first appear, not simply because the themes of the text spoke to a popular sense of discontent concerning the nature, direction, and consequences of the 'neo-liberal' experiment (in France, as elsewhere), but also because this massive book offered a comprehensive and subtle series of discrete but inter-related arguments (it is really several books under one set of covers)—combining sociological and cultural analysis, socio-historical narrative, political economy, and engaged advocacy (Budgen, 2000: 149)—that chimed with ongoing debates about the meaning, significance, and effects of changing forms of capitalism and the role of neo-liberalism as these were being articulated in a disparate range of fields (Blackledge, 2007; Budgen, 2000; Fligstein, 2006; Guilhot,

2000; Katz, 2007; Kemple, 2007; Kogut, 2000; McTavish, 2009; Mohanty, 2010; Parker, 2008; Piore, 2000; Reid, 2000; Ross, 2000; Turner, 2007). When taken together, these arguments offered some important clues as to how and why neo-liberalism has proven so resilient and adaptable when faced with evidence of its own hubris. This edited book was therefore born out of the effort to interrogate the perspectives, tools, and techniques developed by Boltanski and Chiapello in relation to the development of neo-liberal capitalism in the period since their original publication and in particular the culmination of these developments in the ongoing crisis since the financial collapse of 2007–8.

The crisis of neo-liberalism and the *New Spirit of Capitalism*

The financial crisis that erupted in 2008–9 and whose latest turn, at the time of writing, has unfolded in the form of the so-called 'sovereign debt crisis' appear to signify the tipping point for a set of ideas and practices that have gained a remarkable hold over the conduct of governments, institutions, organizations, and individuals since the late 1970s. These ideas and practices are often gathered together under the heading of 'neo-liberalism', though they have elicited many categorizations—'advanced liberalism' (Rose, 1999), 'turbo capitalism' (Luttwak, 1999), 'knowing capitalism' (Thrift, 2005, and this volume), and 'the new spirit of capitalism' (Boltanski and Chiapello, 2005), to name but a few. While there are clearly explanatory dangers in grouping an often quite heterogeneous range of ideas, norms, devices, and techniques, frequently lashed up in contingent ways to address quite specific problems, in particular locales, under a single amorphous heading (thereby overplaying their coherence and homogeneity), it is not too fanciful to claim that the different branches and brands of this 'neo-liberalism' do share a certain family resemblance, thematically at least (Blyth, 2002; Burchell, 1996; Harvey, 2005; Peck, 2010; see also Foucault, 2008 for an early and prescient analysis of forms of neo-liberalism—the book is based on lectures delivered in 1978–9). Indeed, the term 'neo-liberalism' in a sense came to provide a certain rationality, a way of linking up these diverse developments so they appeared to partake of a coherent logic. And once they did so, once a kind of rationality could be extracted from them, allowing translations between them, it could itself be redirected towards both them and other objects and persons, which were able to be thought about in the same way—as for example, with the various uses of the term 'entrepreneurship', 'empowerment', 'market', and 'choice'. And such rationalities came to be embodied in or infused a range of practices for governing economic life, public management, medical care, welfare policy, and so on (du Gay, 1996; Foucault, 2008; Rose, 1999).

This neo-liberal rationality holds few surprises now. Indeed, its basic assumptions and technical repertoire are both relatively limited and easily delineated. They have not altered much over time, though their reach has expanded considerably. One of the dominant themes of this rationality, simply expressed, relates to what we might term 'the imagined market' (Mac-Kenzie, 2005, 2006): the basic assumption that 'marketization' provides the best means of satisfying a range of aspirations, collective and individual, and that markets are in particular to be preferred to states and politics, which are at best inefficient and sclerotic, and at worst threats to liberty and freedom (Peck, 2010). The embeddedness of this approach in the discipline of economics, most particularly in the Chicago School, and its strong association with a politics that sought to shrink the state, at least in terms of its regulation of business and its provision of welfare and other collective services, created powerful coalitions of politicians, experts, and corporate interests at national and international levels that pushed forward forms of neo-liberal policies in many countries and international institutions from the 1980s onwards (on neo-liberalism and the discipline of economics, see Peck, 2010; also Fourcade, 2009; on the diffusion of neo-liberal ideas and their differential adoption in distinctive national contexts, see Blyth, 2002; Fourcade-Gourinchas and Babb, 2002; Prasad, 2006; Simmons et al., 2008; Streeck, 2009; on the role of international bodies such as the European Union (EU), the World Trade Organization (WTO), and the World Bank in these processes, see Abdelal, 2007; Chwieroth, 2010; Jabko, 2006).

The ongoing financial crisis has challenged many of the tropes of this rationality—how could it be that contemporary financial markets, perhaps some of the most complex and sophisticated market forms ever invented, could cause such untold trouble on such a massive scale, when economic theory, for instance, had demonstrated time and again that unregulated financial markets would be self-correcting? Similarly, how was it that financial institutions facing imminent collapse had to rely upon states—those sclerotic and inflexible enemies of liberty and efficiency—to rescue them? Surely, these dramatic events alone attest to certain problems with the tropes of marketization and thus point to some severe limits to the rationality of neo-liberalism to which they are attached. As Colin Crouch (2011) among others has indicated, though, such severe testing of neo-liberal rationality has had some perverse outcomes. States, for instance, hailed in 2008–9 as saviours of the financial system from its own self-destructiveness and thus as guarantors of social peace in Western societies (without the authoritative action that only states are capable of it is not difficult to imagine what the consequences for civic life would have been) have quite quickly found themselves under pressure once again to offload crucial aspects of their 'stateness' to the very markets they helped save from disaster. As the financial crisis has transmuted

3

into a 'sovereign debt crisis', the very basis of state authority and political life and capacity has once again been put into question. Thus, both Greece and Italy have been forced to establish 'technocratic' governments committed to 'austerity' and massive reductions of the public sector budget in order to cut deficits and pay interest on government bonds. In Spain and Ireland, elected governments based on party allegiances rather than technocratic selection have nevertheless sought to appease the financial markets and their representatives in the International Monetary Fund (IMF) and the EU by imposing similarly stringent austerity packages. Elsewhere around Europe, governments have also been seeking to cope with this pressure to reduce deficits whilst maintaining popular legitimacy. Trade union action on specific issues such as job losses, wage cuts, changes in the employment rights of part-time and temporary workers, pension downgrades, etc., along with wider based protests against austerity and finance (e.g. as in the Occupy movement or the Indignados in Spain) as well as outbreaks of undirected, violent disorder, as in London, Madrid, Paris, and Athens in the period since 2010 attest to the stress which this conjuncture is placing on state authority and political life. National electorates feel they are being by-passed as governments develop austerity packages and policies designed in the first instance to appeal to (and to appease) financial market participants (Streeck, 2011). Many of the governing parties at the time of the financial crisis in 2007–8 have been turned out of office by disillusioned electorates, only to be replaced by other parties that have implemented swingeing austerity measures. Maintaining political legitimacy and support in these contexts has been highly precarious, dependent on the state of the opposition and the ability to mobilize specific discourses of 'national emergency' that fit with particular historical experiences and societal trajectories (see e.g. the discussions in Grant and Wilson, 2012). In many countries, extreme left and right wing parties seek to build on this disillusion with the existing political leadership, frequently through rejecting globalization and advocating renewed forms of national self-determination (often in conjunction with anti-immigrant rhetoric). In the European context, this is frequently articulated as part of a broader rejection of the economic, political, and social institutions of the EU in favour of a narrow nationalism or 'economic patriotism' (see Clift and Woll, 2012). The current situation therefore appears as a crisis in the relationship between the economic imperatives of neo-liberal capitalism and the political institutions of democracy, the welfare state, and the legitimacy processes that provide the necessary social cohesion for property rights, contracts, and the operation of capitalist markets (Streeck, 2011).

In 1944, reflecting on the depression of the inter-war years and the reforms of the New Deal, Polanyi identified the potential for combined crises of politics and the market in capitalism as leading to a double movement in which markets were 'tamed' by institutions that set limits on their extension and application, by, for example, establishing collective welfare provision, rights to trade union organization, taxation systems based on the ability to pay, regulation of financial institutions, etc. (Polanyi, 2001; first published in 1944). In the subsequent 'trentes glorieuses' in the developed economies, this taming could be seen as, in Streeck's terms, a 'beneficial constraint' (Streeck, 1997) that allowed a reformed capitalism to grow at least in part through releasing the consumption potential of the population as a whole, a point emphasized by members of the French 'regulationist' school such as Aglietta (1979) and Boyer (1990). The state played a central role in this by regulating the labour market in ways that increased nominal and, for a period, real wages, expanded employment through the public sector, managed output through manipulating the availability of credit as well as the broader fiscal context of economic growth, and, crucially, implemented a welfare system that provided a floor beneath which families could not fall as well as an educational and training system that increased the quality of 'human capital' and the possibilities of social mobility. For a time, this form of capitalism also enabled a stabilization in the rate of profit, though this was gradually undermined by the growth of trade union and employee power under Keynesian conditions leading to inflation and a struggle over distribution which led to what was labelled by the early 1970s as 'the profits squeeze' (Glyn and Sutcliffe, 1972), a phenomenon particularly associated with the United Kingdom and the United States but present also during the 1970s in other more corporatist societies such as France, Germany, Denmark, and Sweden.

The crisis of Keynesianism in the 1970s and its gradual replacement by neo-liberalism undermined each of these pillars and reflected the stagflation that emerged in this period, leading to declining real wages, increasing unemployment, decreased investment, and cuts in state expenditure. Even during the triumph of Keynesianism, neo-liberal economists drawing on Hayek, the polemical skills of Friedman, and the broad network of think-tanks and policy institutes built from the Mont Pelerin Society (see Mirowski and Plehwe, 2009; Peck, 2010) had argued that the policies of this era had reduced market incentives and this was leading to low productivity, low innovation, and low profits, all of which further reduced investment and increased unemployment. The resultant increases in state expenditure on social programmes led to high taxes and high inflation, further reducing incentives for investment. Therefore, governments needed to reduce taxation, increase labour market incentives, control the money supply, deregulate markets, cut barriers to foreign trade, and, above all, allow competition full rein between firms and in the labour and capital markets. These authors also articulated this as a critique of the politics of the era. Hayek's *The Road to Serfdom* (originally published in both the United Kingdom and the United States in 1944—the same year as Polanyi's *The Great Transformation*: both originated from Vienna where they moved in the same circles of intellectuals during the 1920s) linked free markets to free individuals and state regulation of markets to a form of state despotism. Therefore, the battle for free markets was a battle for liberalism and individualism against the state and socialism. For Hayek, there was no middle ground (see the discussion in Peck, 2010).

From the period of Thatcher and Reagan in the late 1970s and early 1980s, these policies became implemented in a range of different countries. In the developed economies, resistance to neo-liberalism and the adaptation of key elements to the path-dependent trajectory of social forces and institutions shaped a process of differential adoption (see Blyth, 2002; Prasad, 2006), though by the 1990s it was clear that most social democratic parties were adjusting to the new reality. Discourses of the Third Way, which circulated particularly around the advisers of Clinton and Blair (reflecting the influence of the sociologist Anthony Giddens: Giddens, 1998), provided a way of superficially distinguishing the social democratic form of neo-liberalism from that instituted by parties of the right whilst still acknowledging the centrality of the 'market' in a way that went beyond the cautious pragmatic acceptance of earlier generations of leftist, non-Marxist politicians. In the developing world, international institutions such as the World Bank and the IMF became active agents in diffusing these policy prescriptions (known as the Washington Consensus) and helping governments to put them into practice as 'structural adjustment policies' in return for various forms of aid (Chwieroth, 2010; Woods, 2006).

By the late 1980s, the impact of these policies was being felt particularly in those developed countries most strongly committed to neo-liberalism, that is, the United Kingdom and the United States, but also in various ways in other Western European economies such as France (Schmidt, 1996, 2002), Germany (Streeck, 2009), and Sweden (Blyth, 2002) where neo-liberalism had to contend with strong path-dependent forces of resistance to its wholesale implementation. Wages in the advanced economies were held down as globalization provided access to cheap labour, through enabling firms to shift production from high-wage areas and to pressurize employees and trade unions in those areas to reduce their expectations of real wage increases in return for maintaining employment. The impact of this varied, but real wages for the bulk of the working population in the United States, for example, have stagnated for the last thirty years (while the rich have got richer) as a result of this interplay between globalization and employer strategies (Hacker and Pierson, 2010). This pointed to a growing divergence within economies in that standardized manufacturing jobs could be easily outsourced but what were becoming known as 'knowledge-worker jobs' (in advanced manufacturing, information technology (IT), professional services, financial services, etc.) were more 'sticky' and relied on the sort of educational and cultural capital that the Western economies still appeared to monopolize, though by the end of the first decade of the twenty-first century, even this was in doubt (Brown et al., 2001, 2011). Thus, those who were less skilled found their employment opportunities shrinking further, whilst the more skilled embedded in globally competitive firms and sectors found their opportunities increasing. Forms of unemployment and under-employment expanded, whilst the core of full-time employees with high wages and benefits failed to grow and in some cases shrank. Many Western societies developed a tier of jobs that were part-time or temporary, low-paid, and low-skilled with limited pension rights—usually in the service sector such as in the expansion of retail and fast-food outlets and in the personal service sector, looking after the old and the infirm. To push workers into these low-paid jobs, conditions for receiving unemployment benefit or other non-work compensation schemes became more restrictive. The resulting dualism and the pressure on the principles of the welfare state have been further exacerbated by the effects of the financial crisis (Palier, 2010; Palier and Thelen, 2010). Only a handful of countries, most particularly the Nordic countries, seemed capable of avoiding this fate, at least to some extent (see Kristensen and Lilja, 2010; also Kristensen in this volume).

At the same time, the state sector itself was becoming increasingly transformed along neo-liberal lines. Four main lines of development can be noted which went furthest in the United Kingdom but also occurred to a varying extent in other countries. The first and most obvious is the process of privatization, the selling off of state assets into the private sector, which occurred in the United Kingdom in the 1980s and more gradually in countries such as France over the next twenty years. The argument here was that market incentives would improve provision for customers through forcing managements to take more responsibility for managing capital requirements and wages. It would also reduce the pressure on state finances. Secondly, those services that could not be sold off wholesale could be subcontracted out to private providers, again providing more market incentives. Thirdly, many other services could be placed at an arm's length from government in the form of public agencies which would have in theory more control over their own management, as in the case in the United Kingdom in terms of various sizes of organization, ranging from the National Health Service at one end through to primary schools at the other (which were allowed to opt out from local authority control). Finally, those services which for whatever reason had to remain within the state sector would be revolutionized by a new public management ethos and set of practices that would draw directly from the private sector in terms of setting performance targets for individuals, adjusting rewards more carefully to marketable skills, and emphasizing a new entrepreneurship in the public sector (see the chapters in this book by Du Gay, Otsche et al., and Serrano-Velade for analyses of different aspects of these changes in the public sector).

In retrospect, there were certain obvious effects of this process. Firstly, it greatly increased inequalities in the public sector as the winners from this supposed market competition were undoubtedly the top executives whose reward packages rose dramatically in contexts where performance measurement and targets were actually poorly set. Secondly, the private sector increasingly penetrated into the heart of government, providing advisers and expertise in all sorts of ways to governments engaged in the marketization process. Thirdly, the private sector frequently shaped the markets in ways that reduced competition over the medium term, for example in public–private financing where governments guaranteed the winning company a long-term rate of return that could not have been achieved had there been more 'real' competition. In effect, as might be expected, 'quasi-markets' were quasi most obviously in this sense—they allowed companies to set their own prices with limited oversight from the new regulatory bodies such as OFCOM and others (see Crouch, 2011 for a clear and devastating account of the consequences of these changes in the UK public sector). Finally, employees in the state sector found themselves the object of much of the reform process, with rewards and conditions of employment and pension rights becoming more 'flexible', that is, being lowered, as a result of these structural changes.

Alongside these changes, however, in particular sectors such as banking and amongst particular groups of top level managers in both the public and the private sectors, salary packages grew hugely in value through the provision of performance-based rewards and annual bonuses. These developments were justified in terms of incentives to top managers to create wealth that would 'trickle down' to other groups in society, a process that for a time during the late 1990s and 2000s had a superficial validity, particularly where the forms of economic growth led to asset price booms as was most obviously the case as the financial industry expanded through encouraging people to take on more debt in the belief that the value of assets purchased in this way would quickly grow. States also reformed their taxation systems to reduce income tax levels on the wealthy, to bring down corporate taxes, and to increase indirect taxes on consumption. Thus, conditions for becoming rich and retaining that wealth became easier under conditions of neo-liberalism, a process that also inevitably led this group and some of the upper middle class to opt out of state provision of personal services such as education and health, thus increasing the tension over the nature and level of these services. This growing inequality made funding of welfare state provision increasingly problematic as life chances diverged.

A central part of this process was the deregulation that occurred in the financial sector. This took many forms, but one of the most crucial was the way in which control over credit provision (and in this sense, the supply of money) has also been privatized. States ceased to regulate tightly the scale and extent of credit provision undertaken by banks and other institutions. As a result, these organizations, encouraged by central bank commitments to fight price inflation whilst keeping interest rates as low as compatible with that objective, have been able to borrow very easily. This has been facilitated by the global circulation of funds from what Schwartz (2009) has labelled the 'repressed rich' countries (where, for various path-dependent political and social reasons, savings are high, access to credit is restricted, and speculative asset booms have been constrained) to those countries less morally circumspect about credit/debt (Garon, 2012) and indeed increasingly dependent on credit and debt to finance consumption (see also Glyn, 2007). Much of this circulation of funds was based on the inability of the United States in particular to pay for its increasing imports of manufactured goods from places like China, Germany, and Japan through equal amounts of exports. The subsequent balance of payments deficit, made worse by the general high price of raw materials (including oil), was covered in effect by the surplus economies accepting payment in dollars and using these dollars to buy bonds in the United States (particularly Treasury Bonds but also bonds issued by banks and other financial institutions) and earn interest on their investments in this way.

Banks in the United States and the United Kingdom borrowed funds from these investors and then lent them out at higher interest rates (often for longer periods of time) to their customers. Banks had traditionally used this model in order to be profitable; they used their short-term deposits where they kept interest rates low in order to lend long term at higher interest rates. Balancing these long- and short-term commitments has been the key to banking stability, with central banks acting as 'lenders of last resort' (usually in secret) in the event of a liquidity crisis for any particular bank. Runs on banks develop when short-term depositors want their money back and the bank is unable to get access to its long-term funds quickly enough. To prevent this, banks had to maintain a certain amount of capital that would be likely to tide them over any short-term problems—the so-called 'capital adequacy' rules. If things looked like temporarily getting out of hand, then the central bank generally came to the rescue. However, in the era of neo-liberalism, holding capital back to cover uncertainty was seen as unproductive for shareholders. This set up multiple tensions between bank regulators at the national and international level with banking institutions reflected in the negotiations of the Basel accords which have currently gone through three rounds including the latest rethink following the financial crisis. Whilst Basel III, as the rules are known, has been agreed by central bankers, national governments (and the EU) are still discussing how to implement it whilst balancing the interests of financial stability with the specific interests of banks to keep reserves low or to count a wider variety of assets than initially agreed as 'reserves' in order to accommodate both the requirements of banks in the private sector to maximize shareholder value and the need of banks such as the German Landesbanken or the Spanish Caja which are state-backed but not state-owned to readjust their balance sheets gradually to the new austerity. Even this set of rules, however, only applied to the formal banking sector (i.e. those organizations which took deposits from retail customers). Institutions such as the investment banks, like Lehman Brothers and Goldman Sachs which prior to the crisis did not hold depositors' funds, were therefore not regulated as 'proper banks' and were free to borrow as much as they wanted subject only to the interest rates at which they could borrow and then lend the money. The concept of 'leverage' described the difference between the total borrowings of these banks and their own capital, which by 2008 had become a ratio of 35:1 for an organization like Lehmans (Sorkin, 2009; on the run on the Northern Rock Building Society in late 2007 and its roots in this mismatch of funding, see Brummer, 2008), meaning that the bank had borrowed more than thirty-five times its own capital. High leverage, usually secured for relatively short-term borrowings that needed to be regularly renewed, allowed banks to lend on the money for longer term periods at higher rates of interest, thus increasing their earnings. The higher the leverage, the more profitable the bank—in theory. However, higher leverage also made these banks increasingly vulnerable if their borrowers started to fail. Their reserves were completely inadequate if borrowers started to fail and lenders proved unwilling to renew loans. By 2007, many banks were thin on capital in reserve and vulnerable to a withdrawal of short-term funds, making the financial system increasingly risky.

This was exacerbated by the fact that innovations in financial markets enabled firms that had made these loans to then package them up into bonds (what are known as asset-backed securities—ABS for short) and sell them to institutional investors (see e.g. the descriptions in Tett, 2009 and Sorkin, 2009 of these processes). With the funds that they received from these sales, they could then lend again. This process of credit creation could proceed ad infinitum as long as there were willing borrowers (which there were in the United States and the United Kingdom, where a house price boom was being created) and willing buyers of the mortgage-based ABS (which there were due to, firstly, the interest rates on these bonds which were high compared to other similar forms of investment and, secondly, the ability to protect against credit loss because of the innovation of credit default swaps). The development of credit default swaps enabled lenders to provide credit and investors to buy these bonds in the belief that they were protected against losses if loans went bad—a judgement which had some truth where each credit failure was idiosyncratic and individual but proved totally wrong where a wider set of factors generated losses across a wide variety of loans—as occurred with the financial crash in 2007–8 (see e.g. Engelen et al., 2011; MacKenzie, 2011; Morgan, 2008, 2010; Roubini, 2011; Sorkin, 2009; Tett, 2009).

This flow of funds and the general belief that credit risk had been traded away facilitated the creation of a wide variety of speculative booms that emerged in housing markets, bond markets, and stock markets over the last thirty years, only to be followed by collapses such as the Asian crisis of 1997–8, the dot-com crash of 2001, and, most spectacularly, the financial crisis beginning in late 2007. This credit creation process has been labelled in various ways such as by Crouch as 'privatized Keynesianism' or by others as 'financialization' (Crouch, 2008; Engelen et al., 2011; Erturk et al., 2008; Froud et al., 2006; Langley, 2008). Credit creation and asset price booms, particularly in housing and shares, bridged the gap in the United States between stagnating real incomes and expectations of increased standards of living. Since 2007, the precarious nature of this bridge has been fully visible, with individuals, firms, and governments revealed to be highly indebted and over-leveraged once the price of these assets crashed.

The dominance of neo-liberalism then provides a paradox. Why did the wider population acquiesce in its rise when the consequences were so problematic for income inequality, the nature of employment, and the provision of welfare services through the state and the housing market? Further, why, when it was so clearly because of neo-liberal policies that the world entered the economic crisis that is still ongoing and causing such devastating consequences to many people, has there been so little determined opposition to imposing neo-liberal solutions to a problem caused by neo-liberalism? The problem to be explained then becomes not why neo-liberalism has bitten the dust but rather how this rationality has proven so robust and continues to exert such remarkable influence. How and why, in other words, has the financial crisis become problematized in such a way that neo-liberal solutions—cuts in public spending, offloading more of the functions of government to private or not for profit providers, the creation of quasi-markets in areas traditionally governed by other logics—present themselves as the obvious remedies to resolve it? As Crouch (2011) puts it, '[W]hat we have to understand today is, therefore, the strange non-death of neo-liberalism' (see also Engelen et al., 2011 for a discussion of what they label *The Great Complacence*).

The contribution of *The New Spirit of Capitalism*

Although Luc Boltanski and Eve Chiapello's *The New Spirit of Capitalism* (NSC) rarely deploys the term 'neo-liberalism', the analysis they undertake offers a distinctive take on the conundrum just posed, though one conducted *avant la lettre*, as it were. NSC is a massive work of synthesis that produces an original and compelling vision of the changing nature of capitalism in the last few decades. This synthesis consists in a distinct historical perspective about the relationship between capitalism and 'spirit', as well as a specific sociological orientation that is both theoretically supple and conceptually sophisticated. In the first part of this section, we examine what Boltanski and Chiapello mean by 'the new spirit of capitalism' and how this offers a novel perspective on the nature of neo-liberalism in the current period. In the following sections, we explore the theoretical basis of this analysis in terms of its distinctive form of sociological framing and mode of critical engagement.

The nature of capitalism and spirits of capitalism

The project of NSC centres on the discourses, norms, and techniques of conduct—the rationality—that not only gird(s) the historical forms of capital accumulation as these have taken shape over the last three decades but also infuse(s) a diverse range of practices in a host of contexts, such as the provision of social welfare and the conduct of public management, for example. The analysis is centred around a—to some—surprisingly old-fashioned invocation of the work of Max Weber. In a nod to the foreword of Weber's *The Protestant Ethic*, Boltanski and Chiapello characterize their central object—capitalism—in a minimalist way as 'an imperative to unlimited capital accumulation by formally peaceful means' (2005: 4). They do so not only in order to distance their analysis from certain accumulated intellectual and ideological baggage, notably of a structural Marxist stamp (of which, more later), but also as a means through which to indicate that this imperative is constantly in need of justification, not least because, in order to work, it has to mobilize fantastic powers and to implicate a very large number of human beings in the overall accumulation process, people whose individual chances of extracting benefit from capitalistic practices are frequently not very great and who are by no means 'particularly motivated to engage in them' (2005: 8). This claim is something like a springboard for the main argument of the thesis: that the capitalistic imperative requires ethical motives of involvement to justify and normalize the individual dispositions and capacities involved in its processes. The quality of these commitments on behalf of those involved in them is thus seen to depend upon 'the arguments that can be cited to bring out not only the advantages which participation in capitalistic processes might afford on an individual basis but the collective benefits, defined in terms of the common good, which it contributes to producing for everyone' (2005: 4). It is the latter that they characterize as 'the spirit of capitalism'. A la Weber, this 'spirit' presupposes the establishment of a certain moral relationship between human beings and their work, one that provides them with 'good reasons' for pursuing certain activities—an ethical and psychological motivation for devoting themselves to the tasks at hand. However, as indicated, this 'spirit' is not simply reducible to the furnishing of 'individual reasons', it also requires justifications in terms of the common good.

It is here that Boltanski and Chiapello turn to a work that might reasonably be considered the finest piece of Weberian historical sociology of the last half century, Albert Hirschman's (1977) *The Passions and the Interests*. Hirschman reformulates Weber's basic question—how does it come about, historically, that an activity barely considered morally tolerable at the time of its emergence, becomes a 'calling'—a 'vocation'—in the following manner: '[h]ow did commercial, banking, and similar money-making pursuits become honorable ... after having stood condemned or despised as greed, love of lucre, and avarice for centuries past?' (1977: 9). For Hirschman, the answer to this question lies in an urgent search undertaken by political elites and their counsellors in Europe in the early modern period 'for a new way of avoiding society's ruin, permanently threatening at the time because of precarious arrangements for internal and external order' (1977: 130). Similar questions were raised by Elias (2000) in *The Civilizing Process*; how was it that societies moved from being driven by warfare and aristocratic ideals of military glory which involved enrichment through acts of plunder, land expansion, and civil war towards societies that valued peace and the ability to grow rich through processes of accumulation and investment? Marx and subsequent theorists of imperialism (most obviously Lenin) doubted this distinction, pointing to the process of 'primitive accumulation' that was necessary to the development and further growth of capitalism and often required coercion and violence at home and in overseas empires as well as leading to wars between imperialist powers. However, sociologists such as Weber, Hirschman, and Elias as well as early political economists, most notably Adam Smith (see e.g. Smith, 1976), preferred to emphasize this process of change from aristocracy, war, and plunder to bourgeois ideals of stable property rights, peaceful coexistence, and the development of conditions to allow capital accumulation and the growth of market society. They saw a distinctive new phase in the management of social order, one associated with the rule of law and forms of representative government, as the basis for market expansion.

According to Hirschman, weary of the destruction caused by the unbridled passions, and bent on reform, these elites of the early modern era became hopeful that the 'mild' passion for money-making and calculation, 'although admittedly ignoble and uncouth, could defeat and bury the violent passion that so ruinously stoked the endless cycles of civil butchery' (Holmes, 1995: 54). This argument reflects what Fourcade and Healy discuss as the *doux commerce* thesis associated with Smith and his contemporaries in which 'markets nurture a long list of *bourgeois* virtues including integrity, honesty, trustworthiness, enterprise, respect, modesty and responsibility' (Fourcade and Healy, 2007: 4) through freeing the individual from status orders based on feudalism and military service.

These attempts to harness the moderating effects of 'enlightened self-interest' were therefore driven by a political need to counteract and neutralize what were seen as the destructive consequences of mobilizing passion in the service of a religious cause and aristocratic ideals. Commerce might be 'low', but in contrast to the bloody and destructive consequences of the pursuit of glory or religious fanaticism, it might be a more civilized and less unpredictable form of life. Interests might be base, but they could also potentially 'raise the comfort level of social interaction' (Holmes, 1995: 54). For Boltanski and Chiapello (2005: 9–10), Hirschman's thesis provides a detailed attempt to think through the justification for capitalistic practices 'before its triumph' in terms of its wider socio-political benefits. It thus offers an important supplement, in their view, to Weber's work on the protestant ethic by highlighting the need for capitalistic practices not only to furnish 'individual reasons' but also justifications in terms of the common good. Central to their analysis is also the idea that this 'spirit' is an energizing force that enters into social actors' sense of themselves as particular sorts of persons. In its early phases, then, the spirit 'moves people', and gets them enthused about building the institutions and practices that become available as possibilities once the 'new spirit' becomes articulated. As we will discuss later, this energizing capacity gradually faces challenges as the initial promises run up against oppositional forces and changes in the broader social and economic context induced by the very success of the 'new spirit'. However, this idea of a particular 'spirit of capitalism' becomes embedded in rules of conduct, in practices, and in institutions as well as in certain forms of legitimatory discourses that explain, normalize, and motivate actors. To shed that 'spirit' or to establish a critique of it then becomes a hugely difficult task as we are seeing with what Crouch calls the 'strange non-death of neo-liberalism' (Crouch, 2011).

The historical work of Weber and others on 'justifications' for capitalistic practices stand as something like the 'foundations' upon which the project of NSC is established. It also functions as a jumping-off point for the project's second main intellectual reference: the Regulation School's account of capitalistic transformations (Aglietta, 1979; Boyer, 1990). This provides a framework for interrogating more closely the dynamics of capitalism in relation to the idea of 'spirit'. Drawing from the Regulationists, Boltanski and Chiapello (2005: 16ff.) argue that each displacement of the forms of capitalistic accumulation requires a 'new spirit of capitalism'. This is a direct echo of the Regulationist maxim that to each 'regime of accumulation' there corresponds, more or less evidently, a number of converging mediations that maintains within the limits of social cohesion the disruptive effects of the accumulation process and thus aids in its reproduction. As Guilhot (2000: 357) points out, 'the idea that capitalism is a blind force that does not find any principle of self-limitation and orientation within itself and needs to be embedded in constraining structures that embody socially legitimate conventions is directly imported from the regulationist account'.

The Regulationist school had in effect extended Polanyi's insight about the double movement; without the development of social movements that seek to build, through the state, institutions that protect citizens to a degree against market forces, capitalism would generate such internal tensions and conflicts that it could not work. It therefore 'needs' institutions, if we understand 'needs' not as essentialist and pre-given or teleological but as emergent from specific forms of political response to crises and conflicts. In the Regulationist school, the inter-relationship between particular forms of capitalist organization and particular forms of social institutions is given a more specific historical context than that proposed by Polanyi which was limited to his reflections on the emergence of the New Deal on one hand and Nazi/Communist forms of totalitarianism on the other as ways of dealing with the 1930s Great Depression. The Regulationists emphasize the way in which phases of capitalism link to consumption processes, both as a means of absorbing a certain level of production and also a route to the promotion of social cohesion by providing improved standards of living for the population.

The post-war period in the major Western economies was characterized variously by Regulationists and others as Fordism or Keynesianism to emphasize the way in which the requirements of capitalist production were moderated and shaped by institutions and normative structures, the role of which was to manage markets in ways that limited their negative consequences and indeed generated positive support and energy for capitalism. Thus, what might be crudely termed, following Boltanski and Chiapello, as the 'second spirit of capitalism' was associated with security at work (employment protection, trade union bargaining, pensionable employment, etc.), security at home (the welfare state for health, education, etc.), participation in a mass consumption society and broader expectations about rising standards of living, increased social mobility, and 'a better life', underpinned by greater equality of opportunity. It is the breakdown of this 'spirit', symbolized by the

May 1968 events in Paris and its replacement by a 'new spirit', that is at the heart of the book.

The Regulationists were also amongst the earliest proponents of the idea of 'post-Fordism' (Boyer and Durand, 1997). Post-Fordism was an early way of describing the decline of large managerial hierarchies and their replacement by networks of small and medium-sized enterprises linked through a variety of institutional, social, and contractual forms of relations (see e.g. the collection of articles in Amin, 1992). Central to these changes was the growing significance of global competition, freedom to locate in different parts of the world (in order both to cheapen production and on the other side to access distinctive new knowledge), and new forms of innovation that undermined the sort of long-term planning characteristic of the large managerial hierarchies. Instead, theorists of post-Fordism emphasized the replacement of large firms by smaller, flexible firms capable, through networking activities, of bringing together knowledge and production processes rapidly and launching highly innovative products into previously untapped markets (as has repeatedly happened in the area of IT-enabled innovations such as the Internet, mobile telephony, etc.). In this form of analysis, these changes presaged similar changes in the structure of the welfare state (towards what Jessop in his critical extension of regulation theory has termed the 'Schumpeterian workfare state'; Jessop and Sum, 2006) as well as in the nature of consumption which was being more individualized and driven by processes of branding and self-identity rather than simply the procurement of consumable goods with specific use values. Many of the tropes of post-Fordism (such as the emphasis on flexibility and mobility) enter directly into Boltanski and Chiapello though without much acknowledgement—as is the case with a number of themes in the book.

Sociological frameworks and the logic of justification

The idea of 'spirit' as well as its relationship to capitalism and processes of crisis and change is given a stronger meaning if we trace its evolution back to Boltanski's earlier work with Thévenot (Boltanski and Thévenot, 2006; first published in French as far back as 1987 and then in a much revised version in 1991). One of the first moves made by Boltanski and Thévenot is to demonstrate that modern economies contain multiple principles of evaluation or what Boltanski and Thévenot refer to as 'orders of worth' (Stark, 2010: 11). In this context, concepts of value and worth play with the two senses of the term in the English language. The first is the idea of esteem, that is, that social actors esteem certain characteristics or forms of practices, behaviours, or institutional structures. They consider them 'valuable' to the form of life in which they are embedded. The second idea of value is that stemming from the idea of evaluation, that is, being able to identify when a characteristic is more or less present. Putting these two aspects together, therefore, orders of worth are 'the very fabric of calculation, of rationality, of value' (Stark, 2010: 11). Hence, for Boltanski and Thévenot, all economies are 'moral economies'. Each of the orders of worth operating within the field of economic life is an economy, and as an economy each is a moral order. In *On Justification*, Boltanski and Thévenot delineate six discrete orders of worth, each epitomized by a distinctive moral philosophy, and illustrate the operation of these within a single domain, that of the large corporation, through a content analysis of six best selling management texts—each embodying a different order as a central generating mechanism. In addition to a *market* rationality, they identify an *industrial* or technological rationality, another organized around a *civic* logic, and others embodying a *reputational*, or *inspirational* logic, or organized according to principles of *renown* or fame. These six 'cities', as they term them, offer philosophical codifications and principles of evaluation for both individual action and a politics of the common good—the just, the fair, and so forth—but according to different, non-reducible criteria of judgement. Each qualifies persons and things with a distinctive grammar.

On Justification also indicates in some detail how these different principles of evaluation entail discrete metrics, measuring instruments, 'tests', and proofs of worth objectified in material cultural artefacts and devices. Much like Weber's focus on *Lebensordnung* and *Lebensführung*, Boltanski and Thévenot indicate precisely how life can be rationalized—philosophically, morally, technically—from a number of different starting points, and in a number of different directions. They emphasize that each order of worth implies certain conventions and tests which have a strategic importance at a given moment in time. In other words, each order of worth implies a specific set of beliefs about how the world works, which in turn lead to expectations about appropriate sets of behaviours, actions, and outcomes that are embedded in specific conventions and tests. By this is meant the idea that these normative structures set limits to what can legitimately be done in a certain context if the central values of the order of worth are to be sustained. Exactly what these limits are is usually unclear, but where social actors that adhere to these orders of worth perceive the limits as being reached (or breached), then they are inclined to protest, to resist, and to question the legitimacy of the system.

The idea that every order of worth has within it a 'test' or a series of tests which can be applied to see whether it is still working appropriately or not is key to understanding the dynamics of change in capitalism. The concept of 'test' implies that actors may begin to doubt the claim that the general good is being served by a particular order of worth. These doubts may focus on a specific set of institutions that become increasingly contested—probably through a process whereby local dissatisfactions build up, coalesce, and

17

extend into broader political and/or social movements. Boltanski and Chiapello, as an example of this process, refer frequently to the case of the French
educational system in the post-war period and its capacity to deliver social
mobility on a meritocratic basis. The 'test' in broad terms revolves around
arguments as to whether this actually occurs; for that reason, Boltanski and
Chiapello sometimes refer to the idea of 'reality tests' to evoke this gap
between rhetoric and what actually happens. The authors make clear that
this is in the first instance an 'internalist' critique; it takes the claims of the
particular order of worth seriously and tests them in the terms that are used
within the discourse. It does not invoke moral orders from outside as criteria
for the test. This 'immanentism' is a tough test; in order for the test itself to
be seen as legitimate, there must be a process of 'qualification', that is,
identifying pertinent and relevant phenomena of the order of worth under
consideration that can be considered serious tests of the validity of the order.
This sort of reality test cannot be undertaken by importing principles and
processes from different orders of worth; there must be an 'equivalence'
identified between the various elements in the test. As Boltanski states in a
later work, 'the social actors whose disputes are observed by the sociologist
are *realistic*. They do not demand the impossible.... Actors, at least when
grasped in the course of their everyday activities, take reality and the real
character of the reality test, seriously' (Boltanski, 2011: 31–2). Testing may
occur in very formal ways, for example through 'testing' the law on the rights
and obligations of certain actors. Or it may occur through public debate and
the actions of groups and movements to challenge justificatory logics with
evidence of various sorts. Efforts by employers to establish new working
conditions or by the state to reshape welfare provision may stimulate actors
to 'test' out how far these fit the prevailing justificatory logic, again a process
that can be brought out formally in the courts or informally through political debates—in formal politics but also in civil society more generally. In
tests, therefore, institutional practices, their outcomes, and their relationship to normative structures become subject to scrutiny. The consequence is
the surfacing of conflict, both over the meaning of the current order of worth
and over the idea that another order of worth or logic of justification may be
more appropriate (see the chapter in this book by Huault and Rainelli-Weiss
for an interesting analysis of the inter-relationship between different logics
of justification in the financial markets). Thus, where an order of worth is
shown to be failing by its own criteria, actors may either seek reform or they
may then start to look at the world in a different way. Chiapello, for example,
in her chapter in this book, argues that there is another order of worth
emergent in the contemporary situation, and this is related to the inability
of any other moral vocabulary to adequately deal with the ecological crisis
that is emerging. In this process of contestation, controversy, and debate,

then, societies undergo change as some orders of worth rise in importance and others decline and are superseded.

In an extension of this framework, Bolktanski and Chiapello distinguish between what they term the social and the artistic critiques of forms of capitalism which are applied to justificatory logics. The former critique focuses on how a particular form of activity or institution generates inequalities beyond those justified by the current legitimatory order. In the twentieth century, this type of critique normally manifested itself in mass movements based on broad common objectives for social reform, that is, trade unions and socialist political parties. The artistic critique, on the other hand, focused on how the nature of the individual was being constructed by mass production and mass consumption and the consequences of this constitution of the self in terms of alienation, commodity fetishism, etc. Thus, artistic critiques, 'pour etaper les bourgeoisies', emerged in the visual arts, in music, and in literature, challenging nineteenth-century conventions of the intimate interconnection between art and moral improvement. The relative neglect of material issues tends to confine the relevance of the artistic critique most of the time to a limited elite of actors, often self-defined avant-garde intellectuals whose critique of the current system of capitalism is reflected in demands for individual freedom and autonomy, a struggle reflected in art work that challenges the status quo by deliberately provocative acts or by-passing altogether generally accepted criteria of 'good taste'.

These two forms of critique coexist, though at particular periods one critique may become more central than the other. As a general expectation, the social critique tends to emerge most strongly when the capitalist economy falters and the struggle over redistribution between employees and owners increases in intensity because there is insufficient growth to allow both sides to feel improvements. When standards of living rise and capitalism seems to be purveying economic improvements, then the tendency is for critique to shift to forms of artistic expression, for example against the emptiness of consumption and commodity fetishism or against the alienation of the work environment or, in the latest period, the performance of authenticity (see Ekman, this volume).

As we show later in the chapter, what Boltanski and Chiapello identify as 'the new spirit' maps on to this framework. What they seek to demonstrate is essentially that the dominant order of worth in the Fordist period which could be characterized as 'the industrial city' increasingly failed to live up to the claims it made to serve the 'common good'. It failed the tests that were put to it during the late 1960s and early 1970s in various institutional arenas by different sorts of actors—employers and owners, employees, women, students, consumers, artists, thinkers, and others. These tests were to a significant extent 'artistic' in their origins. As Western societies got richer, questions of survival and the social critique of inequality lost ground. Instead, concerns about the quality of life created by these newly affluent societies came into focus. Did the large corporate hierarchies enable individuals to express themselves? The cultural politics of opposition to 'the man', to sexual repression, to all aspects of conformity, consumption, and massification became stronger. The graffiti of the Paris streets in 1968 and the antics of the Situationists were symbolic of this cultural politics. One representative (if relatively long) graffiti from the streets ran:

> Since 1936 I have fought for wage increases.
> My father before me fought for wage increases,
> Now I have a TV, a fridge, a Volkswagen.
> Yet my whole life has been a drag.
> Don't negotiate with the bosses. Abolish them (from www.bopsecrets.org/CF/
>   graffiti.htm, accessed 23 March 2012)

It was out of this ferment that a new form of capitalism emerged with a new 'spirit' or 'order of worth'—the projective city characterized by a discourse of freedom, autonomy, and self-expression. How this happened is discussed in more detail in the next section.

Put simply, Boltanski and Chiapello argue that, because of its inherent ethical underdetermination, capitalism as a way of life is open to a plurality of potential normative constructions, including elements that, at first sight, appear to be far from functional for processes of accumulation—those that are non-capitalistic or even openly anti-capitalistic. It is this lack of an ethical 'essence' that makes the critique of capitalism contingently constitutive of its spirit—contingent because the nature of the critique and the context of its reception matter. A specific 'spirit' of capitalism is always a construction site, not a finished building, even if it looks remarkably solid and a 'constant'. Critique is continuously probing capitalism, requiring it to justify itself and to stay aligned with the self-professed principles of justice infusing its 'spirit' at a given time, through conventionalized tests, or attempting to discredit these tests and the norms framing them by positing alternative conceptions of worth to which capitalism is represented as inimical, antithetical, blind, or some combination thereof, and to which it must respond, not least through creative assimilation, in order to prove its worth, and thus stay legitimate. In this way, even the most radical of critiques can be put to the service of capitalism, while modifications of capitalism can be traced back to the travail of its critiques.

The sociology of critique and critical sociology

At this point, it is important to note that, as well as providing a conceptual language for discussing and analysing change, these authors are also elaborating a particular view of the nature of the social world. In particular, as has already been mentioned, they wish to avoid structuralist accounts of society and social change. Boltanski and Chiapello deploy the main theoretical tropes developed in *On Justification* to construct a framework 'that makes it possible to combine approaches in terms of *critical sociology*, referring to supra-individual entities (especially capitalism) with the capacity to affect a large number of people over a long period, and approaches derived from pragmatic sociology, stressing action, the normative exigencies that intentional actions claim to be inspired by, and critical operations in particular, by pursuing a programme of a *sociology of critique*' (2005: xii). In *On Justification*, Boltanski and Thévenot (2006) attempt to develop a sociological theory of value, one that attempts to formulate a language that makes it possible to describe people's actions not 'as the realization of potentialities inscribed in structures, or as the execution of a ready-made programme (which boils down to denying that such things as actions actually exist), but inasmuch as they presuppose that decisions and risks are taken in the light of the uncertain situations in which people find themselves' (Boltanski and Chiapello, 2005: xi). In the field of moral values, then, Boltanski and Thévenot are interested in taking the normative principles and ideals that people claim to adhere to seriously, without reducing them to ideological masks or expressions of false consciousness. This necessitates approaching the creation of social order as an ongoing achievement, not as a once and for all given, without reducing it a priori to an interplay of forces over which actors have no control. It is no surprise then that this pragmatist abandonment of a certain critical sociological stance has endeared *On Justification* to proponents of pragmatist sociology in France and the United States (Callon, 2005; Latour, 2005; Stark, 2010).

In his most recently translated book (see also his contribution in this volume), Boltanski spells this out in more detail. He states that 'in a pragmatist sociology of critique, the metacritical position will therefore consist in *making use of the point of view of the actors*—that is to say, base itself on their moral sense and, in particular, on their ordinary sense of justice, to expose the discrepancy between the social world as it is and as it should be in order to satisfy people's moral expectations. By adopting the viewpoint of the actor, the sociologist can in fact cast a normative glance at the world, without it being guided either by her personal prejudices (bound up, for example, with a cultural affiliation or political commitment or specific religion), or by the adoption of a substantive moral philosophy (e.g. utilitarianism)' (Boltanski, 2011: 30). As Boltanski recognizes, this perspective, which he describes as the 'pragmatic sociology of critique', is a far cry from 'critical sociology' whether this is taken in its French meaning drawn primarily from Bourdieu or in the German Frankfurt School inflection or in the more recent versions of critique developed in variants of post-structuralist Marxism (see the chapters by

Willmott and Parker for a critical response to these arguments). Boltanski argues that, contrary to these theories which assume the ideological pacification of social actors through immutable structures of domination, 'one of the contributions of the pragmatic sociology of critique has been to show that actors are *not* abused (in any event not to the extent that critical sociology gave it to be understood) and that, as regards everything which concerns real life and the injustices they might suffer in everyday life, they harbour no *illusions*' (Boltanski, 2011: 129). He recognizes that 'ordinary people rarely call into question, at least in the normal course of social life, the general framework in which the situations that provoke their indignation and protest are inscribed—that is the set of *established* test formats and qualifications.... Above all because actors know implicitly that tests based on established formats are stronger than they are, so that it would be utter folly to demand for themselves changes in their life that presuppose a radical transformation of this framework' (Boltanski, 2011: 32). Following pragmatist sociology, therefore, Boltanski focuses on actors and how they struggle with uncertainty and change within the contexts of particular orders of worth. What he terms the 'overarching' view of critical sociology with its emphasis on the structures of domination that impose themselves on actors continues to influence Boltanski even whilst he seeks to establish a contrary position in what he terms the 'pragmatic sociology of critique'. He continues to recognize the significance of a totalizing vision going beyond particular tests and particular orders of worth to one which offers the possibility of a sociology of emancipation. Ultimately, this comes back to an emphasis on institutions as 'nothing but arrangements, always more or less lousy, between impermanent beings to slow the pace of change and try to give it a form' leading to what he describes as 'no other road than the road of eternal revolt' and 'to help' society—that is people, the people who are called "ordinary"—deliberately maintain themselves in the state of constant imbalance in the absence of which, as the direst prophecies announce, domination would in fact seize hold of everything' (Boltanski, 2011: 158, 160). The result is a sociology that listens closely to actors, observes how they engage in debate and controversies, and examines the instruments and techniques that they use. It recognizes the existence of domination and inequality and the role that these play in building institutions and resisting demands for change and emancipation. It is, as Boltanski continuously invokes and emphasizes, 'realistic' and 'pragmatic', open to possibilities and placing social actors at the centre of the analysis.

Understanding the emergence of the New Spirit of Capitalism

What sort of analysis of contemporary capitalism emerges from this distinctive combination of historical perspective and sociological framing? There is

22

no doubt that part of the interest in the book derives from the unique manner in which these underpinnings become articulated and combined to provide a distinct perspective on developments in the period from the 1960s through to the late 1990s (when the book was first published in France). Whereas *On Justification* highlighted the critical and justificatory operations performed by people on an everyday basis, and proffered a model of general conventions and forms of equivalence that made it possible to confer legitimacy on justification and critique, in NSC, rather than describing critical operations on a case by case basis, in limited situations, Boltanski and Chiapello focus upon the role played by critique in the dynamic of capitalism since the late 1960s, specifically its French variant, and from this suggest a more general model of change. The book is therefore very much a meditation on the role played by the coexistence of relatively incompatible forms of critique in the dynamic relationship between capitalism and critique. It is undoubtedly this dynamic that has received the most attention in the critical reception of NSC in France, not least, perhaps, because those on the left hoped that the text could offer some pre-cooked recipes for a new politics. It is also, however, the strand of argument that has spurred the most commentary within Anglo-American sociology and organization studies, where the future of radical as opposed to 'merely' reformist critique is a hot topic, and where demands for practical utility (impact) from academic research are high on the policy agenda (Parker, 2008 and this volume; also Willmott in this volume).

According to Boltanski and Chiapello, at a certain historical juncture in France, when a distinctive 'spirit' of capitalism appeared to be exhausting its possibilities, critique became an important part of the deconstruction of older tests and norms and the building of new and different ones with some remarkable, and remarkably disturbing, consequences. With their conceptual architecture in place, Boltanski and Chiapello pursue a line of inquiry that seeks to describe the types of justification that the contemporary spirit of capitalism provides some of its key agents, notably the *cadres* in France. They delineate the model of justice implied therein, and trace its historical emergence in France since the late 1960. They trace the substance of this new spirit in large part through an analysis of a sample of management texts marketed to the *cadres* in the 1990s, which are represented as something akin to manuals of conduct, interpellating their readers through a proselytizing rhetoric of ethical exhortation. These tomes are subsequently compared with the equivalent literature in the 1960s, aimed at the same category of persons, and categorized as an embodiment of the 'second spirit of capitalism'. To the extent that it provides mobilization techniques, ethical motivations, and conceptions of the common good, the highly normative literature of the 1990s both expresses and constitutes the new spirit.

Rejecting bureaucratic hierarchy, seen as the epitome of personally uncreative and socially harmful organization (inefficient, uncompetitive, sclerotic), the new managerial order reframes work relations in terms of horizontal networks, emancipated from the ills of hierarchy and old style 'top-down' controls, in which work is increasingly represented as individually empowering and 'creative', involving the 'whole person', and a certain sort of freedom understood as self-organization and self-actualization. The positive models are no longer the 'organization man' (*sic*) of the 1960s, the stable organization, planning, and the separation of conception and execution, or some derivation thereof, but the charismatic leader of an often intangible organizational process framed as a 'project' (hence the extension of the terminology of cities in *On Justification* to the idea of the 'projective city'). The project is of limited duration, developing a 'culture' inspired by a 'vision' shared with 'partners' each of whom is seen as a self-actualizing individual, with their own unique contribution to make. The costs of social control are increasingly offloaded to employees themselves—who have to constantly prove their worth, an activity deemed in itself 'empowering' as it helps individuals build resources in themselves ('employability', 'personal capital')—or to 'customers', for not entirely dissimilar reasons. In this way, separations between 'work' and 'life' characteristic of an earlier spirit are diminished or, in extreme cases, obliterated (Du Gay, 1996; Ekman, this volume).

Boltanski and Chiapello conclude their analysis of the forms of normativity infusing the new spirit by proclaiming that a 'profound change' in values has occurred. In a manner once again reminiscent of Weber's historical anthropology of *Lebensführung*, they particularize this order of worth by offering a stylized characterological portrait of, in the words of Weber, 'the human type to which these developments give the greatest chance of becoming dominant'—the 'connexionist' (2005: 107ff.). This 'ideal typical' figure is a nomadic 'network-extender', mobile, tolerant of difference and ambivalence, realistic about people's desires (and weaknesses), informal and friendly, with a less rigid relationship to property. Those lacking the requisite flexibility, who cannot become the nodal point of various networks, thus generating the necessary activity, or otherwise engage, communicate, market, innovate, add value, and so on and so forth, have little hope of success in this emergent 'projective city' (see Du Gay's chapters in this book for a critical engagement with this argument at both a general level and in relation to the struggle within the public sector over the new public management inflection of the 'new spirit'; also the chapters in this book by Serrano-Velarde and Ötsch et al.).

It is at this point that Boltanski and Chiapello most explicitly connect the emergence of this novel normative universe to the critiques of capitalism that emerged in the 1960s reaching their zenith in France in the form of *soixante-huitard* criticism. Up to this point, the Fourth (to a limited extent) and then the reformed Fifth Republic (established in France under De Gaulle in 1958) had followed a technocratic path of dirigiste planning. The weaknesses of the French economy in the inter-war years had been blamed in part on the failure of its ownership class to modernize industry, agriculture, and public services in the wake of the devastation wreaked on French society by the disaster of the First World War. In the post-1945 period and particularly in the period from 1958 when De Gaulle led the creation of the Fifth Republic which took power away from Parliament and strengthened the executive and the bureaucracy in order to counterbalance the instability of the legislature with its multiple small parties and unstable coalitions, the French state began to step in to initiate and encourage the modernization process. Through its control and direction over large areas of the economy, sometimes directly through nation-alization and sometimes indirectly through state control of banking and finance, the state shaped French economic growth (Schmidt, 1996; Shonfield, 1965; Zysman, 1983).

France was unique amongst the industrialized countries in that it had a tradition of (and a structure to match) a highly centralized state together with a set of mechanisms for producing the elite who would manage that state. This elite was deeply embedded in an ideology of sustaining what was perceived as being the unique civilizational qualities of the French nation (Bourdieu, 1984, 1996). Central to this process was the formation of the French elite through the Parisian grandes écoles and particularly ENA, École Polytechnique, École Centrale, École de Mines and École des Ponts et des Chausées. This elite was a combination of meritocracy (entry to the écoles was determined by rigorous examinations though this was supplemented by orals which focused more on investigating the social and cultural capital of the applicant—often dependent on family background) and wealth (preparation for the entry exam required an extra year or two at school, usually in a handful of lycées in central Paris that were seen as the best places to learn how to pass the exam and this required parental financial support). Graduates of the écoles went into key positions in the civil service, nationalized industries, finance, and large cor-porations. The senior management of French organizations therefore took for granted their rights to lead and direct.

French employers (in small and large firms) had a long tradition of resist-ance to trade unions and trade union demands. Unlike their counterparts in other countries where either willingly or unwillingly employers had been forced to share power with workers in a variety of ways, employers defended this strongly in the private sector and, because of divisions within the trade union movement, faced only intermittent and poorly coordinated challenges to their authority. Class conflict, therefore, lacked the 'institutionalized' nature of many Western societies in the era of Keynesianism; it was not regulated and controlled by trade unions. Occasionally, it would break to

25

the surface in forms of industrial rebellion, most noticeably of course in 1968 and its immediate aftermath. As French industry grew and the units of production became larger under the guidance of the dirigiste state, these tensions existed under the surface, quelled in part by the broader economic expansion and increased living standards of the period but also, in part, by the presidential structure of the Fifth Republic which reduced the power of the legislature and political parties to reflect these discontents effectively.

In France, Boltanski and Chiapello suggest, the second 'spirit of capitalism' was first threatened by an explosion of critical social mobilization in and around May–June, 1968. The 'critique' registered by students, workers, and others in this 'crucible moment' (Ross, 2000: 105) combined two very different logics of justification that Boltanski and Chiapello term 'social' and 'artistic'. The 'social' demanded greater distributive justice on matters of authority, inequality, and power. The artistic, with its roots in romanticism, demanded autonomy, authenticity, and self-realization. Both offered a serious challenge to the second 'spirit', the authors argue, obliging elites, corporate and political, to respond to their injunctions. Initial responses, in the Chaban–Delmas 'new society' era (1969–72), were largely 'social', but also largely ineffective. Increasingly, decision-makers, especially innovative fractions of the *patronat*, began to focus on elements of the 'artistic' critique, eventuating in the 'new spirit' (Ross, 2000: 105). Boltanski and Chiapello then chart the playing out of the artistic critique in the socio-economic and political transformation of capitalism in France after 1968. Putting it in a nutshell, their argument is that the displacement of capitalism beginning in the 1970s increasingly came to found its justifications in the demands of the artistic critique, whose exponents were progressively to contribute to the promotion of capitalist restructuring and the emergence of 'the new spirit'. At the same time, the dissolution of the artistic critique into a normative justification of the new spirit of capitalism also contributed to the crisis of social critique, since it made possible an effective side-stepping of the conventional tests and the material objects and sites in which they were infused, where capitalism was somehow held in check.

Boltanski and Chiapello offer a detailed and systematic review of the diverse transformations that, in France, have affected the organization of work: the individualization of tasks, the development of outsourcing and subcontracting, the re-engineering of firms, and the progressive substitution of labour law by commercial law and of legislated rights by negotiated ones (Guilhot, 2000: 361). In so doing, they highlight the effects of these developments on the categories through which the social world has been perceived and stabilized. In particular, they focus upon the growing obsolescence of the notion of 'class'. To the extent that such grids of intelligibility and stability were deployed in collective bargaining, for example, and that they helped to secure a *de facto* solidarity between workers in the same sectors (in the case of wage negotiations, for instance), they have quickly been re-presented and come to appear as anachronisms enforcing 'rigidities' that had to be dismantled. The dissolution of these collective identities has not only effected a significant de-unionization (aided by the artistic critique of unions—and of the state—as bureaucratic apparatuses inhibiting individual freedom and initiative) but has also effectively substituted established notions of exploitation and inequality by the tropes of 'exclusion', which emphasize the singularity of each situation as well as its remoteness from aggregates of social relations (Guilhot, 2000: 361). This, according to Boltanski and Chiapello (2005: 325), has led to the effective paralysis of social critique in French political discourse. Indeed, they go further, state and hierarchical bureaucracy, the very institutions that had helped further the social critique in various of its manifestations, themselves lost ground to the artistic critique for whom they were anathema, a process ironically encouraged by the Auroux laws promulgated by the Socialists in 1981 (see Hancké, 2002 for a discussion of these reforms and their impact on the organization of French capitalism). Subcontracting, outsourcing, flexible hours, and the increased use of temporary labour, all legitimated by an emphasis on autonomy and liberty, values championed by the non-Communist left, crippled the social democratic response to the resulting division of employees into the stable and the precarious (see in particular the work of Palier and others on recent developments in the French economy and what he refers to as a growing dualization between these insecure jobs and those in more secure positions; Culpepper et al., 2008; Morel et al., 2012; Palier, 2010; Palier and Thelen, 2010). 'It was by opposing a social capitalism planned and supervised by the state—treated as obsolete, cramped and constraining—and leaning on the artistic critique (autonomy and creativity) that the new spirit of capitalism gradually took shape' (Boltanski and Chiapello, 2005: 201). Boltanski and Chiapello are anxious to emphasize that this new spirit is at least in part energizing, giving a new boost to capitalism by linking the aspirations of social actors to new forms of capitalist activity and organization.

It is worth noting that Boltanski and Chiapello's presentation is an unusual combination. On the one hand, the authors present a detailed analysis of developments in France that fit this connexionist logic; but on the other, they draw on US-based popular management literature to exemplify the discourse of the new 'connexionist', projective city. This discourse in the hands of self-publicists such as Tom Peters pictures a world of possibilities in which individuals are emancipated from the domination of big bureaucracies and are able to forge their own futures through innovation, creativity, and networks. It is a world in which the large organizations that are left are seen as subject to some form of 'permanent revolution' induced externally by heightened global competition and technological change and internally by empowered employees breaking through barriers of habit and routine to 'intrapreneurialism' and customer-facing activities. Alongside these actors, however, is a world of small firms, experts for hire, and knowledge-creating social settings where flexibility of response allows speed of movement to market gaps through market-based solutions (see Thrift's chapter in this book for the link between more recent popular texts emphasizing technological change and virtual worlds and the perspective developed by Boltanski and Chiapello). This combination, however, sidesteps almost entirely the extensive debate within Anglo-American organization studies of the reality of post-bureaucratic structures, as it does also the closely associated debate on post-Fordism discussed earlier. As many authors have argued, this change is firstly exaggerated, secondly strongly resisted, and thirdly has complex and often perverse consequences for the identity of employees and managers as well as for the way in which tasks are performed (as well as the chapters in this volume by Willmott and Parker, see the review of the literature by Alvesson and Thompson, 2005; also the recent book by Clegg et al., 2011). Similarly, the analysis of France, whilst convincing in terms of how the new spirit weakens traditional forms of opposition to capitalism, seems to marginalize the continued resistance in French society to unrestrained forms of capitalism (notable in the oft-repeated rejection of the Anglo-American model of capitalism) and to globalization. Thus, the complexity of the French situation and its path-dependent trajectory seem to be underplayed as does the general issue about comparative differences in the way in which the 'new spirit' evolves (see e.g. Kristensen's chapter in this book on the Danish labour market).

Critique and crisis in the New Spirit

Having outlined both a historical analysis of the emergence of the 'New Spirit' and a description of its content, Boltanski and Chiapello conclude their argument by suggesting the potential forms that both a renewed social and artistic critique of capitalism could take. The final chapters of the book are thus focused on exploring the revival of critical capacities in order to identify the behaviours that contravene the normativity exemplified by the 'projective city'. A key feature of a renewed social critique, they suggest, must be a revived conception of 'exploitation', one freed of much of its historical subsumption under Marxism. Here, their theoretical and pragmatic—politico-legal, technical—efforts aim at surfacing a conception of 'exploitation' that fits with and can thus 'test' the 'new spirit' of a networked capitalism. This is a self-confessed immanentist move, for Boltanski and Chiapello see an effective critique emerging only along the lines drawn by the new spirit, one that can initiate tests to force it to live up to its own professed ideal of the common good. Of crucial concern here is the question of mobility. For Boltanski and Chiapello, a connexionist world is one that valorizes mobility extremely highly, and it is the lines of flight of mobility along which innumerable relations of exploitation are to be charted: financial markets versus states, financial markets versus firms; multinational corporations versus states, large principals versus small subcontractors; the firm versus the casual workforce; the consumer versus the firm; and so on (2005: 371). Those who are exploited in a connexionist world are the immobile sedentary persons and things, which constitute the stabilization of the world in which others move swiftly. 'At all levels of the chain, those who are more mobile extort surplus value from the less mobile, in exchange for a slackening in their own mobility. In exchange for a temporary suspension of the threat to relocate, the firm pays its workforce less, or casualizes it' (2005: 371). Immobile employees, for example, increase the mobility of their employers to the point of ubiquity by fulfilling the function of 'stand-ins', who ensure the maintenance of network connections and the valorization of others' social capital. Their wages and work conditions are lowered because they cannot credibly threaten to move elsewhere as is the common explanation for the rising rewards of senior managers. Thanks to this, their wages can be cheapened, and labour-intensive services that had seemed to be reducing in number in the developed economies have consequently increased with the rise of a new 'servant class'. The low-paid, immobile can be put to work in looking after the sick, the weak, and the disabled. They can take over the functions of maintaining the family, providing cheap childcare to those at work. They can work in personal services such as restaurants, fast foods, entertainment complexes, as cleaners in homes, hotels, and offices, and as employees in public transport in the big cities. Because their wages can be kept low, they serve two functions. Firstly, they enable the organizers of these services to make profits; secondly, at the same time, they keep the costs within a range that the newly mobile can still see as affordable. For Boltanski and Chiapello, this points to the fundamental failure of the connexionist world under conditions of neo-liberalism; it can deliver its promise only to a small part of the population that is indeed dependent on the existence of the mass of the population for the achievement of that promise. The projective city is failing its tests, its own logic of justification.

This is a powerful critique of aspects of inequality under the neo-liberal system, and Boltanski and Chiapello take seriously their own arguments about an immanentist critique by suggesting how this system can be reformed. In order to be corrected, these and other forms of exploitation and injustice immanent to the 'new spirit' would require a number of politico-legal and technical measures (and metrics) that take the norm of justice embodied by the projective city seriously, so that the norms of tests pertaining to this norm are actually geared towards justice (2005: 375). In terms of the form of exploitation specific to the connexionist world, one rooted in the mobility/ immobility differential, what is needed, the authors argue, are tests clarifying mobility as it is, and establishing mechanisms that aim to control it. One aspect of such an endeavour would be the establishment of 'a vast mechanism of *accounting equivalences*', by which means for example, the discrepancy between currently existing accounting systems at level of the firm, which remunerate working time although it no longer relates realistically to production time, might be reduced. Production time, indeed, Boltanski and Chiapello argue, has been extended way beyond the boundaries of the organization as a discrete entity to the entirety of social life, in the course of which individuals acquire the generic human qualities valorized—and exploited—in contemporary capitalism, the paradox of which is that the intensification of the exploitation of singular individual capacities corresponds to a decrease in overall wage costs (Du Gay, 1996; Guilhot, 2000: 362). In keeping with their immanentist inclination, Boltanski and Chiapello propose tests and metrics appropriate to them which 'are not intended to protect people from being mobile, which would thwart the aspirations to autonomy or the requirement of flexibility that have become central in neo-capitalism, but to organize this mobility in a fair and equal way'. In his chapter in this book, Kristensen shows how, in Denmark, labour market policy and broader policies of state provision of nursery care and associated rights of parental leave and replacement income ratios at times of unemployment or ill-health have managed to make a large proportion of the labour force 'mobile' in the terms discussed by Boltanski and Chiapello.

In keeping with their pragmatist approach, Boltanski and Chiapello argue fervently against looking backwards to older 'spirits' and 'tests' in generating the mechanisms of justice that will reduce connexionist exploitation. In keeping with their logic, they do not believe it is possible to offer workers lifetime careers or re-invigorate older forms of job security under the new spirit. Instead, they recommend a politico-legal framework in which, for instance, workers who are intermittently unemployed would have recourse to an 'activity contract', allowing them to amass mobile credits both for training and for prior work experience—a sort of professional patrimony— that could compare favourably with the skills, education, and networking common among elites. Similarly, in order to redistribute wealth from the mobile few who maximize their power in the labour market and give it to the immobile, many of whom live under different labour market conditions or indeed may be denied access to the labour market at all, Boltanski and Chiapello argue for guaranteed and universal incomes, paid to the rich as well as the poor. These do not represent compensatory social benefits but instead decouple income from the opportunity for work and training. These and other politico-legal devices, which represent crucial elements in the development of 'mechanisms of accounting equivalences', are viewed by Boltanski and Chiapello as the lines along which a renewed social critique could be effectively revived. In this, they draw on a line of European social policy which calls for this radical rethink of the role of wages and labour markets, for example in the work of Alain Supiot (2001), an engagement often rooted in analyses of women's role in the labour market in the current era.

As far as a revival of the artistic critique is concerned, Boltanski and Chiapello (2005: 419ff.) acknowledge that the job might be somewhat harder, not least because the 'new spirit' has so successfully incorporated 'whole sections of the critique...subordinating it to profit-making'. It would be possible to point, for example, to the way in which the Young British Artists of the 1990s such as Damien Hirst and Tracey Emin, who shocked the contemporary art world of the time with their use of new and disturbing images, have by 2012 not only become members of the 'arts establishment' but, in Hirst's case in particular, celebrators of the power of wealth and money, even if this is supposedly covered over with heavy lashings of 'post-modern irony'. The question Boltanski and Chiapello pose is whether the success (or failure, depending on point of view adopted) of the artistic critique has emptied 'its demands for liberation and authenticity...of what gave them substance'. Boltanski and Chiapello argue that a revival of the artistic critique is possible as long as it is framed in such a way as to 'bring out the potential for oppression contained in the new mechanisms of accumulation' by identifying 'their perils for authentic relationships, while taking the generalization of demands for liberation and authenticity as established' (2005: 420). Here, a focus on the capitalization and commodification of social relations and the limits of its values lies at the centre of Boltanski and Chiapello's proposals. Suitably reconfigured so as to highlight certain conceptions of liberty and authenticity and to downplay others (the more romantic) that have historically been part of its critical repertoire, the artistic critique does have the capacity to offer tests to the new spirit along its own justificatory axis. Thus, while reforms of the workplace have been conducted in the name of liberation, for instance, highlighting freedom, creativity, and enhanced autonomy, work itself has become a site of an intense capitalization of human attributes and exploitation through constant self-entrepreneurship, where every personal characteristic is assessed on its potentialities for accumulation, and where identification with and loyalty to the values of the corporation or the project trump other forms of attachment. The anti-hierarchical critique may have promised human liberation and authenticity via a reintegration of conception and execution at work, for instance, but the main outcome has been a submission by the individual of their energies, enthusiasms, and identifications to the requirements of their job, now extended to cover all areas of their existence, thereby contributing to a dissolution of distinctions and separations between work and life (Du Gay, 1996; see also Ekman's chapter in this book). No longer do people work to live, but they live to work. Indeed, life is work of a rapacious, financialized, and increasingly boundaryless form. Not only does the autonomy and authenticity promised by the anti-hierarchical organization of economic life correspond to the development of increased financialization, commodification, and self-exploitation, but also the trade-off between liberty and security it has generated has created a situation in which the demand for security can become recognized once again (à la Hobbes) as a prerequisite for autonomy, thus opening a renewed form of connection between the artistic and the social critique.

While Boltanski and Chiapello (2005: 523) are keen to stress the importance of the constitution of a 'projective city' which can generate legitimate tests that are effective in a connexionist world, they are more than aware that this is 'only one of the outcomes that can be envisaged'. Another possibility that cannot be excluded is of 'an increasing degradation in the conditions of existence of the greatest number, rising social inequality, and the generation of a kind of political nihilism'.

As the financial crisis has evolved, these issues have developed in complex and interesting ways. There is no doubt that the struggle over justifications has become even more intense. In country after country, the 'fairness' of government policies of austerity is debated in contexts where banks and their shareholders as well as their highest earning employees have been rescued by the state (Grant and Wilson, 2012). The social questions have come to the fore again as described earlier with rising numbers of unemployed and in some countries a drastic rise in poverty as real living standards are cut (Engelen et al., 2011). It is also clear that, as Boltanski and Chiapello suggest, much of this debate is about the role of mobilities. Thus, the huge salary of some bankers and corporate executives is justified on the grounds that they might move elsewhere if they were not rewarded in this way and such moves would undermine growth prospects. Similar arguments are put forward at the level of corporations and taxation. Meanwhile, those searching for work are being forced to move more rapidly and with less protection onto the labour market by the tightening of benefit regulations. In some countries, definitions of being disabled or unfit for work are being reformed to push individuals into labour market mobility. Increasing the potential pool of low-skilled, low-paid employees enables the high-paid and the wealthy to enjoy cheaper services in many respects and reinforces the exploitative relationship between the mobile and the immobile that Boltanski and Chiapello identify. However, at the same time, the promise of self-autonomy and creativity that comes with the projective city is increasingly out of reach of the many. The connexionist world cannot meet its own tests, and the crisis deepens whilst governments and international economic institutions cling to the belief that eventually economic growth will come from somewhere.

Boltanski and Chiapello suggest that the process of testing the limits to particular logics of justification leads in two directions. One direction is reform and a restructuring that puts into place processes that enable capitalism to restart itself. The other direction is the emergence of a new logic of justification that creates a new spurt of energy and change. In addition to this, however, is the possibility of a long period of uncertainty, increased social conflict, and geopolitical struggle as different societies adjust socially, politically, and militarily to the new situation. In the midst of this uncertainty, positive visions of the future, whether reformist or more radical, are hard to find.

Conclusions

Boltanski and Chiapello's account of the heyday of neo-liberalism in the period up to the late 1990s is a careful attempt to take seriously the discourse of autonomy and networks that emerged, at the same time showing the inherent controversies in this new spirit. Like many such gargantuan efforts, it is necessary to distinguish the underlying logic and concepts that they develop from their actual empirical analysis. The former is probably of much more long-lasting value than the latter. For example, Boltanski and Chiapello spend much time on the issue of labour and mobility and thinking about how a new form of living wage (for those both on and off the actual labour market) could be implemented that would reduce the inequality suffered by the most immobile. From the perspective of the decade that began in 2010, this seems so far off the agenda as to be unreal. However, whilst this way of dealing with the justifications and failures of the projective city may seem less relevant, the issue of how to build such a justificatory logic still remains. Similarly, although their empirical focus was predominantly on France with its very distinct history and social structure, the concepts that they developed and the critique of current practices have been shown to be of more general applicability. As some of the authors in this collection point out, there are strong (though unfortunately unacknowledged) resonances between the arguments made by Boltanski and Chiapello regarding the new forms of organization and their problems and the debates in Anglo-American sociology of work and organizations around the theme of 'post-bureaucracy' and 'post-Fordism'. In all these perspectives, there is a recognition that there have been changes in organization and work and that social actors experience some of these effects through a discourse of empowerment and autonomy, whilst at the same time the reality appears somewhat different. Undoubtedly, Boltanski and Chiapello's critique of the new spirit speaks strongly to issues of labour markets and the organization of work in both the public and private sectors even though their particular solutions of 'accounting equivalences' seem less feasible when the problem is simply defending the gains of the welfare state when it is under such a massive attack in the era of austerity.

Some gaps in the analysis are, however, perhaps more significant. Most obviously, one has to recognize that Boltanski and Chiapello present an account in which the nature of capital itself is strikingly absent. Their project takes, as a base point of the current period, capital's ability under conditions of neo-liberal deregulation to be highly fungible and mobile, moving from one part of the globe to another, from one form of investment to another. However, there is also a substantial gap in their analysis that arises from a failure to interrogate the nature of capital mobility and the international political and economic regime, which underpins it in the current era and has specific conditions of existence in the flows of capital between countries (see e.g. the discussions in Glyn, 2007; Morgan and Goyer, 2012; Schwartz, 2009). Capital has proved to be much more fungible and mobile than labour. The way it has flowed across the world, the way it has been changed into different forms, and the impact which this has had on firms, states, and social actors are not discussed in Boltanski and Chiapello. No doubt this arises again from the unacknowledged blinkering that occurs from the way in which the book is based primarily on the French experience, though, as Goyer (2011) shows, it is possible to develop an analysis of the specificities of French society and economy that shows how global financial flows have been reconstructing and reshaping long-existing relations between managers, employees, and owners. The dynamics of financialization undoubtedly spread out from the deregulation of the United States in particular but also from the United Kingdom (see, most obviously, the highly influential writing of Karel Williams and colleagues which, beginning with the concept of shareholder value and its growth in the United States and the United Kingdom, showed how this was just one part of a wider process of financialization; Engelen et al., 2011; Erturk et al., 2008; Froud et al., 2006).

In the 1990s when *New Spirits* was being conceived, France still seemed to stand to one side of that process. Its banking sector, although mainly denationalized, remained heavily dependent on state support. Only in the 2000s did the banks become fully independent of the state and begin to engage in the forms of high-risk financial market activities that gave rise to the crisis of 2007–8. This is, however, a fundamental lacuna in the *New Spirits* project since the world which was being created by the financialization process was not one in which any developed economy could avoid the consequences as the 2008 crisis showed. Understanding how finance transformed the ground on which capitalism stood was essential if the roots of the contemporary crisis were to be fully grasped.

There is, however, no doubt that NSC represents a remarkable achievement not least in its efforts to systematize a wealth of literature, empirical data, and research from a wide range of disciplinary fields (sociology, management and organizations studies, law, and so forth) within a supple theoretical framework. However, the sheer scope of the enterprise clearly leaves it open to all sorts of criticisms and facilitates the task of those tempted to find fault. On the other hand, it also opens a window on to the processes whereby capitalism is reproducing itself and changing in the current era.

In the chapters that follow, the authors seek to outline certain lines of engagement with the text that have provoked the most sustained commentary within the social sciences, broadly conceived. These relate, firstly, to the conceptual architecture and theoretical and methodological injunctions framing the text and their explanatory reach (see the chapters by Du Gay, Willmott, Parker, and Thrift, as well as the restatements and developments of their position in the separate chapters by Boltanski and Chiapello); secondly, there are a series of chapters that engage directly with the arguments in NSC about the changing nature of capitalism, work, and organizations in the public and private sectors (Huault and Rainelli-Weiss, Kristensen, Ötsch et al., Serrano-Velarde, Du Gay, and Ekman). The chapters reveal the many influences of Boltanski and Chiapello in a variety of different fields ranging from the analysis of financial markets, the nature of the public sector and office holding, the role of labour market policy, and the nature of authenticity at work. The purpose of this book is to highlight the significance of the contributions of NSC. Boltanski and Chiapello's book has provided a highly stimulating approach to how forms of capitalism reproduce themselves, the role that logics of justifications have in this process, the ways justifications break down, and the ability of social actors to engage in critique and change.

References

Abdelal, R. (2007) *Capital Rules: The Construction of Global Finance*. Cambridge, MA: Harvard University Press.

Aglietta, M. (1979) *A Theory of Capitalist Regulation: The US Experience*. London: New Left Books.

Alvesson, M. and Thompson, P. (2005) 'Post-Bureaucracy'. In S. Ackroyd, R. Batt, P. Thompson, and P. Tolbert (eds.), *The Oxford Handbook of Work and Organization*. Oxford: Oxford University Press, 48–507.

Amin, A. (ed.) (1992) *Post-Fordism*. Oxford: Blackwell.

Blackledge, P. (2007) 'Review: The New Spirit of Capitalism', *Capital and Class*, 92, 198–201.

Blyth, M. (2002) *Great Transformations: Economic Ideas and Institutional Change in the Twentieth Century*. Cambridge: Cambridge University Press.

Boltanski, L. (2011) *On Critique: A Sociology of Emancipation*. Cambridge: Polity Press.

—— Chiapello, E. (2005) *The New Spirit of Capitalism*. London: Verso.

—— Thévenot, L. (2006) *On Justification: Economies of Worth* (trans. C. Porter). Princeton, NJ: Princeton University Press.

Bourdieu, P. (1984) *Distinction: A Social Critique of the Judgement of Taste*. London: Routledge & Kegan Paul.

—— (1996) *The State Nobility: Elite Schools in the Field of Power*. Oxford: Polity Press.

Boyer, R. (1990) *The Regulation School: A Critical Introduction*. New York: Columbia University Press.

—— Durand, J.-P. (1997) *After Fordism*. Basingstoke: Macmillan.

Brown, P., Green, A., and Lauder, H. (2001) *High Skills: Globalization, Competitiveness, and Skill Formation*. Oxford: Oxford University Press.

—— Lauder, H., and Ashton, D. (2011) *The Global Auction: The Broken Promises of Education, Jobs, and Incomes*. New York and Oxford: Oxford University Press.

Brummer, A. (2008) *The Crunch: The Scandal of Northern Rock and the Escalating Credit Crisis*. London: Random House Business Books.

Budgen, S. (2000) 'A New Spirit of Capitalism', *New Left Review*, January–February, 149–56.

Burchell, G. (1996) 'Liberal Government and Techniques of the Self'. In A. Barry et al. (eds.), *Foucault and Political Reason*. London: University College Press, 19–36.

Callon, M. (2005) 'Why Virtualism Paves the Way to Political Impotence: A Reply to Daniel Miller's Critique of The Laws of the Markets', *Economic Sociology: European ElectronicNewsletter*, 26, 3–20.

Chwieroth, J. M. (2010) *Capital Ideas: The IMF and the Rise of Financial Liberalization*. Princeton, NJ: Princeton University Press.

Clegg, S., Harris, M., and Höpfl, H. (2011) *Managing Modernity: Beyond Bureaucracy?* New York and Oxford: Oxford University Press.

Clift, B. and Woll, C. (2012) 'Economic Patriotism: Reinventing Control over Markets', *Journal of European Public Policy*, 19(3), 307–23.

Crouch, C. (2008) 'What will Follow the Demise of Privatised Keynesianism?' *The Political Quarterly*, 79(4), 476–87.

—— (2011) *The Strange Non-death of Neo-liberalism*. Cambridge: Polity Press.

Culpepper, P. D., Hall, P. A., and Palier, B. (2008) *Changing France: The Politics that Markets Make*. Basingstoke: Palgrave Macmillan.

Du Gay, P. (1996) *Consumption and Identity at Work*. London: Sage.

—— (2000) *In Praise of Bureaucracy: Weber/Organization/Ethics*. London: Sage.

Elias, N. (2000) *The Civilizing Process: Sociogenetic and Psychogenetic Investigations* (rev. edn.). Oxford: Blackwell.

Engelen, E., Erturk, I., Froud, J., Johal, S., Leaver, A., Moran, M., Nillson, A., and Williams, K. (2011) *After the Great Complacence: Financial Crisis and the Politics of Reform*. Oxford: Oxford University Press.

Erturk, I., Froud, J., Johal, S., Leaver, A., and Williams, K. (2008) *Financialization at Work: Key Texts and Commentary*. London: Routledge.

Fligstein, N. (2006) 'Review: The New Spirit of Capitalism', *Contemporary Sociology*, 35(6), 384–5.

Foucault, M. (1986) *The Care of the Self: The History of Sexuality*, Vol. 3. Harmondsworth: Penguin.

—— (2008) *The Birth of Biopolitics: Lectures at the Collège de France, 1978–79*. Basingstoke and New York: Palgrave Macmillan.

Fourcade, M. (2009) *Economists and Societies: Discipline and Profession in the United States, Britain and France, 1890s to 1990s*. Princeton, NJ: Princeton University Press.

—— Healy, K. (2007) 'Moral Views of Market Society', *Annual Review of Sociology*, 33, 285–311.

Fourcade-Gourinchas, M. and Babb, S. L. (2002) 'The Rebirth of the Liberal Creed: Paths to Neoliberalism in Four Countries', *American Journal of Sociology*, 108(3), 533–79.

Froud, J., Johal, S., Leaver, A., and Williams, K. (2006) *Financialization and Strategy: Narrative and Numbers*. London: Routledge.

Garon, S. M. (2012) *Beyond Our Means: Why America Spends While the World Saves*. Princeton, NJ: Princeton University Press.

Giddens, A. (1998) *The Third Way: The Renewal of Social Democracy*. Cambridge: Polity Press.

Glyn, A. (2007) *Capitalism Unleashed: Finance, Globalization, and Welfare*. Oxford: Oxford University Press.

—— Sutcliffe, R. B. (1972) *British Capitalism, Workers and the Profits Squeeze*. Harmondsworth: Penguin.

Goyer, M. (2011) *Contingent Capital*. Oxford: Oxford University Press.

Grant, W. and Wilson, G. (eds.) (2012) *The Consequences of the Global Financial Crisis: The Rhetoric of Reform and Regulation*. Oxford: Oxford University Press.

Guilhot, N. (2000) 'Review Essay: *Le nouvel esprit du capitalisme*', *European Journal of Social Theory*, 3(3), 355–79.

Hacker, J. S. and Pierson, P. (2010) *Winner-Take-All Politics: How Washington Made the Rich Richer and Turned its Back on the Middle Class*. New York: Simon & Schustser.

Hancké, B. (2002) *Large Firms and Institutional Change: Industrial Renewal and Economic Restructuring in France*. Oxford: Oxford University Press.

Harvey, D. (2005) *A Brief History of Neoliberalism*. Oxford and New York: Oxford University Press.

Hirschman, A. (1977) *The Passions and the Interests*. Princeton, NJ: Princeton University Press.

Holmes, S. (1995) *Passions and Constraint*. Chicago: University of Chicago Press.

Jabko, N. (2006) *Playing the Market: A Political Strategy for Uniting Europe, 1985–2005*. Ithaca, NY and London: Cornell University Press.

Jessop, B. and Sum, N.-L. (2006) *Beyond the Regulation Approach*. Cheltenham: Edward Elgar.

Katz, W. (2007) 'Democracy and the New Capitalism?', *New Labour Forum*, 16(2), 126–30.

Kemple, T. (2007) 'Spirits of Late Capitalism', *Theory, Culture and Society*, 24(3), 147–59.

Kogut, B. (2000) 'Making Networks Accountable', *French Politics, Culture and Society*, 18(3), 123–8.

Kristensen, P. H. and Lilja, K. (eds.) (2010) *Nordic Capitalisms and Globalization: New Forms of Economic Organization and Welfare Institutions*. Oxford: Oxford University Press.

Langley, P. (2008) *The Everyday Life of Global Finance: Saving and Borrowing in Anglo-America*. Oxford: Oxford University Press.

Latour, B. (2005) *Reassembling the Social*. Oxford: Oxford University Press.

Leca, B. and Naccache, P. (2006) ' "Le Nouvel Espirit du Capitalism": Some Reflections from France', *Organization*, 15(4), 614–20.

Luttwak, E. (1999) *Turbo Capitalism*. London: HarperCollins.

MacKenzie, D. (2005) 'The Imagined Market', *London Review of Books*, 24(21), 22–4.

—— (2006) *An Engine, not a Camera: How Financial Models Shape Markets*. Cambridge, MA and London: MIT Press.

—— (2011) 'The Credit Crisis as a Problem in the Sociology of Knowledge', *American Journal of Sociology*, 116(6), 1778–1841.

McTavish, D. (2009) 'Review: The New Spirit of Capitalism', *Business History Review*, 83 (1), 183–5.

Mirowski, P. and Plehwe, D. (eds.) (2009) *The Road from Mont Pelerin: The Making of the Neo-Liberal Thought Collective*. Cambridge, MA: Harvard University Press.

Mohanty, T. (2010) 'Review: The New Spirit of Capitalism', *Capital and Class*, 34(2), 301–3.

Morel, N., Palier, B., and Palme, J. (2012) *Towards a Social Investment Welfare State? Ideas, Policies and Challenges*. Bristol: Policy Press.

Morgan, G. (2008) 'Market Formation and Governance in International Financial Markets: The Case of OTC Derivatives', *Human Relations*, 61(5), 637–60.

—— (2010) 'Legitimacy in Financial Markets: Credit Default Swaps in the Current Crisis', *Socio-Economic Review*, 8(1), 17–45.

—— Goyer, M. (2012) 'Is there a Global Financial System? The Locational Antecedents and Institutionally Bounded Consequences of the Financial Crisis'. In M. Morgan and R. Whitley (eds.), *Capitalisms and Capitalism in the Twenty-First Century*. Oxford: Oxford University Press, 119–45.

Palier, B. (2010) *A Long Goodbye to Bismarck? The Politics of Welfare Reforms in Continental Europe*. Amsterdam: Amsterdam University Press.

—— Thelen, K. (2010) 'Institutionalizing Dualism: Complementarities in and Change in France and Germany', *Politics and Society*, 38(1), 119–48.

Parker, M. (2008) 'The Seventh City', *Organization*, 15(4), 610–14.

Peck, J. (2010) *Constructions of Neoliberal Reason*. Oxford: Oxford University Press.

Peters, T. (1992) *Liberation Management*. Basingstoke: Macmillan.

Piore, M. (2000) 'Deconstructing the Reconstruction of Capitalism', *French Politics, Culture and Society*, 18(3), 109–14.

Polanyi, K. (2001) *The Great Transformation: The Political and Economic Origins of Our Time* (2nd Beacon pbk. edn.). Boston, MA: Beacon Press.

Prasad, M. (2006) *The Politics of Free Markets: The Rise of Neoliberal Economic Policies in Britain, France, Germany and the United States*. Chicago: University of Chicago Press.

Reid, D. (2000) 'Not Your Father's Capitalism', *French Politics, Culture and Society*, 18(3), 115–22.

Rose, N. (1999) 'Inventiveness in Politics', *Economy and Society*, 28(3), 467–96.

Ross, G. (2000) 'Capitalism and Its Spirits', *French Politics, Culture and Society*, 18(3), 103–8.

Roubini, N. (2011) *Crisis Economics: A Crash Course in the Future of Finance* (updated with a new afterword edition). New York: Penguin Press.

Schmidt, V. A. (1996) *From State to Market? The Transformation of French Business and Government*. New York: Cambridge University Press.

—— (2002) *The Futures of European Capitalism*. Oxford: Oxford University Press.

Schwartz, H. (2009) *Subprime Nation: American Power, Global Capital and the Housing Bubble*. Ithaca, NY: Cornell University Press.

Shonfield, A. (1965) *Modern Capitalism: The Changing Balance of Public and Private Power*. London: Oxford University Press.

Simmons, B. A., Dobbin, F., and Garrett, G. (eds.) (2008) *The Global Diffusion of Markets and Democracy*. Cambridge: Cambridge University Press.

Smith, A. (1976) *The Theory of Moral Sentiments* (Glasgow edn.). Oxford: Clarendon Press.

Sorkin, A. R. (2009) *Too Big to Fail: Inside the Battle to Save Wall Street*. London: Allen Lane.

Stark, D. (2010) *A Sense of Dissonance: Accounts of Worth in Economic Life*. Princeton, NJ: Princeton University Press.

Streeck, W. (1997) 'Beneficial Constraints: On the Economic Limits of Rational Voluntarism'. In J. R. Hollingsworth and R. Boyer (eds.), *Contemporary Capitalism: The Embeddedness of Institutions*. Cambridge and New York: Cambridge University Press, 197–219.

—— (2009) *Re-forming Capitalism: Institutional Change in the German Political Economy*. Oxford: Oxford University Press.

—— (2011) 'The Crises of Democratic Capitalism', *New Left Review*, 71, September–October, 5–29.

Supiot, A. (2001) *Beyond Employment*. Oxford: Oxford University Press.

Tett, G. (2009) *Fool's Gold*. London: Little, Brown.

Thrift, N. (2005) *Knowing Capitalism*. London: Sage.

Turner, B. S. (2007) 'Extended Review: Justification, the City and Late Capitalism', *Sociological Review*, 55(2), 410–15.

Woods, N. (2006) *The Globalizers: The IMF, the World Bank, and their Borrowers*. Ithaca, NY and London: Cornell University Press.

Zysman, J. (1983) *Governments, Markets, and Growth: Financial Systems and the Politics of Industrial Change*. Ithaca, NY: Cornell University Press.

Section 1
New Spirits of Capitalism: Developments and Critique

2

A Journey Through French-Style Critique

Luc Boltanski

French sociology, having lost after the Second World War the prominence it claimed during the Durkheimian era, regained international recognition—especially in the United States—by taking up a programme of critical sociology which had been, until then, associated with the Frankfurt School. This re-implementation of a critical orientation, launched in the French context of May 1968, has taken a different path, however, from the one followed by the German heirs of the Frankfurt School.

Specific to the *French style* of critical sociology is the attempt to build a synthesis between Marxist and Durkheimian traditions, centred on the notion of institution. This synthesis entailed elements borrowed from Weberian sociology as well as approaches rooted in the phenomenological tradition. One can say without reservation that Pierre Bourdieu's sociology presented the most visible aspect, both in France and abroad, of this diverse and proliferating archipelago constituted by the new French critical sociology of the 1970s.

This new critical sociology became, in turn, the target of numerous critiques. Some were inspired by political considerations that amounted, briefly, to a purely conservative dismissal of critical sociology for targeting the established political and social order. Other critiques, however, were grounded not in political but instead in basic theoretical disagreements. These internal critiques were sometimes developed by sociologists who had been—as was my case—close collaborators of Pierre Bourdieu, but were at odds with some of the theoretical postulates underlying the Bourdieusian conceptual system.

Such theoretically inspired critical stances did not imply, however, giving up the project of associating sociology and social critique. These critiques recognized, at least implicitly, the legitimacy of such a project, as old as sociology itself. Despite the inner tensions and perhaps internal contradictions of such a project, it has defined what is unique to the sociological discipline. Arguably, sociology has always been caught, as in a pincer, between, on one hand, the requirement for scientific description from an objective distance and, on the other, the need to adopt a normative stance allowing judgement of the prevailing social order.

It is in this context of debates about the relations between sociology and social critique that another programme—in which I was involved—took form during the 1980s, namely, the pragmatic turn to *a sociology of critical practice*. This programme was not oriented against critique—contrary to what has often been said—either in reproach or in praise. On the contrary, one of its main aims was to renew the possibility of a critical sociology, and this by focusing on the critical capacities of ordinary actors and by taking as the subject of empirical research those situations, abounding in ordinary life, in which actors put into play these capacities, especially in the course of disputes (Boltanski and Thévenot, 2006).

I will not recall the now well-known objections opposed to the Bourdieusian scheme, for example, by Jeffrey Alexander in the United States (Alexander, 1995) and Jacques Rancière in France (Rancière, 2004). What was particularly objectionable for us was the excessive weight placed on the delusion of the agents and the deep asymmetry between deluded actors and the clear-minded sociologist.

Such a paradigm, moreover, by stressing a circular relationship between, on one side, underlying structures and, on the other, embedded dispositions, tends to ignore or underestimate the state of uncertainty that persons frequently face when they are acting. Consequently, it precludes the possibility of taking into account the very logic of social action and, thereby, analysing and understanding the disputes in which actors become engaged.

The programme of a sociology of critical practices

The main orientation of the programme of a sociology of critical practices was to pursue and enhance a critical sociology grounded in rigorous empirical fieldwork by offering fine-grained accounts of actors engaged in situations. The strategy implemented consisted of a *return to the things themselves*, as phenomenology used to say. In the case of criticism, it meant taking as one's main object of research those situations in which people are producing criticisms and justifications, in other words, studying *disputes*. We thus launched a series of ethnographic fieldwork studies, implementing methods of direct observation borrowed from the anthropological tradition. The ethnographic field sites were deliberately chosen to provide access to a wide array of disputes emanating from domains as diverse as possible, such as firms, media, schools and universities, town councils, trade unions, commissions for health or welfare, etc.

Another part of the programme was devoted to the study of 'affairs'. By this term, we mean, in France, a big public debate, triggered by a case entailing uncertain features and involving a question of justice, of which the famous Dreyfus affair remains, up to our time, the paradigm. In the course of these affairs, a conflict, which is originally local, spreads and takes on a general significance. The conflicting parties seek, then, to mobilize as large a group of actors as possible in support of their cause. Different incompatible accounts are publicly advocated, resulting in a persisting uncertainty about 'what really happened'.

The *actors* revealed by these inquiries were very different from the *agents* to which the critical sociology of domination had accustomed us. They were always active, not passive. They were openly critical, almost in the style of critical sociologists, continuously unmasking the hidden foibles and intentions of their opponents, and, furthermore, not hesitating to adopt, when it suited them, the schemata of critical sociology that could have been popularized by education (often by post-school education) and by the media. They pressed home their demands, condemned injustices, produced evidence to support their complaints, or developed arguments to defend themselves against criticisms levelled against them. From this alternative standpoint, the social world no longer seemed a place of passively accepted domination, or even of domination suffered unconsciously, but instead a site full of disputes, critiques, disagreements, and attempts to restore local, always contestable, harmony, that is, a scene more in line with a lawsuit.

On methodological and theoretical grounds, this programme has drawn resources from different trends more or less inspired by the pragmatist tradition. These trends, taking different paths, were united in directing sociological attention towards actors in situations, and in viewing them as the principal agencies performing the social. Inversely, they discouraged sociology from producing quasi-cartographic descriptions of the social world viewed from an overhanging point of view and described as an already formed solidified entity. Some of the trends informing our approach were inspired by American pragmatism, such as interactionism or, less directly, ethnomethodology. But one must also mention other variants that were rooted in the French intellectual context. These approaches reprocessed a part of the pragmatist legacy frequently via tortuous paths by way of the work of Gilles Deleuze (e.g. as in Bruno Latour's effort; Latour, 2005). One must mention also other orientations which, although not directly connected to pragmatism, nonetheless directed sociological attention towards language and the interpretative work implemented by actors in situations, as, for example, analytical philosophy, the second Wittgenstein, or the attempts, developed in France by Paul Ricoeur, at merging analytical philosophy and phenomenology (Ricoeur, 2008).

Among this disparate array, we made particular use of linguistics. We first drew elements from pragmatic linguistics aimed at analysing indexicality and the process of making sense within situations. But we also drew upon generative linguistics, from which we borrowed (in a somewhat unorthodox manner) the notion of *competence*. This notion allowed us to infer the presence of underlying cognitive schemes displayed in the capacity of actors to produce criticisms and justifications within situations as well as their ability to discriminate between those that were appropriate to the situation and those that were not. We started then to build models of the manifested sense of justice, or moral sense. One can also attribute to the pragmatist influence the tendency of the sociology of critical practices to describe the social world as if it were the *scene* of a *trial*, in the course of which actors, plunged in *uncertain* situations, implement *inquiries*, develop *experiments*, formalize their interpretations of the state of affairs into *reports*, determine *qualifications*, and subject one another to *tests*.

I would add that the programme of a sociology of critical practices maintained an objectivistic orientation, and even remained, in some aspects, rooted in the structuralist tradition. Such structuralist orientation, however, was redirected, by shifting the focus from the mapping of a social morphology, to modelling the cognitive resources and *normative* tools available to actors. Relying upon these models, we tried to understand the way in which actors succeed in reaching a loose coordination of their actions and making their interpretations more or less convergent, in the course of the disputing process. The main task of sociology, considered from this epistemological position, is, then, to make explicit the methods implemented by actors themselves by which they select a meaning from among a large array of possible interpretations and, by this same operation, create or sever social ties. From this perspective, the object of sociological research lay in rendering explicit and delineating the generative grammar yielding the operations implemented by actors in the process of making and unmaking social ties and associations. Thus, the kind of truth that such analysis sought to reach can be compared to the notion of acceptability as it is used in linguistics.

In terms of advancing a critical orientation, our intention was to make normative stances emerge from the description itself. We thought that analysing disputes and clarifying the moral sense and the sense of justice practised by actors would, in the long run, provide a firm ground on which sociology could base its claim to participate in social change. This participation would take the form of rendering generally accessible the frustrations and aspirations expressed by actors by translating such local claims into formulations whose general meaning could be recognized and validated and hence have warranted political significance.

On Justification, a book originally published in French in 1991 and translated and published in English only in 2006 by Laurent Thévenot and myself (Boltanski and Thévenot, 2006), can be seen as the core example of such an approach. It develops a theoretical model, based on extensive fieldworks, of the sense of justice in our society. It outlines the cognitive tools implemented by people so as to generate criticisms and justifications and lays stress on the plurality of the principles of evaluation and interpreted criticisms as based on a conflict between these.

Without going into the details of the model, I will just point out that it seeks to describe not only the argumentation but also the procedures people use to support their claims. We refer to these procedures as *reality tests*. These tests (e.g. exams or other selecting procedures) can be more or less institutionalized and are more or less bound to conform to certain formats. Using such a frame, one can analyse the criticisms developed by the actors in the course of their disputes. They can take two different directions: either challenge the specific way in which the test is implemented by showing that it does not conform to the approved correct format; or question the test format itself.

Can a critical sociology be developed on the basis of a sociology of critical practice?

This research programme has undoubtedly achieved a better description of the various critical practices evident in everyday life. Moreover, it facilitated the spelling out and modelling of the collective resources available to disputants. One can say, then, that the programme reached its objectives, at least on the ground of descriptive adequacy. But, can we say the same thing with regard to our second objective, which was to renew the contribution of sociology to social critique by relying directly upon the criticism formulated by the actors?

In terms of this second aim, the results seem rather modest. The programme makes it possible to rely on the actor's criticisms such as might be directed, for example, against selection tests in school or work that fail to conform to their correct format. But, unlike a critical sociology of domination, it does not permit mounting a wider critique encompassing social reality regarded in its *totality*, with different components systematically linked one to another, a critique that would consequently advocate for a drastic change of the political order.

We have then to face a kind of paradox. We reproached critical sociology for presenting people as subjected to mighty structures and for ignoring their critical capacities as agents. But it seems that this critical sociology did open the way to a radical critique, which could be appropriated by ordinary actors in order to support their own bluntly critical claims.

Inversely, the sociology of critical practices wanted to really listen to the critical activity developed by ordinary actors. But, it seems that it did not succeed in fostering a form of critique of more salient potency that could supply actors with the resources needed to reinforce their critical will and their critical efficiency. This outcome is rather easy to understand and can be attributed to the fact that, in ordinary times as opposed to exceptional periods of uprising or revolution, the critical stances formulated by social actors and collected by the social scientist tend to be relatively limited and directed towards local settings. Must we conclude from this, then, that critical sociology was right when it considered social actors to be plunged in a world of illusion, blinded by dominant ideologies, and not capable of gaining an awareness of their subjected state?

Our interpretation is different. As frequently demonstrated by the sociology and anthropology of resistance, actors can be aware of the general forms of injustice they suffer, without expressing strong claims, as individuals and in face-to-face interactions. And this can be noticed even when they are not paralysed by fear, enjoying political contexts where free speech is a right. And the reason for this, we would argue, is that actors are *realistic*. They do not ask for the impossible. Their sense of reality is constantly reinforced by their ordinary experiences. They can appreciate to what extent their condition can be said to be just or unjust, privileged or disadvantaged, by referring to the situations of other actors they regard as comparable in various respects.

Ordinary persons, at least in daily life, are rarely driven to question the general frame that informs their particular state of affairs leading to protest or indignation. They can judge unjust the way a certain test was performed in a certain situation, but without questioning, for all that, the institutionalized formats of tests and qualifications, taken as a whole. A first reason is that they do not have access to the kind of tools necessary to totalize. But the primary reason is, more probably, that actors implicitly know that the tests and their institutionalized formats are stronger than they are as individuals and, hence, it would be irrational to demand, on their own behalf, effective changes that would require a drastic transformation of this wider frame. The actors, considered in the course of their ordinary life, seem to take seriously the mere fact that what we call *reality tests* are grounded upon reality. A waiter in a café knows implicitly that it would make no sense to consider unjust the fact of not being a university professor, because he realizes that, if tested, he would not, for instance, be able to cope with trigonometry. Although, of course, it would be another matter if he took a correspondence course and obtained a diploma. In such a case, his denial of opportunities normally opened up by the professional exam would be a matter of discrimination, for example, for being a Jew in Vichy France, an Afro-American person in the racist states of the United States, or else a woman or a homosexual, etc.

Granting that actors are realistic does not mean, however, that reality, as such, will always hold them prisoners as in an iron cage. As demonstrated by the literature on revolt and uprising, the pressure that reality imposes upon the aspirations and claims of actors is variable in different historical contexts. One can suggest that it depends, mainly, on the degree to which reality appears robust or, seems to *hold*. Reality is robust when the very existence of each of its components is symbolically and practically sustained and, consequently, confirmed by others. Inversely, it becomes fragile when this solidarity is weakened and the necessity of existing reality is no longer constantly auto-confirmed; reality seems, then, to break up. Such contexts are favourable to the development of critique, seen as a questioning of *the reality of reality*. Similarly, what actors could only have considered, up to that moment, as pure dreams can be transformed into aspirations, and then into claims.

Up to this point, I have used the word *reality* to mean what sociology has referred to for nearly forty years as the 'construction of social reality'. By reality, I designate the social context in which actors are involved. But I must point out that, by context, I mean a network of qualifications, definitions, standards, test formats, rules, selection procedures, etc. In contemporary societies, these different formats rely mainly upon a juridical logic, which is not reducible to the laws of the state.

However, my position is that this constructed reality does not determine in a mechanical way all of an actor's experiences. Certain experiences can be authentically lived, even if they cannot be formulated in terms of, or given a place within, the web of constructed reality. The construction of social reality—a process that involves symbolic operations of qualification and agency—makes it necessary to select, in the continuous flow of events, some elements treated as if they were the only relevant ones. In consequence, one can say that reality is far from incorporating all that is happening, namely, the *world*. The experiences of persons are, thus, at the same time, rooted in *reality* and in the *world*, regarded—in Wittgenstein's terms—as 'all that is happening'. Thus, against *social reality*, which can be mapped in a quasi-cartographic way, I oppose the *world*, which no one can conceivably totalize. If the project of building a representation of reality, as it unfolds in a certain historical context, does not seem absurd, all attempts to delineate the contents of the world are doomed.

I think that this distinction between reality and world can be used in order to get a better understanding of the role played by critical activity in the processes of social change. One would not be able to understand how, in certain situations, actors manage to access desires which seem the least realizable, consider them seriously, and, on this basis, launch a radical critique of a reality that denies the satisfaction of these desires if the experience of actors were entirely restricted within the shackles of reality. But these border situations become understandable if one acknowledges that the field of experience is also rooted in the world. Actors, relying upon their experiences, reveal themselves capable of drawing from the world arguments and examples that do not fit in with the qualifications, definitions, and test formats on which current social reality is based. They would, then, be able to question its necessity, to expose its arbitrary nature, and, finally, to propose other kinds of social arrangements.

The model proposed in *On Critique*

In order to develop this idea, I will outline now, very schematically, a theoretical frame (sketched in my last book, *On Critique*, published in France in 2009 and in English in 2011; Boltanski, 2011). This frame is rather different from the one presented, twenty years ago, in *On Justification*, but not contradictory. It aims at designing a larger scheme that would make it possible to integrate elements drawn, on one hand, from the critical sociology of the 1970s and, on the other, from the more recently developed sociology of critical practices. It represents, by some of its aspects, an attempt at giving a theoretical basis to the analysis of the recent change of capitalism presented in *The New Spirit of Capitalism*, in which these two kinds of perspectives were implemented but loosely integrated on theoretical grounds (Boltanski and Chiapello, 2005).

This framework starts from the question of institutions. Institutions, seen mainly from the point of view of critical sociology as a source of symbolic violence, have been largely ignored by the sociology of critical practices. In the frame that I will outline now, institutions are two-sided. Their negative aspects, namely, as sources of *symbolic violence*, are maintained. But, on the other side, we recognize their positive functions, which are to provide beings, and, particularly, persons, with *semantic security*. One can say, briefly, that human beings enjoy semantic security when their social identity, and the social properties attached to it, are maintained whatever the context in which they are plunged.

My argument will be that the pre-eminence given, in any specific context, to either negative or positive aspects of institutions will depend on the place given to critical practices in the social setting. The research would then be centred on the relations between institutions and critique. Institutions have the task of maintaining in working order the current formats and rules and, hence, the task of *confirmation* of the *reality of the reality*. But critique, drawing new resources from the world, questions this socially constructed reality and, when it succeeds in gaining a listening, transforms it.

The frame outlined in *On Critique* starts from a statement, which has the status of a postulate. This statement lays stress on a radical uncertainty concerning *'the what is it of what is'*. This uncertainty is seen as continuously besieging the course of social life. Such a statement challenges numerous positions that take as granted that social life relies on a kind of tacit agreement which could be seen as original, even as quasi-natural, and consubstantial to sociality. It puts into brackets, first, the approaches that consider *meaning* as relying on the presupposition of a *common sense* (borrowed from phenomenology and/or from analytical philosophy). Second, it puts aside the approaches that focus on the certainty of group membership (as developed in social anthropology). This postulate of uncertainty must be seen as a thought experiment (rather like the state of nature in contractualist political philosophy). The aim of such a strategy is to compel us to problematize the making of arrangements that must be built in order to create a common social world.

This postulate of uncertainty does not lay stress on the competition of interests but, instead, on the incapability of human beings to reach spontaneously an agreement on a determinate way of fixing a relationship between *symbolic forms* and *state of affairs*—to use a distinction borrowed—once again—from Wittgenstein (Wittgenstein, 1958). Given such uncertainty, these differences of interpretations and, consequently, of usages always involve the risk of dispute, which can lead to violence. A consequence of this postulate is that different registers framing action—which I will examine now—will be regarded as tools aimed at reducing the effects of this uncertainty.

Practical and metapragmatical registers of action

The first register considered is *practice*. It implies, more or less, physical proximity and is particularly activated in the course of interactions and encounters. During these practical moments, persons cooperate actively in order to reduce the anxiety about the *what is it of what is*, which constantly jeopardizes interaction. Interacting persons actively strive to ignore possible differences of interpretation about what is really happening and, above all, shut their eyes on the misbehaviours that might increase uncertainty. *Tolerance*, which is one of the main characteristics of this register, is linked to a low level of reflexivity. One can say that, during such moments, actors collaborate tacitly so as to reduce the level of reflexivity or, at least, its public expression.

In this register, language, of course, is made use of, but rather in an indexical way combining naming and pointing towards what is referred to. The discourse includes few reports from a general point of view, either to recall past actions or to describe the current course of action, or, still more, to evoke future plans of action. Finally, the relation between symbolic forms and states of affairs is not explicitly addressed, so as to avoid questioning the connection between, on one hand, the objects and, on the other, the terms used to qualify them.

This way of averting the possibility of a dispute and of maintaining the appearance of an agreement is rather efficient. However, it cannot be sustained when there is too great a divergence in the interpretations given by actors of what is really happening and the way they make use of the common surroundings. A dispute, or the threat of one, enforces, therefore, a shift towards other registers, which I call *metapragmatic* (a term borrowed from linguistic anthropology). These moments can be characterized, in particular, by a change in the way language is used and its metaproperties are activated, that is, the possibility of referring, at the same time, to an object and to language itself (e.g. when one speaks of 'a poet in the full sense of the term'). During these metapragmatic moments, the level of reflexivity tends to increase and to take public forms. One witnesses, then, a reshuffling of the dispute which amounts to questioning the way in which the relation between symbolic forms and states of affairs must be recalibrated to be judged acceptable.

Two opposite modalities of metapragmatic interventions are proposed. The first ones are forms devoted to the establishing of *what is*, and to the maintaining of what has been established as really being, through time. I will call these forms *confirmative agencies* because they reduce uncertainty by continuously confirming what is. These forms make a great use of quasi-tautologies. Epidictic discourses, which, according to Aristotelian Poetics, serve to announce publicly statements that everybody already knows, are typical instances of this form.

The second are forms that enhance factors of uncertainty present in the setting in order to contest the reality of what is given as really being. In these cases, I will speak of forms oriented towards *critique*.

These two opposite modalities, namely confirmation and critique, are interdependent and, thus, must be considered in their dialogic relationship. The main task of confirmation is to prevent critique. As for critique, it would lose its orientation and turn into a kind of nihilism if it cannot target confirmed statements. Confirming and maintaining reality can be seen as constituting the main task of *institutions*. In our framework, institutions are thus considered, above all—as in John Searle's work—from the point of view of their *semantic functions* (Searle, 1969, 1971). They have to establish and constantly confirm the relationship between symbolic forms and states of affairs, and to make it acceptable.

Why are institutions necessary to social life? The argument developed in this frame starts from the question of the body. No individual has the authority, and perhaps even the power, to state on behalf of others the *what is it of what is*, and this for a very simple reason: because he/she has a body. Having a body, each person is necessarily situated in external time and space, but also, in a way, relative to his or her own interiority, desires, tastes, dislikes, etc. In ordinary situations of interaction, the only thing that an individual can do is to present his or her 'point of view'. But, especially when a dispute is becoming explicit and threatens to lead to violence, confronting views are not sufficient to reach an agreement. I think that the rationalist hypothesis, which relies on the mere power of discussion as a device capable of selecting among different views, or of reaching a synthesis, is too strong and hardly realistic.

The main characteristic of an institution, seen as such, is to be *a bodiless being*. And it is because institutions are bodiless beings that mere human beings—that is all of us—delegate to them the task of stipulating the *what is it of what is*. It follows that institutions must be seen, above all, as operators implementing semantic functions, for example, when they set references or control qualifications. Allocating this role to institutions prevents us from confusing them with two other types of entities with which they are often associated but from which they must be analytically differentiated: first, *organizations*, which carry out functions of coordination and, second, *administrations*, which carry out police functions.

It is because institutions are bodiless beings that, frequently, the phenomenological approach to institutions attaches to them the capacity of settled, long-lasting, and even eternal entities. Unlike the individual bodies of those who speak on their behalf—their spokespersons—institutions are supposed, at least ideally, to escape from the corruption of time. We will add that institutions, being bodiless beings, are the only ones capable of making real those *non-existing beings* that sociology cannot afford to ignore, namely nations, social classes, ethnic groups, etc. Institutions give to these beings (much contested by the approaches stemming from positivist logic) an opportunity to reach modes of existence far from being purely illusory.

The hermeneutical contradiction

The problem with institutions is that they are simultaneously both necessary and fragile, useful, and always prone to abuse. Being bodiless, institutions cannot speak, except through their spokespersons—persons made of flesh and blood like you and me—such as judges, priests, deputies, professors, etc. These persons, even when delegated and legally authorized are, nevertheless, nothing but ordinary bodily people and, hence, situated and equipped with a libido, interests, tastes, etc. They are, for this very reason, doomed to express nothing more than a point of view, at least when they are not supposed to

53

speak on behalf of the institution. It is for this reason that they generally assume specific symbolic marks (such as uniforms, turns of phrase, tones of voice, etc.) so as to make manifest the case that they do not speak personally but instead on behalf of an institution. Institutional delegation is supposed to invest their earthly frame with the properties of a bodiless being (according to the twin bodies logic made famous by the work of Ernst Kantorowicz; Kantorowicz, 1957). Nonetheless, the appearance of these spokespersons cannot be thoroughly transformed. No sign can possibly give direct access to their interiority and intentionality and, hence, assure the absence of deception. How can we know if the one who is speaking is an incarnation of the bodiless institution or if he is nothing more than a 'nobody' like you and me carrying on in a perishable body?

From this follows a profound ambivalence with regard to institutions, which is inherent to all social life. Moreover, this ambivalence increases when the size of the settings considered is larger, so that anxiety can no longer be soothed by local arrangement as in the case of an interactive context. On the one hand, hence, we trust the institutions, we 'believe' in them. How could we do otherwise, given that without their intervention our concern about *what is* could only increase, with all the risks of discord or dissipation into private language that this would entail? But, on the other hand, we know all too well that they are fictions and that the only real beings are the humans they are made of, who speak for them and who, having bodies, desires, impulses, etc. do not have any robust property that would allow us to trust them.

I propose to see in this tension a kind of contradiction which lies at the very core of common social life and which we must tackle, at this moment of our analysis, as impassable. I will call it the *hermeneutical contradiction*. By this term, I do not merely mean the divergence between different interpretations, which becomes evident in the course of disputes. I mean, rather, a problem inherent to the interpretation process, posing the following dilemma: On one side, we can renounce the task of saying the *what is it of what is* in favour of a mere exchange of points of views, with the risk of never reaching closure, even a temporary one. Here the danger is, above all, the awakening of uncertainty, whose effect would be to trigger an anxiety of fragmentation, the outcome of which could be the use of violence to impose an interpretation. The alternative side is—as we have seen—to delegate the task of saying the *what it is of what is* to disincarnated beings, namely, to institutions, but, then, running the risk of another kind of anxiety no less disturbing. This anxiety regards the question of not knowing whether the spokespersons are really expressing the will of the bodiless being or whether they are doing nothing more, actually, than manifesting their proper will so as to satisfy their selfish desires.

We must also note that the hermeneutical contradiction is not extraneous to the relation between semantic and pragmatic dimensions of meaning. Instead, institutional operations, when involved in the circumstances of ordinary life, come into tension—given their basically semantic nature—with the pragmatic dimensions of interpretation and action. The way people grasp qualifications in the course of action has a pragmatic character. It follows that the tension between semantic qualifications and situated usages plays an important role in the uncertainties of social life. If a conception of social activity completely based upon pragmatics is, as we have seen, unrealistic, it remains that it is impossible to conceive a social world in which the manufacture of meaning could be thoroughly stabilized by semantic devices. Qualifications, definitions, test formats, rules, etc. generated by the institutions are not, as such, susceptible of being processed in real situations. Their implementation requires a process of interpretation that relies upon context. It follows that the maintenance of reality, particularly when it is jeopardized by critique, entails the dilemma of having determinate but easily criticized formats, or of opening the stream of interpretation. But given the interminable character of the latter, there is a risk of constant distortion of semantic marks.

Critique and emancipation

This tension embedded in institutions opens a breach within which critique can develop. In the absence of the hermeneutical contradiction, persons would continuously be under the regime of formats generated by institutions and, consequently, completely immersed in a social reality taken as granted. It would be impossible for them to consider these formats from an exteriority, that is, to make them relative and call the social reality into question. Critique can then be seen as the only defence against the kind of domination that institutions would, in its absence, necessarily exert.

Emancipation—in the sense given in our work—ensues from the defence and extension of the critical practices that contest and unsettle those formats on which reality relies. The implementation of these formats has, for the most part, asymmetrical outcomes, in the form of uneven distribution and recognition and, thus, in many cases, strengthens exploitation. Critique is thus the main weapon that can be used by exploited or scorned people, or by groups, so as to change the outlines of reality.

In more radical forms, critical practices draw from experiences of the world heterodox elements that do not conform to the existing formats. This process can, in the beginning, have an individual character and, for example, be triggered by works of art. Art, probably because it is not limited

55

by argumentative constraints, offers the possibility of outlining forms of life that are not yet encapsulated in the web of reality. But this process takes a political expression when, through the mediation of inter-subjectivity, personal experiences are shared and associated with principles of equivalence which inform them and make possible their circulation in the public sphere.

Emancipation and hermeneutical contradiction

We will argue now that different kinds of asymmetries (between social classes, gender, ethnic groups, etc.) are linked to a more general one regarding institutions considered as the main sources of qualifications, test formats, and rules. The analysis of that asymmetry could, perhaps, shed light on the rather obscure notion of 'symbolic violence'. The basic assumption is that the relationship people have with institutional rules is utterly unequal according to the position they occupy in power relationships. A way of giving sense to the notion of 'domination' and of clarifying a label such as 'dominant classes' (or dominant gender or dominant ethnic group, etc.) consists of examining the practical relations persons have with rules. Inequality in terms of rules is something evident in societies in which a different and unequal status is attached to different categories of agents, allowing different degrees of autonomy, even threatening thereby the idea of a common humanity (e.g. as in a caste system). But the asymmetry regarding rules, supposedly common to all, is particularly thorny in the formally egalitarian and, even more, democratic societies, where important asymmetries towards rules can be observed. Such tacit asymmetries rely, particularly, upon the distinction between the *letter of the rules* and the *spirit of the rules* and, for this reason, involve the question of interpretation.

In these societies, the activities of actors occupying a dominant position, as well as the actions of the dominated actors, are supposed to be framed by rules. But, with regard to those in a dominant position, the net of the regulatory frame is loose enough to tolerate a very large range of actions, implemented according to diverse modalities. This state of affairs, when criticized, is generally justified by arguing that actors in a position of power must be evaluated according to their ability to attain large objectives in uncertain situations. One of the outcomes is that the success or failure of a series of moves depends, largely, on a global appraisal effected at the game's end.

It is not unusual that actors who have occupied dominant positions come to confide in private encounters (or, e.g., in memoirs written at the end of one's life) the way in which they managed to perform great things. By doing so, they frequently disclose information that they could not publicly reveal during the course of action. They describe, for example, how they were compelled to circumvent some rules, or to overstep them, in order to reach their objectives. Nevertheless, they can justify afterwards these infringements of the rules by arguing that they would never have succeeded in realizing such efficient actions—so useful, not only for themselves but, above all, for the common good—if they had remained trapped in the cage of rules. But frequently, they also seem eager to mark the difference between these mere 'arrangements' and what could be seen as clear transgressions, arguing that they had to withdraw from the 'letter of the rule' but did so with the intention of remaining as close as possible to the 'spirit of the rule'.

This fuzzy appreciation of the rules echoes the relation—not cynical but just, instrumental, and devoid of any sacred aura—that the dominant ones frequently adopt towards institutions—at least when they are not within sight of the dominated. They can then, rather easily, recognize that institutions are nothing more than *artefacts*. And this disillusioned knowledge comes out from one of their very specific experiences, consisting in producing and imposing rules and in manufacturing institutions. They do not ignore that institutions are human devices which can be built, transformed, or abolished. Their mode of relation to reality places them in connivance with the hermeneutical contradiction. This contradiction is not altogether abolished nor even disclosed, but—so to speak—tamed. And, as to the distinction between the letter of the rule and the spirit of the rule, it endows them with a kind of moral plasticity, which is very convenient in order to cope with the tension between uncertainty and rules.

If we turn now towards the dominated, we have to face a very different situation. In this case, the network of rules surrounding actions is tighter and the control to which they are subjected is operated on a narrower scale. They are supposed to 'obey', which means to respect the letter of the rules imposed from above, and they are also supposed to believe that the institutions supporting these rules are something similar to real beings, immutable and inviolable.

It is, of course, evident that the dominated can, no more than the dominating, pursue actions and remain in strict conformity with the rules, something well described by the anthropology of resistance or by the sociology of Taylorism. But, in this case, the distance they must necessarily take with rules, if they want truly to act, is socially labelled as transgressing, and must, therefore, be masked so as to escape sanction.

These asymmetries regarding rules and institutions must be connected with the capabilities of intervening upon reality. The mere fact of enjoying the possibility of modifying rules and institutions is the basis of the subjective and objective autonomy characterizing the dominants. But, vice versa, it is because they take liberties with the rules that they can effectively intervene upon reality, modifying not only the course of their own life but also the lives of a more or less important number of other persons.

Emancipation in a pragmatic meaning

These brief remarks help us to see how emancipation must be understood in this frame. It does not call for an appeal against the dominants requiring them to respect, *in fact*, the rules they recognize as valid, *in principle*. Such exigencies, marked by moral indignation, are, nowadays, very frequent, at least verbally. It is the case, for example, when one demands a strengthening of the power of the state in order to compel the persons in charge to respect the common rules and to give more transparency to their actions. These proclamations are doomed either to remain wishful thinking or to lead to authoritarianism.

The direction we suggest is the opposite. A move towards emancipation would consist in establishing a political context in which the dominated could demand and acquire the same kind of freedom with regard to rules that characterizes the freedom enjoyed by the dominants. Such a conception of emancipation does not however imply a radical contestation of institutions, the necessity of which we stressed. But the process of emancipation, considered at least since the Enlightenment as a path towards equality, supposes that everyone equally can establish the same kind of relationship with the hermeneutic contradiction and its outcomes. In other words, it means that those who are now dominated would be recognized as having the same capacities of action and, thus, of interpretation, which currently constitute the privilege of the dominants. A move in this direction requires two things: first, everyone would be entitled to criticize the rules and, even more, to interpret and to adjust them, as the dominants actually do. Second, institutions, without being abolished, would be deprived of their intangible and quasi-sacred aura so that everyone could regard them from the same distance and with the same flexibility already assumed by those who have control and power.

Such a decrease of asymmetry regarding the hermeneutic contradiction would not suppress, all at once, all the different kinds of asymmetries, particularly the ones that derive from a very unequal distribution of property rights. But one can surmise that it would constitute, at least partly, a sort of pre-condition in this direction, by releasing capacities of acting that could serve the struggles aimed at decreasing such inequalities. If one admits that the relation to rules and institutions is closely linked to the power of acting, one must recognize that the development of the capabilities of action of ordinary people would be both the condition and the result of such a turn.

One of the consequences of the process of emancipation, expressed in these terms would be, probably, to modify the outlines of the sovereign nation state. This last form is still conceived as the institution of institutions or, if one prefers, as the legitimate foundation of the administrative and organizing powers which ensure, *de facto*, the maintenance of reality and the perpetuation of social asymmetries. A policy aimed at equalizing the relation towards rules, and at establishing a dialogical relationship between institutional forms of confirmation and devices devoted to critique, would, perhaps, contribute to a weakening of state violence, thereby maintaining the peacemaking and unifying functions fulfilled by institutions—functions that only institutions can ensure.

References

Alexander, J. C. (1995) *Fin de Siècle Social Theory*. New York: Verso.

Boltanski, L. (2011) *On Critique: A Sociology of Emancipation*. Cambridge: Polity Press.

—— Chiapello, E. (2005) *The New Spirit of Capitalism*. London and New York: Verso.

—— Thévenot, L. (2006) *On Justification: Economies of Worth*. Princeton, NJ: Princeton University Press.

Kantorowicz, E. H. (1957) *The King's Two Bodies: A Study in Mediaeval Political Theology*. Princeton, NJ: Princeton University Press.

Latour, B. (2005) *Reassembling the Social: An Introduction to Actor-Network-Theory*. Oxford: Oxford University Press.

Rancière, J. (2004) *The Philosopher and his Poor*. Durham, NC: Duke University Press.

Ricoeur, P. (2008) *From Text to Action: Essays in Hermeneutics, II*. London: Continuum.

Searle, J. R. (1969) *Speech Acts: An Essay in the Philosophy of Language*. Cambridge: Cambridge University Press.

—— (1971) *The Philosophy of Language*. London: Oxford University Press.

Wittgenstein, L. (1958) *Philosophical Investigations* (2nd edn.). Oxford: Blackwell.

3

Capitalism and Its Criticisms

Eve Chiapello

Introduction

The history of capitalism cannot be separated from the history of its criticisms. Many social innovations were initially conceived and tried out by reformers who were sometimes considered utopian dreamers by their contemporaries, before being put into practice and encouraged by enlightened business managers or incorporated into law by progressive politicians. Transformation of the economic system has always partly arisen through the recuperation of critical ideas, often in a time of crisis when the search for alternatives intensifies because the usual remedies are no longer working.

An increasing number of conferences, books, and special editions are currently trying to diagnose the ills afflicting us and assess the emerging proposals. For, capitalism is undergoing an unprecedented crisis, at once social, ecological, moral, economic, and financial. Ecological disasters (of natural causes or resulting from technical attempts at risk control, as demonstrated by the BP oil platform leak in the Gulf of Mexico) are on the rise, the risk of further financial collapse continues, and most populations are finding it hard to make ends meet or are sliding into poverty. Against this background, there is a proliferation of initiatives and ideas for reform and change. Similar moments have occurred in the history of capitalism when what Topalov calls 'reforming nebula' (Topalov, 1999) appeared, for example, in the late nineteenth century, the 1930s (Boltanski, 1987; Kuisel, 1981), and the 1970s (Boltanski and Chiapello, 2005*a*). These moments are characterized by an intense period of collective work, involving political and administrative personnel, trade unions, think-tanks, intellectuals, schools, non-governmental organizations (NGOs), consultants, managers and manager groups, and more. This is largely happening as a result of pressure from critical social movements, some of which can be very radical in order to identify what should be changed in capitalism and how those changes should be achieved. Identification of problems is principally left to the critics, but the responses are constructed collectively by the various actors. One of the results is the construction of compromises between the capitalist logic (profit) and the amendments proposed by the criticism, not all of which are adopted. Most participants in these nebulae are searching for a 'third way', so named for its similarities with the projects of the 1930s that helped to invent the post-Second World War planned market economy (Berland and Chiapello, 2009; Kuisel, 1981) and sought to avoid both the excesses of economic liberalism and the state socialism of communist countries.

Capitalism seems, thus, to be embarking on a new cycle of recuperation, during which a criticism will be assimilated. In the book I wrote with Luc Boltanski (Boltanski and Chiapello, 2005a), we were concerned by a movement whereby the 1970s protests were being appropriated for incorporation into capitalist systems. I am convinced that we are now seeing the beginning of a new cycle of recuperation and appropriation. This chapter examines that argument and extends it by suggesting that a new form of criticism—ecological criticism—which was very much present in the 1970s unrest—but not to a point where it could reorient capitalism—has now become a central element in the recuperation and restructuring of capitalism. What are the differences between this cycle of recuperation and its predecessors?

To answer this question, I will first give a more detailed presentation of the framework I intend to use for the analysis of the changes in capitalism. I will then give a detailed review of the history and propositions of the different criticisms of capitalism, and end by identifying the 'third ways' currently under discussion to reform capitalism.

The framework of analysis

The theoretical framework used as a basis here was initially developed to propose an interpretation of changes in business management methods and the accompanying ideologies over a period prior to that concerned in this chapter (Boltanski and Chiapello, 2005a). The aim was to understand the shift in France from the post-May 1968 years, with their loudly asserted criticism of capitalism, to the 1980s, when criticism fell silent and the organizational forms on which capitalism's operation depended underwent profound change, up to the hesitant search for new critical bases in the second half of the 1990s. However, the model goes beyond the merely descriptive, as we also intended to propose a more general theoretical model through this historical example.

One major characteristic of the model of change developed in this way is the role it attributes to the criticism of capitalism in the change in corporate practices and the related ideologies. This criticism is produced by social reformers and the social networks they belong to. Their output is of course theoretical, aiming to diagnose problems, draw attention to situations considered negative, propose modifications, etc., but also practical, with the implementation of various campaigns belonging to what Tilly (1986) calls the 'repertoires of collective action' (propaganda, training courses, demonstrations, strikes, boycotts, etc.).

Criticism of capitalism is as old as capitalism itself. We focused in Boltanski and Chiapello (2005a) on two types of criticism that have developed since the nineteenth century, the social criticism and the artistic criticism, which were both very active in the 1970s. This chapter also looks at two other types of criticism: the conservative criticism and the ecological criticism. According to this framework, the forms in which capital accumulation exists at a given time greatly depend on the type and virulence of the criticism levelled at it. Some of the transformations undergone by capitalism since May 1968 can thus be analysed as a clever integration of the 'artistic critique' and its demands for autonomy, creativity, more authentic interpersonal relationships, etc.

The interaction between capitalism on one side and criticisms of capitalism on the other gives rise to the spirit of capitalism of a given period. The spirit of capitalism is an ideological configuration situated in space and time, which provides

- a stylistic description of certain features of business operations at a given time (e.g. today we talk of cognitive or informational, international, flexible, connexionist, or financial capitalism as opposed to Taylorian, industrial, hierarchical, or national capitalism); and

- a normative indication of the right way to behave in order to succeed in this world, explaining how this is fitting, fair, and legitimate.

The spirit of capitalism operates both as a source of understanding and legitimization of capitalism and an active constraint on capitalism, as legitimization can work only as long as the reality is not too far from the ideal model. This is where criticism has a role to play: its accusations force capitalism to mend or justify its ways. Failure to do either could cost its legitimacy, and ultimately its operative capacity. Clear-sightedness and dynamism are required if a criticism is to achieve the following: first, narrow the gap between the wonderful world of the spirit of capitalism and the real world; and, second, incorporate new constraints into capitalist systems, to compensate for various problems pointed out and monitored by the criticism.

This framework gives criticism a partly functional role in relation to capitalism. Being blind to all the forms of disaster it generates, capitalism benefits from the monitoring and inventions of the critical movements. As long as its profit-based dynamic can continue to operate, it can integrate various constraints and try out a range of systems. This capacity for assimilation is one of the reasons for the impressive longevity of this economic system, which Marx considered doomed to a rapid demise.

But although this role for criticism in the dynamics of capitalism is striking, it is not the only one. Regardless of whether it is appropriated by capitalism or not, criticism plays several roles in the change process. This is why, more generally, the forms in which capital accumulation exists at a given time greatly depend on the type and virulence of the criticism levelled at it.

First, criticism produces ungovernability, a situation that naturally encourages changes of method, particularly by business managers, in order to regain the capacity to govern. It can itself produce a crisis, as occurred at the end of the 1960s (the governability crisis came before the economic crisis, which happened only in 1973). Criticism is a reason for change.

Secondly, criticism also produces ideas, with the essential part of the reforming vision probably concentrating on the problematic aspects revealed. Some of these ideas will be taken on board and integrated into management practices, maybe because while satisfying the criticism they also serve profit, or because they provide a means of motivating people in a change process (even if the change is desired for reasons other than the pressure exerted by the critics), or even because integration is the only way to silence persistent, inventive criticism whose virulence is beginning to undermine employee motivation and cause disorganization in the enterprise. It can thus be said that a successful criticism is fated to be taken over and adapted. This, strictly speaking, is the recuperation process.

Thirdly, criticism also contributes to the construction of the normativity that accompanies capitalism, and consequently justifies it while placing constraints on it, making capitalism incorporate the values that just a short while before served to criticize it. Through this shift, capitalism incorporates its enemy's value system to survive, making a compromise between its tendency to accumulation and the necessity of being able to commit enough people to function and thus respond satisfactorily to criticism. This is another aspect of the appropriation process.

Fourthly, criticism has another very different role as a source of 'displacement', motivating capitalism to 'escape' to another method or location. If the cost of responding to criticism is considered too high, and if capitalism can find another way of making money, organizing production, and managing its workforce, it will do so (without assimilating any of the criticism). Relocating manufacturing to countries with lower wages and social security costs is a typical example of such displacement. Criticism can even provide a justification for this displacement process. Because capitalism faces more than one stream of criticism, it can escape from certain criticisms in a move that provides a satisfactory response to another kind of criticism.

Three main forms of criticism that appeared in the mid-nineteenth century and have continued to be central can be identified: I call them the 'conserva-tive criticism', the 'social criticism', and the 'artistic criticism'. These first criticisms were joined in the twentieth century by a fourth, the ecological criticism. This classification of criticisms of capitalism is based on two major criteria:

- What phenomena attributed to capitalism does the criticism aim to denounce? These are called the 'causes of indignation': not only are these factors judged negative, they are also considered as the consequences of the capitalist economic system, although the label 'capitalist' is not necessarily used by the principal authors. The causes of indignation are not always rooted in concrete descriptions intended to arouse indignation, but are themselves often theoretically constructed and expressed in the form of mega-concepts such as the class struggle or alienation. This is why identification of what arouses the indignation of the critical authors cannot be separated from identification of their conceptual universe.

- What are the underlying values in the name of which the criticism is operating? These are not always easily identifiable, and are often deduced from analysing the objects of the authors' indignation and what they appear to be proposing instead. Careful analysis is often necessary to bring out the underlying values. Boltanski (2009) has shown that not all critical arguments are constructed in the same way.

Table 3.1 gives a brief and concise overview of the various criticisms, putting to one side the different types of critique and argument within each broad category.

The following section elaborates these forms of criticisms in more detail, in particular providing a more detailed account of the 'ecological criticism', before in the final section examining how the ecological criticism is being brought into the process of recuperating capitalism in the current period.

The history and current situation of the four criticisms

The social criticism

We actually owe the concept of capitalism to the social criticism, and that is why no critical movement of capitalism can really afford to ignore this criti-cism. The social criticism is concerned with what capitalism imposes on the people whose labour is used: they are reduced to production components in

Table 3.1. The four types of criticism

	Conservative criticism	Social criticism	Artistic criticism	Ecological criticism
Causes of indignation	Poverty/insecurity, moral disorder, destruction of solidarity, class struggle	Poverty/inequalities, wage relationships, exploitation, command of capital, class domination	Mediocrity, stupidity; uniformization, massification, commodification, conditioning; alienation	Destruction of ecosystem, species, and human habitats
Underlying values	Shared dignity common to all human beings, class interdependence, moral duty of the elite	Labour, equality (in economic terms and in decision-making) as the necessary condition for a true freedom	Personal autonomy (internal and external), taste and refined existence (art, philosophy, truth, etc.)	Shared dignity common to all living beings, life of future generations

the economic machinery, and lose all value if they cannot find employment. With the social criticism, labour takes on a glorious status and is celebrated as the creative activity *par excellence*, and the source of the value of things. The essence of man is labour. Man's history is the history of his self-production via his creative activity. Consequently, any examination of 'real' labour and the conditions of the workers who in fact embody the greatness of man reveals several scandals that the social criticism constantly exposes. Not only do the people who are the source of all value draw no benefit from it, being confined to unbearable poverty with no power to decide what they should do (heteronomy at work), while others who do no work but simply own the capital become richer and have the power to command the workers; in addition, the work the workers are asked to do uses only a tiny part of their creative potential, and mistreats or permanently cripples what forms the very core of their humanity. The social criticism cannot be dissociated from a profound Labour philosophy.

This rooting in the question of labour goes hand in hand with the central importance for this criticism of the question of exploitation. Exploitation is the schema that can connect the poverty of poor workers and the wealth of the idle rich: under this analysis, revenues from capital are 'in fact' produced by labour that is not remunerated on a level commensurate with the full value it produces, since some is taken up by the capital.

The Labour philosophy of the social criticism explains why the most recent attempts at reformulation have strived to extend the notion of labour to situations other than that of wage labour. This is the case for Negri and Hardt (2000), who explain that what is being exploited is now social labour as a whole, and therefore the activity of human beings in its entirety, and Holloway (2005), who bases part of his book on the distinction between 'doing' and 'done', a direct reference to the traditional distinction between labour (doing) and the product of labour (done). Moulier-Boutang (2007) is also faced with this difficulty, and identifies a new type of exploitation, 'degree 2 exploitation', in which it is no longer the labour force that is being exploited but the 'invention force'. What is subject to exploitation is thus the availability in people of the knowledge, skills, and capacities for invention accumulated within them (and thus not directly appropriable), which can be profitable for those who buy their labour, but more importantly lie at the source of many 'positive externalities'. The cognitive worker is in fact producing something for which he is not being paid.

The social criticism reached an unprecedented scale with the works and militant positions of Karl Marx, forcing everyone to take a position. Through their scope and depth, Marx's analyses remain a central reference for the social criticism. The history of the social criticism is thus partly the history of the study of Marx, of how his analysis was adapted to a changing economic world, and how his ideas were hybridized with new theoretical frameworks.

The indignation that runs through the social criticism in response to the real situation of labour in the capitalist world (exploitation, which explains the inequality between the working poor and the non-working rich, domination at work, and alienation) lies at the heart of its eventful history and highlights why the social criticism is multi-faceted, with sub-groups fighting tooth and nail over questions such as the role and relevance of the state, trade unions, the general strike, revolution or reform, and the necessary degree of liberty as a principle of social organization.

There are two major groups within the social criticism.

- The first made the exploitation issue its main battleground. Its supporters thought that collectivization of production means and elimination of market mechanisms would put an end to exploitation by abolishing private monopolization of the surplus and price-setting determined by competition. This was the path chosen by socialist countries that were unable to abolish either wage labour and work subject to command or the bureaucratic and hierarchical form of the enterprise and could only distribute economic flows differently.

In these analyses, economic inequality is the mother of all evils, and should therefore be the first target for action if we are to put an end to domination and alienation. It is because capital is initially unequally distributed that some people must work to live while others can use their capital to buy machines, resources, and labour, and combine them to make products that will then be sold at a profit on the market. People endowed with capital can make investments, and have the time to wait for returns on their investments. This initial inequality in ownership is also the source of the domination of capital:

because it pays, it can command labour and make it undertake tasks that cripple creative capacities (alienation).

- The second considered that the most urgent need was to release labour from the oppression it suffered, and fought all forms of heteronomy affecting the worker, who never chooses what she or he will do or how she or he will do it but must always obey: obey the employer at work and obey the state outside work. For this libertarian type of social criticism, collectivization without elimination of heteronomy is simply a continuation of oppression by other means. The state planning, which replaced market forces, in fact increased this oppression. Clearly, after the failed experiments of the socialist countries which not only abolished exploitation at the price of intolerable oppression but also—and this must have been a particularly bitter lesson for the most fervent believers— managed to stifle their country's whole wealth-creation process, the social criticism of today finds itself forced to incorporate a large share of anarchy-inspired propositions in order to retain its credibility. This is the case for an interesting fringe of the social criticism's intellectual production (see e.g. Holloway, 2005), as illustrated by the success of Negri and Hardt's *Empire* (2000).

It is interesting to note that the state-control type of social criticism, which believed that the state could be relied on to solve the social question, did not only give rise to the experiments of the socialist countries. It also inspired a formidable wave of adoption of its proposals for assimilation into capitalism, and construction of what is now known as 'social democracy'. Thus social criticism also encompasses non-Marxists, the most famous of whom historic-ally are the social technocrats: in the nineteenth century they were Saint-Simonians; they became proponents of state planning in the 1930s, and then Keynesians after the Second World War; they believed that only technological and economic progress would bring social progress, and that the state and its engineers can and must intervene in the economy to rationalize it and prevent it from producing social disasters. What the economists called 'Fordism' can also be seen as incorporation into capitalism of planning processes of a range of social protection measures that socialism also promised. The reformers of capitalism who constructed Fordism after the Second World War also sought to abolish exploitation by influencing the distribution processes for the wealth created by enterprises' economic activities (Berland and Chiapello, 2009).

The success of the statist social criticism after the Second World War in both capitalist and communist countries can be credited with pushing aside the libertarian social criticism, which was also savagely repressed on both sides, making its current renaissance partly attributable to the crisis of the statist solution, not only in communist countries but also in capitalist countries.

67

The current ideological situation is one of mistrust towards all forms of state regulation, which are under attack from all sides:

- from proponents of free market economics, who consider that the state should not obstruct the workings of the market and free competition between economic agents. According to these ideologists, the role of the state is, on the contrary, to improve the operation of existing markets and help create others whenever there are trade-offs to be made between divergent private interests. The law of the market is the only law that respects individual choices, which can all be expressed, and it must apply to all possible choices, and therefore also to activities that were formerly governed by the public authorities;

- from critics (on both the right and the left) of the experiments of the state socialism countries, accused of creating a new totalitarianism, who believe the state can only ever be oppressive; and

- finally, from analysts of contemporary states, who note that these states are in any case incapable of regulating capitalism, which is totally beyond their control and shows no respect for national frontiers. These analysts attribute the crisis in nation states' regulatory capacity to globalization (which also results from the firms' progressive release from their legal and political shackles).

This loss of credibility for the state control approach has nonetheless arisen concomitantly with a renewal in the social question in the most traditional sense of the term. Although globalization made possible a worldwide recovery for growth and a renewal of entrepreneurial activity, it has ultimately led to an unprecedented return of the most traditional forms of exploitation. The capacity for monopolization of wealth associated with control of capital (I am thinking of actors on the financial markets, or the business management elites) and possession of capital is once again at a high point in its history, breathing new life into the old criticism of exploitation that social democracy thought for a while it could hold in check. In many countries, globalization has not fulfilled its promises: 'labour and environmental conditions deteriorated, the number of people living in extreme poverty failed to decline, and inequality increased. Global awareness of such imbalances and regulatory deficits, and of the need for institutional reform, was reinforced through a series of UN summits and commissions, as well as through the "anti-globalisation" movement' (Utting, 2005: 377).

This spurs the social criticism into action, although it is put in an awkward position by the loss of legitimacy of the statist solution. Of course, the statist social criticism has found new reason to act in this situation and is lobbying for the construction of a supranational government. The plan to construct a more unified Europe has been a vehicle for a great many such hopes. Some would also like the United Nations institutions to be able to create 'hard law'. However, the partisans of such solutions are having trouble making themselves heard and have to propose more 'transparent', 'participatory', and 'accountable' arrangements than the public solutions of the Fordist age.

Libertarian proposals, meanwhile, although experimented with by small groups on the margins of the globalized economy (e.g. the Zapatista movement in Mexico's Chiapas region or the Brazilian Landless Workers movement), are not considered capable of supporting societies as intensive as our own in financial, technological, and human capital.

The propositions of the social criticism in response to the crisis are thus not unique. As in the past, we find ideas from anarchist-type movements that want to do away with the state and construct a self-managed society, as well as ideas from neo-Fordists who think that regulation of capitalism can be reconstructed at supranational level.

The conservative criticism

The conservative criticism, like the social criticism, is preoccupied with the social question, but, in contrast to the social criticism, associates these concerns closely with the question of moral order. This heterogeneous current includes, in France, social Catholics[1] and 1930s corporatists, some of whose ideas were put into practice under the Vichy government. The works of Frédéric Le Play are a good example of this criticism, and the writings of Alexis de Tocqueville and Edmund Burke paved the way. Criticism of the disappearance of the nobility of duty and the old feudal, knightly spirit of loyalty characteristic of the *ancien régime* is one of their common features.

---

[1] Christian movements, both Catholic and Protestant, were more broadly behind this criticism in the capitalist West. For example, dissenters (radical protestants) concerned for Christian values and saving souls were to be found in England's first Fabian Society, and one of the books considered a founding work in 'corporate social responsibility' in the United States (Bowen, 1953) was commissioned by the Federal Council of the Churches of Christ in America. The concern for the poorer members of society which is supposed to go with Christian faith has always led some Christians to examine the social question and propose reforms. Since the first social Encyclical of 1891 (Rerum Novarum), the Catholic church has constantly updated its 'social doctrine'. Clearly, the view of business taken by religions in general tends to discredit its aim (making profits) as divergent from the means. At best, profit is a means or a constraint. This explains why religions are sources of inspiration for the criticism of capitalism. However, the conservative criticism cannot be assumed to be a synonym for all religion-inspired criticisms. Our concept of the conservative criticism is more precise in its analysis and proposals. It can be supported by people with no religious faith, and does not claim to cover all the protests inspired by one religion or another. Case-by-case examination is necessary to decide whether the criticism by a given religious movement can be considered equivalent to the conservative criticism that emerged among European Christians concerned with the social question in the late nineteenth century.

For conservatives, labour is precious because it contributes to moral educa-tion and provides a path to a virtuous life, not because, as in social criticism, it is through labour that man expresses his humanity. This leads to criticism of the idle lifestyle of the rich, who have time to develop animal passions and sensual appetites. Wealth creates bad morals. The lack of work for the poor, who depend on the rich for their work, is also the source of moral disorder, encouraging drunkenness and immoral behaviour.

Capitalism—because it accelerates impoverishment by encouraging the rural exodus and the abandonment of working the land, increases the vulner-ability of all existence, makes it easier to become rich in a short time, and fosters construction of gigantic enterprises which through the effect of numbers and geographical distance prevent the upkeep of personal connec-tions between rich and poor—is reprehensible. The problem does not lie in the unfair distribution of economic value and the lack of freedom for the masses. It lies in the disintegration and moral decline of society. Conservative thought is organic and functionalist. The classes are interdependent, parts of a whole that are naturally differentiated; they experience unequal conditions, but all have equal dignity. A man's dignity depends on his morals, his virtues, and his merits, which are accessible to all, rich or poor. And the virtue of the rich is to understand that it is their duty to look after those who are poorer.

Consequently, the solutions put forward by the conservative criticism are very different from those of the social criticism. It argues that a spirit of duty should be restored to the governing classes.[2] In day-to-day business manage-ment, development of personal connections and affection towards employees is recommended, and the firm owner should have a duty to live on the same territory as his workers, so that he (conservatives generally have a strictly gender-segregated view of the world) will retain a permanent concern for their living conditions and safety. In particular, it is desirable that a worker should have a small plot of land to cultivate, giving him a guaranteed food supply independent of the wage relationship, through work of his own that no one can take from him. Finally, various measures should be taken for the education and moral edification of workers.

The conception, characteristic of the conservative criticism, of an elite whose domination is counterbalanced by duties to the less fortunate and an obligation to construct a fairer world is still with us today. The modern incantations calling for 'responsible' or 'moral' capitalism are one of its current forms. The conservative criticism is still active today, and as in the nineteenth century continues to be linked to the religious question. Employers and executives with no publicly declared Christian faith but

---

[2] These ideas were also developed in England in the early twentieth century by Alfred Marshall in his 'economic chivalry' concept. In fact, a large part of the European elites agreed with these analyses.

whose actions are nonetheless inspired by religious commitments are often at the forefront in promotion of more 'responsible' practices or campaigning for a new corporate philanthropy. In the United States, many support services for the unemployed are connected with churches. The religious factor thus remains an important factor in the elite's commitment to reforming practices, and the conservative criticism has the advantage of involving them without challenging the legitimacy of their command.

Being closely related to the protestant work ethic with which Max Weber (1992) is considered to have encouraged the development of a disposition favourable to capitalism, the conservative criticism cannot be a channel for criticism of capitalism's underlying dynamics. In particular, it does not criticize the right to private ownership, which, in contrast, is seen as the instrument of appropriation of surplus and lies at the core of the social criticism. Nor does it criticize the command of capital, so long as it is moral. For the conservative criticism, it is normal for positions in society to be unequal: what is important is to entrust government to the best. Provided a society is able to put the most worthy and most humane people in positions of power, nothing needs to change structurally in the current economic system. The subordinate levels of society must also learn that what is essential in life is not personal fulfilment and the extension of personal freedom, but a moral life 'with meaning', which relates back to an ascetic ethic of work and a frugal life; poor people's aspirations to consumerism are unanimously denounced. This model focuses less on the way the business functions than on the sharing of the surplus. Thus, what the conservative criticism calls into question is not the enterprise or its operation, but mainly the morals of the people. Although not a radical criticism of capitalism, it remains very powerful and useful for involving the dominant classes in cycles of reform. It can be considered to have been at work in each cycle of recuperation of criticism by capitalism.

The artistic criticism

In contrast to the previous two criticisms, the artistic criticism shows very little concern for the social question or the workers' lot. Its main concern is the transformation of lifestyles in a capitalist society. The whole life of a human being finds itself shaped by capitalist processes: not only his working life but even his consumption patterns and education. Everyday life is taken over by the capitalist machine. Life has lost all authenticity, depth, and unexpectedness. The useful and the functional reign supreme. This is recognizable as a criticism of mass society, the consumer society (Baudrillard, 1970), the self-perpetuating growth of the technical (Ellul, 1964), societies of control and discipline (Deleuze, 1990; Foucault, 1975), submission to the logic of the tool (Illich, 1973), learned needs, and indoctrination (Marcuse,1964).

The artistic criticism is a criticism of alienation, making it an ally of the social criticism which points a finger at alienation in work, but here the accent is on general, widespread alienation, the imprisonment of the human being in a world of commodities. This is an awkward critical position, as it requires the critic to look down from above on the general conditioning. The critic has come out of his cavern and is no longer like his fellow men. This is an aristocratic position (Chiapello, 1998). It knows that a more refined culture exists and that it is possible to gain access to authentic pleasures that have not been manufactured by the mass society. The artistic criticism will push for elitist cultural policies that do not depend on industries, and school curricula focusing on education of taste and artistic practices. It takes action through creative hijacking of advertising messages, festive occupation of the symbols of modern society (Klein, 2000), a refusal to consume the products of capitalism (particularly television), and possibly modern education and health services (Illich, 1973). But despite all this potential for action, the artistic criticism is often associated simply with a disillusioned view of the world as it stands, considered as inescapable.

While the first two criticisms inspired the whole reformist effort up to the 1960s, the artistic criticism—which argued more for withdrawing from the world than for reforming action—only became a real threat for capitalism in the 1970s, attacking simultaneously on the fronts of labour (with the development of a refusal to take orders, and also to give them) and consumption (rejection of standardized products). As analysed in *The New Spirit of Capitalism* (Boltanski and Chiapello, 2005a), this sudden movement inspired relatively large-scale transformations in behaviours, the organization of work, and product design. The last cycle of appropriation by capitalism fed on the anti-authoritarian mood to construct a more flexible world in which life was organized by projects, bringing about more individualized, creative, and fulfilling careers, with employers no longer telling workers what to do but stimulating their energies.

Unfortunately, these transformations came about at the cost of much lower job security, as all projects come to an end one day. The hoped-for liberation of labour was only partial, and only concerned those who were best endowed with the skills prized by capitalism. In consumption, a marketing movement began for systematic adoption of challenges and creative hijacking (Klein, 2000). Everything could be marketed, and some market study bureaux spent their time scrutinizing the smallest avant-garde inventions, the latest youth protest movement, the clothes and music found in trouble-spot neighbourhoods, and more. Enterprises, too, sought to offer consumers something different, more attention, a personal relationship, authenticity—a tall order when the aim is for constant quality at reasonable cost (which tends to be achieved through standardization). These transformations fostered development of lifestyles since denigrated as 'bourgeois-bohemian' (Brooks, 2000), in which money makes it possible to buy a certain quantity of authentic, unique products which can never become accessible to all consumers.

Despite the efforts made in recent decades to incorporate more authenticity into labour and consumption, it seems that, as analysed in Boltanski and Chiapello (2005a), the task is unending, because the very instrumentalization of the desire for authenticity in managerial practices causes an act to lose its authenticity. Conversely, any attempt to invent cultural forms that are divorced from merchandise is quickly hijacked by marketing, and does not remain long outside the sphere of merchandise (Klein, 2000). The cycle of recuperation has become both very short and rapidly inefficient.

It also appears that, after a period of expansion and autonomy at work, since 2000 we have been witnessing a reinforcement of corporate control, which is by no means unconnected to the digital and Internet revolution. The forms of control have changed profoundly, shifting from hierarchical supervision towards a combination of a self-produced visibility (i.e. a source of auto-control) and more systematic market relationships. Paradoxically, business managers have succeeded in increasing both autonomy at work and control (which is a negation of autonomy). The forms of autonomy and control change over time, under the pressure of the demands of the artistic criticism and because of the opportunities opened up by new technologies, but the core demands of the artistic criticism (i.e. self-determination) appear in the end to be impossible for capitalism to incorporate.

The artistic criticism is still alive, reflected, for example, in the Adbusters movement. But in several aspects it can be considered that its hybridization with the ecological criticism is what really keeps it going. Both criticisms share a dislike of the technical (dehumanizing and alienating for the artistic criticism, blinding technophilia for the ecological criticism), consumerism (meaningless and numbing for the artistic criticism, source of excessive pressure on the biosphere for the ecological criticism), and the industrial system (oppressive for the artistic criticism, oriented towards an impossible, endless accumulation of material things in a finite world, in the ecological view). Finally, nature offers a form of authenticity that may be sought by the artistic criticism.

The ecological criticism

This criticism, which in my opinion lies at the heart of the new cycle of appropriation we have now entered, puts the question in yet another way. Quite simply, it challenges the ability of the capitalist system to guarantee the future of mankind, beginning with its reproducibility. The focus is no longer on indignation at the worker's lot, the destructive selfishness of the dominant classes, or the disciplinary nature of society. Capitalism, by its very operation, is leading directly to destruction of our civilization.

One specificity of the ecological criticism in the strictest sense is that it appears to have no preference for any particular political model. It is possible, for instance, to be anti-democracy and pro-ecology. Some even think that only a strong authoritarian state will be capable of preventing the disaster and accumulated effects of individual selfishness (Jonas, 1984). Individual liberty can be a bad counsellor, and in deep ecology equality is to be shared with all living species, who have an equal claim to life. Will human beings be capable of such sharing without being constrained to do so? In contrast, there are many ecologists who combine their criticism with the libertarian social criticism and promote the opposite political model (Naess, 1989). These ecologists consider that the problem lies in large-scale industrialization and the mass society, which can be effectively fought only by challenging the hierarchical and technocratic political model that makes them function.

The fact remains that the lack of any embedded political model makes the ecological criticism highly adaptable to all regimes and all types of labour management. Since capitalism depends on a lack of democracy in working life, and therefore has categorically no need for political democracy, there is a definite risk that assimilation of the ecological criticism will continue to erode current liberties. The 'risk society' focuses on a lost security to be regained and feeds on fear, which rarely goes well with political freedom (Beck, 1992).

The ecological criticism is also divided between advocates of a return to the organization models of traditional societies that use fewer resources and are more respectful of nature with their modestly sized self-governing communities (a utopian idea attractive to both the conservative criticism and the artistic criticism, as well as certain libertarian sections of the social criticism), and modernists who believe that only technical progress can help us to save the planet through renewable energies, advances in genetic engineering and agronomy, and information technologies (this option is more compatible with capitalism and the social criticism's faith in progress). Both these models are gaining ground: on one hand, social self-government, seen as a remedy for the capitalism practised by large businesses that are rejecting more and more workers and making all life artificial; and on the other, colossal technical investments to cope with the issues, without bringing about any change in the basic rules of the economic system.

Searchers for a third way find themselves, I believe, in a totally new situation: they are facing two major questions at once. The older 'social question', the first to arouse anti-capitalist and reforming thought from the mid-nineteenth century, reappeared a while ago and is reflected in all the indicators of social exclusion, poverty, inequalities, and social insecurity. In the meantime, we have come to understand the seriousness of the 'ecological question'. Sooner or later, global warming will force us to drastically reduce greenhouse gas emissions. As for the prospect of using up the earth's natural resources in a few decades, it raises profound questions about our technological society and the durability of existing economic models.

This new situation calls for a more in-depth combination of the social criticism and the ecological criticism, as proposed by eco-socialism. Sociological reasons make this difficult. As the ecological movement tends to draw its members from the middle and upper classes rather than the working classes, it has long been accused of being created by and for the planet's rich elites, who can 'afford the luxury' of worrying about the environment. The social criticism is only just beginning to realize that the poor will be the first to suffer from the ecological question, and that it must therefore extend its concern for social justice to the ecological question. Meanwhile, the ecological movements have long chosen to ignore the risk their demands involve for workers in certain sectors, who could lose their jobs to save certain animal species, or even be prevented from having food and warmth (as illustrated by the arguments over destruction of primary forests) (see Foster, 2002 for an analysis of these problems). Another major obstacle is the social-democratic compromise signed by the social criticism with capitalism, in a plan for indefinite economic growth that is to solve the social question by future increases in wealth and sharing of that wealth. Growth is still today synonymous with job creation and therefore social benefit. The ecological criticism will be able to support this plan only if there is a drastic change in the idea of growth. Considered in its current form involving accumulation of goods and extensive, not to say organized, waste in order to stimulate the desire to buy, it is a plan that quite simply makes no sense for the ecological movement, and furthermore is criminal because it accelerates emergence of the crisis.

But combining the social criticism and the ecological criticism could be made easier, because on two points the ecological criticism's analysis structures are reminiscent of those developed a century earlier by the social criticism:

- Capitalism can operate only because it procures resources for which it pays less than the true value. This is the case for most natural resources, whose finite nature is never taken into account, but also applies to damage that is never repaired or paid for by enterprises. All that is needed is to extend the theme of exploitation.

- Internal contradictions are so intense and systemic that capitalism will self-destruct. Much more worrying than this, however, is the nature of the coming cataclysm, as no radiant future is predicted to follow. All the talk is of wars, famine, epidemics, and a return to medieval lifestyles. At least in the social criticism, the advent of communism was only seen as a cataclysm by a fraction of the population. If criticism must use apocalyptic language to make itself heard, then the ecological criticism is off to a good start.

The ecological criticism, like the original Marxist social criticism, also takes a determinedly materialistic approach in its demonstration methods, and this certainly has its advantages. As long as it can rely on highlighting insurmountable contradictions, it has no need to brandish values in the name of which capitalism is criticized. All that is needed to convince its audience is to patiently describe the workings of the economic machine and scientifically demonstrate their consequences. The critic is no longer a person who tries to impose his values; he is simply a well-informed observer warning you of the risks you run. On this point, the artistic criticism and the conservative criticism with their clearly visible values are more problematic than the social criticism, which uses economic discourse, or the ecological criticism, which uses the discourse of the life sciences.

It now remains to identify the various 'third ways' that are being devised at the intersections between the four criticisms described.

The current reforming nebula

In the current period, these forms of criticism are combining and evolving in three distinctive ways.

Green capitalism and the CSR debate

Modern capitalism could evolve towards 'green capitalism', continuing to pursue economic accumulation through technological solutions to the ecological challenge and adaptation of the social model based on philanthropic practices and 'corporate social responsibility' (CSR). Some enterprises are trying to gain a position on the newly emerging green markets, and design new ranges of services. Rather than a technophobic retreat, priority is being given to the search for alternative technologies and financial investment in research. Businesses are also calling for worldwide governance that can level the field for competition and avoid their competitiveness being eroded by environmental obligations that are not compulsory for all. This is the multinationals' favourite scenario. Large financial investors also support it, because it is the only way forward that does not endanger their power or the 'financialization' of the economy.

This scenario has the approval of the conservative criticism (which has faith in the elites' good intentions) and appears fairly realistic in the globalized world. However, the level of investment and the level of constraints on the economic system may, for ecological reasons in particular, be too low to avoid accentuation of the crisis.

Most CSR initiatives tend to give large multinational companies a role in society that they had not previously sought. The title of a recent book published in 2007 to mark the 25th anniversary of a group of socially committed French companies (*IMS Entreprendre pour la cité*) is significant in this respect: 'Society—is it the firm's business?'[3] The aim is to campaign for businesses to be socially committed, and some companies were already engaged in this orientation before there were any threats from social movements. The determination to construct more responsible firms without state-imposed obligation has also been taken up by some large international NGOs, which long ago abandoned a mere posture of criticism to help firms change and incorporate more responsible practices into their management (e.g. UNICEF, WWF, FIDH). In many respects, 'the CSR agenda, based as it is on voluntary approaches and a critique of government regulation, is often perceived as an alternative to law. A series of recent proposal are attempting to construct a "post-voluntarist" agenda in which CSR is articulated with (*a*) complaints procedures associated with a variety of regulatory institutions, and (*b*) "soft" and "hard" law, which lays down obligations, international standards, rewards, and penalties in relation to corporate transparency, accountability, and performance' (Utting, 2005: 384). It is therefore possible to see the CSR movement as a form of response to the new social and ecological criticisms, which does not seek to abolish wage labour or withdraw from capitalism, in a world in which states are considered powerless and perceived as illegitimate, leaving the obligation of constructing new regulations up to the companies themselves.

The local economy on a human scale

Another possible world is the world of the local economy on a human scale, democratic, 'inclusive', and environmentally friendly. This economy would focus on fundamental material needs and education in a local loop. Local authorities would have a stronger role, in partnership with the economic and social fabric. This is the solidarity-based economy, which can boast of some impressive achievements but still has to gain in visibility and credibility. Nonetheless, the project is acceptable to a social criticism with libertarian tendencies, updating one of its hybrid forms with the artistic criticism (self-management). It can also satisfy the ecological criticism (through its aim of local autonomy for production and supply).

---

[3] *La société, une affaire d'entreprise?*

The specific hybrid of self-management between the libertarian social criticism and the artistic criticism headed the agenda of part of the social movement in France in the 1970s, but has not succeeded in transforming the capitalist world. To succeed, a radical transformation in domination relationships at work would have been required, and such a change is contrary to the capitalist logic of command entrusted to capital or its representatives. The same difficulties still exist today: in fact the current balance of power is even less favourable to social movements, which lack the energy to bring about large-scale change.

The self-management ideal is nevertheless back in fashion among proponents of a solidarity-based economy,[4] but, probably due to the aforesaid unfavourable balance of power, they are more interested in constructing another economy alongside the capitalist economy than in achieving change from within. We know that competition from a different form of economic organization can be an incentive for capitalist enterprises to change, as demonstrated by the years when the communist bloc countries presented a potentially attractive model, and this is the approach currently favoured by some of the critical movements. The renewed interest in old organizational forms such as cooperatives or mutual societies covered by the current nebula should, in my opinion, be seen as related to the inability of capitalist forms of organization to deliver what they want and to the social criticism's search for non-state-controlled alternatives. These alternatives, in actuality, seem so far to have posed no challenge to large companies, which are even developing a certain interest in cooperative forms with a view to accelerating organization in developing countries where they wish to set up establishments. Some, for instance, intend to promote supplier groupings in the form of cooperatives (in the absence of capitalists able to construct large groups by takeovers) in order to have local partners of suitable size and conquer new markets.

It might be considered that the capacity of this 'alternative economy' to threaten capitalism lies either in its large-scale development and competition, or in harder line movements starting with expropriation to take possession of properties (freeing them from the tutelage of a few major owners to hand them over to the greater number, with different management rules). That competition can arouse concern was observed in the late nineteenth and early twentieth centuries when buyers' cooperatives and cooperative bakeries won large market shares in certain areas. These forms spread so widely that some commentators, such as the economist Charles Gide in France (who even occupied a Chair of Social Economy at the Collège de France), were able to

---

[4] See the writings of Paul Singer in Brazil, who can be considered as an ideologist of solidarity-based economy (see e.g. *Introdução à Economia Solidária*. São Paulo: Editora Fundação Perseu Abramo, 2002).

interpret the expansion of buyers' cooperatives as heralding the advent of a new society. The traditional economy's response consisted of tradesmen setting up business cooperatives and central buying offices. Also in France, mutual insurance (from the establishment of the MAIF by the teachers' body in the early twentieth century to the bikers' *Mutuelle des motards* in the late twentieth century) was developed from the outset with a view to reducing market prices for insurance, which were considered unacceptable for future members; these entities were therefore in head-on competition with capitalist insurance. The second type of concern had been aroused by the solidarity-based economic movements in South America, particularly the Brazilian Landless Workers movement.

This type of project for an economy on a human scale could also be popular with certain supporters of the conservative criticism. After all, is not the easiest way to have responsible managers to refuse overexpansion and organize matters so that there is a personal link between the different stakeholders? The potential dispute between the conservatives and the libertarian social criticism would concern decision-making powers, which the libertarians want to see shared by all, while the conservatives want them entrusted to the 'best'.

The return of the state to manage social and ecological issues

Lastly, one final possibility is to have a powerful, restrictive state overseeing the economy for management of shortages and environmental protection, and using robust taxation for redistribution purposes. This is a return to Fordism, but this time ecological as well as social. The level of constraints to place on capitalism would theoretically be higher than in post-war Fordism, as now both the social and ecological questions must be addressed. This will require either a withdrawal of globalization to allow the state to take control of businesses, which will take time, or else construction of restrictive regulations at world level. Whatever solution is adopted, the difficulties of the international climate negotiations (even though everyone agrees on their importance) show that the mentalities, sense of urgency, and pressure of social movements are not enough to elicit firm commitments of this sort from politicians. However, some sections of research in economics, social criticism favouring state control, and the professional interests of civil servants and political staff are encouraging a move in this direction.

Conclusion

The future will show whether capitalism has once more managed to get out of the tight spot it put itself into, once again at the price of a large-scale transformation in its internal operation and game rules. This is why the term 'recuperation', which we use for convenience, cannot be considered totally satisfactory. Once the transformations are complete, we are faced with a capitalism that is no longer quite the same, meaning that the criticism must constantly adjust its position and rework its ideas.

In conclusion, this chapter has aimed:

1. to identify the various ideal types of criticism of capitalism put forward at different points in history, with a clear statement of their specificity. These clarifications are analytically very useful in examining the history of critical doctrines and making history understandable.

2. to retrace the history of these criticisms through the periods in which they influence capitalism and force it to change, sometimes by assimilating part of the criticism; each one has had its hour of glory, and the history of capitalism can be read as the history of its interactions with its criticism. My aim has thus been to extend the model of change in *The New Spirit of Capitalism* beyond the period it was originally designed for.

3. to understand the specific combination in the current revival of the criticism of capitalism, bearing in mind that it relates to the visible problems of the new capitalism, but also to the history of its critical currents. Some options pushed aside for almost seventy years—such as reliance on non-profit-making, small self-governing production units— may resurface as confidence wanes in the state-controlled solutions that dominated twentieth-century reforms. The ecological criticism, which wants to see production and consumption processes that use less transport and are therefore built on local networks and small-scale production, finds itself here in alliance with the libertarian plans to involve every member of small-scale units in decision-making. The conservatives, who advocate solidarity-based capitalism with a human face rather than anonymous gigantism that discourages individual responsibility, may also find this period favourable.

References

Baudrillard, J. (1970) *La société de consommation*. Paris: Gallimard (English translation; London: Sage, 1998).

Beck, U. (1992) *Risk Society: Towards a New Modernity*. London: Sage.

Berland, N. and Chiapello, E. (2009) 'Criticisms of Capitalism, Budgeting and the Double Enrolment: Budgetary Control Rhetoric and Social Reform in France in the 1930s and 1950s', *Accounting, Organizations and Society*, 34(1), 28–57.

Boltanski, L. (1987) *The Making of a Class*. Cambridge: Cambridge University Press (first edition in French, 1982).

—— (2009) *De la critique. Précis de sociologie de l'émancipation*. Paris: Gallimard.

—— Chiapello, E. (2005a) *The New Spirit of Capitalism*. London: Verso (first edition in French, 1999).

—————— (2005b) 'The Role of Criticism in the Dynamics of Capitalism'. In Max Miller (ed.), *Worlds of Capitalism: Institutions, Economics, Performance and Governance in the Era of Globalisation*. London: Routledge Economics, 237–67.

Bowen Howard, R. (1953) *Social Responsibilities of the Businessman*. New York: Harper and Brothers Publishers.

Brooks, D. (2000) *Bobos in Paradise: The New Upper Class and How They Got There*. New York: Simon & Schuster.

Chiapello, E. (1998) *Artistes versus Managers*. Paris: Métailié.

—— (2006) 'Capitalism'. In J. Beckert and M. Zafirovski (eds.), *Encyclopedia of Economic Sociology*. London: Routledge, 35–40.

Deleuze, G. (1990) 'Post scriptum sur les sociétés de contrôle'. In *Pourparlers*. Paris: Editions de Minuit, 240–7.

Ellul, J. (1964) *The Technological Society*. New York: Vintage (first French edition, *La technique ou l'enjeu du siècle*, 1954).

Foster, J. B. (2002) *Ecology Against Capitalism*. New York: Monthly Review Press.

Foucault, M. (1975) *Surveiller et Punir*. Paris: Gallimard (translated to English: *Discipline and Punish, The Birth of the Prison*. New York: Vintage, 1977).

Holloway, J. (2005) *Change the World without Taking Power*. libcom, online.

Illich, I. (1973) *Tools for Conviviality*. New York: Harper & Row Publishers.

Jonas, H. (1984) *The Imperative of Responsibility: In Search of an Ethics for the Technological Age*. Chicago: University of Chicago Press.

Klein, N. (2000) *No Logo: Taking Aim at the Corporate Bullies*. London: Flamingo.

Kuisel, R. (1981) *Capitalism and State in Modern France*. Cambridge: Cambridge University Press.

Marcuse, H. (1964) *One-Dimensional Man: Studies in the Ideology of Advanced Industrial Society*. Boston: Beacon Press.

Moulier-Boutang, Y. (2007) *Le capitalisme cognitif. La nouvelle grande transformation*. Paris: Editions Amsterdam.

Naess, A. (1989) *Ecology, Community and Lifestyle*. Cambridge: Cambridge University Press.

Negri, T. and Hardt, M. (2000) *Empire*. Cambridge, MA: Harvard University Press.

Nisbet, R. (1966) *The Sociological Tradition*. New York: Basic Books.

Perroux, F. (1937) *Capitalisme et communauté de travail*. Paris: Sirey.

Tilly, C. (1986) *The Contentious French*. Cambridge, MA: Harvard University Press.

Topalov, C. (ed.) (1999) *Laboratoires du nouveau siècle. La nébuleuse réformatrice et ses réseaux en France, 1880–1914*. Paris: Editions de l'EHESS.

Utting, P. (2005) 'Corporate Responsibility and the Movement of Business', *Development in Practice*, 15(3/4), 275–388.

Weber, M. (1992) *The Protestant Ethic and the Spirit of Capitalism*. London: Routledge (first edition 1930, HarperCollins Academic, translated by Talcott Parsons).

4

Notes on Aspects of the Conceptual Architecture of the 'New Spirit': Weber and Hirschman

Paul du Gay

Introduction

Of all of Max Weber's texts, one alone has been attributed a special signifi-cance across the social and human sciences: *The Protestant Ethic and the Spirit of Capitalism*. This truly canonical text, frequently referred to as sociology's 'most famous work', was published in English in 1939 with Talcott Parsons as the translator. It was the second of Weber's texts to appear in English, following Knight's translation of *General Economic History*, and the two were, for some time, the only texts in English widely available until the post-war cascade of translations that began with the selection of writings edited by Hans Gerth and C. Wright Mills, *From Max Weber: Essays in Sociology*. Parsons's translation reigned for seventy-two years as the sole authority for the Anglo-phone world until new editions emerged from Peter Baehr and Gordon Wells, based on Weber's original for *Archiv für Sozialwissenschaft und Sozialpolitik* essays of 1904–5, and by Stephen Kalberg using Weber's 1920 revised text, favoured by Parsons (Scaff, 2011: 211). The early translations became the basis of the post-war permeation of Weber's work into the social sciences, in gen-eral, and sociology, in particular. As Wilhelm Hennis (1988), among others, has argued, these translations often ended up attaching Weber's work to the intellectual preoccupations of their translators, thus setting the scene for a series of battles in which Weber and his body of work occupied the part of 'stand-ins' for a set of struggles often far removed from the concrete problem-oriented investigations characterizing his thinking. That said, in the decades since, the underlying issues connected to Weber's thought have never entirely vanished, and those defined by the problematics of 'statecraft and soulcraft', of 'rationality', and that 'most fateful force in our modern life, capitalism', have returned with a vengeance in the opening decade of the current century (Scaff, 2011: 247). Indeed, judging by the numerous edited collections and articles that have appeared over the last decade, there has been not only a renewed interest in many of Weber's specific 'problematics', but also considerable attention directed towards uncovering the 'central generating mechanism' of his entire *oeuvre*. But what exactly would a Weberian 'theory' or 'research programme' signify, given Weber's incomplete, exploratory, and unsystematic writings and his precise (and obsessive) focus on specific problems rather than on generating a general 'theory'? Putting all doubts about the very possibility of such an endeavour aside for one moment, one might, just might, be tempted to say that Weber's central questions were always directed towards investigating developmental dynamics and understanding their consequences for the conduct of life in different (and non-reducible) socio-historical contexts. This is such a broad and abstract rendition that it almost hurts to specify it in such terms. However, let us proceed in a stoical manner. In Weber's work, such questioning is irreducibly singular. However, viewed through the lens of such an expository synthesis as that animating contemporary Weberian sociological scholarship, we might wish to suggest that 'Weberian' analysis is thought to be concerned with three central problems and their relationship to one another: the problem of the *material* form (or *structuring*) in which action occurs, the problem of the *rationality* of action, and the problem of *cultural* 'meanings' and 'significance'. From the perspective of a demand for 'theory', then, the Weberian 'project' seems to straddle analytic approaches in the social sciences that often remain somewhat separate or pose themselves as alternatives to one another: the structural, the institutional, the action-oriented, and the cultural (Scaff, 2011: 247). Furthermore, in posing the matter in this way, it also becomes possible to point out that, in this synthetic Weberian view, the relationship between what we might term 'problem complexes' is worked out at different levels of analysis: at the level of the *individual* as a *certain sort* (or category, in the Maussian sense) *of person*; at something like a *'social'* level of associations, organizations, and institutions; and at the *cultural* level of legitimation processes and disputes over *'value'* and *normative ordering* (Scaff, 2011: 248). What is more, seen in this way, no single problem complex can claim a logical priority either, for to do so would be to prejudge the relationships and dynamics that any specific investigation aims to surface. This insistence on a 'configurational' (or, in the terms of much contemporary social science, 'multilevel' or 'multicausal') analysis or 'stance' highlights the importance of looking for and respecting the unique particularities and differences in any specific configuration—on what Weber termed 'the concatenation of circumstances'. Summarized in this reductive manner (i.e. abstracted from its concrete problematics), the hypostatized 'Weberian' project is amenable to generating modes of analysis and pathways of investigation applicable to the most varied problematics and 'problem complexes'.

It takes little imagination to see that Boltanski and Chiapello's programme is firmly located within this abstracted 'Weberian' paradigm in all its main component dimensions, exhibiting a complex synthesis formed from combining structural and institutional analysis; notions of rationality ('reasons' and 'justifications'); propositions about social action; awareness of cultural particularities, normative ordering, disputes over 'value'; and an appreciation of the importance of historical inquiry and evidence (the 'specificity' of the French road to 'the New Spirit'). However, in adopting this sort of 'Weberian' sociological synthesis, Boltanski and Chiapello inadvertently cut themselves off from perhaps the most consequential re-reading of Weber's work, including *The Protestant Ethic and the Spirit of Capitalism*, currently being undertaken in the humanities and social sciences. In so doing, they may also have blunted both Weber's and their own critical edge in significant ways. Well, how so?

'Office' as a vocation: Max Weber, soulcraft, and statecraft

The ongoing battle for the 'soul' of Weber's work has charted a double course. On one hand, as we indicated above, it has resulted in a Weberian sociology which seeks to recast Weber's work as canonical for the social sciences and central to providing it with a wide-ranging analytic synthesis. On the other hand, notably through the obsessive and singular focus of Wilhelm Hennis (1988, 2000, 2009), a rather different picture of Weber is emerging as a historical anthropologist of *Lebensführung* ('conduct of life') and *Lebensordnung* ('orders of life') and a late, great exponent of a distinctive ethical tradition: that of 'the ethics of office' (Condren, 2006; Du Gay, 2000, 2008, this volume; Hennis, 2009). For Hennis (1988: 104), Max Weber's work is only amenable to some sort of 'sociological synthesis' once his central problems, methods, and concerns are neglected. The 'spirit' animating Hennis's perspective has encouraged a subtle re-orientation, a shift of focus towards Weber's preoccupation with 'statecraft and soulcraft'. If we wish to divine Weber's abiding concerns, then the answer from this perspective is, succinctly put, the formation of the personality and character of the individual within the different orders of life. This emphasis can be represented as a 'singular preoccupation with ethical characterology' (Scaff, 2011: 250) and an attempt, under remarkably unfavourable circumstances, to breathe new life into the practice of casuistry, and to retrieve and re-state the significance of an ethics of office (Condren, 2006; Du Gay, 2008; Hennis, 2009).

These concerns are threaded throughout Weber's work, notably in *The Protestant Ethic and the Spirit of Capitalism*, but find their most telling expression perhaps in the political writings and the two remarkable lectures/essays, *The Profession and Vocation of Politics* and *Science as a Vocation*. In the latter, Weber encourages his audience to be 'polytheistic', and to take on the *persona* specific to the life-order within which they are engaged. In the absence of a universal moral norm, or a conclusive victory for one form of organized rationality over all others, Weber asks: how are individuals to develop 'character' or 'personality' (*Persönlichkeit*)? In considering the future of modern societies, and the individuals existing within them, Weber's deepest concern is the cultivation of individuals with 'personality': those willing and able to live up to the ethical demands placed upon them by their location within particular life-orders, whose life-conduct within those distinctive orders and powers—the public bureau, the firm, the parliament—can combine practical rationality with ethical seriousness (Darmon, 2011).

In *Science as a Vocation*, Weber's answer to this problem is clear and direct: 'Ladies and gentlemen: Personality is possessed in science by the man (*sic*) who serves only the needs of his subject, and this is true not only in science' (1989: 11). The individual with 'personality' is one who is capable of personal dedication to a cause (*Sache*), or the instituted purposes of a given life-order, in a manner that 'transcends individuality' (Hennis, 1988: 88). It is in this sense that it is possible, for example, for bureaucrats to be 'personally' committed to the ethos and purposes of their distinctive office even though that ethos lies outside of their own personal (i.e. individual) moral predilections or principles. This has a number of important implications. First, the possibility of different categories and practices of personhood requiring and expressing distinctive ethical comportments, irreducible to common underlying principles, appears quite foreign to those for whom a common or universal form of moral judgement is held to reside in the figure and capacities of the self-reflective person or individual (e.g. Habermas). This context-specific, and thus 'limited', conception of 'personality' cautions against the siren-calls of those political romantics—socialists, anarchists, the *littérateurs*—seeking to hold on to, or re-establish, the idea of the 'complete' human being: an ultimate, supra-regional persona that could function as the normative benchmark for all others. Here, in his guise of an ethicist of office, Weber's work certainly provides resources for surfacing the 'magical thinking' underpinning the artistic critique of capitalism and the 'romanticism' of certain facets of contemporary popular management theorizing. However, this Weber also seems somewhat less amenable to being enrolled in Boltanski and Chiapello's project, not least because his work appears antithetical to the latter's reflex critical sociological belief in 'human agency' as a universal datum of experience, and to their abiding affection for aspects of the 'artistic' critique (as an embodiment of this reflex), specifically the notion of the authentic 'full human personality'. Indeed, this is something that Hirschman's work (1977) also latches on to, a point we will return to in due course. Despite their avowed pragmatism and reformism, Boltanski and Chiapello hold on to a number of basic assumptions about agency and personhood that lie at some critical distance from Weber's own and which he may well have categorized as 'metaphysical' and 'unworldly' in the manner in which he chastised the *littérateurs* of his own time (see Du Gay, Ötsch, Pasqualoni, and Scott, this volume).

The ongoing obsession with individual creativity and autonomy, 'break-though thinking', and expressivism in both public and private sector management literature, and the current commanding position occupied by the concept of moral autonomy in contemporary Western ethical culture, are probably not entirely unrelated. The concept of moral autonomy involves the supposition, which is common to all the leading moral theories, that people should only be subject to moral constraints that they could have rationally or consensually formulated for themselves. On this assumption, authentic moral deliberation requires detachment from institutionally given obligations—bureaucratic roles are often a paradigm instance in both philosophical and management literatures—in order to 'think for themselves' about right conduct. Within such a framework, the ethics of office finds little or no place.

It was precisely such supra-regional obsessions with moral autonomy and expressivism—assumptions that Boltanski and Chiapello appear to hold to in their advocacy of a sociology of action and justification in which human agency is given its full recognition—that Weber's work was concerned to negate. His theorization and description of bureaucracy as *officium* and of science and politics as vocations offers an alternative to these obsessions, indicating, instead, the importance and indeed indispensability of office-specific conceptions of moral agency and ethical substance. It is this that leads us to locate Weber as a late practitioner of the ethics of office as this becomes a defensive doctrine—defensive, that is, in the context of the overwhelming dominance of moral autonomy as a value criterion.

Early in the twentieth century, we find Weber railing against the various political romanticisms that sought to do away with bureaucracy and the other detritus of the liberal state in pursuit of their own radical and metaphysical 'visions'. Weber was quite clear that the ethos of bureaucratic office, for instance, constituted a virtue that a liberal regime, with a parliamentary democracy and market economy, could not afford to dispense with. Indeed, he was adamant that 'without this supremely ethical discipline and self-denial the whole apparatus would disintegrate' (1994*b*: 331). It is not simply public or state bureaux to which this injunction would still apply. After many years in which bureaucracy and office-based ethical constraints more generally have been represented in a variety of management literatures precisely as stumbling blocks to those wishing to display initiative and exercise autonomy at work, a point Boltanski and Chiapello emphasize, the corporate scandals at Enron and elsewhere engendered a period of reflection on the wisdom of this reflex anti-bureaucratic sentiment. Even the fulsomely anti-bureaucratic *The Economist* magazine noted evidence of a 'return to values that we thought were gone forever' (2002: 118). These included a new-found respect for hierarchy, attention to detail, and the importance of people acting within the confines of their office, so as to be on their guard against temptations to impetuosity and other heart-felt enthusiasms—the very passions on which management gurus such as Tom Peters had built a career urging organizations to let loose (2002: 118).

We clearly do not have to rely only upon Weber's work alone to evidence the continuing significance, practically, normatively, and intellectually, of office-specific concepts of moral agency. Organizational cases as diverse as the Enron scandal, the official (*sic*) inquiries on both sides of the Atlantic into events surrounding the decision to go to war in Iraq, and the collapse of Lehman Brothers have shown what happens when office-specific rights, duties, and obligations are over-ridden, whether in the pursuit of private policies by stealth, or, in the governmental context, as part and parcel of a demand from the central executive for more 'responsive' forms of management conduct, or from a desire to create an 'all on one team' mentality. It is by no means 'reactionary' or 'conservative' (though it may well be 'conservational') to highlight the continuing significance of office-based forms of ethical agency and the purposes or 'core tasks' which they are designed to fulfil (not least the responsible and effective running of the state as a state). In other words, they offer a 'political' resource to those seeking to critically engage with the hubris of neo-liberalism or 'the New Spirit', but one which avoids the pitfalls of political romanticism, including an attachment to the metaphysical possibility of people 'realizing their humanity' (Boltanski and Chiapello, 2005: 491), not least because they are in certain important respects radically opposed to 'adaptation' (Darmon, 2011: 214; see also Ötsch, Pasqualoni, and Scott, this volume).

Given their continued adherence to the state and its agencies as crucial vehicles in the mitigation of the worst excesses of the 'New Spirit', it seems strange that Boltanski and Chiapello appear to view any continued adherence to the ethos of bureaucratic office-holding, for instance, as 'reactionary' or 'nostalgic', rather than seeing it as constitutive of political life and state capacity (see, by contrast, Latour's remarkable ethnography (2009) of the *Conseil d'Etat*: 'Above this somewhat derisory'—because seemingly anachronistic and conservative—'institution, there is nothing better, quicker, more efficient, more economical, and, above all, nothing that would be more just'); nor do they pay any attention to the frontal assault launched upon state administration and indeed notions of 'stateness' by the public sector vanguard of the 'New Spirit', the New Public Management movement and its offspring ('network governance'), in the name of economy, efficiency, responsiveness, creativity, and enterprise (see Du Gay, and Serrano-Velarde, this volume). Moral expressivists—be they philosophers like Alasdair MacIntyre (1981) or management 'gurus' such as Tom Peters (1992)—require institutions to express certain moral ideals, such as an all-pervading spirit of community, or an inalienable right to personal autonomy. In making such demands, they fail to appreciate that different institutions heed different priorities, and that these differing purposes and priorities are routinely formatted into the personal dispositions and competences required of the office-holders charged with fulfilling them. If we wish to see states operating as states, it is important to maintain the language of stateness (sovereignty, impersonality, authority, and so forth) and to foster the comportments and dispositions amongst those in its employ necessary to its practical operation as just such an entity. Indeed, we can scarcely hope to talk coherently about the nature of public (as opposed to private) power without making some reference to the idea of the state as a fictive moral persona distinct from both the rulers and the ruled. Maintaining a categorical distinction between the apparatus of government and the person of the state is an important aspect of this endeavour (something a number of theorists, Boltanski and Chiapello included, signally fail to do). Maintaining such a distinction helps to provide a means of testing the legitimacy of the actions that governments undertake. According to Hobbes and Pufendorf, for example, the conduct of government is morally acceptable if and only if it serves to promote the safety and welfare of the person of the state, and in consequence, the common good, or public interest. As Pufendorf summarizes, echoing Hobbes, as ever, 'the general Rule which Sovereigns are to proceed by is *Salus Populi suprema lex esto. Let the safety of the People be the Supreme Law'* (quoted in Skinner, 2009: 362).

As Boltanski and Chiapello (2005) make clear on a number of occasions, the 'New Spirit' of capitalism is one with a distinctive anti-statist genealogy. If capitalism has been intent, to paraphrase Foucault, on liberating itself from the very laws that made it possible, one might be forgiven for thinking that it is important for the minimum security and welfare of a given population that it be organized as a state, not least because such an independent power, whatever faults it may possess, is one of the few artificial entities on earth that can intervene in an economy to prevent it from self-destruction (Geuss, 2001). One of the many reasons for wishing to re-introduce the figure and practice of the Leviathan into the heart of our political discourse is that this would provide us with a means of not only testing the legitimacy of government conduct but also vindicating ('justifying') the actions that governments are sometimes obliged to take in times of emergency. If there is a genuine crisis, as there has been and continues to be in the financial system, there must be a strong case for stating that the person whose life most needs saving is the person of the state. After all, governments and individuals come and go; in this case, the only person sufficiently enduring to be capable of owning and eventually repaying a national debt, for instance, must be the person of the state. As a *persona ficta*, the state is able to incur obligations that no government and no single generation of citizens could ever hope to discharge (Skinner, 2009: 363–4).

In the United Kingdom, for example, the Conservative Prime Minister, David Cameron, and the Liberal deputy Prime Minister, Nick Clegg, are both products of and allied to certain neo-liberal ideas of the 1980s as embodying the only progressive political philosophy. But if, as John Gray (2010: 7) has persuasively argued, there is nothing certain about progress, with the latter's meaning shifting with events, then there is nothing to suggest that their conception of 'progress', allied as it is with the main tenets of the New Spirit, will not be consigned to the backburner as a result of the self-defeating effects of (metaphysical and romantic) market liberal policies. Gray (2010) believes this is quite likely if, as seems plausible, the consequences of contemporary fiscal orthodoxy are to exacerbate the fragilities of capitalism. In contrast to everything they believe, Gray (2010: 7) argues, Cameron and Clegg 'may turn out to be the politicians who lead Britain into a new era of statism'. This, in turn, suggests that Boltanski and Chiapello's continued adherence to aspects of the artistic critique (whose anti-statist, romantic, and metaphysical credentials are impeccable), no matter how nuanced (as in their discussion of security as the basis of freedom, and their comments on the limits of commodification, e.g. Boltanski and Chiapello, 2005: 468–72), and their immanentist take on critique more generally, working with the grain of the contemporary 'spirit' in order to make it live up to its own promises, may be somewhat problematic (see Ötsch, Pasqualoni, and Scott; and Parker, this volume). As Darmon (2011: 213–14) has argued, 'Weber's teaching had sought ... to ground challenges to capitalist rule in terrains of vocation subtracted from the capitalist spirit, that is, in radical opposition to adaptation'. Here, as Hennis (2009: ch. 2) suggests, the idea of office is crucial, with its legitimate elements of non-adaptation to leaders' orders and 'environmental' demands, for instance. Politically, Weber's doctrine of 'office' is at least disconcerting and seemingly ill-suited to a 'connexionist' age. However, as he would no doubt have remarked, not liking is hardly refuting.

Some not entirely dissimilar points emerge from a close reading of the second key reference point informing the conceptual architecture of *The New Spirit of Capitalism*, Albert Hirschman's *The Passions and the Interests* (1977). While Boltanski and Chiapello rely heavily upon a number of

Hirschman's texts, including notably the theory of organizational decline and the concepts of exit and voice he developed in his classic essay, *Exit, Voice and Loyalty* (for a full discussion of this engagement, and its lacunae, see Christiansen, 2010), it is *The Passions and the Interests*, and particularly its attempt to historicize justifications for capitalistic practices in terms of their wider 'sociopolitical' benefits, or the 'common good', that is a central resource for, or component element in, their overall thesis. It is therefore worth spending a little time on the argument Hirschman advances not only to see how it connects with Weber's concerns with 'statecraft and soulcraft' but also to indicate the extent to which it can, or cannot, serve the purposes to which Boltanski and Chiapello put it.

The stoic 'self' of 'self-interest': on 'avoiding society's ruin'

In *The Passions and the Interests*, subtitled 'arguments for capitalism before its triumph', Hirschman (1977) explored why and how certain, frequently commercial, ideas of self-interest were popularized, and particular self-interested conducts endorsed, by a wide variety of seventeenth- and eighteenth-century thinkers. The latter, many of whom were personally antithetical to money-making and commerce, came to look favourably upon commercial self-interest, he argues, because they saw it as a relatively peaceful and harmless alternative to the violent passions that had fuelled the European wars of religion and inspired military and aristocratic adventurism. Weary of the destruction caused by the unbridled passions, and bent on reform, a number of these thinkers were hopeful that the 'mild' passion for money-making and calculation, 'although admittedly ignoble and uncouth, could defeat and bury the violent passions that so ruinously stoked the endless cycles of civil butchery' (Holmes, 1995: 54). These attempts to harness the moderating effects of enlightened self-interest were therefore driven by a need to counteract and neutralize what were seen as the destructive consequences of mobilizing passion in the service of a religious cause and aristocratic ideals. Given this context, it seems unsurprising that 'interest' could come to assume a 'curative' connotation which its prehistory and established meanings would otherwise have rendered unthinkable. And, that, in turn, the association of 'interest' with a more enlightened idea of governing human affairs and attenuating some of the latter's more destructive propensities, helped to bestow upon certain practices of 'interest' governed conduct, a similarly positive and 'curative' set of meanings—as enhancing the 'public interest' or 'common good'.

Self-interested agents, whether commercially oriented or not, were regarded as acting with a certain coolness and deliberation, cultivating a particular approach to human affairs which appeared to be the very antithesis of that expected from a 'full human personality'. Interest thus assumed a certain standing because it seemed to offer a counterweight to pre-eminent—dangerous and unpredictable—human motivations. Here lies the heart of Hirschman's argument. By failing to discern the implicit contrast with the violent passions, and continuing, therefore, to conceive of interest as fundamentally inhumane, we may be at a loss to explain the positive and curative attitude towards 'interest' and 'interests' displayed by a wide range of thinkers in seventeenth- and eighteenth-century Europe. Moreover, by ignoring the irrational and destructive antonyms of self-interest, we might fall into the sort of error popularized by Tawney (1926) and Macpherson (1964), for instance, and continuing today in the work of critical intellectuals such as Jürgen Habermas (1997), where affirmations of calculating self-interest end up being represented as a mean-spirited repudiation of the common good. Indeed, for as long as sociology, for example, has been practised, as Boltanski and Chiapello indicate, capitalism, or markets, or rational self-interested conducts have been the target of considerable critical opprobrium/denunciation. The mode of critique has varied with the theoretical position favoured, from Marx's theory of alienation, Durkheim's *anomie*, or Freud's thesis of libidinal repression, up to, and including, more recent visions of contemporary economic conducts as destructive of morality. In these and other implicit or explicit critiques of capitalism, the stress, more often than not, is on the repressive, alienating, or otherwise inhibiting aspects of economic conducts on the development of, what we might term, 'the full human personality'. It is nonetheless worth pointing out that, rather than being an unforeseen side-effect of 'self-interested' conduct, one to be denounced and eradicated at the earliest opportunity, the one-sided, predictable, rational, and in some senses 'repressed' personality it produced was exactly what its advocates trusted it would accomplish. And this for good reasons, as Hirschman (1977: 132) indicated:

> This position, which seems so strange today, arose from extreme anguish over the clear and present dangers of a certain historical period, from concern over the destructive forces unleashed by the human passions with the only exception, so it seemed at the time, of "innocuous" avarice. In sum, capitalism was supposed to accomplish exactly what was soon to be denounced as its worst feature.

From this perspective, the focus on interest-governed conduct, commercial or otherwise, was a product of an urgent quest 'for a new way of *avoiding society's ruin*, permanently threatening at the time because of precarious arrangements for internal and external order' (Hirschman, 1977: 130). For its advocates, 'self-interested' conduct appeared as a potential cultural counterweight to the menace posed by the world of the 'full human personality', replete with its destructive passions; yet, as Hirschman suggests, if we exercise our historical imaginations just a little, we might also wonder at contemporary critics' forgetfulness of the dire consequences of a time when social and political existence was dominated by rival religious zealotries and the search for 'glory'. Hirschman (1977: 132) has the 'romantic' critique in his sights here, and his warning is clear and evident: only by forgetting the desperate conditions that had fostered the emergence of early modern doctrines of 'self-interest' could the Romantic critique represent the latter as incredibly impoverished in relation to an earlier age of freedom, spontaneity, and passion. Hirschman's account in many ways mirrors that provided by Reinhard Koselleck (1998) in *Critique and Crisis*, where 'romantic' critics of state and law, keen to represent the latter as immoral and oppressive, successfully forgot their own historical dependence on that same state and law: '[to] the extent to which the initial situation, the religious civil war to which [the] State owed its existence and its form, was forgotten, *raison d'etat* looked like downright immorality' (Koselleck, 1998: 39; see also, Saunders, 1997: ch. 9). Both Hirschman and Koselleck indicate how appeals to 'humanity' or the 'full human being' within the romantic critique function as forms of future moral subject deployed against existing 'amoral' institutions, such as the state, and conducts, such as calculating 'self-interest'; and both also indicate where such metaphysical appeals can lead—to a potential fanaticism.

Such sentiments could equally apply to the 'artistic critique' emerging in the late 1960s, with its accusations levelled against capitalism, bureaucracy, law, and the state as vehicles of human oppression, voiced in the name of liberation, autonomy, and spontaneity. As Hirschman (1977: 133) suggests, in these critiques one is hard-pressed to find any historical recognition that, in an earlier age, the 'full human personality' appeared as a menace that needed to be exorcized to the greatest degree possible, and that such forgetfulness can have some serious consequences, giving rise, for example, to 'identical and identically flawed' thought responses, without any reference to the encounter they had already had with reality, 'an encounter that is seldom wholly satisfactory'. Boltanski and Chiapello's text, in many ways, testifies to the predictable, and predictably destructive, consequences that arise from attempts to revive politically 'romantic' ideas whose confrontation with reality had indeed, historically, been less than 'wholly satisfactory'. They indicate clearly, for instance, how, in incorporating the values of the artistic critique, capitalist conduct reconnected with the tropes of the 'full human personality', 'natural liberty', and other metaphysical themes, to produce, as they put it, various 'forms of oppression' that run directly counter to the public interest or common good (Boltanski and Chiapello, 2005: 468). The performative effects of this re-romanticization can, as we have already suggested, also be hinted at in the corporate scandals that surfaced at the beginning of the current millennium, and those associated with the ongoing financial crisis, though it may take some time to delineate more precisely the distinctive role of metaphysical ideals of liberty and 'the whole person', for instance, in these and other related developments within economic and organizational life.

For Hirschman (1977: 129), in the context of enduring religiously motivated bloodshed and civil war in early modern Europe, the search 'for new rules of conduct and devices that would impose much needed constraints on rulers and ruled' was at a premium, and it is this that helps to explain why doctrines and practices of 'self-interest' were thought to hold much promise in this regard as beneficial mechanisms by which such restraint was to be engendered. As Hirschman indicates, however, the 'self' of 'self-interest' bears little comparison to the conception of the person animating contemporary justifications of capitalism or, indeed, modern notions of individuals as integrated, autonomous agents more generally. In fact, it is usually a denial of what we might today conceive of as 'autonomy'. 'Self-control', self-command', 'self-government', and 'self-interest' all designate forms of inner discipline as an expression of something else, namely, à la Weber, the internalization of the expectations of *office*. Autonomy, here, is probably about the worst term we can find to level at a person, as it is fundamentally linked to notions of office abuse, to the idea of protean or autonomous identities as quintessentially villainous because floating free of the duties and obligations consequent upon their occupation of an office (Condren, 2006: 144).

As Hirschman indicates, Hobbes's so-called 'ego-istic' model in *Leviathan*, for instance, far from expressing the appearance of modern individuality, as has frequently been suggested, is rather intended to explain and promote the necessity of offices. Hobbes's dramatic descriptions of a natural condition comprised of 'un-socialized' individuals can be plausibly taken as presenting a vision of a world of persons armed with rights. Coming from an office-driven and framed environment, Hobbes's natural condition is indeed a remarkably imaginative conceptual achievement, an example of what he would call an act of privation, imagining the empirical world away in order to imagine a cogent explanation for it. For Hobbes, all variations of natural condition were intended to explain the necessity of offices: the horrors of that condition are threatened by people not accepting the reciprocities of there being a ruling office. For Hobbes, everything hung on understanding aright the idea of office as well as the language and conducts appropriate to it. Only then would people begin to possess those characteristics required of political subjects in the Sovereign State, which Hobbes represented as necessary conditions for the securing of civil peace (Johnston, 1986: 215–16). In making this point, Hirschman also acknowledges the role of stoic thought and practice in Hobbes's programme, not least in his discussion of the relationship between liberty and self-interest. Indeed, the application of questions and devices derived from classical thought to the 'urgent problems' besetting early modern Europe, not least the profound political crisis that developed in the age of the religious wars, can be traced in a host of areas, from jurisprudence to military organization and warfare. As Oestreich (1982) has argued in this respect, imitation did not mean blind adoption, but critical adaptation and transformation of classical precepts and practices with the concrete aim of constructively assisting in the establishment of political order in the face of the threat of its perpetual disintegration.

Of foremost import, here, was the role of neo-stoicism in the shaping of the sovereign state and its legal, administrative, and military arms. Indeed, the revival of stoic thought and the practical and pedagogical orientation of the 'spiritual exercises' associated with it (Hadot, 2002), not least those relating to notions of *auctoritas*, *disciplina*, and *constantia*, thus 'became fundamental to the historico-political thinking of the age' (Oestreich, 1982: 6). In all countries of Europe, the seventeenth-century 'ideal' of conduct, whether institutional, military, economic, intellectual, political, or legal, was associated with the cultivation of stoic personae able to approach the duties associated with the offices they occupied with a combination of practical wisdom and ethical seriousness (Oestreich, 1982: 6). Here, we find a remarkable echo of Weber's central concern with 'statecraft and soulcraft'—that singular preoccupation with ethical characterology noted above, and in particular with the quality of 'non-adaptation' of particular instituted persona to certain demands—to be, for example, as Boltanski and Chiapello (2005: 536) put it in relation to the New Spirit, 'subject to an exigency of incessant change'. As Hadot's work (2002, 2011) has consistently indicated, the tenets and practices of both stoicism and epicureanism have been constantly revived and re-employed, not least at times of worldly chaos, when the pursuit of security, peace, and order has been at a premium. This is why, perhaps, in approaching the ancient 'techniques of self' as aesthetic rather than purposive, Foucault (1986) missed what Hadot sees: that at times of social instability, nothing might be more 'other' than the ethos of those engaged in producing order (Saunders, 1997: 114). As Hadot (2011: 101) puts it, there is little more opposed to the contemporary spirit of capitalism than stoic morality and practical wisdom. The latter has historically played a crucial role in the 'character' formation and office-based forms of ethical agency associated with various state persona—bureaucrats, judges, and military officers, for example—as well as having a clear influence on the protreptics of 'classic' management and organizational theorizing, such as that advanced by Chester Barnard (1968), for instance. The 'self' of stoic 'techniques of self', where discipline, authority, and constancy occupy pre-eminent positions and ridding oneself of 'the partiality of the individual, impassioned ego' is an imperative in order to achieve the detachment necessary to live up to the obligations of the office one occupies, therefore stands in direct opposition to the 'self' of contemporary 'self management', where flexibility, involvement, enthusiasm, constant activity, potentiality, and an abnegation of limits hold sway (Boltanski and Chiapello, 2005: 108–21).

Hirschman's genealogy of 'self-interest' indicates the significance of the neo-stoic revival in early modern Europe as a key element in the struggle for stability and order in a period of unremitting conflict. He also shows how the association of 'self' with office, and thus with the knowledge of limits and duties, is gradually transmuted in the late eighteenth century into something altogether different. Before then, selves approaching 'autonomy' are likely not to be viewed as positive indications of a 'freeing up' of relations of domination or the validation of an inner conscience or capacity for agency, but as moral accusations levelled by others against persons deemed unable or unwilling to live up to the obligations of office. Once interest and office are detached from one another, and the stoic conception of self as a persona associated with the former is replaced by notions of persons as autonomous individuals, it becomes unsurprising then, as Hirschman (1977: 135) succinctly puts it, that 'the passions are not to be counted out in situations where interest-motivated behaviour is considered to be the rule'. It is in this context, perhaps, that his comments concerning the dangers of 'trotting out' old ideas about the essentially socially harmless and potentially politically beneficial conse-quences of the individual accumulation of wealth have considerable purchase. In other words, Hirschman's genealogy indicates that the problems that interest was designed to counteract are still with us; and, moreover, that they may well have intensified precisely because the neo-stoic conceptions of the 'self' of self-interest he delineates, and the justification of the common good to which they were historically attached, have, under the sway of a romantic conception of the whole human being associated with the 'artistic' critique of 'instrumental rationality', given way to an 'enriched' metaphysical conception of personhood whose 'agency' is held to heed no artificial bound-aries and whose 'civilizing' effects are far from obvious (Du Gay, 2008). The critical possibilities that might be associated with a revived 'neo-stoic' concep-tion of persona, and its association with the language of office (not least in its 'statist' Hobbesian variant) in particular, remain curiously unexplored by Boltanski and Chiapello, perhaps, again, because they appear so 'anachronis-tic' and out of step with the norms and ideals of the 'projective city'. If we exercise our historical imaginations just a little, though, and remember how seemingly inhospitable such notions were at the time of their recuperation by some of the writers Hirschman focuses on, we might once again begin to see their potential.

Indeed, Boltanski and Chiapello (2005: 470) come close to acknowledging the enduring significance of office, persona, and the relations of liberty and authority attached to them, in their discussion of security as a factor of liberation. Here, they re-emphasize the importance of detachment, as embodied in legal and bureaucratic conducts, and the 'professional conscience' associated with them in 'the slowing down of the pace of connections', and thus enhancing 'the security and stability of people at work', for instance. In so doing, they allot renewed recognition to such institutions of state authority and authorization as the only bodies 'capable of legitimating the tests and sanctions' required to constrain the worst excesses of the New Spirit, not least in providing and exercising 'an external constraint in the form of obligations and sanctions' (2005: 468–70). As they indicate (2005: 470), this 'conservational' shift clearly presupposes an abandonment of the 'quest for liberation defined as absolute autonomy, simultaneously free of any interference from others and any form of obligation laid down by an external authority'. Here at least, Weber and Hirschman's programmes would tend to be one with that advanced by Boltanski and Chiapello.

References

Barnard, C. (1968) *The Functions of the Executive* (2nd edn.). Cambridge, MA: Harvard University Press.

Boltanski, L. and Chiapello, E. (2005) *The New Spirit of Capitalism*. London: Verso.

Christiansen, C.-O. (2010) 'Lost in Translation: Bringing Hirschman's Concept of Voice Back into the Spirit of Capitalism', *Management and Organization History*, 5, 19–35.

Condren, C. (2006) *Argument and Authority in Early Modern England*. Cambridge: Cambridge University Press.

Darmon, I. (2011) 'No "New Spirit"? Max Weber's Account of the Dynamic of Contemporary Capitalism through "Pure Adaptation" and the Shaping of Adequate Subjects', *Max Weber Studies*, 11(1), 193–216.

Du Gay, P. (2000) *In Praise of Bureaucracy: Weber/Organization/Ethics*. London: Sage.

——(2008) 'Max Weber and the Moral Economy of Office', *Journal of Cultural Economy*, 1(2), 129–44.

Foucault, M. (1986) *The Care of the Self: The History of Sexuality*, Vol. 3. Harmondsworth: Penguin.

Geuss, R. (2001) *History and Illusion in Politics*. Cambridge: Cambridge University Press.

Gray, J. (2010) 'Progressive, Like the 1980s', *London Review of Books*, 32(20), 3–7.

Habermas, J. (1997) *Between Facts and Norms: Contributions to a Discourse Theory of Law and Democracy*. Cambridge: Polity Press.

Hadot, P. (2002) *What is Ancient Philosophy?* Cambridge, MA: Harvard University Press.

——(2011) *The Present Alone is Our Happiness*. Stanford: Stanford University Press.

Hennis, W. (1988) *Max Weber: Essays in Reconstruction*. London, Allen & Unwin.

——(2000) *Max Weber's Science of Man*. Newbury, Berks: Threshold Press.

——(2009) *Politics as a Practical Science*. Basingstoke: Palgrave Macmillan.

Hirschman, A. (1977) *The Passions and the Interests*. Princeton, NJ: Princeton University Press.

Holmes, S. (1995) *Passions and Constraint*. Chicago: University of Chicago Press.

Johnston, D. (1986) *The Rhetoric of Leviathan*. Princeton, NJ: Princeton University Press.

Koselleck, R. (1998) *Critique and Crisis: Enlightenment and the Pathogenesis of Modern Society*. Boston, MA: MIT Press.

Latour, B. (2009) *The Making of Law*. Cambridge: Polity Press.

MacIntyre, A. (1981) *After Virtue*. London: Duckworth.

Macpherson, C. B. (1964) *The Political Theory of Possessive Individualism*. Oxford: Oxford University Press.

Oestreich, G. (1982) *Neostoicism and the Early Modern State*. Cambridge: Cambridge University Press.

Peters, T. (1992) *Liberation Management*. Basingstoke: Macmillan.

Saunders, D. (1997) *The Anti-Lawyers: Religion and the Critics of Law and State*. London: Routledge.

Scaff, L. (2011) *Max Weber in America*. Princeton, NJ: Princeton University Press.

Skinner, Q. (2009) 'A Genealogy of the Modern State', *Proceedings of the British Academy*, 162, 325–70.

Tawney, R. H. (1926) *Religion and the Rise of Capitalism*. New York: Harcourt, Brace and World.

The Economist (2002) *The World in 2003*. London: The Economist.

Weber, M. (1989) 'Science as a Vocation'. In P. Lassman and I. Velody (eds.), *Max Weber's Science as a Vocation*. London: Unwin, Hyman.

——(1994a) 'Parliament and Government in Germany under a New Political Order'. In P. Lassman and R. Speirs (eds.), *Weber: Political Writings*. Cambridge: Cambridge University Press.

——(1994b) 'The Profession and Vocation of Politics'. In P. Lassman and R. Speirs (eds.), *Weber: Political Writings*. Cambridge: Cambridge University Press.

5

Spirited Away: When Political Economy Becomes Culturalized[1] . . .

Hugh Willmott

Introduction

Is it not ironic that it has taken the work of two French academics, writing almost exclusively about contemporary changes in France, to engage the interest of Anglophone social scientists in the field of management? *The New Spirit of Capitalism* (hereafter NSC) has also been celebrated as 'a powerful and comprehensive account of modern society' comparable in significance to Schumpeter's *Capitalism, Socialism and Democracy* (1943), Aron's *18 Lectures on Industrial Society* (1967), or Mandel's *Late Capitalism* (1975) (Turner, 2007: 413), and as impressive in 'scope and ambition' as Castells's *The Information Age* and Hardt and Negri's *Empire* (Wolfreys, 2008). Remarkably, NSC has attracted limited critical attention even from those who might be expected to challenge it (e.g. Callinicos, 2006).

For students of management, such unqualified acclaim is surprising, as Boltanski and Chiapello's sprawling 600-page book offers comparatively little that is particularly novel or exceptionally instructive. The story told by the empirical material, much of it extracted from pop management texts, is unengagingly familiar, and NSC's theoretical framing is shallow. Where Boltanski and Chiapello offer some originality and insight is in offering heuristically useful distinctions—for instance, between types of indignation and associated kinds of critique; and, more prominently, in presenting detailed

---

[1] I would like to thank Glenn Morgan for his detailed comments on an earlier draft of this chapter. Contributions from participants at events dedicated to discussion of *The New Spirit of Capitalism* held at Warwick University and Essex University were also influential in shaping my reading and assessment of the book.

examples of how, by becoming selectively engaged to produce a new 'spirit', critique contributes to capitalist renewal by addressing legitimacy deficits and thereby 'justify(ing) people's commitment to capitalism' (Boltanski and Chiapello, 2005b: 162). It is not as a critique of contemporary capitalism, nor as a contribution to the revival of critique, but as a sociology of critique that NSC offers something distinctive.

This unflattering but not dismissive assessment of a book touted as a 'classic' (Farris, 2010: 297) attracting 'the epithets "monumental" and "path-breaking"' (Kemple, 2007: 151) is perhaps, to invoke NSC, expressive of the 'indignation' that 'continually fuels criticism' (Boltanski and Chiapello, 2005a: 37). I find it dispiriting and irritating that *this* book, which has been most influential in drawing the importance of management and organization to the attention of a wide audience of social scientists, presents such a superficial stock of material; and so it reinforces prejudices about the unscholarly calibre of research and poverty of analysis in this field. It might concluded, on the basis of these peevish and possibly touchy comments, that NSC should find its place on some dusty shelf reserved for overblown tomes. There is indeed a case for casting much of the book into oblivion or at least declining to add to the attention already devoted to it.[2] The problem with ignoring NSC, however, is that, by default, reverential readings and reviews are uncontested. In the absence of critique, the grandiose edifice of NSC conceals an unconvincing account of the development and reproduction of capitalism and allows NSC's weak analysis of the current conjuncture to go unchallenged. Without more ado, I now elaborate upon, and hope to justify, these disappointments and frustrations.

Critique: some initial reflections

Boltanski and Chiapello connect types of critique to forms of indignation.[3] *Social critique* is piqued by, and directed at, institutionalized inequality and

---

[2] It would be remiss to omit reference to criticisms that have been made of NSC, usually in passing or as a qualification to a generally positive review. Commentaries that appeared in French following its initial publication in 1999 are summarized by Leca and Naccache (2006). These included concerns about how the management texts had been selected and how the periods under examination had been differentiated. Others have commented upon the implausibility of the omission of analysis of the public sector from NSC because, according to Boltanski and Chiapello (2005a: 267, note 127), 'it does not form part of "capitalism"' (ibid.), and the lack of information about the analysis of their content of texts using a software programme.

[3] Distinguishing between forms of critique has some heuristic value. But it risks overlooking how, in practice, critique comprises a dynamic assemblage of diverse properties to which specific constituent identities—'social' and 'artistic', 'conservative' and 'ecological', etc.—are retrospectively ascribed. These labels are not 'descriptive', as Boltanski and Chiapello (2005a) invite us to believe, but are inescapably imbued with particular, ethical-analytic purposes (Ezzamel and Willmott, 2012). The distinction drawn between artistic and social critique, for example, fashions a particular kind of

Hugh Willmott

Table 5.1. Four criticisms of capitalism

	Social criticism	Artistic criticism	Conservative criticism	Ecological criticism
Causes of indignation	Poverty/inequalities, wage relationships, exploitation, class domination	Uniformization, massification, commodification, alienation	Moral disorder, destruction of solidarity	Destruction of ecosystems and species, human habitats
Underlying values	Labour, equality (in economic terms and in decision-making) as the necessary condition of freedom	Personal autonomy (internal and external), refined existence (art, philosophy, truth, etc.)	Moral duty of the elite, shared dignity common to all human beings	Shared dignity common to all living beings, life of future generations

Adapted from Chiapello (n.d.: 10).

self-interestedness. It censures capitalism for its material disparities and divisions, and for its destruction of community and solidarity. *Artistic critique*, in contrast, is ignited by, and directed at, the erosion of authenticity and/or the oppressive denial of freedom and creativity. Its target is capitalism's commodifying of everything, including the commodification of people whose lives become drained of other sources of value and beauty. Elements of artistic critique, Boltanski and Chiapello argue, were recuperated in the post-1970s era to bestow legitimacy upon capitalism, and thereby facilitate the development of its current 'connexionist' phase. In addition, Boltanski and Chiapello identify two other—'conservative' and 'ecological'—kinds of critique which I consider later. They are summarized in Table 5.1.

Given the focus and length of NSC, it is disconcerting to find no engagement with literatures—such as the labour process tradition (Thompson, 1983) and contributions to critical management studies (Alvesson and Willmott, 1992, 1996, 2012), to which I return when referring to recent studies of the managerial cadres (e.g. Hassard et al., 2012; McCann et al., 2008, 2010)—that explore issues at the heart of NSC (see also Parker, 2008). Their omission makes it irresistible to apply two elements of Boltanski and Chiapello's typology of indignation (2005a: 36 et seq.)—'inauthenticity' and 'opportunism'—to reflect upon this lacuna.

argument, provides a specific form of analysis, and potentially inspires and guides a 'reconstruct(ion) of critical forces' (Boltanski and Chiapello, 2005a: 531).

Inauthenticity, opportunism

The charge of 'inauthenticity' is directed at Boltanski and Chiapello's claims concerning the novelty of the contents of NSC. Since the 1980s, very similar empirical material and associated arguments have been available in abundance in management journals (e.g. *Human Relations, Journal of Management Studies, Organization, Organization Studies,* and occasionally in *Academy of Management Review* and *Administrative Science Quarterly*) as well as in numerous edited collections and monographs. Boltanski and Chiapello's explanation of their absence from NSC is a lack of resources which obliged them 'to restrict ourselves for the most part to the French case' (ibid.: xiv). That restriction may be defensible with regard to their decision—albeit a rather eccentric one given their purpose to develop a broad-brush account of capitalist development—to focus on French material. The restriction is completely unconvincing with regard to the neglect of substantial bodies of literature that are of direct relevance for their thesis.

Turning to what Boltanski and Chiapello term *'opportunism'/'egoism'*, this signals the 'destruction of social bonds and collective solidarity especially between the rich and poor' (ibid.: 37). NSC does not destroy social bonds; but it does divide critiques developed within critical social science from those advanced by students of management and business. In doing so, the prejudices of many social scientists are reinforced. Lacking the sociological imagination or dialectical sensibility to reflect critically upon their prejudices, many social scientists are content to assume that research undertaken from within business schools comprises *only* forms of consultancy thinly disguised by a scholarly veneer. By excluding all material, including critical studies of management, from NSC, Boltanski and Chiapello unhelpfully reinforce established scholarly divisions.

Where do Boltanski and Chiapello stand theoretically?

Boltanski and Chiapello parse social theory into two opposing positions. On one side, they place theories 'in which only capitalism's tendency to unlimited accumulation at any price is real' and 'the sole function of ideologies is to conceal the reality of all-powerful economic relations of force' (ibid.: 26; see also note 59, p. 50). On the other side, they assemble theories that 'confuse normative supports and reality, ignore the imperatives of profit and accumulation, and place the demands for justice faced by capitalism at its heart' (ibid.; see also note 60, p. 51). By placing social theories in polarized camps, Boltanski and Chiapello give the impression that numerous analyses of modern society and contemporary workplaces inspired by the thinking of Gramsci and Foucault, for example, are either irrelevant, or perhaps unknown, to them.

Our authors then cast themselves in the heroic role of Odysseus who navigates between Scylla and Charybdis.

Most conspicuously, given the focus of their project upon the world of work and knowledge of management, Boltanski and Chiapello overlook the many contributions to post-Bravermanian labour process analysis (see contributions to Knights and Willmott, 1990) in which sustained attempts have been made to *draw together* and *begin to move beyond* what they term 'the importance of interests and relations of force' (Boltanski and Chiapello, 2005a: 59) with 'the intricate conventions on which social order always rests' (ibid.: 60; see e.g. Burawoy, 1986). A potent effect of this omission of such contributions is to make NSC appear path-breaking—a 'magnificent work of social theory', as one reviewer (Davies, 2007, n.d.) effusively describes it. This assessment verges on the farcical, as NSC's theoretical contribution amounts to little more, and indeed offers a good deal less, than is available from other frameworks in which the coexistence of elements of 'voluntarism' and 'determinism' is appreciated within the dynamics of social action without polarizing them into opposing sociologies (Dawe, 1970). Numerous frameworks—such as those commended by Giddens (1984) and Glynos and Haworth (2007)—offer more robust, if imperfect, vessels for traversing the perilous seas navigated by social theorists. What these frameworks share, in contrast to NSC, is a sustained effort to combine attentiveness to 'relations of force' with an appreciation of the 'normative dimension' of those relations (Boltanski and Chiapello, 2005a: 27; see also p. 486). At the very least, they do not get into the embarrassing position of simultaneously privileging the views of actors when advancing a pragmatic sociology of critique, thereby distancing analysis from 'critical sociology', while implicitly relying upon critical sociology to align NSC to a sociology of emancipation (see 'Introduction' to this volume).

Boltanski and Chiapello's reluctance to engage with contemporary social theory when setting out their own Odyssean position makes it difficult to tease out more precisely where they stand. Perhaps their readers are expected to be familiar with Boltanski and Thévenot (2006/1991), first published in English a year after the appearance of NSC. One discernible feature of their approach is a welcome recommendation, albeit one that is shared by diverse post-Marxisms and post-structuralisms, that ideology, including 'spirit', is best understood not as something confected to veil or mystify reality (e.g. the 'dominant ideology thesis', Abercrombie et al., 1984) but, rather, is woven together by actors who draw upon diverse logics of justification, to reproduce, contest, and/or transform realities (see also Chiapello, 2003). This understanding of ideology is endlessly illustrated in NSC but is left neither explicated nor justified, as its presentation and positioning is confined to less than a handful of pages (e.g. Boltanski and Chiapello, 2005a: x–xi, 26–7, 46, note 22). Perhaps its scanty treatment is a casualty of an intention 'to be descriptive' (ibid.: xv).

Or, perhaps, it simply betrays a lack of reflexivity for which the torrent of empirical detail in NSC is a decoy. This suspicion finds some confirmation in Boltanski and Chiapello's remarkable claim that, in principle, it is possible to be 'in full possession of the facts' (ibid.: 535)—as if what counts as a 'fact' is self-evident; or as if the claim to 'full possession' is beyond contestation.

Such jaw-dropping assertions drain confidence in Boltanski and Chiapello's scholarship and, more particularly, in their proposition that '*the spirit of capitalism makes it possible to surmount an opposition that has dominated a considerable amount of the sociology and philosophy of the last thirty years*, at least when it comes to works at the intersection of the social and political' (ibid.: 26–7, emphasis added). Whether it is arrogance or naïveté, such extravagant claims deserve Parker's razor-sharp verdict (2008: 613) on NSC as a work of 'pompous certainty'. There is, nonetheless, an interesting, if not especially nourishing, kernel to be extracted from its husk—in the form of a discussion of how critique plays a significant role in the creation, as well as the destruction, of the 'spirits' that, according to Boltanski and Chiapello, furnish capitalism with normative legitimacy. This 'normative dimension' (2005a: 486) is, as Boltanski and Chiapello argue, important because without it key agents (e.g. managerial cadres) would lack the motivation to enact the reproduction of capitalism (see also Chiapello, 2003: esp. 163). A normative dimension is undoubtedly involved in the reproduction and transformation of capitalism. But I will question whether it can support the explanatory burden that Boltanski and Chiapello seek to place upon it.

Capitalism and mixed spirits

A primary point of reference for Boltanski and Chiapello, signalled by the title of their book, is Weber's *The Protestant Ethic and the Spirit of Capitalism* (see also Boltanski and Chiapello, 2005a: 100, note 6). Whether deferential, ironic, or self-aggrandizing, the gesture towards Weber invites confusion because Weber's *Protestant Ethic* and NSC differ significantly in their respective conceptions of 'spirit'. For Weber, the significance of 'spirit' resides in its deeply corrosive effects upon tradition and its associated institutionalization of the calling to make money.[4] For Boltanski and Chiapello, in contrast, 'spirit' supplies 'the moral foundations that [capitalism] lacks' (Boltanski and Chiapello, 2005b: 163). The two are related inasmuch as the emphasis Boltanski and Chiapello place upon the normative dimension is, in effect, responsive to

---

[4] Of course, avarice is historically commonplace. What is new is the modern normalization of money-making as an ethos (see Fullerton, 1928).

the disenchantment of the world resulting from the corrosion of traditional values and norms by the capitalist spirit addressed by Weber.

Weber's spirit

The practices of early capitalism, Weber (1992) contends, were 'foreign to all people's not under [its] influence' (ibid.: 52). More specifically, it made no sense for a 'man' (*sic*) living in a pre-capitalist era to aspire to more than 'to live as he is accustomed to live and to earn as much as is necessary for that purpose' (ibid.: 60). To such a man, '*acquisition* as the ultimate purpose of [one's] life' (ibid.: 52, emphasis added) was not just 'incomprehensible' but 'unworthy and contemptible' (ibid.: 71). Capitalism, Weber argues, was possessed of a 'spirit' that *defied and disarmed tradition*, and so promoted and facilitated a process of rationalization that gradually installed it as the dominant political economic system. The spirit of capitalism, supported by the Protestant ethic,[5] was condensed in 'that attitude which seeks profit rationally and systematically' (ibid.: 64) and, in this pursuit, it overturned '*traditionalistic business*' (ibid.: 67, emphasis added) where considerations of surplus, work, and relationships were *settled by reference to custom*. This process of rationalization geared to capitalist priorities, in the form of the embrace of a work ethic that provided the most reliable sign of salvation, was arguably as much a means of counteracting traditionalist resistance to the personal accumulation of wealth as it was taken to be 'proof of rebirth and genuine faith' (ibid.: 172; see also below). Responsiveness to the 'calling for making money', rather than a Calvinist belief in the significance of wealth accumulation as an indicator of rebirth, was set to become the more important impetus of capitalist development.

Consider briefly the use of the piece-rate method of remuneration. For a worker rooted in traditionalism, this method might be acceptable *if* in all other respects it allowed him (or her) to 'live as he is accustomed to live' (ibid.: 60) while reducing his (or her) hours of work. However, the latter requirement is in tension with the priorities of capitalism, as it places an 'irrational' constraint upon the extraction of productive effort from which private wealth is accumulated. The work ethic of Protestantism was undoubtedly important in facilitating the development of capitalism (Fullerton, 1928). But the meaningfulness of making money (as income or capital) soon came to displace the meaning of work as a virtue or as a sign of salvation:

---

[5] For Weber (1992), the ethic of Protestantism (largely unintentionally) groomed believers for productive activities, including employment as wage labourers. The ethic is seen to have fostered a post-traditional capacity for 'mental concentration, as well as the absolutely essential feeling of obligation to one's job . . . combined with a strict economy which calculates the possibility of high earnings, and a cool self-control and frugality which enormously increase performance' (ibid.: 63).

The capitalist system so needs [the] devotion to *the calling of making money* . . . there can to-day no longer be any question of a necessary connection of that acquisitive manner of life with any single *Weltanschauung*. In fact it no longer needs the support of any religious forces . . . these are phenomena of a time in which modern capitalism has become dominant and has become emancipated from its old supports. (Weber, 1992: 73, emphasis added)

For Weber, then, *'the calling of making money'*—not simply for purposes of accumulating private wealth and improving individuals' material standard of living but as *the equivalent of spiritual devotion*—is key to understanding the potent appeal and grip of the practices which enable capitalist development and its reproduction.[6] It is this materialist 'calling', rather than any other ideological support or justification of this pursuit, that primarily accounts for capitalism's institutionalization and continuation. As Fullerton (1928: 182) has observed of Western economies, and can be extended globally today,

> Economic reasons alone cannot account for the extraordinary power in the western civilization . . . which the money-making motive exerts. The whole point of Weber's essay is to show that something deeper, more transcendental, more idealistic, is at work here, and must be reckoned with if the psychology of capitalism, its spirit and temper, is to be adequately explained.

In order for capitalism to become established and maintained as the dominant politico-economic system, sufficient opportunities to respond to this call must be recurrently created and protected—for example, by establishing and preserving a regulatory apparatus of education and consumerism, as well as a legal framework that makes the call sufficiently calculable as well as audible and meaningful. In this respect, the materialist calling to make money is inextricably intertwined with institutions that facilitate and legitimize its pursuit. Today, the calling is manifest in diverse forms of financialization that are at the centre of 'connexionism' (see 'Introduction' to this volume). The footloose banker or financial trader—Masters of the Universe—exemplify 'the mobility and ultra-commodification of the connexionist world in which 'the mobile', discussed by Boltanski and Chiapello (2005*a*), threaten to move their operations to whatever location offers them the most materially advantageous regime of (labour/capital) market regulation and taxation. It is the call to make money, exemplified in processes of domestic as well as corporate and state modalities of financialization, rather than the confection of a new spirit from residues of artistic and/or social critique, that better accounts for the

---

[6] To construct, support, and illustrate his account in *The Protestant Ethic and the Spirit of Capitalism*, Weber relied very heavily upon a single source—the writings of Benjamin Franklin. A close reading of these writings suggests that Franklin's 'attachment to capitalist values of profit accumulation was wholly pragmatic rather than being linked to, or deriving from his religious beliefs' (Dickson and McLachlan, 1989: 81).

contemporary dynamics of capitalist development, including the increasing divisions between the mobile and the immobile to which NSC usefully points.

In sum, Weber invites us to appreciate how capitalism is legitimized by ensuring that the calling to make money is continuously renewed and answered; conversely, the reproduction of capitalism is most at risk when this process is interrupted or frustrated—for example, when a lack of opportunities to affirm devotion to the call results in it becoming drained of meaning, with the consequence that the guardians of capitalism are faced by a scale of mass resistance that they struggle to recuperate. Capitalism is most vulnerable when fulfilment of the materialist 'calling' is impeded—notably, during periods of recession (and 'austerity') and/or when alternative 'callings' (e.g. ecocentrism) that are resistant to accumulation and acquisitiveness become persuasively articulated and embraced.

Boltanski and Chiapello's spirit

What do Boltanski and Chiapello mean by the 'spirit of capitalism'? For them, it comprises a series of ideologies which 'legitimate the accumulation process' in a manner that simultaneously 'constrains it' (2005a: xx). It comprises a fungible 'set of beliefs' that, in 'justify(ing) this order . . . sustain(s) the forms of action and predispositions compatible with it' (ibid.: 10; see also 485–6). Notably, such beliefs offer and incorporate assurances of security, excitement, fairness, etc. but, in doing so, they invite 'tests' in relation to such promises and assurances (see Table 5.1). One area of concern, and associated test, is the issue of how participation in capitalism is made personally meaningful—for example, by designing work in ways that offer opportunities for *autonomy* and 'self-realization'. Another is the issue of whether the participation of employees will provide *security*, including 'guaranteeing their children access to positions that allow them to preserve the same privileges' (ibid.: 14). And the third concerns how, in the face of criticisms of injustice, actions can be justified 'in terms of the *common good*' (ibid.).[7]

Boltanski and Chiapello's conception of 'spirit' follows, I suggest, from their understanding of 'capitalism'. For them, capitalism is a (reified) system driven by its own distinctive 'logic'. The legitimation provided by 'spirit' is then functionally necessary to animate this system, the alternative being '"enforced commitment" under the threat of hunger and unemployment [which] does not seem to us to be very plausible' (Boltanski and Chiapello,

---

[7] These concerns, it might be imagined, are historically contingent—so that, for example, a concern with work as a source of personal meaning would be regarded as a comparatively recent preoccupation (Fox, 1971)—but Boltanski and Chiapello assume that the three concerns addressed by different 'spirits' are ahistorical.

2005*a*: 8). In Boltanski and Chiapello's conception of spirit, the reality of capitalism is abstracted from the social relations in which it is embedded, and out of which capitalist reality emerges and mutates. Not only is it disenchanted, in Weber's sense, but there is no equivalent to 'the calling to make money'. For this reason, 'spirit' (or a succession of 'spirits') is functionally necessary to remedy the normative deficit, and thereby support and justify capitalism's continuation. Spirit serves to 'elicit the good will of those on whom it is based, and ensure their engagement' (ibid.: 12). I take the following passage to condense Boltanski and Chiapello's thesis:

> Unable to discover a moral basis in the logic of the insatiable accumulation process (which is itself, on its own, amoral), capitalism must borrow the legitimating principles *it lacks* from orders of justification *external to it*. . . . Through the intermediary of the spirit of capitalism, capitalism thus in a way incorporates its own critique, since it incorporates moral principles on which people can depend to denounce those of its aspects which do not reflect the values it has annexed to itself. (ibid.: 487, emphasis added)

Note how capitalism, as a reified system, is anthropomorphized—it 'must borrow', it 'lacks from orders of justification', it 'incorporates its own critique', it 'incorporates moral principles', etc. I accept that 'spirits' and associated ideologies are important in rendering participation in capitalist relations meaningful; and also that 'spirits' are double-edged—constraining as well as supportive; reassuring as well as risky for future legitimation—in the way that Boltanski and Chiapello describe. But it seems to me that Weber is right to identify and prioritize 'the calling of making money', while recognizing that this is articulated, historically and culturally, in a variety of ways that may be illuminated by reference to the influence of Boltanski and Chiapello's 'spirits'; and, relatedly, by paying attention to how critique is recuperated to legitimize capitalist relations. The values that justify these relations are deeply materialistic. As Weber also emphasized, life becomes disenchanted where these relations become established; in turn, this begs the question, posed by Boltanski and Chiapello, of how it is legitimized. I have suggested that Weber offers the key to this conundrum when he ascribes to the 'calling to make money' a quasi-religious meaning and significance. Developing and safeguarding ways of realizing this calling, and thereby enhancement of self and social esteem (e.g. by acquiring assets, however small and transient), is key to capitalism's legitimacy, and thus to its reinvention and reproduction. So long as the means are available to pursue this calling—for example, by creating opportunities for employment, investment, and speculation through the privatization of public assets or the financialization of private assets—then critiques of capitalism are absorbed or disarmed before they escalate into widespread, popular demands for radical reform or revolutionary change.

Cadres and connexionism

Boltanski and Chiapello's stance (2005*a*) can be further illuminated by considering their examination of the 'cadres'[8] as targets and consumers of 'spirit', amongst whom are included those groomed for managerial and administrative positions. Eliciting engagement of the cadres in the reproduction of contemporary capitalism is understood to be particularly critical because, according to Boltanski and Chiapello, their members feel the normative deficit of capitalism (see above) most keenly. The cadres, they write,

> cannot make do with the material benefits granted them . . . [they] require personal reasons for commitment. To make commitment to [capitalism] worthwhile, to be attractive, capitalism must be capable of being presented to them in the form of activities which, by comparison with alternative opportunities, can be characterized as 'stimulating' . . . as containing possibilities for self-realization and room for freedom for action. (ibid.: 15–16)

A 'high level of commitment' is required of the cadres that, Boltanski and Chiapello argue, 'cannot be obtained purely through duress; moreover, less subject to immediate necessity than blue-collar workers, they can mount passive resistance, engage only reluctantly, even undermine the capitalist order by criticizing it from within' (ibid.: 14–15). It may indeed be difficult, and perhaps impossible, to obtain the 'commitment' of the cadres through 'duress' (ibid.: 14; see also earlier), but should it be assumed that they are 'less subject to immediate necessity than blue-collar workers' (ibid.)? Perhaps the situation is very different in France, but, since the 1980s, have not many managers and other cadre members become increasingly materially stretched and vulnerable as their security of employment has been eroded by the dismantling of 'Fordism' following the deregulation of labour and capital markets by proponents of neo-liberalism? Boltanski and Chiapello also contend that 'the spirit of capitalism is expressed in a *certainty* imparted to cadres about the "right" actions to be performed to make a profit, *and* the legitimacy of these actions' (ibid.: 16, emphasis added). I question whether members of the cadres have to be assured that such actions are inherently 'right' or 'legitimate', let alone exude 'certainty' in order to obtain their engagement. It is to be expected, of course, that world-weary cadre members will be sceptical, and they may participate in forms of resistance, usually of an individualistic and 'de-caff' variety' (Contu, 2008). But managers learn or calculate that a tolerably convincing display of commitment (for themselves and their

---

[8] The term is distinctively French and resists translation. Boltanski and Chiapello (2005*a*: 306 et seq) offer an extended discussion of its relevance for understanding the 'new spirit'. See also Boltanski (1987).

audience) soothes the pain of any personal and social dissonance and lack of more 'stimulating' possibilities, thereby enabling them to hold down their jobs and climb career ladders, and so act as effective functionaries of capitalism (see Jackall, 1988). If this quasi-ironic stratagem is widespread, then obtaining the unequivocal *'commitment'* of cadres may be difficult but it is also unnecessary when their willing, and even grudging, *compliance* is forthcoming (see Gratton et al., 1999).

It is also relevant to remember that cadre members are comparatively privileged, symbolically and materially, and so are amongst those with the most to lose from politico-economic convulsions. To suggest that they are poised to 'undermine the capitalist order by criticizing it from within' (Boltanski and Chiapello, 2005a: 14), unless checked by an interceding 'spirit', is, I suggest, a little far-fetched. Increased opportunities for self-fulfilment would doubtless be welcomed. But, in the absence of identification with a counter-materialist (e.g. collectivist) ideology, the prospect of 'making money' by selling their labour (to pay the mortgage on the property they aspire to own, etc.) is likely to prove more important but also sufficient, if imperfect, for most cadre members. In short, the 'calling to make money' exerts a powerful appeal, irrespective of the provision of 'personal reasons for commitment . . . arising from whatever might be ' "stimulating" . . . as containing possibilities for self-realization and room for freedom for action' (ibid.: 15–16).

Some empirical evidence

To illuminate the position of cadre members, it is relevant to refer to some empirical research. Studies informed by a labour process tradition (e.g. Hassard et al., 2012; McCann et al., 2008, 2010)[9] are perhaps closest (politically) to what could be characterized as Boltanski and Chiapello's 'left progressive' stance.[10] These studies lend some support to Boltanski and Chiapello's thesis inasmuch as they confirm that 'middle managers', who form a substantial part of the cadres, continue to have *formal* 'responsibility and authority over their subordinates' but that *substantively* their work, 'in some aspects,

---

[9] The research reported in Morris et al. (2006) was based upon sixty-four interviews with managers in five in-depth case studies of organizations in the United Kingdom undergoing restructuring (four in the private sector, one in the public sector). See McCann et al. (2006: 348 et seq.). The research reported in McCann et al. (2008, 2010) incorporates findings from the earlier study but extends this to cover five comparable companies in both the United States and Japan. A total of 142 formal interviews were conducted with 259 informants in total being consulted (see Morris et al., 2006: 578 et seq.).

[10] Boltanski and Chiapello's leftist stance is deduced from statements such as 'in a capitalist society, the strong are first and foremost the owners of capital, and history has repeatedly shown that in the absence of legislative and regulatory obstacles they tend to use their economic power to wrest a dominant position on all spheres, leaving wage-earners with only the meanest share of the value added that has been created' (Boltanski and Chiapello, 2005: 34).

resembles a form of degraded labour—the affliction Braverman describes affecting blue-collar employees' (McCann et al., 2010: 349). McCann et al. (2008) conclude that cadre members are encountering a combination of work intensification, a blurring of established divisions, and reduced social distance between workers and (middle) managers,[11] but also up-skilling. Work intensification is broadly consistent with an orthodox Bravermanian degradation thesis. But up-skilling indicates how much managerial work (like much 'blue-collar' work) has been 'enriched'—in the sense of an expansion of responsibilities and associated skills arising from the removal of layers of management. Of particular relevance, I suggest, is McCann et al.'s finding (2008) that 'salaries and bonuses have been improved after structural transformation' (ibid.: 365). In effect, there has been a willingness amongst middle managers, albeit under some duress, to trade off elements of 'degradation'—in terms of work intensification, greater performance pressures, reduced security, and reduced promotion opportunities—for increased compensation and enticingly large jumps in salary for top performers.[12] In short, there have been opportunities, met by a positive response, to realize the 'calling to make money' even when accompanied by elements of proletarianization, including 'a heightened sense of anxiety and uncertainty' which managers associate with 'the challenges of working in large organizations under the heavy demands and risks of the shift from managerial to investor capitalism' (Hassard et al., 2012; see also 'Introduction' to this volume and later sections of this chapter).

If we adhere to the central thesis of NSC, then it might be imagined that, for middle managers, the opportunity to undertake more personally meaningful projects or the chance to develop and harness their 'potential' would be a very important, and perhaps the primary, source of motivation. According to McCann et al. (2008), however, 'attempts at ameliorating the harshest effects of the new organizational demands did not provide solace for overworked managers juggling with uncertainty and transformation' (ibid.: 366). This being the case, and again following the NSC thesis, it might be expected that increased pressures would strain the commitment of managerial cadres who, experiencing a loss of status as well as security, would be inclined, in Boltanski and Chiapello's words, to 'mount passive resistance, engage only reluctantly, even undermine the capitalist order by criticizing it from

---

[11] Indicators of such 'proletarianization' include the use of open-plan offices and hot desks as well as the withdrawal of differentiating privileges from middle management, such as the use of separate facilities (e.g. toilets, canteen, etc.).

[12] At the time of the study, some private sector middle managers are reported to have earned as much as £70,000 per annum, with the possibility of a further £30,000 in performance-related annual bonus. In contrast, the equivalent public sector manager might be earning closer to £30,000 with no bonus.

within' (2005*a*: 14–15). But there is little evidence of much 'passive resistance', as contrasted to a degree of cynicism and resignation, amongst the cadres. McCann et al. (2008) conclude that despite 'the personal pressures, many of these managers appear to remain focused, committed and enthusiastic' (ibid.: 366), which they attribute to 'the relatively higher wages and bonuses on offer' (ibid.).

McCann et al.'s in-depth empirical study suggests that, in response to the challenge of intensified competition, members of the cadres are pursuing individualistic strategies of survival and advancement geared to opportunities that are responsive to a 'calling to make money' emphasized by Weber. In addition to its exemplification of this calling, the orientation of the managers studied by McCann et al. (2008, 2010) and Hassard et al. (2012) echoes Weber's description (1992) of the early champions of capitalism who, through a process of rationalization, expanded and perfected its forms:

> calculating and daring at the same time, above all temperate and reliable, shrewd and completely devoted to their business, with strictly bourgeois opinions and principles. (Weber, 1992: 69)

Perhaps the contemporary cadres of management are not always so 'temperate' especially when anxiety and uncertainty get the better of them, but in *what they do* they act as if they are, in effect, 'completely devoted to their business', or at least to the demands of their immediate boss (see Jackall, 2008; Žižek, 1989). Privately, cadre members may be critical and resentful of pressures placed upon them, and recognize how their conditions of work are being degraded, but they continue to manage 'as if they did not know' (Žižek, 1989: 32). The opportunity to undertake more 'challenging and varied' work (Boltanski and Chiapello, 2005*a*: 366) is afforded by flattened hierarchies inspired by the strategic intent to reduce 'managerial overload'. But this change is addressed principally as an opportunity for displaying superior 'fitness' as a means to the end of making more money through career progression within a new, networked world. In this respect at least, a parallel may be drawn between the benefits of self-denial attributed by Weber to the puritanical impulses of early capitalists and the deferred gratification of cadres as they make their aspirational, social Darwinian ascent up corporate hierarchies.

The new capitalism

Accounting for change

Boltanski and Chiapello argue that the new (spirit of) capitalism is integral to a shift from 'managerialist' to 'connexionist' (not investor) capitalism (see

Table 5.2. Three spirits of capitalism

	First (*bourgeois*) spirit	Second (*managerialist*) spirit	Third (*connexionist*) spirit
	End of nineteenth century	1940–70	Since 1980s
Forms of the capital accumulation process	Small family firms Bourgeois capitalism	Big industrial companies Mass production	• Network firms • Varying and differentiated production
Autonomy	Freedom from local communities	Career opportunities	• Innovation and creativity • Permanent change
Security	Personal relationships Paternalism	Long-term planning	For the mobile and the adaptable: • Companies will provide self-help resources to manage oneself
Common good/fairness	A mix of domestic and market production	Management by objectives	• New form of meritocracy that values mobility and ability to nourish networks • Each project is an opportunity to develop one's employability

Adapted from Boltanski and Chiapello (2002).

Table 5.2). The shift is seen to have emerged from the crisis of the 1970s when the unsustainability of the corporatist, post-war settlement was, Boltanski and Chiapello argue, initially (mis)interpreted by government and employers in terms of *social critique* (see Table 5.1). Social critique, it will be recalled, censures capitalism for its material inequalities, social divisions, and self-interestedness, which destroy community and solidarity. Social critique proposes that legitimacy can be restored by making concessions to organized labour in the form of protecting benefits, safeguarding the social wage, etc. In the mid-1970s, applying these favoured remedies 'did not succeed in halting protest or reasserting control over behaviour at work' (Boltanski and Chiapello, 2005*a*: 177); but the failure opened up a space for an alternative diagnosis and associated remedy advanced by 'innovative fractions among the employer class' (ibid.). These fractions construed the crisis 'in terms of the *artistic critique*—as a revolt against oppressive working conditions and traditional forms of authority' (ibid., emphasis added)—and commended a restructuring of work to incorporate increased scope for autonomy and creativity. As Boltanski and Chiapello describe the dynamics of this shift:

at the end of the 1960s and the beginning of the 1970s, social critique in its most classical form, articulated by the working-class movement...underwent a revival to the point of eclipsing the artistic critique, which had unquestionably been more in evidence during the May [1968] events. The artistic critique was to have its revenge in the second half of the 1970s, when the social critique seemed to be exhausted. (ibid.: 178)

More specifically, NSC highlights autonomy-expanding innovations in job design and organizational structure as demonstrations of the recuperation of artistic critique. In doing so, Boltanski and Chiapello omit consideration of connections (or elective affinities, as Weber would say) between these innovations and politico-economic pressures to raise the productivity of labour without significantly increasing its cost. To the extent that changes in the organization of work—such as the flattening of hierarchies, strengthening corporate cultures, and enriching jobs—were accompanied by greater autonomy, I suggest that this smoothed the path of forms of work intensification and restructuring that have delivered cuts in costs passed on mainly to shareholders but also to key cadre members (e.g. strategically important specialists as well as senior executives with stock options). The bigger picture is that the 1970s profits squeeze was relieved by an expansion and redistribution of wealth arising from the project of neo-liberalism that combined privatization and marketization with the turbo-charged process of financialization. It is highly questionable whether elements of the 'artistic critique' of the late 1960s were the chief inspiration, or provided key raw materials, for Boltanski and Chiapello's 'new spirit'. But elements of the artistic critique were clearly resonant with, and supportive of, a neo-liberal project which promoted greater 'flexibility' and championed 'employability' as well as 'the virtues of mobility and adaptability' (ibid.: 199; see also pp. 193–4, 324–7, 467) to which Boltanski and Chiapello instructively point. Such innovations were, I suggest, manifestations of the fumbling efforts, pursued through the 1970s and 1980s, to establish a viable replacement for post-war Keynesian corporatism. Keynesianism had become enfeebled and discredited as investment opportunities and associated taxation revenues proved insufficient to sustain expected levels of public expenditure and associated forms of 'security' and 'common good', to adopt Boltanski and Chiapello's terminology. Keynesian policy was gradually dismantled by an enlivening monetarism that mutated into practices of neo-liberalism which penetrated and recomposed, to a greater or less extent, the advanced capitalist economies (see 'Introduction' to this volume).

This post-1970s reconfiguration of capitalism, I suggest, has been corrosive of forms of corporatist security and associated notions of the common good and social justice. Is it not the reassertion of market discipline that has impelled or accelerated what Boltanski and Chiapello characterize as 'disaffiliation' and increased 'mobility'? Although somewhat lubricated by the libertarian thinking of new managerialism, which counter-posed increased scope for autonomy and empowerment in (and outside) the workplace against what it (conveniently) redefined as the suffocating security of Fordist corporatism and the 'Nanny State', the chief propellant of what Boltanski and Chiapello call connexionism was not, and is not, the recuperation of the 'artistic critique'. Rather, it is the contested efforts of the advocates and apologists of capitalism to save it from a self-destructive cyclical tendency to spiral, as boom turns to bust, into contraction and recession. In this effort, individualism and enterprise ('Stand on your own two feet!'; 'Be Empowered!') have been advocated and valorized in support of a neo-liberal crusade for capitalist revitalization. Their appeal is, I suggest, more closely related to the 'call to make money' (see above), notably through a liberalization of markets, than with the (recuperation of) 'artistic critique'. To suggest otherwise is to supplant political economy by cultural economy, instead of appreciating the centrality of the latter for the organization and development of the former (Willmott, 2010, 2012). This brings us to a consideration of Boltanski and Chiapello's characterization of the current era as 'connexionist' rather than, say, 'investor capitalism' (Hassard et al., 2012: 593).

Connexionism or financialization?

Characterized as a connexionist era of networks, Boltanski and Chiapello argue that in ' "globalized" capitalism' (2005*a*: 19) a 'new spirit' has emerged that they distinguish from two previous—'bourgeois' and 'managerial/bureaucratic' spirits (see Table 5.2). Even allowing for some hyperbole, Boltanksi and Chiapello convey something of the distinctive mood of connexionist times when they observe that

> everyone lives in a sense of permanent anxiety about being disconnected, rejected, abandoned on the spot by those who move around. This is why today local roots, loyalty and stability paradoxically constitute factors of *job insecurity* and are, moreover, increasingly experienced as such ... [In response to this] 'disaffiliation' can be initiated by self-defensive behaviour in a situation of job insecurity, the paradoxical result of which is to increase the insecurity. (ibid.: 364)

What, ironically, Boltanski and Chiapello do not appreciate is how anxieties 'about being disconnected' (ibid.: 364), for example, can, perversely enough, become normalized and even celebrated, rather than fuel nostalgia for a more secure, or immobile past. That is to say, as Morris et al. (2006) and Hassard et al. (2012) indicate, these concerns can be recuperated as valued features of a dynamic, challenging, and exciting world of (ultra-competitive) possibilities. For Boltanski and Chiapello, anxieties about becoming disconnected and/or insufficiently mobile to avoid rejection are identified as features of a new era called connexionism. In contrast, I find it more plausible to regard them as symptomatic of, but not reducible to, a neo-liberal celebration of risk-taking associated with processes of financialization (to be discussed below) facilitated by developments in information and communications technologies.[13]

I have noted already that McCann et al.'s research (2008, 2010) on the work of middle managers offers some confirmation of Boltanski and Chiapello's description (2005a) of the inhabitants of connexionism who live 'in a sense of permanent anxiety about being disconnected, rejected, abandoned on the spot' (364). Their research also offers a measure of corroboration for Boltanski and Chiapello's description of the 'networker' who works flexibly, is responsible for a portfolio of projects, and is 'possessed of the art of establishing and maintaining numerous diverse, enriching connections, and of the ability to extend networks' (ibid.: 355; see also pp. 359, 377). In contrast to Boltanski and Chiapello, however, McCann et al. (2008, 2010) and Hassard et al. (2012) make a connection between the growing dominance of the financial sector in capitalist development and changes in the work of the cadres. More specifically, they relate these changes to pressures to increase 'shareholder value' through cost cutting and improved capacity utilization.

In NSC, the lack of any sustained or substantive consideration of financialized capitalism exists in some tension with the 'deregulation' and 'decompartmentalization' of financial markets to which passing reference is made in its Prologue. There Boltanski and Chiapello (2005a) usefully note how the creation of new financial products results in 'multiplied possibilities of purely speculative profits, whereby capital expands without taking the form of investment in productive activity' (ibid.: xxxvii). It is worth recalling that a shift form Keynesianism to neo-liberalism and associated processes of financialization were well under way by the time of NSC's preparation. Yet, after the brief mention of financial products in the Prologue, there is no further reference to them or to the wider role of financial institutions and markets for several hundred pages. The silence is broken when financial markets are described as 'premier exploiters' because they are the 'most mobile in a long chain of sequential exploitation' (ibid.: 365). This insight is welcome, but it lacks connection to, or integration with, the increasing centrality of financial markets with their analysis of 'spirit'(s) (see 'Introduction' to this volume).

---

[13] It is also relevant to note how the post-bureaucratic features of connexionism identified by Boltanski and Chiapello have been accompanied by some strengthening of certain 'bureaucratic' elements (e.g. the widespread use of bureaucratic performance measures, such as audit (Power, 1999) and forms of McDonaldization, especially in the growing service sectors (Ritzer, 2011)).

If we follow Boltanski and Chiapello's own logic, then the effects of the 2008 financial crisis—notably, the economic downturn and the socialization of private losses—should have precipitated widespread social critique and related policies directed at reducing inequality—for example, the nationalization of failed financial institutions to secure employment, the improvement of lines of credit to small businesses, and the curbing of excessive bonuses paid to traders and bankers. To date, such critique has been comparatively muted and policies have been more responsive to powerful lobbies comprising the most 'mobile' who demand a return to the status quo *ante*. There has been considerable anger but, as yet, a lack of political will to make substantial changes, and even less inclination amongst bankers to introduce, rather than endlessly explore and thereby postpone, the possibility of more effective forms of (self) regulation such that financial institutions and markets become the servants, and not the masters, of capitalist revitalization (Glynos et al., in press). As I write, a movement against austerity in 'Eurozone' countries is growing in which there are signs of social polarization (e.g. increased popular support for the far right, at least in the United Kingdom and France, as well as the centre left) but, with the exception of Greece, no mass popular dissent. For the moment, perhaps because the austerity measures have been lagged in the expectation that they would be buffered by growth that has not materialized, there appears to be little appetite or political will for challenging a conjuncture of the debt crisis in which the dominance of financial institutions and financial markets has been buffeted but ultimately strengthened. The banks are permitted, and even encouraged, to prioritize the rebuilding of their balance sheets; public sector and welfare spending is slashed in order to pay down the debt incurred by bailing out the banks and compensating for the subsequent economic slump; employees and savers are squeezed; corporations hoard cash; many corporate executives continue to enjoy double digit pay increases; and borrowers struggle to obtain loans—all with predictable consequences for economic activity. It is hard to see what distinctive light NSC can shed upon on this New Capitalism.

Other critiques: conservative and ecological

A difficulty facing efforts to mount an effective challenge to contemporary politico-economic crises, which Chiapello (n.d.) usefully acknowledges but declines to explore, is the strength of appeal of 'conservative critique' (see Table 5.1). Conservative critique, Chiapello argues, diagnoses problems of capitalism in terms of a moral decline of its economic and political leadership, resulting in a failure to 'look after' those less fortunate than themselves. With regard to the financial crisis of 2008, for instance, conservative critique would, and does, point to the immorality (e.g. greed or recklessness) of individuals or groups—bankers, regulators, and politicians. Such critique is, in principle, readily disarmed simply by placing more 'worthy and human people in positions of power' (ibid.)—for example, by voting out governing parties or substituting high ranking technocrats for politicians—so that 'nothing needs to change structurally in the current economic system' (ibid.). Such stratagems may encounter greater difficulties when *many* of the members of an elite are criticized for failing in their patrician and/or patriotic duty to provide sufficient opportunities (e.g. jobs) for the masses, and also to take care of the deserving poor and vulnerable. Note, especially, how these responsibilities are framed materially in terms of responsiveness to what Weber terms 'the calling to make money' (see above), or to compensate for the lack of such opportunities. Capitalist elites are at greatest risk when they are shown to behave in ways that cheat on this responsibility—for example, when they are found to fiddle expenses; minimize their tax contributions (which support the funding of educational and welfare provision); tolerate and conceal forms of corruption; and so on. At that point, conservative critique can mutate into social critique, but with uncertain consequences with regard to the kind of collectivist/populist/nationalist remedy that finds popular support.

Ecological critique addresses irresponsibility in relation to the preservation of the biosphere and its life forms. This critique is directed at capitalism insofar as pursuing profitable growth is associated with neglectful husbandry of finite resources and/or the destructive effects of relentless expansion (e.g. global warming). To the extent that this connection becomes more evident and potent, and so attracts and affirms ecological critique, Chiapello (n.d.) notes that it is difficult to imagine how proponents of capitalism will 'get out of this tight spot'. To date, the most common response to ecological critique—from politicians, media, and corporations—has been to marginalize, obfuscate, trivialize, or simply deny its concerns, and also to develop self-serving remedies (e.g. carbon trading) that may actually exacerbate the problems (Bohm and Dabhi, 2009). A dystopic scenario suggests 'the generalization of a kind of political nihilism' (Boltanski and Chiapello, 2005a: 523) as growing social inequality and widespread degradation of the conditions of existence are accompanied by fatalism, despair, and/or overpowering subjugation. Alternatively, there is the possibility of an ecocentric, global movement away from dependence upon currently entrenched elites (e.g. ecologically irresponsible politicians, indifferent financiers, and 'greenwashing' business leaders) towards greater reliance upon 'local networks and small scale production' (Chiapello, n.d.) in which priority is given to the quality of life, and not to the 'calling to make money' (see above) exemplified in a preoccupation with accumulation and consumption.

A 'local' and 'small scale' approach to sustainable development is arguably more consistent with lifting out of poverty half of the world's population who currently live on $2 per day or less (Kerbo, 2006 cited in Del Gandio,

2008) as well as with an emancipatory quest for greater autonomy and self-determination. Amongst the millions living in poverty are those whose greatest vulnerability is not the kind of immobility identified by Boltanski and Chiapello but, rather, a local rootedness which renders them defenceless against severe disruptions wrought by climate change. Here the inequality is not only, or primarily, within nation-states between the comparatively mobile and immobile but, rather, between 'North' and 'South'—the grossly overdeveloped nations that have produced most of the 'greenhouse' emissions and the inhabitants of scandalously pillaged, undeveloped nations which are most adversely affected by climate change.[14] Notwithstanding the opportunities for the development (and premium pricing) of 'green' products, the distinctiveness of the ecological critique is that it cannot readily be recuperated so that, in Chiapello's words (n.d.), 'Capitalism, by its very operation, is leading directly to destruction of our civilisation.' For the moment, however, a compelling, quasi-religious fixation upon the 'calling to make money' supplants and dims attentiveness to such destruction. A condition of possibility of such a shift of priorities is an antidote to

---

[14] The background to this scandal is that, in 1992, the United Nations Framework Convention on Climate Change (UNFCCC) reached an agreement in Rio de Janeiro to adopt measures calculated to prevent dangerous anthropogenic interference with the climate system. The Rio agreement determined that nations would reduce their greenhouse gas (ghg) emissions based upon the principle of equity, with the developed, higher polluting countries taking the first steps to prevent dangerous climate change. The Kyoto Protocol, which was passed in 2005 and eventually ratified by every developed nation except the United States, requires that, on average, the developed countries agree to reduce six greenhouse gases to 5.2 per cent below 1990 levels by 2008–2012. Meetings of UNFCCC have continued on an annual basis to monitor and update progress. At the Copenhagen meeting in 2009, scientists were asserting the need to reduce ghg omissions by 25–40 per cent below 1990 levels in order to limit warming to 2 per cent-C or less, which they believed would trigger dangerous climate change. At the Copenhagen meeting, the United States took the weakest position of the developed countries by offering a 4 per cent reduction. President Obama's hands were effectively tied as the House of Representatives had pre-empted the Copenhagen meeting by passing a bill that required a 17 per cent reduction below 2005 levels by 2020. So, twenty years after the first meeting of the UNFCCC to determine enforceable greenhouse gas emissions reduction targets for the developed countries, these targets have yet to be agreed. Following the Copenhagen meeting in 2009, forty-two industrialized countries submitted their emissions targets for 2020. Using this data, it is possible to calculate that *if* all nations meet equivalent projections, the emissions will reduce from a business-as-usual figure of 56 Gt of CO_2 by 2020 to around 49 Gt. This would be 5 Gt short of what scientists believe to be necessary to limit temperature rise to under 2 per cent-C, and thereby avoid very dangerous climate change. If, however, the pledges of these nations are only partially fulfilled, then the gap rises to nearer 10 Gt, with predicted catastrophic effects for millions of the poorest people and with the prospect of accelerating warming after a tipping point is exceeded. A Royal Society report has suggested that the opportunity to reduce emissions to a level necessary to limit temperature rises to 2 per cent-C may already have been squandered—unless, of course, the scientific predictions turn out to be erroneous or actual emissions from developed nations are revised downwards. It would seem that a majority of those who live in the North/developed world are disinclined fully to register the implications of climate change, or to mitigate the death and destruction predicted for others when this means damaging our own economic prospects. The irony, of course, is that the failure to change the game, or to radically revise its rules, has consequences—such as rises in commodity prices and the migration of peoples—that are not confined to the South/undeveloped nations as they adversely affect the growth rates of advanced economies.

the calling of capitalism, involving processes of struggle and transformation equivalent to the historical destruction of traditionalist totems addressed by Weber in the *Protestant Ethic*.

Conclusion

This chapter has examined some key propositions of NSC, focusing primarily upon its consideration of 'spirit' and 'critique'. I have not, for example, examined Boltanski and Chiapello's emphasis upon exclusion, rather than exploitation, as the focus for critique. Instead, I have pointed to NSC's neglect of studies of management that are often more penetrating than literatures that Boltanski and Chiapello cite; drawn attention to the weak articulation, positioning, and justification of the book's theoretical stance; explicated Boltanski and Chiapello's confusing conception of 'spirit' in relation to Weber's very different formulation of the same term; exposed NSC's neglect of neoliberalism and financialization when accounting for the most recent 'connexionist' phase of capitalism; and, finally, commented on the failure in NSC to incorporate consideration of the ecological critique that has been developing since the late 1980s.

In addressing these limitations, I have sought to respond to Boltanski and Chiapello's (2005*a*: xxvii) invitation to read NSC 'as a research programme rather than a fully finished work; as a summons to future work for the purposes of extending, clarifying or invalidating our suggestions . . . '. I have questioned their assumption that critique can invalidate, rather than problematize, social analysis while respecting their plea not to read NSC as 'a dogmatic, self-sufficient *summa*' (ibid.). In this 'spirit', it is relevant to acknowledge and appreciate how my criticisms of NSC are articulated from a particular standpoint that invites further explication and critique.

The most basic and pervasive limitation of NSC, I have suggested, flows from Boltanski and Chiapello's disinclination to situate the significance which they ascribe to 'spirit' within a discussion of political economy. The importance of appreciating how notions of autonomy, security, and fairness, for example, serve to lubricate the reproduction of capitalism can be affirmed without overlooking how the most potent and enduring source of legitimacy for capitalism is widespread identification—amounting to secular devotion—with what Weber (1992: 73) identifies as the 'calling to make money'. It is a devotion that clearly extends to members of the cadres studied by McCann et al. (2008, 2010) and Hassard et al. (2012). Its secular appeal, as well as the fetishism of commodities which supports it, resides at the heart of capitalism as a distinctive mode of production. And, in the contemporary context, it has been amplified by neo-liberalism's populist appeal to 'better oneself' through individual endeavour framed by opportunities to become a player in financial, as well as labour and product, markets.

This is not to deny that varieties of capitalism[15] are embedded in normative frameworks which enable and constrain their specific forms of articulation. But Boltanski and Chiapello's claim that capitalism *'requires'* a normative dimension should be placed in scare quotes. It reflects their functionalist conception of capitalism as an abstract, 'absurd system'[16] (2005a: 7) governed by impersonal forces which, because it operates independently of everyday relations and mundane practices, lacks normative ballast that is supplied by repeated injections of 'spirit' to remedy this deficiency. It has been shown that the earliest phase of modern capitalist development, studied by Weber (1992), did not *'require'* the normative framework provided by the Protestant ethic. The normative order, comprising practices that articulate different 'spirits' associated with successive eras of capitalism (see Table 5.2), is not equivalent to a mantle draped over a 'naked' capitalism to provide some modest legitimacy, and thereby remedy an endemic normative deficit.[17] Everyday practices of production and exchange are accomplished within institutionalized relations that are *integral* to the (re)production of capitalism. Far from being supplied to meet a functional requirement, normative frameworks, including the compelling 'call to make money', become objectified, internalized, and legitimized within the institutions of civil society (e.g. family, community, mass media). Capitalist relations emerge out of, and are indivisible from, the institutions in which they take shape, where some (religious) 'spirits' are disenchanted and other secular ones are sanctified. It makes little analytical or political sense to conceive of 'capitalism' as an abstract system driven by logics that operate independently of the institutional conditions of their possibility.

Conceiving of 'capitalism' as a disembedded system populated by reified firms and markets, Boltanski and Chiapello fall well short of their ambition to 'engage with the complexity and indeterminacy of the production of historical realities' (2005a: xx). In effect, Boltanski and Chiapello adopt and reinforce a conventional (bourgeois) understanding of social relations in which the 'political' is partitioned from the 'economy', only to be reconnected by an invocation of 'spirit' to supply its means of animation and justification. When responding to such criticisms, Boltanski and Chiapello have insisted that NSC

---

[15] For example, market economies that are identified as liberal or coordinated (Hall and Gingerich, 2004; Hall and Soskice, 2001).

[16] This characterization is repeated in NSC but also softened in Boltanski and Chiapello (2005b: 162) where capitalism is described as 'in many ways' absurd.

[17] There is something of a disconnect here between Boltanski and Chiapello's understanding (2005a: xxi) that (a) ideology is not so much a mask that veils reality as a resource engaged in the constitution of reality, and (b) their conceptualization of capitalism as an abstracted, absurd system.

does not make '"spiritual tendencies" the motor of history' (ibid.: xix). Perversely, this defence is credible but only because the dynamic role in processes of capitalist development is ascribed to the disembedded machinations of an 'imperative' to pursue 'unlimited accumulation of capital' (ibid.: 4).

To conclude, it is necessary to situate the significance of 'the cultural' *within* the study of political economy in an integrated manner, and not to treat 'the cultural'—in the form of 'spirit'—as a discrete activity, or as something that accounts for the development of different phases of capitalism. Otherwise, phases of capitalist development are understood to be driven not by struggles to address and survive *material* crises (e.g. stagflation, unsustainable levels of debt, financial meltdown) but, instead, by the appearance of a *normative* deficit for which the recuperation of critique, and the associated rise of a new 'spirit', presents a revitalizing remedy. Material crises and normative deficits are, of course, interrelated—not least because the nature of 'crisis' as well as the means of responding to it is not self-evident; and, indeed, this uncertainty is a defining feature of 'crises' (Gamble, 2009: 38–43). Unfortunately, NSC spirits away an appreciation of how the changing materialization of politico-economic relations is always already embedded in a normative order that it rearticulated, rather than destroyed, by these relations. Forms of 'spirit' explored by Boltanski and Chiapello contribute to revitalizing these relations, in addition to providing legitimacy and justifications. It is an enduring devotion to the 'calling to make money', harnessed to policies of politico-economic governance (e.g. Keynesianism, neo-liberalism), that ensures their reproduction.

References

Abercrombie, N., Hill, S. and Turner, B. S. (1984) *The Dominant Ideology Thesis* (2nd edn.). London: Routledge.

Alvesson, M. and Willmott, H. C. (1992) *Critical Management Studies*. London: Sage.

——— (1996) *Making Sense of Management: A Critical Introduction*. London: Sage.

——— (2012) *Making Sense of Management: A Critical Introduction* (2nd edn.). London: Sage.

Bohm, S. and Dabhi, S. (eds.) (2009) *Upsetting the Offset: The Political Economy of Carbon Markets*. London: Mayfly Books.

Boltanski, L. (1987) *The Making of a Class: Cadres in French Society*, trans. A. Goldhammer. Cambridge: Cambridge University Press.

——Chiapello, E. (2002) 'The New Spirit of Capitalism'. Paper given at the Conference of Europeanistis, Chicago. Available at http://www.frontdeskapparatus.com/files/boltanskiNewSpirit.pdf.

——— (2005a) *The New Spirit of Capitalism*. London: Verso.

——— (2005b) 'The New Spirit of Capitalism', *International Journal of Politics, Culture and Society*, 18, 161–88.

——and Thévenot, L. (2006/1991) *On Justification: Economies of Worth*. Princeton, NJ: Princeton University Press.

Burawoy, M. (1986) *The Politics of Production*. London: Verso.

Callinicos, A. (2006) *The Resources of Critique*. Cambridge: Polity Press.

Chiapello, E. (2003) 'Reconciling the Two Principal Meanings of the Notion of Ideology: The Example of the Concept of the "Spirit of Capitalism"', *European Journal of Social Theory*, 6(2), 155–71.

——(n.d.) 'Understanding the New Cycle of Recuperation of Criticism in the Age of Cognitive Capitalism', unpublished mimeo.

Contu, A. (2008) 'Decaf Resistance: On Misbehavior, Cynicism, and Desire in Liberal Workplaces', *Management Communication Quarterly*, 21(3), 364–79.

Davies, W. (2007) 'Luc Boltanski and Eve Chiapello: The New Spirit of Capitalism', *Renewal: A Journal of Social Democracy*, 15(2/3). Available at http://potlatch.typepad.com/weblog/files/renewal_boltanski_review.doc (accessed 30 January 2011).

Dawe, A. (1970) 'The Two Sociologies', *British Journal of Sociology*, 21(2), 207–18.

Del Gandio, J. (2008) 'Global Justice Rhetoric: Observations and Suggestions', *Ephemera*, 8(2), 182–203.

Dickson, T. and McLachlan, H. V. (1989) 'In Search of "The Spirit of Capitalism": Weber's Misinterpretation of Franklin', *Sociology*, 23(1), 81–9.

Ezzamel, M. and Willmott, H. C. (2012) 'Registering "The Ethical" in Organization Theory Formation: Towards the Disclosure of an "Invisible Force"', Working Paper available from the author.

Farris, S. R. (2010) 'Review Essay: New and Old Spirits of Capitalism', *International Review of Social History*, 55, 297–306.

Fox, A. (1971) *A Sociology of Work in Industry*. London: Collier-Macmillan.

Fullerton, K. (1928) 'Calvinism and Capitalism', *Harvard Theological Review*, 21(3), 163–95.

Gamble, A. (2009) *The Spectre at the Feast: Capitalist Crisis and the Politics of Recession*. Basingstoke: Palgrave Macmillan.

Giddens, A. (1984) *The Constitution of Society: Outline of the Theory of Structuration*. Cambridge: Polity Press.

Glynos, J. and Howarth, D. (2007) *Logics of Critical Explanation in Social and Political Theory*. London: Routledge.

——Klimecki, R., and Willmott, H. C. (in press) 'Cooling out the Marks: The Ideology and Politics of the Financial Crisis', *Journal of Cultural Economy*, 5(3), 297–32.

Gratton, L., Hope-Hailey, V., Stiles, P., and Truss, C. (1999) *Strategic Human Resource Management: Corporate Rhetoric and Human Reality*. Oxford: Oxford University Press.

Hall, P. A. and Gingerich, D. W. (2004) 'Varieties of Capitalism and Institutional Complementarities in the Macroeconomy'. Available at http://www-old.gov.harvard.edu/faculty/phall/BVCmp.pdf (accessed 27 January 2011).

——and Soskice, D. (eds.) (2001) *Varieties of Capitalism: The Institutional Foundations of Comparative Advantage*. Oxford: Oxford University Press.

Hassard, J., Morris, J., and McCann, L. (2012) '"My Brilliant Career?" New Organizational Forms and Changing Managerial Careers in Japan, the UK and USA', *Journal of Management Studies*, 49(3), 571–99.

Jackall, R. (1988) *Moral Mazes: The World of Corporate Managers*. Oxford: Oxford University Press.

Kemple, T. M. (2007) 'Spirits of Late Capitalism', *Theory, Culture and Society*, 24(3), 147–59.

Kerbo, H. R. (2006) *World Poverty: Global Inequality and the Modern World*. New York: McGraw-Hill.

Knights, D. and Willmott, H. C. (1990) *Labour Process Theory*. Baingstoke: Macmillan.

Leca, B. and Naccache, P. (2006) ' "Le Nouvel Esprit du Capitalism": Some Reflections from France', *Organization*, 15(4), 614–20.

McCann, L., Hassard, J. and Morris, J. (2008) Normalized Intensity: The New Labour Process of Middle Management', *Journal of Management Studies*, 45(2), 3–371.

—————(2010) 'Restructuring Managerial Labour in the USA, the UK and Japan: Challenging the Salience of "Varieties of Capitalism"', *British Journal of Industrial Relations*, 48(2), 347–74.

Morris, J., Hassard, J., and McCann, L. (2006) 'New Organizational Forms, Human Resource Management and Structural Convergence? A Study of Japanese Organizations', Oraganization Studies, 27(10), 1485–1511.

Parker, M. (2008) 'The Seventh City: The New Spirit of Capitalism', *Organization*, 15(4), 610–20.

Power, M. (1999) *The Audit Society: Rituals of Verification*. Oxford: Oxford University Press.

Ritzer, G. (2011) *The McDonaldization of Society* (6th edn.). London: Sage.

Thompson, P. (1983) *The Nature of Work*. Basingstoke: Macmillan.

Turner, B. (2007) 'Justification, the City and Late Capitalism: Extended Book Review of *The New Spirit of Capitalism*', *Sociological Review*, 55(2), 410–14.

Weber, M. (1992) *The Protestant Ethic and the Spirit of Capitalism*. London: Routledge.

Willmott, H. C. (2010) 'Brandization Creating "Value" Beyond the Point of Production: Branding, Financialization and Market Capitalization', *Organization*, 17(5): 517–42.

——(2011) 'Making Sense of the Financial Meltdown—An Extended Review of *The Spectre at the Feast: Capitalist Crisis and the Politics of Recession*', *Organization*, 18(2), 239–60.

——(2012) 'The Financialized Corporation: Re-visioning Analysis by Correcting the "Political Economy" Deficit'. Paper presented at the 50th anniversary of the *Journal of Management Studies* Conference, St Anne's College, Oxford, April 2012. Available from the Author.

Wolfreys, J. (2008) 'Won't Get Fooled Again', *International Socialism*, 118. Available at http://www.isj.org.uk/index.php4?s=contents&issue=118 (accessed 27 January 2011).

Žižek, S. (1989) *The Sublime Object of Ideology*. London: Verso.

6

Beyond Justification: Dietrologic and the Sociology of Critique

Martin Parker

> There's a word in Italian. Dietrologia. It means the science of what is behind something. A suspicious event. The science of what is behind an event.
>
> Don DeLillo *Underworld* (1997: 280)

Sociology, perhaps like any other intellectual project, sometimes implicitly expresses a sense that it could be completed, and, hence, that the problem of 'the social' could be solved.[1] From Condorcet, Saint-Simon, and Comte onwards, there is a stream of thinking that attempts to grasp everything about the social within one definitive theory, an explanation of society that bridges the gap between psychology and history, between the stuff in our heads and the rise and fall of empires. It is a big gap of course, and there have been many big books with big titles that have attempted to fill it—*The Rules of Sociological Method*, *The Structure of Social Action*, *The Constitution of Society*. In this chapter, I want to think about what it means to have a comprehensive set of explanations for the sorts of things that social actors might do and the patterns that they make. The big question lurking here is not in itself a new one, but concerns the relation between general descriptions and social change. *The New Spirit of Capitalism*, it seems to me, is another book that seeks to explain pretty much everything, and once everything is explained, what room is there for something new?

This idea of filling up the world with explanations owes something to rational thinking in the very broadest sense, but I want to use a different

[1] Thanks to Glenn Morgan for his very insightful comments on an earlier draft of this chapter. A few parts of this chapter are based on 'The Seventh City', an extended review of NSC which appeared in *Organization* 15(4) (2008), 610–14.

term—'dietrologic'. Writing about conspiracy theories, Alasdair Spark wishes us to embrace this term for thinking about the practice of finding explanations that are assumed to be hidden. The term literally translates as 'behindology' (Knight, 2000: 230; Parker, 2001; Spark, 2001). Spark borrowed it from Don DeLillo's *Underworld*, a labyrinthine novel about the Cold War, but it is a word commonly enough used in Italian—*dietrologia*—to refer to the uncovering of explanations related to their underworld—the Mafia, Camorra, church, politicians, Masonic lodges, police, military, intelligence services, bankers, and industrialists, who are entangled with each other in multiple ways (Dickie, 2004: 239). Dietrologic suggests that you should not believe what you are told because the world is a place of secret powers and hidden motives. All is not as it seems, and explanations are creatures of hindsight. Often, this is not groundless fantasy but empirical fact—as the story of Roberto Calvi, the P2 Masonic Lodge, and the Banco Ambrosiano clearly indicated (Durden Smith, 2003: 183 *passim*). In such circumstances, only the naïve or stupid believe what they are told, and we should always be attentive to the machinery that moves behind our backs.

Theoretically, this chapter engages with an interesting logic puzzle for anyone who is persuaded by a sociological explanation of explanations, that is to say, with the dietrologic that motivates much sociology. If we start off by saying that our explanations for the way that the social world works are themselves given to us by that social world, then on this basis witchcraft, conspiracy theory, and sociology are all potentially equivalent forms of knowledge (Horton, 1984). We might try to make sociology distinctive by claiming that it can reflect on its own explanations, as in Giddens's 'double hermeneutic', but it also seems to be true that a belief in witchcraft can be explained by witchcraft, and conspiracy theories can certainly explain other conspiracy theories. A more sustainable difference could be the comprehensiveness and ambition of explanations. Paranoids aside, reasonable adherents of witchcraft or conspiracy theory would not assume that their explanations were needed for every social phenomenon that they encountered. Spells and UFOs are not needed to explain the fact that the bus arrives on time. Sociologists often lack such inhibitions. Durkheim, Parsons, and Giddens—as well as Boltanski and Chiapello—claim a degree of comprehensiveness for their accounts that far exceeds that of other explanations. The latter go even further by claiming to offer a 'sociology of critique', in the sense of explaining why some people articulate ideas that they believe to be critical of established explanations, but that can actually be explained by the workings of Boltanski and Chiapello's explanation of those explanations. In that sense, their dietrologic, their insistence on providing accounts for the status quo, as well as those voices that speak against it, is either admirable in its consistency, or rather mad, depending on which way you look at it. I will also suggest that it has some rather damaging political consequences. I think that their framework produces a kind of fatalism because thinking about, or even recognizing, radical alterity then becomes very difficult indeed.

I will begin by summarizing the argument in *The New Spirit of Capitalism*, as I read it, and then develop some ideas about its political consequences. These seem to me to concern the costs of thinking within such a dietrological framework. If everything is explained by recourse to existing mechanisms of power, including resistance to that power, then it is unclear how such a charmed circle might be broken. There appears to be nothing 'external' to the explanation that could cause it to fail because everything is included. This appears to mean that the future must be more of the same, and that all the vibrant forms of intellectual and practical resistance to contemporary capitalist forms are doomed to be incorporated too. I conclude by noting a series of problems with the sort of evidence that Boltanski and Chiapello admit, and suggesting that there are actually many alternatives to the new spirit of capitalism, should we care to look for them. In part, this is an attempt to counter Boltanski and Chiapello's sociologic with empirical evidence, but it is also to insist that there are already existing forms of action and justification that cannot be explained (away) by their argument, or indeed within the covers of any big book. And that, I believe, should give us cause for considerable optimism.

Locating the spirit

The New Spirit of Capitalism (NSC) is a big book which proclaims its importance. In an age when academics often read abstracts instead of journal articles, this book proposes a diagnosis of the present which updates Weber, corrects Marx, builds on Durkheim, and offers a new way to think about social critique. It is chastening to be reminded that such ambitions are possible, that thought and words can attempt so much. The political economy of the university in the global North now means that many of us spend much time worrying whether one journal has better impact factors than another, whether we will get that grant, or what our citation scores are. Boltanski and Chiapello seem unconcerned with satisfying the tests that dominate academic capitalism, and perhaps that is a good thing. Much contemporary social science is gap-filling in tiny subfields of normal scientific inquiry, published in journals that no one reads. This book claims to be doing something much grander, and I find its ambition laudable. Even though the sociological version of 'the Great American Novel' will probably never get written, it is perhaps an ambition worth burning the candle for.

Nonetheless, I think that NSC would have been better if it was less certain of its ground, and more alert to the dangers of claiming that the world you know is the same for everyone else. Some modest reflexivity might have encouraged me to be less struck by the way in which Boltanski and Chiapello generalize their Parisian experience to everyone else, and then claim that the world has changed. They claim (in the preface to the English edition) that when they began this research in 1994 'virtually no one... referred to capitalism any longer' (2005: x). A remarkable claim, if it was correct. So have a look for Braverman's *Labor and Monopoly Capital* (1974) in the text. You would not find it. Neither will you find any reference to Alvesson, Armstrong, Barley, Burrell, Clegg, Czarniawska, Deetz, Du Gay, Grey, Hassard, Knights, Linstead, Kunda, Morgan, Reed, Thompson, Townley, Willmott, and others, or almost any 'English speaking' critics of work organizations over the last thirty years. Entire intellectual traditions are absent—industrial relations, industrial sociology, labour process theory, critical management studies, critical accounting. Now, this might not be a problem if such work were irrelevant to their project, but this is a claim that is difficult to sustain because they do not qualify their arguments as being ones that originate or refer to particular social locations. It is ironic, to say the least, that an argument that seeks to sociologize so much ends up being so forgetful of its own small place in the scheme of things—a moral that is very germane to the argument in this chapter.

Let us locate these arguments then. The book was originally published in France by two French academics in 1999, the year of the 17th Labour Process Conference in London, the 18th Standing Conference on Organizational Symbolism in Edinburgh, and the first Critical Management Studies conference in Manchester. They have written about what they know, French sociology of work, and some US sociology too. When they deploy their impressive knowledge of unions, labour struggles, political parties, employment statistics, and so on, they are writing about France. Even their suicide statistics are French (2005: 423), which would be a problem even for Durkheim's comparative analysis of how the world behind our backs appears to compel us to make the most personal decisions. In various places in the book, such as the preface to the English edition, they wonder about this insularity themselves, but it does not seem to temper their view of the world and suggest some moderation in its claims. So, parts of NSC should really be a book titled *The New Spirit of Capitalism in France*, and it would probably be quite a good book too, but not one that claimed too much about the things which were happening anywhere else.

Another possible way to locate the arguments is to consider the evidence. In large part, these are textual materials that form the basis of a 'corpus' of work from the 1960s and from the 1990s. These are extracts from management guru type books (both translations from English, and French works), some articles from academic and popular journals, and even a brochure, all pulled from the HEC library shelves and then put through a qualitative software programme.

We are not really told how the books were chosen, or how the extracts were chosen, or whether there was any consideration of the issues that might come up when dealing with translations. Neither is there much speculation concerning the different sites of production of these texts, or how they circulate and are read, and by whom, and so on. Even more bizarrely, the confusion over texts spills over into the confusion over location, so that they appear at some points to be claiming that Tom Peters's *Liberation Management* (1992) was directly influenced by a French language post-1968 critique of work organizations. Well, perhaps, but my guess is that Bob Dylan and the Weather Underground mattered more. Just like the claims about France being the world, these are claims that a particular pile of evidence represents the world. It does not, any more than we would claim that what is ordered by the librarian at London Business School is representative of anything but the interests of the staff and students at London Business School.

The point of my cautions here is to remind ourselves that general claims are very often grounded in some rather specific ones, and that when someone tries to claim that the world has a particular shape, they are almost always claiming that their world is the same as yours. That might be the case, but it might not, and it is always worth considering the specificity of any claim, particularly if it is embedded in a big book that claims to be a theory of everything. The paradox of the social theory put forward in NSC is that it does claim to be attentive to particulars, and to the potential illuminations that empirical evidence might provide for understanding different worlds. Indeed, as I will argue later in the chapter, its origins are a long way from where it ends up. In order to understand this movement, I think we probably need to begin with Boltanski and Thévenot (2006), originally published in French in 1991. This is a work of Durkheimian moral sociology, which uses an ideal type methodology in order to conduct a series of thought experiments about justification, or legitimation in Weberian terms. This work is structuralist, in the sense that it is attempting to uncover the rules for social order as a set of largely agreed prescriptions and prohibitions, as a skeleton that holds the social world in a certain form. On the basis that a social order based on pure coercion cannot last for long, they ask how different social orders justify themselves to their participants. What rules for justification of worth and the common good can be legitimately employed in terms of the sorts of virtues that different social orders celebrate, or the sins they punish?

Boltanski and Thévenot suggest six ideal type 'worlds', 'cities', or 'polities', each coexisting in modern society, but each with different logics of justification. So, we have a world of inspiration, where status goes to those open to the sublime; a polity based on domesticity, with status based on some version of the ancestor figure; and a world of reputation, in which the opinion and trust of others is what matters. Fourth is a civic city, in which the great man represents the general will; whilst the commercial world provides status for those who supply desirable commodities. Finally, the industrial city values efficiency and professionalism. What NSC does is to add to these arguments a further city, the networked, projective, or connexionist polity, in which the great people are those with the most connections, and hence mobility, both social and spatial. These are people involved in projects, and who can exploit the holes in networks (Boltanski and Chiapello, 2005: 405) to their advantage. And the audience for (and actors within) this talk of a new world are the *cadres* (Boltanski, 1987), the managerial and professional classes whose consent, and even enthusiasm, is needed for this new spirit to have effects. These are the networked knowledge workers of globalizing capitalism, symbolic analysts who demand relative autonomy and assume that the time clock has been replaced by personal motivation and company culture.

However, this development is not a simple act of addition that produces the magic number seven. Rather like Weber's ideal types of charismatic, traditional, and legal-rationality authority, there is a tension between the connexionist logic of justification and the others, and the beginnings of a sort of teleology in which one city replaces others. Indeed, according to Boltanski and Chiapello, it is this historicism that (in a sense) makes for the possibility of critique. We cannot criticize from nowhere, because the very idea that a particular world fails a specific test requires an agreement that the test matters in the first place. And here we get to the heart of the matter, because critique, to do anything useful or significant, must also be embedded in a logic of justification. In other words, for some social phenomenon to be articulated as inadequate, it must fail a test of legitimacy within a particular social context. There are no trans-historical tests, no place outside the social where critique can be aimed in the name of a transcendent subject, class, epistemological position, and so on. Critics, like the modern press in times of war, must be embedded, otherwise they end up merely raving to themselves. So a networked city can only be critiqued on the basis of its own logic, not a logic which would only make sense somewhere else: just as French academics should only be critiqued by other French academics, perhaps (Leca and Naccache, 2008).

The tests of critique

So let us begin again with a more located understanding of their project. The reason that Boltanski and Chiapello appear to claim that critique needed revitalizing in 1990s France is actually rather predictable in terms of the longstanding division between a materialist position, which points at the cruelties of the world and shouts its outrage, and an idealist standpoint, which begins with language and reflects that 'cruelty' and 'outrage' are

129

words with many meanings (Parker, 1999). In other words, they wish to beat a path between theorists of power who think that things are obvious, and stargazing deconstructionists who appear to be claiming that there is nothing outside the text. Pierre Bourdieu is used as a representative of the former tendency and Jacques Derrida and Gilles Deleuze of the latter. All, according to Boltanski and Chiapello, no longer listen to the voices of ordinary people, and instead claim to understand the 'code, spectacle or simulacrum' which governs the social world, whether that be the hidden mechanisms of capital or of thought. The aporia is clear enough. For a sociology of critique, 'from what external position can critique denounce an illusion that is one with the totality of what exists?' (2005: 543–55). How can these 'critics' claim their position when there is no outside to the social, and no privileged position that allows tablets to be brought down from the mountain? In his later book *On Critique*, Boltanski is even more explicit in his renunciation of the 'cultural dopes' who are produced by Bourdieu's sociology of domination, a 'metacritical' position which is at once 'too powerful and vague in character' and seeks to 'explain how and why actors are dominated without knowing it' (2011: 20). Eschewing such supposedly arrogant and grandiose positions, Boltanski and Chiapello pursue a pragmatic strategy, based on studying what can be done within a particular logic of justification. By pragmatism, here they mean looking at language in context and seeing what it does, but the more common use of the word seems appropriate here too in terms of a certain sort of grounded practicality that eschews utopian schemes. This is a rationalism which is hostile to sentimental indignation and religious protest, too (2005: 325). Do not waste time trying to create a bloody revolution, or write manifestos aimed at inventing a new sort of human; just work with what we have now in order to ferment reform that could decrease suffering.

Crucially, their justification for their own position is not termed a 'critical sociology', but a 'sociology of critique' (2005: xi). If the former tends to presuppose a transcendental meaning to criticism, and elevates the importance of the critic, then the latter is based on observations of what happens when something people called critique is deployed. It is a sociology of knowledge, and involves treating critical claims as if they were the same sort of thing as witchcraft claims. Never mind the grandstanding, what does this language say, what claims does it make, and what effects does it have? Because Boltanski and Chiapello *do* believe that critique has consequences, but they might not be what the critics (or critical sociologists) would like to believe that they are. Indeed, they claim that it has been capitalism's response to embedded criticism that has produced the connexionist city as new regime of justification. It was the social and artistic critiques of 1968 (Illich, Marcuse, the situationists, and so on) that actually provoked the social change they identify as so important, yet also so impotent (Chiapello, 1998). The demands for flexibility, a general hostility to bureaucracy and 'working for the man', the inclusion of women in the workplace, claims for autonomy, creativity, and self-expression—all these emerge from the social and artistic critique only to be translated into new forms of organizing capitalism, for this is the new culturally driven workplace, with dress down Fridays, games rooms, a passion for customer satisfaction, and a workplace nursery. This is the basis of the new city, and this is precisely how Tom Peters and others justify their putatively new form of management and organization.

This story of the incorporation of resistance, of what autonomists now call recuperation, is a common one in critical work on organizations over the past twenty years or so (Hancock and Tyler, 2009; Kunda, 1992; Parker, 2000). Things that look like fun, that smell of freedom and dissent, are employed by capital to increase productivity and profit. It is not even a very new story, because the company picnic and song certainly predate *les événements* of 1968 by half a century (Beder, 2000). What Boltanski and Chiapello add is a caution. If the connexionist city is itself to be criticized, it must happen on its own terms, with tests of legitimacy that open the possibility for reforms that will ameliorate suffering. Tom Peters must be used against Tom Peters, because neither Bourdieu nor Derrida will be able to do the job. What is wrong with having fun at work? Why should we not be passionate about our product or service? What is wrong with thinking of yourself as being a project, like a career, with clear goals and an MBA along the way?

The problem they formulate here is clear, and it is a taxing one. If the critic is to contest the connexionist city, they must either buy into its language and assumptions and suggest that work might be more fun if it was done like this rather than like that, or rely on a different logic of justification. But the different logic might end up sounding antique, pompous, impractical, or whatever. To suggest, for example, that being passionate about selling mobile phones is a questionable use of human emotion might easily provoke a connexionist to ask whether you wanted people to do their jobs badly. Or, if a critic observed that the workplace nursery appeared to be allowing carers to self-exploit, they might ask whether you thought it was better that women stayed at home. The problem is that the tests of justice employed in one context are not the same as those employed in another and so the very words that we might celebrate—'freedom' and 'authenticity' for example— do not even mean the same things. This is an Aristotelian point, and it embeds us neatly within a sociological universe from which there appears to be no escape. There are no metaphysical trapdoors, no philosophical referee who can be called on 'at fear of contradiction', no skyhooks to rescue us from our location as human beings in the middle of other human beings. Boltanski and Chiapello's argument seems to have the sociologic worked out well, and it certainly exposes the grandstanding of those who wish to embrace the 'great refusal', but without thinking very hard about what *exactly* they are refusing.

In empirical terms, this sort of argument does echo elements of Hardt and Negri (2000) in their autonomist reworking of Marxism. Capitalism responds to proletarian demands, the master relies on the slave, and the slaves might take matters into their own hands. Yet where it differs is in Boltanski and Chiapello's dogged refusal to endorse any sort of political utopianism in the guise of Hardt and Negri's version of the mob—'the multitude'—as the agent of social change. The seven cities of NSC are only ideal cities in Weberian terms, not in any sense of Piero della Francesca's architectural city state ('La città ideale') and its lineage from Plato to H. G. Wells to the intentional community. No one is being invited to believe that any one city is better than any other, despite the gradual social changes that have brought connexionism into being. There is no perfectionism in these arguments, just a pragmatic description of where we are now. We can only deploy critique if we attend to the tests that matter here and now, not the tests we would like to deploy, or those that might have worked in the past. So we can point out, and Boltanski and Chiapello do, that the bad side of the connexionist city means that networked flexibility converts into job insecurity. It means trade unions are shrinking, wages are being driven down, and that creativity is appropriated and sold (see also Sennett, 2006, for a similar diagnosis). Boltanski and Chiapello are reformists and not revolutionaries, and their convincing empirical documentation of the many cruelties of connexionism certainly shows them to be clear-eyed observers of the French scene. The problem is that they, unlike Hardt and Negri, do little to inspire us with the possibility of a new social order. The question that remains, the nagging doubt in the face of such an impressive argument, is whether their 'sociology of critique' inevitably explains away a 'critical sociology'.

Conspiracy theory

Another way of putting this is to ask whether NSC leaves space for any other sorts of arguments or possibilities. One of the problems with dietrologic, if it is taken to an extreme, is that nothing escapes its explanatory scope. It fills the world with a significance that is already prefigured, and the smallest matter then becomes explicable in terms of some already existing mechanism. Why did the butterfly flap its wings? Why do suicide rates differ? How can unit acts be explained in terms of functional prerequisites? Now, whether or not something was actually caused is not the issue here. I do not want to make this into a question of choice versus determination on an ontological level, because I do not think we are in a position to answer that one, but instead wish to consider what dietrologic does at a social and political level. If we treat sociology as we would witchcraft or conspiracy theory, then we can note that it is a form of explanation that produces certain effects, just as Boltanski and Chiapello do, without commenting on whether the substance of the theory is correct or not (Horton, 1984).

I will distinguish between two versions of dietrologic here, and call them 'weak' and 'strong'. Weak dietrologic proposes that the world in general should be approached with suspicion, but that powerful interests and their institutions should be treated with particular care. If our government tells us that there is a heightened risk of a terrorist attack by fundamentalists, or a newspaper claims that all the social housing is being taken by migrants, or our employer indicates that they wish to empower us, we would be wise to be sceptical. Their interests are clear enough, and an account of heightened control measures leading to higher funding for the security services, an atmosphere of racialized resentment leading to higher sales for the newspaper, or work intensification leading to higher profits would seem to be good candidates for an explanation. Simply because something is a conspiracy theory does not mean that it is untrue, and in an era of mass communication and marketing, much that we are told is designed to persuade us to think, see, and consume in ways that are helpful for powerful interests. This is an understanding of knowledge that links it with power, and assumes that truth claims are often related to interests. It seems a broadly sensible approach for a citizen or social scientist to take if they live in complex societies.

The strong version of dietrologic runs along similar lines of course, but essentially assumes that *all* claims reflect the operation of a particular mechanism. It replaces a suspicion with certainty, and refuses the possibility that there could be events and actions that cannot be explained by the theory. In the background, or below consciousness, the causes of the social world are already prefigured. If this were a mental state, it would be paranoia, a disabling condition in which no one can really be trusted, yet where the logic of hidden cameras or secret policemen is unfalsifiable. Again, to be clear, I am not concerned here with whether there are hidden cameras or secret policemen, but with what such a belief does to explanation. Essentially, and this is my key point, it denies the possibility of events that might not be explained by the theory. This has some very important consequences, both relegating things that do not fit to relative invisibility, and assuming explanations for things that might be explained in other ways. If the sociologic is locked up in such a way that there appears to be no alternative, then no alternative will be visible. For example, if there are only seven cities, then it becomes difficult to imagine an outside, let alone see it.

As I noted, a weak dietrologic seems a sensible position for any sceptic, but it seems to me that Boltanski and Chiapello end up positing a strong dietrologic, even though they begin by insisting that they are pragmatists who understand accounts as locally specific. They almost certainly do not mean to do this, because they spend time criticizing others (particularly Bourdieu) on pretty much the same grounds. Though the logic of justification argument begins by insisting that it is sensitive to context, in NSC the argument goes on to build from a corpus of materials that represent certain forms of French managerial thought, and then generalizes those to become something as grand as a new spirit of capitalism. We have come a long way from a located pragmatism in a few jumps there, and now arrived at a position in which forms of critical thought (presumably expressed by people who are not cultural dopes) are either dismissed as metacritical arrogant waffle or described as incorporated. The only form of explanation left standing is one that denies that there can be any other form of explanation. As I said, there is a substantial irony in this diagnosis, if it is accepted, because Boltanski in particular claims to be in search of a theory of critique which builds on actors' explanations. From this entirely laudable starting point, what he ends up with is a theory of the incorporation of critique, regardless of actors' explanations. So in making its claims about 'the new', NSC puts forward an explanation that crowds out the possibility of difference, and only leaves space for the reproduction of the same.

Outside the seven cities

It seems to me that Boltanski and Chiapello's dietrologic is sociologically impeccable, essentially because it refuses any position, any platform, outside the social. It is an attempt to think about justifications from within, and consequently makes a splendid job of making explanations relative, or symmetrical (Law, 2004). This is undoubtedly a very important move, because it closes the door on forms of metaphysics that would arbitrarily give certain signifiers, agencies, or locations a particular transcendental priority—whether they be God, progress, the working class, or whatever. It simply insists on a version of Occam's razor for the social—admit no more entities or explanations than you already have within the description itself. So, if you observe patterns to the generation and dissemination of consent and dissent, then you are forced (at fear of contradiction) to apply those to your own arguments. So far so good, and it becomes clear enough how a 'critical sociology' must then take its place as an exemplar within 'the sociology of critique'. There is no other place to stand.

However, the compelling nature of this argument conceals one really important point, that it is not possible to 'see' the entire social. Theoretically, it is entirely legitimate to assert that there is no act that is not social, but empirically it is quite a different claim to say that you have observed the logic of all acts. The example needs to come from no further than NSC itself. We could accept that these two French sociologists know French sociology and French society, and that their descriptions are hence largely comprehensive and convincing for people who exist within that context. (I am not commenting on whether they are or not, simply on whether they could be.) It is clear that the same cannot be claimed about their knowledge of the English business school, of Labour Process Theory, Critical Management Studies, and so on. Or, at the very least, that such knowledge is not accounted for within their story of changes in the theory and practice of work organizations for the past thirty years or so. Now this might not be a problem, because it is theoretically probable that such forms of knowledge are also subject to some sort of regime of justification, and there is no reason to provide English sociology with any priority over the French variety. But, and this is the key point, Boltanski and Chiapello have not observed the logics of justification within the English context. This means that they might be the same as the French one, or that they might not. As I hope they would agree, the only way to tell is empirically.

If we did decide to explore these assertions comparatively, it would be possible to argue that the putative dominance of connexionism might differ depending on local context, and there are chapters in this volume which make that argument. At the same time, we might also assert that all seven different regimes of justification might be found in contemporary social orders, and it is an empirical question as to their relative weights in each different society. These would be possible articulations of the NSC project that are sensitive to difference, and to the forms of evidence, argument, and testing which locals use in different contexts. This is to make Boltanski and Chiapello into institutionalists who are pursuing a project that explains varieties of capitalism within a broad theoretical structure which begins with actors' explanations. Whilst I quite like this description of a possible project, my reading of NSC does not support it as a claim about what this book actually does. I do not think it is a book that opens up empirical questions, but rather one that prefigures the answers to these questions based on some very thin empirical evidence. To put it bluntly, the book tells us that connexionism is the dominant logic nowadays, and that it incorporates critique. This is a dietrologic that asserts the endurance of sameness and sadly opines that there can be no difference, both theoretically and empirically.

But Boltanski and Chiapello cannot be everywhere, and hence they cannot make assertions about everywhere. They simply do not know whether the logics of justification in their seven cities apply in other places—across the channel, in the *banlieus*, in a Spanish cooperative, or a community enterprise in Thailand. The problem with strong dietrologic, or this rapacious sociologic, is that it tends to be inductive. It fills the world with the same sort of explanations, when something different might be happening for entirely different reasons. The observer theorist might assume that they already know the reasons, but they lack social context, and hence might easily be wrong. Right to say that there are rules and reasons, but wrong to say that they know them. So if you want to understand a cockfight, you will need to spend some time in one, observing what people do and say, and asking them for their justifications of particular sequences of action (Geertz, 1973). No inductive generalizations will allow you to claim, from a desk in Paris, that you understand the logics of justification that pertain in a village in Bali.

It might be answered that the seven cities are 'ideal types', models that approximate to forms of action but that do not describe what actually happens, and that this gap between concept and action is precisely the right place for a sociology that generalizes on the basis of empirical evidence. This is fair enough, but it also allows for inductive generalizations to be contested with empirical evidence from other places. The strength of the ideal type is precisely that it generates questions that can be empirically tested and, as the lengthy post-Second World War debate on the dysfunctions of the bureaucratic ideal type clearly showed (Albrow, 1970), ideal types can be found wanting as descriptions of action and belief. If the seven cities are ideal types, then they can be tested with respect to their accuracy in describing and predicting what people do. If the connexionist city is putatively increasingly dominant in the global North, then it can in principle be tested against other contemporary practices to see whether it can explain them, either to the sociologist or to the actor.

The general problem with Boltanski and Chiapello's model, like pretty much any model, is that it tends to 'internal' explanations. Causes and phenomena tend to be those that fit, like the depictions of the world found in the documents from the HEC library. The reasons for things that happen, and the identification of the things that count, are already shaped by the theory. The paranoid already knows that their dietrologic applies. So, for example, if we accept Boltanski and Chiapello's claim that criticism deemed to be legitimate is the motor of social change, then a whole range of other potential candidates tend to recede into the distance. Social orders might change because of war, disease, technology, and climate change. They might change because the powerful organize themselves with guns and a secret police. Legitimacy is clearly important in the maintenance of the capitalist hegemony, but even social orders that lack legitimacy seem to be able to hold on to power—particularly if they can do their dirty business elsewhere in the globe, and prevent the very need for justification to take place. For example, globalization does not figure that much in the book, but I do not see how the building of a factory in a 'Free Trade Zone' in the Philippines to replace French workers could really be an example of capitalists responding to post-1968 criticism. Just as Hardt and Negri overstate the hegemony of immaterial labour (Camfield, 2007), so do Boltanski and Chiapello appear to assume that certain locations and forms of labour in the global North explain global capitalism. Richard Sennett produces a similar diagnosis of the culture of the new capitalism, but he is clear to say in several places in his book that 'the new economy is only a small part of the whole economy' (2006: 10). I do not remember such qualifications in NSC, and if it were an empirical project, I would expect to see them.

Second, and this is the standard critique of the ideal type form of analysis, is the connexionist city a useful empirical or political tool? The danger of the ideal type is that readers begin to assume that it is a description, rather than a model, for helping understanding. Boltanski and Chiapello are clear that work organizations in France are not enlightened hubs of creativity but there is a clear implication that elements of the older cities (patriarchy, bureaucracy, inherited wealth) are somehow on the wane. Though Boltanksi and Thévenot (2006) may be clear that the six polities can more or less coexist, depending on local contingencies, NSC asserts with few qualifications that connexionism is the new logic which replaces all the others. I have already heard people discussing this book as if it were empirical proof of the dominance of the new capitalism, or even (as the authors themselves recognize and regret) a hymn in its praise (Boltanski and Chiapello, 2005: xv; Leca and Naccache, 2008). The grounded sociology of critique that the book explores might never even be read, because (as the authors would again realize, but too late) another sort of incorporation has already happened. The ideal type has become idealized. Not a condensation of tendencies that need to be empirically tested, but an assertion about the way that the world is, and why it cannot be otherwise.

And that makes me wonder whether sometimes the oppositional voices actually do come from 'outside' a particular regime of justification, which is to say, from somewhere else than the connexionist city, and outside the Parisian academy, and in the name of a different way of life. Not always, because this is an empirical matter, but sometimes. Because if the 'test' is only possible on the grounds already established by pre-existing institutions, then recuperation seems likely, and the possibility of radical alternatives seems slim. My point is not that such critiques could come from outside the social itself, but that the social is not exhausted by the new spirit. In order to make their claim about incorporation and critique, Boltanski and Chiapello have simply glossed over the matters that do not fit, or that they did not see. For example, in the late 1990s in France, as they acknowledge, they did not see the arrival of Seattle, Genoa, or Porto Alegre (2005: xvi). And if we read NSC now, and do not look up from our reading and notice the Occupy movements, we might believe that there is still no significant alternative to the seventh city. On the other hand, if we put connexionism in its place,[2]

---

[2] And its place might actually be *La Défense*, the skyscrapering office city on the edge of Paris.

different socio-economic practices come into view—anti-capitalism, charity, communes, cooperatives, credit unions, eco-villages, fair trade, indymedia, intentional communities, Islamic finance, local exchange trading schemes, mutualism, open source software, permaculture, slow food, squatting, scrounging, time banks, voluntary work, worker self-management, and so on (Parker et al., 2007, 2013).

It is easy enough to suggest that all these are too small to matter, but I could just as easily keep on extending this list until non-capitalist economic and social relations begin to look like more than a series of isolated and marginal alternatives (Williams, 2005). This is an empirical question, and I suggest that it is odd that Boltanski and Chiapello seem to put more weight on what Tom Peters says than, for example, what hundreds of thousands of cooperatives and 800 million cooperators[3] do across the world. Tragically, they seem aware of the problem, and write in a postscript entitled 'Sociology *contra* Fatalism', that '... it is definitely more effective to create a multiplicity of changes that might seem small-scale from some overarching grandiose viewpoint' (2006: 533). The problem appears to be that they cannot see the small-scale changes because their theory has already assumed them away, and hence are themselves the ones who tend towards grand fatalism.

It is quite possible to dismiss my list of non-commodified forms, from ATTAC (*Association pour une Taxation des Transactions financières pour l'Aide aux Citoyens*)[4] to Zapatista, by saying that they are all on the way to being incorporated. Whilst this is a possibility and, as Boltanski and Chiapello demonstrate, has certainly been a way of understanding many oppositional critiques from the 1960s onwards, to assert it is to repeat the dietrological problem. If the theory predicts that critical positions will be recuperated and become tools for the marketing of capitalism 2.0, then that is what will happen. Longstanding examples of very large producer co-ops, a bank, and university (like Mondragón in the Basque region); consumer co-ops (like Suma in Northern England); partnerships like the John Lewis department store or the Scott Bader Commonwealth; Italian social centres; worker-managed organizations; squats and co-housing; and well over 1,000 intentional communities such as Findhorn, Auroville, and Crystal Waters simply disappear from view (Bunker et al., 2006; Erdal, 2011; Fellowship for Intentional Communities, 2010; Parker et al., 2007, 2013; Volker and Stengel, 2005). Of course, just like capitalist firms, there are also plenty of these forms of organizing that grow and die, but the continuing endurance of such a huge

---

[3] See www.ica.coop/statistics.html, accessed 14/11/10.

[4] The Association for a Taxation of Financial Transactions and for the Aid of Citizens, a radical French anti-capitalist group established in 1998, the year before the publication of NSC. For more details of this organization, see the chapter in this volume on ATTAC by Ötsch, Pasqualoni, and Scott.

variety of alternatives to capitalist forms of management and commodification, which seem to me to provide counter-examples to the incorporation argument, is an empirical fact and not a prediction from theory. These examples, and many others, have their own logics of justification too, of course. They are not external to the social, not alternatives in the sense that they are outside sociological analysis, but they do not appear to be easily accounted for within Boltanski and Chiapello's story of the dominance of connexionism.

To go back to where I started, as a host of philosophers of social science from Popper onwards have observed, your theory structures your observations, which in turn results in observations that confirm the theory. Strong dietrologic is merely an intense form of this process, in which one theory assumes meta-theoretical status, and hence explains all observations. So it is, I think, with the NSC. This is a theoretically sophisticated attempt to understand what happened to the spirit of 1968, and which makes some compelling arguments against metacritical positions. However, in doing so it leaves no outside, no space where a 'critical sociology' is not corrosively dissolved into a 'sociology of critique'. To their credit, Boltanski and Chiapello are aware of this, and it seems to be a problem that continues to haunt Luc Boltanski's *On Critique* (2011) and his essay in this volume. When he notes in the latter that the 'sociology of critical practices' ends up doing pretty much what Bourdieu et al. are accused of doing—'presenting people as subjected to almighty structures and of ignoring their critical capacities as agents'—he is acknowledging the political problems that his epistemological arguments lead to—a sort of fatalism, in which we already know that resistance is pointless.[5] However, for myself and for millions of organizers of alternatives to capitalist commodification, the world is not explained away by a Parisian sociologic in which no space is left for anything else. Boltanski and Chiapello might claim that it is, and make us into cultural dopes, but this is both contradictory to their theory, and politically tragic. The idea of a big book that ends the sociological project is a seductive one, but it always runs the danger of closing the politics of the social within its covers, and hence refusing any space for concepts and evidence that challenge its central thesis. This is a question of the limits to any dietrologic, or to reverse Boltanski and Chiapello, the point at which a critical sociology must and will always exceed a sociology of critique. For, if we stay within the seven cities, we might never be able to imagine life outside them.

---

[5] The argument that he then develops in that chapter is one that is intended to open the sort of space I am thinking about here, but assumes that alternatives can never become institutionalized. Whilst there is certainly a tension here, the empirical examples I have provided in this chapter go some way to questioning this assertion.

References

Albrow, M. (1970) *Bureaucracy*. Basingstoke: Macmillan.
Beder, S. (2000) *Selling the Work Ethic: From Puritan Pulpit to Corporate PR*. London: Zed Books.
Boltanski, L. (1987) *The Making of a Class: Cadres in French Society*. Cambridge: Cambridge University Press.
—— (2011) *On Critique: A Sociology of Emancipation*. Oxford: Polity Press.
—— Chiapello, E. (2005) *The New Spirit of Capitalism*. London: Verso.
—— Thévenot, L. (2006) *On Justification: Economies of Worth*. Princeton, NJ: Princeton University Press.
Braverman, H. (1974) *Labor and Monopoly Capital*. New York: Monthly Review Press.
Bunker, S., Coates, C., and How, J. (2006) *Diggers and Dreamers: The Guide to Communal Living in Britain*. London: D&D Publications.
Camfield, D. (2007) 'The Multitude and the Kangaroo: A Critique of Hardt and Negri's Theory of Immaterial Labour', *Historical Materialism*, 15, 21–52.
Chiapello, E. (1998) *Artistes versus Managers. Le Management Culturel Face à La Critique Artiste*. Paris: Métailié.
Dickie, J. (2004) *Cosa Nostra: A History of the Sicilian Mafia*. London: Hodder & Stoughton.
Durden Smith, J. (2003) *The Mafia*. London: Arcturus.
Erdal, D. (2011) *Beyond the Corporation*. London: Bodley Head.
Fellowship for Intentional Communities (FIC) (2010) *Communities Directory: A Comprehensive Guide to Intentional Communities and Co-operative Living*. Rutledge, MO: FIC.
Geertz, C. (1973) 'Deep Play: Notes on a Balinese Cockfight'. In *The Interpretation of Cultures*. New York: Basic Books, 412–54.
Hancock, P. and Tyler, M. (eds.) (2009) *The Management of Everyday Life*. Basingstoke: Palgrave Macmillan.
Hardt, M. and Negri, A. (2000) *Empire*. Cambridge, MA: Harvard University Press.
Horton, R. (1984) 'African Traditional Thought and Western Science'. In B. Wilson (ed.), *Rationality*. Oxford: Blackwell.
Knight, P. (2000) *Conspiracy Culture*. London: Routledge.
Kunda, G. (1992) *Engineering Culture*. Philadelphia: Temple University Press.
Law, J. (2004) *After Method*. London: Routledge.
Leca, B. and Naccache, P. (2008) '*La Nouvel Espirit du Capitalisme*: Some Reflections from France', *Organization* 15(4), 614–20.
Parker, M. (1999) 'Capitalism, Subjectivity and Ethics: Debating Labour Process Analysis', *Organization Studies* 20(1), 25–45.
—— (2000) *Organizational Culture and Identity*. London: Sage.
—— (2001) 'Human Science as Conspiracy Theory'. In J. Parish and M. Parker (eds.), *The Age of Anxiety: Conspiracy Theory and the Human Sciences*. Oxford: Blackwell, 191–207.
—— Fournier, V., and Reedy, P. (2007) *The Dictionary of Alternatives: Utopianism and Organization*. London: Zed Books.

—— Cheney, G., Fournier, V., and Land, C. (eds.) (2013) *The Routledge Companion to Alternative Organization*. London: Routledge.

Peters, T. (1992) *Liberation Management*. New York: Knopf.

Sennett, R. (2006) *The Culture of the New Capitalism*. New Haven, CT: Yale University Press.

Spark, A. (2001) 'Conspiracy Thinking and Conspiracy Studying'. Internet document accessed 15 March 2001 at http://www.wkac.ac.uk/research/ccc/index2.htm.

Volker, P. and Stengel, M. (2005) *Eurotopia*. London: Edge of Time.

Williams, C. C. (2005) *A Commodified World?* London: Zed Books.

7

The Insubstantial Pageant: Producing an Untoward Land[1]

Nigel Thrift

My sense of the bodily unconscious is that it now holds the future of the world in the balance as much as the other way around; that we have reached a time in world history when we can choose to press forward with the exploration of this 'last frontier' which would, like the study of work habits by scientific management from Taylorism to the present, exploit and disfigure and even destroy it, or else we can figure out a way of mastering our drive for mastery. (Taussig, 2009: 16).

We now have a new spatial, religious, or anthropological foundation for tenancy. No longer is there a here or appropriation; we live as transients or tenants, deprived of a fixed abode. (Serres, 2011: 20).

The envious have inherited the earth. (Clark, 2007: 16).

So on the one hand I really believe in empty spaces, but on the other hand, because I'm still making some art, I'm still making junk for people to put in their spaces that I believe should be empty: i.e. I'm helping people waste their space when what I really want to do is to help them empty their space. (Warhol, 1975: 144).

Introduction

Over the last ten years, in a good part of the social sciences concerned with what we might loosely call the economy, the spotlight has tended to focus on finance. Indeed, there was a moment not so long ago when there was even a

---

[1] William Shakespeare. *The Tempest.* Act 4, Scene 1.

kind of love affair with finance, especially by those who belonged to the social studies of finance school which had transported the protocols of science studies into finance. Finance seemed to be something almost scientific in its attention to models and data. It was complex and intricate, something you could really get your teeth into. But the bust has revealed finance for what it was and is: some very clever people doing some not particularly clever things in a smokestack industry which has a lethal capacity to pollute its surroundings and which has produced a banking system which is probably more dangerous now than before the financial crisis began in 2008 (French et al., 2009 Thrift, 2010).

Of course, none of this is meant to suggest that finance is anything other than a vital source of economic governance but, in this moment of disillusionment, perhaps it would be interesting to step back and think about what some other parts of the economy have been doing and, in particular, to consider again the production of commodities by means of commodities. For, I will argue that, in its latest incarnation, capitalism is not just busily manufacturing commodities, already understood for some time as no longer simply goods but as shapers of and solutions to experience. Rather, it is attempting to manufacture rolling worlds within which 'communities of sense' (Hinderliter et al., 2009) can be catalysed which can act to furnish the world anew through a process that might be understood as a reinvention of the commodity itself. That is, or so I will argue, industry is trying, through a continual process of world-making, to commodify the push of will[2] with the aim of producing enhanced 'invention-power'. Of course, such a project can only ever work imperfectly and patchily, but to be able to see such a process of creating process in the throes of what Peter Sloterdijk calls 'explicitation' is surely not only worthwhile but crucial if it is to be modulated or, indeed, opposed.

I therefore want to ask a question: 'where does the leading edge of capitalism want to go next?' What might its new 'New Spirit' look like? Of course, I am aware that 'capitalism' does not have well-formed and articulated wants or goals, but that is the point.[3] By speculating about what those wants or goals might be, perhaps it is possible to get a clearer picture of what is, so to speak, in store as capitalism aims to make the whole world not just into a continually evolving and involving store—through increasing not simply what is saleable but what is appropriable to be sold in the world (Serres, 2011)—but also into a

---

[2] It is about the noun and verb 'the will' and 'to will' in several senses, as we shall see. I understand the will as the bridge between mental activity and outward conduct. Unlike James, I take the will to constitute both the power of reflex action or habit and acts which can only be attentively performed—James concentrated only on the latter category.

[3] The evidence for this chapter comes from three main sources. First, extensive reading of academic books and papers. Second, and as importantly, reading of all manner of press articles, websites, and general business magazines. Third, discussions with numerous industry leaders across industry.

means of continually generating ideas which can, in turn, continually restock this restore: this is all about knowledge oriented towards the future. It is world as laboratory, feasting on space (McNeely and Wolverton, 2008).[4]

I want to argue that it is a peculiarly appropriate time to try to answer this question because capitalism's need for an answer has become more and more pressing. I think it is possible to argue that capitalism has reached a technological plateau in that it is finding it increasingly difficult to squeeze value out of innovation—which no doubt explains why innovation has become such a watchword, even an obsession. At least in the developed countries, capitalism has picked off the 'low-hanging fruit' (Cowen, 2011; Mirowski, 2011), the most apparent opportunities for rapid development—like free land or immigrant labour or educational gains or the most productive new technological ideas—and is often simply skimming the past.

To escape this technological plateau and to produce a new round of accelerated productivity and profitability born out of gains from knowledge and innovation, therefore, requires a fundamental reorganization of how the world is. I argue in this chapter that to achieve this reorganization means redefining the commodity world such that this reorganization produces new possibilities for what a commodity and commodification might be—as complex collective goods—in a kind of baroque transformation (Scarpellini, 2011) brought about by two different tendencies: one, the production of a new infrastructural project, the formation of an expressive infrastructure; the other, the formation of a continuously migratory land out of this project, land which can run and run and in doing so act as a new source of value as it is tenanted and tilled.

In other words, capitalism has embarked on a huge experiment. As we shall see, the outcome is fundamentally uncertain in the sense that it is not clear whether it will produce elevated levels of invention and hence profit, but without it capitalism can only fall back on what are now tired solutions that are likely to lead to stagnation (Boltanski and Chiapello, 2005).

Thus, I want to go back to the commodity. Commodities have always come with extension in space and time. So far as *spatial* extent is concerned, commodities have been systematically wrapped and packaged in various forms since the nineteenth century. Gradually, they attained more grip on the world as they became linked in to experience in multiple ways, most notably through a panoply of consumer spaces like shops, arcades, supermarkets, malls, and shopping villages. Commodities had to have affective purchase,

---

[4] For a long time, it was assumed that economies have to have goals. But this is only one model of how an economy has to function and, increasingly, it is being challenged. Economies are becoming seen as much looser aggregates which only periodically act in concert, as in the case of the industrial revolution (Clark, 2007). Economies are no longer seen as necessarily going towards a state which is somehow fuller or more finished. Rather, they are seen as patchworks in both space and time which never click entirely into place.

which initially meant the growth of advertising through which publics could be formed but since the 1980s has come to mean associating the commodity with all manner of experiences: indeed, the commodity is increasingly understood as a part of a more generalized experience of a world.

So far as *temporal* extension is concerned, commodities equally have been extending their range. Whereas they were associated simply with the point of sale and their subsequent consumption, increasingly, driven by financial and marketing innovations, commodities are understood as personalized processes, as a flow of services of which the commodity understood as a physical object for sale is but a part of a wider experience. The commodity becomes a kind of tenancy, in other words, that is rented out. Equally, inhabitation comes to mean valuing habitat as a time-limited experience—on the model of a franchise or a lease or a subscription. 'Like victory, the terrain changes hands with each match and every half-time. It is paid in rent' (Serres, 2011: 22). Increasingly, consumers no longer keep what they buy, but rent it out for a defined period as a cluster of possessions that have shorter or longer temporal signatures.[5]

As spatial and temporal extension have both grown, so commodities have taken the next step. They have started to package the world so that they can nestle more deeply within it. The world is wrapped up in the cellophane of commodity worlds as complex collectivities which flicker into and out of being as different cues are formed, in a filmic process of movement *and* engagement which is part of why this process can be compelling: 'perception can grasp movement only as the displacement of a moving body or the development of a form' (Deleuze and Guattari, 1987: 177). To achieve this state, not only perceptions of space (and especially what we understand as framing) but also of time have altered in lockstep with the development of the commodity. Our habits of viewing the world mutate. For example, time has become increasingly cut up and breathless as a result of the techniques of fast art found in recent film and video, games and music which redefine what is meant by a lasting experience (Mullarkey, 2009). But this process of producing a new *land*, as I will call it, is *not* a process of alienation. It requires buy-in, literally and metaphorically, and the reason for the battery of methods that have been invented recently can be seen as marshalling the means to produce precisely this sense of grip. In turn, it produces a new form of ground rent in that the proportion of property value attributable to location is redefined by continually reworking what counts as location, thus producing a world which allows new claims to be made on future profits arising out of the ability to put investment together with labour (for the new location demands labour by consumers at all points) by relying on moving, relative location.

---

[5] The growing cluster of work in geography, anthropology, and history that documents the afterlife of commodities is symptomatic of this tendency.

So the answer to my question is that the leading edge of capitalism is involved in a process of engineering worlds such that every moment becomes an opportunity to both make a sale and explore the subsequent moment: capitalism wants to run at the rate of life itself. This is a project that both seeks out intelligence on consumers in a kind of renovation of bookkeeping and tries to tap consumer intelligence in a way which can be thought of as the modern equivalent of the novel.[6] This also suggests the need for the formation of a long-term infrastructural project which would require the construction of what we might term an *expressive infrastructure* in that it is meant to act as a pipeline for affect and imagination. But the project of channelling and damming affect and imagination through the laying down of technology and the practices associated with it demands much more than a simple concentration and acceleration of what already exists. It requires, instead, capitalism reworking the substance of what we regard as the world down to the smallest grain of interaction through an architecture of intimacy (Turkle, 2011) which enables a company or companies to focus on one consumer interaction from among the millions taking place at any time as though this were the only interaction that mattered. To explain this ambition means calling not just on the obvious sources of inspiration like Michel Foucault but also, as we shall see, on luminaries like William James and Andy Warhol. James allows us to understand the construction of this moment of interaction as an intensification of his likening of life to a frontier of flame making its way rapidly through the stubble in a cornfield as the field is burnt off, whereas Warhol allows us to understand that commerce is increasingly taking on many of the attributes of art: art does not simulate commerce so much as commerce simulates art.

In other papers, I have tried to show that the way in which the world turns up is changing as firms begin this process of redefining process (Thrift, 2009, 2010, 2011). This chapter follows on from them, in that it looks at and summarizes the broader issues that result from this thesis. In particular, it considers the way in which a certain kind of stance to the world, an *environmental* stance, has changed the terms of trade. In making this claim, I am in the company of a number of other authors who want to show how modern cultures are moving from a closed-off and circumscribed to an atmospheric means of understanding what is in the world and how to control it.

I will make my case in three parts. In the first part of the chapter, I will examine the main changes that have been taking place in the economy as they relate to innovation. I will argue that these changes might be thought of as a second industrial revolution based around the growth of an expressive infrastructure. Then, in the second part, I will consider how these changes are

---

[6] The two practices of bookkeeping and the novel have been brought together by Batuman (2007), suggesting that technical and affective practices have always been a feature of capitalism.

producing a different kind of production—of worlds premised upon a different way of combining capital and labour, worlds which attempt to direct populations in ways that simultaneously call on all of their qualities and try to pre-empt them, a naturalistic process akin to Foucault's idea of 'normation'.

The industrial revolution is often characterized as the first break in human history with the natural economy. But what if the natural economy was now being recovered—but by other means—as a redefinition of what constitutes land? But if a new land is coming into existence, the problem still exists of how to extract surplus from it. In the final part, I will therefore turn to a series of halting experiments in how to extract surplus from this new land by surveying the imprint that these changes are making upon cities as part of an ecology of innovation and a corresponding form of consciousness in motion.

One important word of warning is in order. I do not take the new ecology of practices I want to outline as simply taking over from a previous order, as if there was some kind of historical queue, with older forms simply dropping away and newer forms unambiguously regnant, an impression often given by extant theoretical accounts which, whilst assiduously denying it, often produce a succession of ideal types. As Gibson-Graham (2006) has pointed out, economies are variegated beasts which at any point in time will consist of many different kinds of economic practice, sometimes replacing other practices but as often coexisting with them and not infrequently producing new economic forms out of this coexistence. Like all things, new orders should not be overdone. Everything matters but everything does not connect. For example, much manufacturing industry remains of a very different kind from what I will describe and will continue to do so. In the region I come from, for example, 18 per cent of small firms still have no internet site.[7] This is not the economy I will be describing here but we should not forget the salutary lesson it serves up. Beware of exaggeration. There is and always will be other modes of production entangled and still potent. The economy I want to describe continues to exist more prominently in some industries than others, in some places rather than others, amongst some populations but not others.

A new industrial revolution

The industrial revolution remains something of an enigma, with all kinds of explanations and interpretations of its genesis and evolution still in play. But we know that it crucially depended upon the invention of productivity-raising

---

[7] But equally, that same region is one of the key nodes for the global computer games industry and the global automotive industry (which is intent on engineering ambience through a profusion of electronics and software).

machinery and the coterminous invention of the railroad and steam-powered ships which created a global economy and an international division of labour which could support the boost it provided by producing the first hints of truly global industry, all set against a background of cheap energy and capital but comparatively expensive labour. More generally, it arose out of the insertion of a process of continuous invention into invention arising out of better communication between those who knew things and those who made things (Allen, 2010; Mokyr, 2010). One thing we also know about the industrial revolution is that it involved new levels of pooling of information. Costs to access knowledge plummeted. Producers, in turn, spent more time seeking access to the best knowledge available at the time. It is important to note that invention here is not considered as bolts from the blue. Rather than these Eureka moments, it 'takes the form of analogies to and combinations of existing techniques, or combined knowledge from diverse fields in what we might call technical hybrids or recombinations' (Mokyr, 2010: 94). That might involve systematic processes or plain and simple tinkering (Mol et al., 2010).

At the same time, the industrial revolution was always coupled with growing consumer demand. As De Vries (2008) and others have shown, the entanglement of supply and demand had already produced sophisticated markets for commodities by the beginning of the industrial revolution along with equally sophisticated consumers 'actively engaged in a process of discovery' (De Vries, 2008: 23), which involved taking risks on new products and new combinations of products. Consumers were consequential from early on in the history of capitalism, not least because they drove invention through a growing insistence on novelty (which drove innovation) and status and other 'tangible intangibles' (which drove quality) and which became more important as a result of the growth of advertising coupled with a more general effect, namely that a rise in material affluence produced less individual self-control (Offer, 2006).

Since the industrial revolution, the process of continuous invention of invention—invention power—has therefore become such a staple of life that we tend to forget its wider historical significance. For example, 'innovation' has become a defining characteristic of what firms are meant to do. Indeed, for some, it has become their core value, part of what, to outsiders, can look like a large, suitably updated cargo cult. Yet, what is termed 'innovation' only rarely includes the initial 1 per cent of innovation, as it is known, the breakthrough ideas that change the nature of what is on offer. It is precisely the continuous invention of invention that is most important, and most firms at least implicitly acknowledge this. For example, starting in the 1980s, firms began to experiment with ways of working that might produce enhanced invention of invention, all the way from learning organizations to communities of practice to what became known as open innovation.[8] At around the same time as these developments, there was a vogue in business and all kinds of other arenas for the construction of inventive spaces at each and every scale. All around the world, spaces were assembled which, it was hoped, would boost inventiveness by increasing the number of creative interactions and general 'buzz', and, by implication, the number of innovations: a kind of turbo-charged inventiveness. Hence the simultaneous vogue for clusters that could maximize the circulation of ideas and promote so-called absorptive capacity (Thrift, 2005). Equally, and from about the same date, many firms started to run down their corporate research and development facilities, outsourcing these capacities to other agents like universities or research facilities held jointly with other companies.[9]

Whilst all this was happening, firms were being restructured in other ways, so that they could bring innovations to market more quickly, redefining what could count as a market in the process. For example, the distinction between production and consumption became even less marked as old 'push' models in which disembedded factories churned out commodities with only limited regard to whether anyone wanted them have been replaced by 'pull' models which use a mixture of new customized manufacturing processes, precise inventory control, large subcontracting networks, extensive logistical net-works which also act as means of gaining market intelligence, cloud comput-ing, and new forms of finding and relating to the consumer. Indeed, a number of commentators have begun to refuse the distinction between production and consumption entirely, substituting the idea of firms as 'network orches-trators' (Fung et al., 2007) which manage variegated webs of circulation that continually prepare the ground for exchange.[10]

So the halcyon days when, in order to stimulate the exchange of ideas, we painted things in primary colours, chucked some bean bags around, and, for the first time, had easy access to computers have gone. Firms have been through this phase and have incorporated its lessons.[11] Their ambition is

---

[8] This interest in enhanced innovation often coincided with a move to export large manufacturing facilities to low-wage locations in the now classic 'burn and move'. What we see is an attempt to produce labour forces that are able to add value in the core (which was, of course, being busily redefined) whilst outsourcing all routine tasks to the periphery, howsoever defined.

[9] More recently, more and more attention has been paid to what Govindajaran and Trimble (2010) call the 'performance engine', the ongoing operations of the firm which have to implement innovation. Much neglected in the literature in the decades of innovation, the 1990s and 2000s, it has now become clear that firms that cannot marry innovation with their performance engines cannot innovate, or can only innovate imperfectly.

[10] For example, on this basis, it would be possible to argue that many large retailers are actually producers in all but name.

[11] Thus, it often now seems as though the whole world has become subject to the rule of innovation. To not be innovative rapidly becomes unthinkable. It can even be counted as a kind of crime against the economy at large.

now much greater. With the advent of more and more information and communications technology—a generation brought up knowing the Internet with all the consequences that are becoming apparent (see Turkle, 2011), such as the growth of social networking as a fount of social knowledge, and the parallel advent of mobile capabilities which index location and 'ground' these networks in new ways are the most important developments—it has become possible to think about extending the world of innovation out from the spaces of the corporation to the spaces of the consumer, by producing both an individual relationship with each consumer and the possibility of exchanging more than goods through the development of what I call an *expressive infrastructure*.[12]

Thus, we reach the age of what we might call knowing or cognitive capitalism in which the essential point is no longer the expenditure of human labour power but what Lazzarato calls intention power, collective, living know-how able to be captured by networked computation. In cognitive capitalism, harvesting the gains from knowledge and invention becomes the central issue for accumulation. Capitalism has to, needs to, intervene in the imagination. Thus, its main interest becomes what Moulier-Boutang (2011) calls 'pollination', the systematic production and management of various kinds of publics and their opinions and affects through all kinds of imitative cascade which act as both supply and demand (Thrift, 2007). As James put it: 'Some of us are in more favourable positions than others to set new fashions. Some are much more striking personally and imitable, so to speak. But no living person is sunk so low as not to be imitated by somebody' (James, 2010: 139).

The result is that companies now explicitly espouse the goal of creating a kind of performative ontology, which consists of laying down a series of 'natural' experiences by drawing on the extensive psycho-cultural knowledge that business now has, a bank of knowledge which dates from as far back as 1930 and Paul Lazarsfeld's clever though ethically problematic idea of boosting the business of laundries by sending letters to all those in an area who had suffered bereavements and needed emergency support (Samuel, 2010). The result is that the old lines between production, consumption, and distribution no longer apply. There is fluidity in what companies do and how they do it, which means that they are likely, directly or indirectly, to operate in each of these domains, naturally mixing and matching them and often moving domains.[13]

---

[12] As Prahalad and Krishnan (2008) would have it, value is based on the unique, personalized experiences of consumers coupled with the fact that no firm is big enough in scope and size to satisfy the experiences of one consumer at a time. The focus is therefore as much on *access to resources* as on ownership of resources.

[13] A defence company like Qinetiq, for example, can suddenly redescribe itself as a consultancy.

It has become clear that this coupling of production and consumption and distribution in networks of circulation produced via the growth of information technology, the intricate complexities of supply chains, bodies of movement knowledge like logistics and movement analysis, and the so-called smart customization have begun to produce a new kind of settlement (if that is the right word) which allows the genesis of small differences to be tracked and traced and continually both sold into and used as a resource in their own right.

Thus, capitalism and academe have alighted on the same issue. For, whereas, at one time, most academic interest was invested in outlining social structure, a good deal of interest nowadays is also being given to the genesis of small differences, stimulated by an interest in the work of Leibniz, Tarde, Deleuze, and Jullien, but also by advances in our understanding of complexity. Deleuze (cited in Dosse, 2010: 161), for example, following Tarde, argues that imitation, understood as a deeply creative process of gradual variation and slippage brought about through small acts of mimicry, 'belongs to a flow or a wave but not to the individual. Imitation is the extension of a flow.' A similar concern with small differences motivates much of the thinking currently taking place in business about markets and consumers which are inevitably concerned with currents of imitation and movements of invention. The intention is clear: to make *involvement* visible and thereby operable by building an expressive infrastructure which continually tracks these differences and is able to operate on them as they unfold. Behind all the technology—the server farms, the vast energy requirements, the endless texts and emails and other communicative acts, the general reshaping of space that arises therefrom—this infrastructure is founded on four different but linked projects, each of which can be seen as founded on the reincarnation of a much earlier historical project. One arose out of early history of economics and statistics and what was often called, after Francis Ysidro Edgworth's notoriously opaque book, 'mathematical psychics' (Edgworth, 1881/2010). What is being aimed for is the ability to meter[14] and analyse feeling through what Edgworth called 'speculative and active instruments' (15)—'to remotely sense and quantify emotional levels, either post hoc or in real time' (Dodds and Danforth, 2010: 442)—so as to be able to increase involvement to order. The hunt is on, in other words, for the hair-triggers of invention in a highly connected world and it has produced a whole new set of economic-cum-social knowledges about what and how to constitute markets and property. The latter are based on new data and new techniques which can track the so-called networked behaviour

---

[14] The importance in this earlier literature of metering is made clear in the work of both Edgworth and Tarde. For example, Edgworth wanted to construct a hedonometer, 'a psychophysical machine, continually registering the height of pleasure experienced by an individual'. It has been renovated by modern happiness studies (see e.g. Dodds and Danforth, 2010).

which is based on the assumption that actions do not exist in isolation but with the expectation that they will react to what others are doing (see Ayres, 2007; Davenport and Harris, 2007; Easley and Kleinberg, 2010).

The second is the revival of aesthetics, understood in Baumgarten's original formulation as the ability to judge according to the senses, instead of according to the intellect, with such a judgement of taste being based on feelings of pleasure or displeasure but filtered through James's later formulation of motion as sensation. That revival has produced a new era of representation which is able to represent the myriad data that have been produced by various meters in inspiring forms that can, in many cases, be returned to sender as stimuli to further action. In turn, aided by software, that has meant a return to drawing and diagramming as both collaborative summaries of system states and tools for intervention which is bent on redefining what is meant by 'ground' (Garner, 2008). Drawing and diagramming is neither medium nor message but something in between, always pointing somewhere else: 'to a chain of serial development, another condition, another state, even when, as a gestural flourish it appears to have said everything in the most economical manner' (Petherbridge, 2008: 37).

Third, it requires a re-examination of the notion of the environment. This is a word in such common coinage that it has become debased since its inception in the nineteenth century. But that is why it is worth recalling one particular strand of meaning as a part of the movement to re-enchant science found most prominently in Germany in the late nineteenth and early twentieth centuries (Harrington, 1996), a movement that intended to nourish the heart as well as the head. This movement required a vocabulary of surrounding which could act as both operator and operand in producing the kind of purposefulness and meaningfulness which could only be known through immediate experience, intuition, and felt imperative. It has been resurrected in various forms of late as a renewed interest in landscape, fieldwork, and 'hauntology', at least in the sense that what is at issue is 'cooking' space by paying attention to the somatic qualities of the body as a means of partnering the environment (Daniels et al., 2010).

Talk of 'hauntology' leads to the last current of thought. One of the first proponents of performative ontology, William James, expressed it well in his own actions. For, this most rational of the new 'psychologists' also had an allegiance to a psychic, Leonora Piper, who he considered to be in touch with his beloved dead son (Myers, 2001; Richardson, 2006). But though we might no longer necessarily be seized by the idea of speaking to the dead, we do want to speak to and enliven dead space through a knowledge of absences and gaps. That knowledge is based on a pluralistic understanding of the ways in which space is activated and deactivated which can key into many different kinds of experience, 'ghosts and all' as James (cited in Myers, 1986: 381) would have had it. That, in turn, requires a better understanding of how to translate different time signatures, clocks that allow different kinds of seeing, so to speak (Lim, 2009), a correspondingly better understanding of gaps in perception that allow perception itself to be switched on and off, and a better understanding of what might be called strategic simplification, that is the ability to characterize and sum up a space through just a few cues of one kind or another. In turn, this knowledge is able to be used to treat the world, producing new means of interference with our sense of what there is and what there must be, and correspondingly new senses of place.

So, how has a new kind of industrial settlement come about which both lays down and literally and metaphorically draws on an expressive infrastructure using these four projects? We can point to at least four principles of *enhanced productivity of expression* that underlie it. The first of these is that capitalism has taken a micro-sociological turn. If we turn to the work of Goffmann and Garfinkel, or even an earlier micro-'sociologist' like Tarde, what we can see is text, blog, Facebook, and Twitter becoming not just a garland to the event but a part of the event in their own right in that they form part of the evolving expressive infrastructure,[15] a means of embedding certain kinds of dramaturgy in everyday life as an explicit technology of response and counter-response which extends or at least augments what we might think of as talk. Indeed, we might well see symbolic interactionism and ethnomethodology and general conversational (and gestural) analysis as one means of understanding how one might produce this aspect of the modern world *avant la lettre* in their close attention to response, signification, and the vagaries and inflections of the situation and the crucial importance of next turns. In particular, in a world in which all goods become creative goods,[16] they became a way to understand not just how to knowingly link talk to the commodity but how to make talk about the commodity into an explicit part of the design of the commodity. In turn, this ambition has been extended to the other somatic registers of communication with the ambition of folding them equally into the envelope of commodities. Thus, commodities become ever more complex collective goods.

It might be objected that the development of these means of understanding of being in touch as expressive artfulness has often been subject to quite severe forms of reductionism, but equally these forms of reductionism have themselves become constitutive of interaction as 'we bind ourselves together through acts of communication' (Harper, 2010: 146). By concentrating relentlessly on the

---

[15] Note the heavily gendered nature of much of this expressive infrastructure which depends on grounding what were traditionally regarded as 'feminine' skills and enthusiasms and making them general.

[16] See Caves (2000: 180–1) on word of mouth.

simple mechanics of individual interactions, and indeed making them as attractive as possible so as to make susceptible and draw in new members, the idea is to produce something akin to a subjectless field of limitless and perpetual activity. 'Logistical' subjects (Harney, 2010) are subjects flattened out by being reduced to the sum of their potential for connectivity and then hyperlinked in such a way that they become nodes in a vast speculative web.[17] Flattened but hyperconnected, subjects are unique, personalized—and multiply positioned as a matter of course. Being in touch becomes serious business, made possible by technologies that add in registers of feeling and speed up reaction times in ways that were not hitherto extant and are able to gauge the feel of an audience at a distance.

Continuing with the pragmatist theme, the second principle recognizes diversity and difference as vital. To understand this principle, we can return to William James journeying to the town of Lilydale in western New York State in 1896. Lilydale was a utopian community founded in 1874 in the belief that everyone 'has a right to be all that he can be—to know all that he can know'. At first, James found the community close to perfection with its excellent health facilities, numerous educational institutions, and a love of learning itself. But he quickly got tired of it. He began to find Lilydale disappointing, even enervating. Why? 'Instead of elevating the human psyche, he determined, the embodiment of perfection deadens it, primarily because such an existence leaves no place for the dissension and friction that ultimately gives life significance' (Ferguson, 2007: 2). In other words, in James's depiction of life, difference and disagreement is central to existence. Any project needs to 'keep the doors and windows open'. It cannot stay fixed, or it will become like utopia, a passive expression of principle without the essential element of invention that arises out of difference and disagreement (Stengers, 2010).

This pragmatist orientation has become a mark of modern economic thinking. Raising the innovation stakes means not being snooty about where new knowledge comes from. Narrow information channels choke off innovation. Diversity of background and view is crucial. Authors such as Page (2007, 2011) and Stark (2009) have pointed to the way in which diversity has become a corporate watchword as companies have moved away from homogeneous hierarchies towards teamwork on the presumption that cognitive diversity improves performance. The idea is straightforward: to build collective intelligence by widening diversity as well as individual ability, systematic heterogenesis, in other words.

Third, and following on, relevant knowledge can be gleaned from anywhere. Collective intelligence depends not just on workers existing within the firm's boundary but can extend to all kinds of populations that may have

---

[17] The links to Whitehead's and Deleuze's transcendental empiricism are clear.

an interest in a product or service. The idea and practice of open innovation might be regarded as the original template, which was intended to draw in populations as an inventive resource intent on co-creation. The idea has become so familiar that it has already led to articles proclaiming 'the next step in open innovation' (Bughin et al., 2008) and inevitably it is now being argued that more is being claimed than has been delivered, notably because of a lack of emphasis on implementation (Govindajaran and Trimble, 2010). That said, open innovation is starting to produce a significant increment of profit for some firms in some sectors. Most particularly, knowledge is being pooled in ways heretofore unconsidered based around the idea of creative spaces which take in large but diffuse scales of activity. These spaces are knowledge ecosystems which not only work within or between formal organizational boundaries but also outside them, so that they are able to reach a more diverse group of participants. And, because of their scale, they are able to sponsor permanently active knowledge flows, much like the permanent flow of foreign currency around the world, not least because they continually prepare the ground by setting up new encounters.

But to achieve these qualities, these spaces still need to be made attractive and sometimes surprising so that they draw in encounters. That requires a mixture of aesthetics, the presence of other like minds, and the ability to attract what Hagel et al. (2010) call 'edge players'; that is, people whose ways of perceiving the world and solving problems may be very different but, as a result, may provide new, innovative fuel by better capturing the unexpected and aleatory. In this way, organizations can be open to unknowns and catch nonlinear multiplier effects.

Fourth, raising the innovation stakes means that, at the same time, people have to be given knowledge in the form of what people think is expected of them: social knowledge, if you like. They need to be able to read signals, decipher the signs, know how to follow a lead. That means promoting 'inter-visibility' (Ober, 2008). Spaces need to be constructed in such a way that everyone can keep an eye on everyone else, and so pick up cues, signals, insights, and experiences and so identify the moments when a creative rush takes place. Designing spaces which allow that kind of open interchange is again important—and difficult to do. It means promoting what is often called, in football argot, the quality of 'bouncebackability' (Runciman, 2009). Spaces need to be designed so that they will attract the kind of verve and drive that builds practical solutions to technical-cum-social problems. Then, spaces need to allow for negotiation and diplomacy, since so much social knowledge is manifested in this way. In the current situation, this is probably the factor that is most lacking: institutions that allow this kind of activity to take place are still relatively thin on the ground.

Producing organizations that can work to these four principles is obviously difficult and progress has been halting.[18] But the overall goal is clear, at least: a system of production without end, of production spurring on production, where 'everything is mobilized', to use the phrase of Ernst Junger, in the cause of invention of more and more commodities pulled into frames that are themselves commodities. The system becomes continuous and continuously inventive. Everything is consumed for production, and everything is produced for consumption. The outside edge is folded into the centre through multiple environments.

> The maximization of production through these networks of circulation includes ultimately the production of not only replaceable objects but objects that are already en route to replacement. To exist within these networks is to be diffused along their paths, to be everywhere at once and nowhere wholly. What is present here is likewise present in a storeroom awaiting the call for delivery, already on its way to delivery, surging along the circuitry. (Mitchell, 2010: 27)

Such an analysis of an economy of spontaneous synthesis might be seen as simply the logical conclusion of a Heideggerian analysis in which

> the will has no other goal than to create conditions that will allow it to will further, ultimately to will only itself insofar as what it wills is the appropriation of what is other (to will that it become stronger). As such, its activity is 'aimless', striving for nothing outside or apart from itself. (Mitchell, 2010: 27)

But this is both too Olympian and too seamless. Numerous ethnographic studies have shown that production is beset by error and braced by all manner of improvisations and consists, as I have already pointed out, of many different forms of production which can gather together as sometimes unlikely hybrids. Meanwhile, the motives that underlie practices of consumption are

---

[18] The nature of the corporate shift has perhaps been best put by Hagel et al. (2010). Though their book is clearly prospective, and ideological, it seems to me to be the best account of how corporations are beginning to think about the world on the ground, so to speak. In particular, the book focuses on three elements. One is the necessity of gaining leverage by mobilizing the passions and interests of other people, many of whom will be without the organization. The goal is to support and amplify the efforts of talented individuals. 'Rather than individuals serving the needs of institutions, our institutions will be recrafted to serve the needs of individuals' (2010: 8). So far, so predictable. This is the standard rhetoric of *Fast Company* capitalism, based on an amalgam of open innovation and actualizing American individualism, that has been in circulation since the 1990s (see Thrift, 2005), and before in earlier variants. Then, and less predictably, the use of edge practices at the core. And bringing up the rear, the need to think of the world not as stock but as flow. Again, not perhaps too surprising in that, stimulated by the examples of service delivery found in domains like logistics, and the attempts to re-engineer manufacturing processes, and the like, corporations might be thought to be thinking along these lines. What is novel, however, is the synthesis of these elements into a hymn to prospecting: the idea is to act out in order to act upon. Yet, at the same time, there are still problems with such an account. It is not clear that shortage of ideas is always the problem. Many corporations have too many ideas and can stagger about in a morass of conflicting claims as to which might be the best to go with.

many and various and can by no means be sheeted home to simple explanations like commodity fetishism or status (Thrift, 2010). But if there is no perfection of the will, the will still persists, however patchily and imperfectly that may be, as James pointed out so frequently. Schopenhauer and Nietzsche and Rank become important points of reference as guides to the creative power of willing will but they must be leavened by authors like Montaigne or James who remain crucial correctives as reminders of how prosaic wilful action can often be.[19]

Herewith, then, is a basic description of the new industrial system which will be familiar to many in one form or another. But what can we see as the spatial correlate of this new system?

The construction of naturalism

In this section, I want to argue that the second industrial revolution depends upon making not just people but environments maximally productive. Of course, designing environments that are more productive has always been a part of capitalism's beat—whether it has been the organization of factories or homes—but the argument of this chapter is that the attempt now being made is to fold all environments, at least potentially, in to part of a system of production and consumption and thereby in to fit (because carefully outfitted) surroundings—by enveloping them in a kind of informational fog which boosts their capacity to integrate and feed back on themselves and so generate new knowledge.

Like the first industrial revolution, this new revolution depends upon the pooling of knowledge. But the means of pooling are both more powerful and more extensive, sufficient to suggest a step change in inventive capacity, what Prahalad and Krishnan (2008) describe as a 'new house of innovation'. This new house of innovation is more concentrated in its ability to generate innovation because it calls to many more actors, human and non-human. It is an ecology of practices sufficiently extensive that it can be called environmental, or as Massumi (2009) might term it, proto-environmental, in that it owns no territory of its own for any length of time. Rather, it exists in a perpetual time of emergence and onflow 'at the leading edge of an incoming event' (Massumi, 2009: 170), always multiplying but never transcendent.

This is a new medium, then, which is neither time nor space nor time-space but something else, something closer to movement moving (Manning, 2009)—James's cornfield fire—which itself constantly squeezes value out of

---

[19] An average CEO is not a Nietzschean visionary!

the world and which can also be worked on so as to squeeze value from itself, on an 'on-all-the-time, everywhere-at-the-ready' (Massumi, 2009: 162) basis. It is a medium that consists of a series of worlds flashing into and out of existence which are able to carry invention to a new level by harnessing the power of what Stengers (2010) calls reciprocal capture.[20] It is *rolling composition* in which life is always a line pointing forward, never a circle. It is *becoming put to work*.

What is being built here are ecologies of commodities and ideas and feelings all mixed together, and these ecologies gain their value from making the most of new interactions, from pre-empting these interactions and steering them on to new, more advantageous courses. This is an art of building attachments, of continually restarting the work of association (Read, 2009; Thrift, 2011). The overall goal is to produce, often for only the briefest of moments, a kind of secular magic by forming collectives, temporary gestalts to use Merleau-Ponty's filmic description, which have pull through their 'whatever singularity' (Agamben, 1993: 21), an internally plural collectivity understood as that which has an 'inessential commonality, a solidarity that in no way concerns an essence'.[21]

That, in turn, requires what we might call a thickening of space in which these brief and contingent unities can then be brewed up. If one was looking for an analogy, one might find it in the Chinese notion of *qi*, the breath of energy, which sometimes disperses itself, so that things become dormant and invisible, and sometimes gathers itself, making things awaken and so visible. In particular, the kind of thickening of space that brings things into visibility— optimal space to summon optimal life—requires five concurrent skills in order to produce a cognitive and affective current, made up out of the props provided by current technology, informed by a wealth of tacit and explicit knowledge.

The first skill is aesthetic. The skill required is to produce a new information landscape. The essential skill required to build this landscape is, as pointed out above, diagrammatic. Thought takes place in diagrams as much as text. Indeed, the text often accompanies the diagram rather than the other way round since standard alphabets cannot convey the richness of the information landscape by themselves. That requires a new lexicon, a stock of diagrammatic terms that will compress and interpret information by spatializing it. The terms are descriptive rather than axiomatic, not so much based on a decision or ontological commitment to found the world as they are intent

---

[20] As I have pointed out previously (Thrift, 2005, 2010), this medium could not have existed without the centuries in which the world's coordinates were transcribed such that a grid now encompasses the earth. But as I have also made clear, this grid is the precondition for what is now taking place, which is the thickening of space.
[21] It is important to note this understanding of 'whatever' as not being about indifference. Rather, it is based on the Latin translation of 'being such that it always matters'.

on redescribing the world so that it is friendly to large flows of information (Mullarkey, 2006). These are descriptive regimes that generate working descriptions for living and for a living. They are 'working objects' which constitute a territory of inquiry, a collage of disparate data and processes of data-gathering, sampling, calculation, and correlation, 'working objects that emerged from contingent systems of knowledge [that] came increasingly to assume material form, and to be accepted as inventions rooted in multiple realms of experience' (Bender and Marrinan, 2010: 210).

The second and related skill I have also mentioned already. It is the ability to create inter-visibility through this logic of appearance (Ober, 2008). It is important to be able to see other members of a community and observe their response. The premium is not just on reaching large numbers of consumers, but on reaching large numbers of consumers each of whom knows that the other consumers are receiving the same message at the same time and each of whom knows that the others know the same things. The Web, for example, is getting better at creating this kind of inter-visibility founded in common knowledge, chiefly through cues which are also a means of feedback on what others are doing. Social networks, new forms of crowd, even some kinds of advertisement, all display this capacity.

The third skill is the corresponding ability to create resonance. As the theoretical line through Tarde and Lazzarato has shown, it is possible to brew up affective storms which push ideas. But that skill requires aggregation and alignment in order to produce pathways that these storms can travel down. In other words, it is possible to engineer situations in which feelings that are weak at first can gradually rise to prominence, prompting others as they do so. This is an attempt to select for particular kinds of feeling over others.

The fourth skill is the bringing into visibility and consideration of non-human actors that have become smart if not awake. In this sense, this is more than a micro-sociological enterprise, since objects are allowed into the conversation. How might we describe such a venture? Perhaps the best description might be as the bringing into being of 'nonobjects'. This term has been used by a number of luminaries to describe the way in which the search for form with clear and distinct contours is being displaced by an attempt to grasp the way in which things pass continually from one state to another, producing different combinations of attachments as they go: 'burying and unearthing—catching and letting go—occur in tandem . . .' (Jullien, 2009: xvi). One version of this story of opening things onto their absence considers the model provided by classical Chinese culture in which much more attention was given to cumulative changes over time in contradistinction to Western thought with its foundations in classical Greek philosophies of being (Thrift, 2009). For Jullien (2009), what we can see in this civilization is a very different way of thinking about representation. In classical China, art was not used to mirror the world around and about but to evoke unfathomable experience. Art lies on a continuum of existence and is therefore not distinct from reality in contradistinction to the Western idea that art remains separate from the world it supposedly represents. Thus, objects are isolated and apprehended in very different ways and the nonobject is

> [that which] is too hazy-indistinct-diffuse-evanescent-confused to keep still and isolated. This nonobject sinks into the undifferentiated and, as a result, cannot be composed of 'being'. It cannot be sharply delineated as a Gegenstand that 'stands before' the Eye or Mind. It is [something] we constantly experience, leading us back to the indefiniteness of the foundational, but which science and philosophy left behind early on in their haste to treat things logically, to constitute a 'this' that could be manipulated by thought, with the aim of replying to the question: 'What is it?'. (Jullien, 2009: xv)

Another version of this story comes from the world of design. It is not, I think, coincidental that at this point in history ideas of things discarded by one civilization are being reinvented by another. This reworking draws a distinction between three approaches: one a human-centred approach which sees in objects human needs and desires, the second an object-centred approach which sees in objects form and function, and a third nonobject-centred approach which wants to work in the space in between the previous two as an 'ergonomics of the mind' (Lukic and Katz, 2011, see also Boradkar, 2010 and Flusser (1999) on 'non-things'). This latter approach wants to concentrate on the emotional space between subject and object by bringing strangeness back into the realm of the artefact, echoing Marx's famous dictum. It uses a series of techniques—humour, and especially parody, disruption of the form of a familiar artefact in order to cast it in a different light, and radical extrapolation—to question the space between commodity and consumer, thus bringing into the light of practice Marx's observation (2005: 163) that the commodity 'is a very strange thing'. Putting these two views of the nonobject together, we are able to see a new stamping ground emerging in which objects have a say which arises out of lapidary processes that include them as 'citizens'. In other words, Latour and Harman's calls to take more note of objects are already being heeded, although perhaps not in the way that they envisaged (Frampton, 2006; Mullarkey, 2009), not just through the fact that objects are becoming nonobjects but also because objects are communicating directly with each other without going through human intermediaries. Indeed, their thoughts seem a little old-fashioned in that what we can start to see is objects and environments becoming minded, able to think in thought-like ways about how the world works and means, through what might be called a doubled phenomenology: our perception and the object's perception which, through the advance of technology, is producing other views of a similar world, new forms of witnessing.

The fifth skill is the most obvious one: the cultivation of an ability to track presence and absence. What arises out of this skill is an ability to rapidly conjure up sufficient locational cues so as to induce in any situation a feeling of reality. In turn, this ability requires constant mapping and remapping. It is no coincidence that there has been a renaissance of mapping (Thrift, 2011). Being able to constantly locate and represent activity—each practice being a side of the same coin—is a vital part of making things appear vital in this new kind of performance art (Turkle, 2011).

To summarize, these changes require skills of what might be called depiction, which write at the rate of life in a world in which simulation is no longer necessarily second best (Turkle, 2011). As I have noted in other papers (Thrift, 2009, 2010), the orthographic traditions of the past are not adequate when the intention is to write worlds through these overlapping skills. Text cannot just be supplemented, however. It has to be reinvented. The practices of worlding demand the use of a much greater sensory palette in order to produce *ambience* as well as message. Background and foreground become an increasingly inseparable part of an art–science of momentary impression and pre-emption. The intention is to produce *atmospheres*—tropic or frozen, cramped or spacious, busy or still—but atmospheres all the same. Thus, all manner of sensory registers are pressed into service which can serve as the walls and furniture of these worlds, so producing from moment to moment a whole, indistinct, animated, chaotic even, but a whole nonetheless. Form gives way to something auratic. Let us consider two of these registers—sound and colour (these out of many others such as smell, touch, temperature, humidity)—for what they can tell us about this process of reinventing sound and vision.

So far as sound is concerned, the need is to create an aether. In the manner of early eighteenth-century tafelmusik or Satie's 'furniture music', the so-called ambient music has become general. Sound is chopped up, shuffled, and laminated on to events in order to produce specific kinds of 'mood music' (Toop, 1995). The intention is no longer to produce coherent musical narrative but instead to use sound to create the body of new worlds. Music increasingly takes on all kinds of sounds as legitimate. Indeed it is becoming 'voracious in its openness' (Toop, 1995: 12). What is equally interesting is the way sound is being carefully designed into space as the dynamics of sound have increasingly become understood, with the aim of leaving a 'soft imprint' on consciousness: 'you'd realize its absence should it not be there but at a level that you are not fully conscious of' (Scanner cited in Battle, 2011: 1). In other words, acoustic channels are coming to be fully used.[22]

---

[22] The games industry, with its need for music that conveys site unobtrusively but definitively, has been another major influence. See also the remarkable radio programme, Radiolab, which makes this ambition fully visible (or rather hearable).

Colour has always been a stalwart of the creation of new worlds but now it is being used in new ways in order to construct convincing images, and, as that happens so our colour vocabulary is changing, as it did in the classical world (Bradley, 2009; Taussig, 2009). For example, whilst remembering that light is made of colour rather than the other way round, precisely those qualities of colour that the Ancients supposedly favoured—luminosity and hue[23]— become more important than formerly since they can be used to heighten and extend colour discrimination. Equally, bold and bright colours have overcome traditional Western chromophobic tendencies and much expanded colour ranges in the process (Thrift, 2009). What has been produced is what might be called a spirited sense of colour which goes beyond colour as such in that it incorporates tactile movement—wheelings, pivotings, and splicings— into its effect (Taussig, 2009): a new art of illumination.

In the case of each register, what is privileged is, in Deleuze's terms, not so much the action-image as the perception-image which makes the affective inside into an actual outside like the face and what is called by Deleuze (see Mullarkey, 2009) the crystal-image, the ability to split and to hold the dimensions of an event several times at once, like the facets of a crystal. In thinking about this shift to a new medium of depicting, which not so much captures movement as is movement, we inevitably have to think analogically, since we are trying to name something that is only just coming into existence. The result is that all kinds of symptomatic names for this proto-environment in which rolling composition is the norm are being articulated. Classically, there are Deleuze and Guattari's thoughts on 'landscapization'. Equally, Sloterdijk's spheres come to mind too as a 'psychotopical' historical anthropology which may be better thought of as symptomatic of the present day. Again, it is possible to consider accounts from art or film as precursors of what is coming about, such as Grusin's account of premediation or Krauss's thoughts (2010) on perpetual inventory, or Frampton's account (2006) of film's 'minded' affective thinking. Or we could even move on to Sebald's thoughts on transfiguration of landscape (Sebald, 2003). In each case, something is struggling to be named, a new kind of way of building communities of sense based on the power provided by a 'myriad tiny architects', to use Darwin's description of a coral reef.

But I also want to think about this process of replacement of a fixed environment by a proto-environment in another way, as the invention of a *new factor of production* which has most affinity to land. Land was, of course, one of the classical factors of production, the source of wealth in all early societies because of the rents that arose from it as the payment for land use and the

---

[23] Recent research suggests that this distinction may have been based on a misunderstanding (Bradley, 2009).

received income of a land owner. It consists of both site and the natural resources within that site: naturally occurring goods such as water, air, soil, minerals, flora, and fauna that are used in the creation of products. Land can be continually reused because of the rise of arts of cultivation.

In the new land, site, organic and inorganic bodies, and information are mixed up in an anorganic mass which is continuously cultivated—but with a much greater turnover time. The new land, as I have pointed out, has no territory of its own. It is a proto-territory in which space is continually being temporarily captured for specific purposes, rather like the kind of military order promoted by insurgent groups (Roberts, 2010), or the use of personal computers as distributed computational networks in their down time, or the attitudes towards risk typical of the classical Chinese culture which entail a gradual convergence on an event (Jullien, 2009; Thrift, 2009). It is a zone of continual emergence which is 'equally produced and presupposed' (Massumi, 2009: 165). Its power is chiefly pre-emptive: 'preemptive power is environmental power. It alters the life environment's conditions of emergence' (Massumi, 2009: 167) via incursive charges which alter the potential of a situation, pointing it in a new direction.

We can see this land as the attempt to construct a new low-hanging fruit which can be continuously cultivated so as to produce new kinds of surplus based on momentum and the new opportunities it provides to generate invention power. The new practices of cultivation run alongside older ideas of how to cultivate land so as to make it more productive, but the cultivation time may only be in seconds rather than the seasonal turnover of the past. It is important to prepare the ground in order that the ground can be prepared for chance encounters so that they can be shaped. This is therefore a constantly moving land that has taken on some of the characteristics of weather.

I want to use two old agricultural terms in new ways to understand what cultivating this new land means, namely 'broadcasting' and 'enclosure'. In this incarnation, the act of scattering seeds, which is akin to Moulier-Boutang's 'pollination'—'to cast or scatter abroad over an area, as seed in sowing'—becomes an act of transmission of ideas and practices in order to produce germination, thus making the land progressively more fertile. But the modern sense of broadcasting as a medium that disseminates ideas and practices via telecommunications is now changing again, to a method of transferring a data message to all recipients simultaneously. At the same time, the new land also depends upon acts of enclosure. What we can see, in effect, is a new round of enclosures. But this is a more open form of enclosure: it is enclosure without fences or hedges or walls. Whereas the first agricultural revolution was based on a combination of productivity-raising machinery and enclosure, putting an end to traditional rights over land by closing land off and asserting ownership, the second aims not so much to close off as to continuously colonize a moving field, asserting ownership over the process itself. The aim is to cultivate this new land more intensively and in a way that can raise productivity. But, by using the form of tenancy known as *syndication* to both broadcast and enclose, it is possible to provide a high degree of mass-produced individuation.[24] In other words, site is composed through a process of *syndication which means that the same content can be used simultaneously in many locations in different ways in order to individuate.*[25]

This new kind of massed and yet also individuated land will feel with us through its ability to pre-empt and nudge our thoughts via four art–sciences of placing consciousness everywhere which can reveal new means of extracting surplus and thereby turning a profit.[26] First, to reprise the points made earlier, the art–science of resonance. Think of an extreme example like a concentration camp and the ability to walk around its strangely manicured grounds. It feels as though every plant and stone ought to shout out what has gone on there but does not. But what if 'inanimate' objects could shout or indeed could nestle meaningfully. What if money really did have a character, a soul as in Marx? What if it were witty or despairing or hopeful or frivolous? I think that is what the new land is aiming for. What if, in turn, human subjects took on the qualities of the inorganic, not as an analogy but as an explicit project of subjectification? As if in affirmation of this point, *We Feel Fine: An Almanac of Human Emotion* (Kamvar and Harris, 2009) takes the data collected from blogs over a three-year period and trawls them for the phrases 'I feel' and 'I am feeling'. The execution is off—the book is a strange mix of all kinds of things. But the ambition is interesting—which is to map out human feeling on the Web as a kind of disinhibited weather system.[27]

---

[24] Originally, syndication arose in print, radio, television, and the Web so that content creators could reach a wider audience. In the case of radio, the United States federal government proposed a syndicate in 1924 so that the nation's politicians could quickly and efficiently reach the entire population. In the case of television, it has often been said that 'Syndication is where the real money is'. So far as commercial Web syndication is concerned, it can be categorized in three ways: by business models, by types of content, and by methods for selecting distribution partners.

[25] Not combinations, since these assume sorting of a finite set. Land's set does not work through permutation since the outcomes of its events are often unknown.

[26] In particular, land is measured out by its connections and its time line. Giving visual form to chronological as well as spatial information becomes crucial. What we see is the recasting of the old historical timeline (Rosenberg and Grafton, 2010) but working with much more varied periods and paces of time.

[27] In the academic realm, MacKerron and Mourato have produced the 'mappiness' project, intent on mapping the UK's happiness through space and time via an iPhone app. The app asks how 'happy', how 'relaxed', and how 'awake' people feel using sliding scales. It also asks for brief contextual information on activity, companionship, and location, whilst users who are outdoors can optionally contribute a photograph. Ambient noise levels are measured using the iPhone's microphone. More generally, all kinds of work are trying to link feeling to location via maps.

The second art–science is amplification. This land grows crops—but of ideas and affects. Taking the large amount of knowledge that has now been generated in this domain, from advertising, from politics, from film, from performance, from architecture and design, from dance and logistics and other movement arts, it has become possible to produce ways of amplifying ideas and affect in a more controlled way with more predictable outcomes which allow sales to be made off the back of them and which allow them to become saleable in their own right.

The third art–science is personification in the sense that all things can be represented as having a degree of agency, insofar as they are extensions or embodiments of persons or can be understood as having person-like qualities (Weiss, 1996). In turn, these things can undo or subvert the identities of those who seek to control them, producing untoward effects which mix and mingle identities in all kinds of ways. Things are no longer 'flat', as Serres (2011) would have it, but are able to call and respond.

The fourth art–science is government. The intention is no longer to exert absolute control but to set parameters. Parameterization is the process of deciding and defining the parameters necessary for a complete or relevant specification of a model or geometric object, thus allowing any point to be uniquely identified. Parameters are not unique. They can be parameterized equally efficiently with different coordinate systems. Thus, the land can be described coherently using a variety of coordinate systems which might vary from group to group. These coordinate systems act as a part of a new art of surveying, which is a means of registering both desire and ownership. According to Massumi (2009), what we can see occurring in the contemporary art–science of government is a gradual unfolding of Foucault's thoughts on a new form of biopower, in the sense of the management of populations, leading to what Foucault called 'normation', rather than normalization, a series of punctuated equilibria in which control is exerted through modulation. Foucault identified a shift in the arts of government from discipline of man-as-species to regularization. As societies have come to be predicated on innovation, understood as 'the discovery of new techniques, sources, and forms of productivity, and also the discovery of new markets or new resources of manpower' (Foucault, 2008: 231), so the norms tended by disciplinary power have to be loosened to admit a wider arc of variation and a quicker turnover of conformities. Normal no longer coincides with fixed norms but becomes punctuated, moving from one state of equilibrium to another, often in short order.[28] The environment becomes permanently non-standard. And the gradual answer is a new concept of nature itself:

---

[28] As a result, the neo-liberal individual is no longer a sovereign subject. Rather, it is a heterogeneous subject of interest, simultaneously flattened and hyperconnected.

a base redefinition of nature is required outside any categorical opposition to the cultural, social or artificial. The overall environment of life now appears as a complex, systemic threat environment, composed of subsystems that are not only complex in their own right but are complexly interconnected. They are all susceptible to self-amplifying irruptive disruption. Given the interconnections, a disruption in one subsystem may propagate into others, and even cascade across them all, reaching higher and wider levels of amplification, up to and including the planetary scale. (Massumi, 2009: 159)

One might challenge whether this way of viewing the economy is actually that new: it bears a striking resemblance to the classical Chinese model of going on but one which applies an art of harvesting the moment to exchange (Jullien, 2009). And it has been explicated many times in different ways, as a Deleuzian model of ambulatory control, as an operaismo model of immaterial labour, and so on. But, whether it is original or not, the point is made, *it lifts what was formerly considered a go-between function into an actor in its own right.* What is required is not so much a skill as an art of balance which takes in states of off-balance as valuable strategic information which can contribute to new balances. The goal is captivation in order to capture.

To summarize this section, what I am suggesting is that a new land is now being invented out of what Massumi (2009) calls 'ontopower'. What is beginning to be produced by firms is a space based on a supercharged naturalism of ideas and affects which is in the business of reloading/recoding on a constant basis, a space of continual composition which has grip through the different textures it produces in the world (Harper, 2010), a never-ending sequence of singular events which must be prepared for. Since uncertainty is everywhere, the main solution is to produce a space that can work one small step in front of the moment in order to be able to charge the moment up with favourable ideas and affects,[29] a space that can be thickened, gathered together, knotted in new ways, flowing through us, buoying us along, drawing us out, and relating us back in new ways, changing our bearings. Such a thickening of space represents a dissolving of human individuality into a new kind of earthliness which wants to eat the knowledge people have in the way that people eat bread.[30]

In turn, this new land produces new forms of *rent*. New forms of land provide new forms of extraction of surplus based on relative location. Classically, rent could take on three forms. But now we can see rent being able to be applied in a new way—as a revenue stream arising out of temporary but continuous encampment. Just as commodities are increasingly thought of as

---

[29] Hence, the rise of a security–entertainment complex which can both keep the population secure and make entertainment from the mechanics of doing so (Thrift, 2011).

[30] Exteriority has always been a part of human embodiment but now we exist more and more outside ourselves. Human identity is stretched, mapped, and remapped and even inverted.

extending in time—think of an aircraft engine which is rented out as a service, for example, with all the ancillary operations and maintenance included in the price, or the myriad forms of leasing which produce a time-limited right to a commodity—so this is the ability to derive an income stream from a resource. But whereas this resource is usually thought of as fixed, now it comes unfixed and fixed simultaneously since the land is in constant movement.

The chief stamping ground of the process of continuous composition and decomposition is the city joined to the Web. The city is the chief arena in which a 'supercharged proto-territory of emergence' can be nurtured (Massumi, 2009: 164). The city becomes an accessory *before* the fact. But the city has no less a variegated geography because of this. Indeed, the footprint of the new territory is often stronger in cities because they provide a means of aggregation which has positive effects and most noticeably the phenomenon of the so-called superlinear scaling: as cities get larger, they generate ideas at a faster rate. Indeed, they seem to conform to a quarter power law such that 'a city that was ten times larger than its neighbour wasn't ten times more innovative; it was seventeen times more innovative. A metropolis fifty times bigger than a town was 130 times more innovative' (Johnson, 2010: 10).

The unburdened city

Early on in 1962, *Dance Magazine* commissioned a young and still relatively unknown artist called Andy Warhol to illustrate an article on movement analysis by Warren Lamb, with sketches of Laban's eight basic efforts (Davies, 2006). The idea was to provide a cartography of movement. It can and should, I think, be argued that these illustrations indicate not so much a new way of capturing and promoting movement—after all, dance notation dates from at least the seventeenth century—as a way in which this notation could be applied in the economic realm. Warhol's sketches accompanied the work of Warren Lamb, one of the founders of movement analysis, an application of Labanotation to the economic realm which would provide one of the impetuses for new forms of thinking about work process in the 1980s. Perhaps this early experience of linking art and the economic realm in a functional moving loop is where Warhol's subsequent imperatives stemmed from: later in 1962 his hugely successful show at the Stable Gallery in New York included not only his serial works of consumer objects but also *Dance Diagram* (Danto, 2009; Indiana, 2010). And by 1964, he was exhibiting a real-life supermarket at the Bianchini Gallery in New York where the goods on display—all for sale—were both works of art and consumer icons and moments in a kind of choreography of art and business; 'tins of Campbell's soup signed by Warhol (18 dollars each), plastic steaks by Mary Inman (27 dollars), chromium-plated melons by Robert Watts (125 dollars) and, if short of money, ... at least one of Watts's eggs could be purchased for 2 dollars' (Scarpellini, 2011: 218–19).

Seen in retrospect, the 1950s and 1960s constituted the first round of a new series of spatio-temporal practices which produced new ways of thinking about what constituted a manufactory. New technologies like the sea container, first used in 1956, started to have their effects in making it easier to make commodity connections around the globe (Levinson, 2008), while advertising was beginning to glimpse what it understood as the connections between motivation and acquisition of commodities in the hemispheres of the brain, typified by Ernest Dichter's research in the 1950s into how we value the things around us (Samuel, 2010). At the same time, the founders of logistics were finally making a serious imprint on the economic world that would come to fruition in the notion of the supply chain in the 1980s, while mass advertising campaigns were swinging into action which would come to an equal fruition as the unofficial government of television produced a new kind of connected citizen (McCarthy, 2010). And, haltingly, in the background, computers were also being used to connect up spaces and represent space anew in a way which would lead to the exponential growth of GIS in the 1980s (Peuquet, 2003), and they were also being used to speed up time in a way that led to the first experiments with concerted financial trading in the 1960s which led on to the informational markets of the 1980s and so, seemingly inexorably, on to developments like high-frequency trading in which the advantages of microseconds can be creamed off by robots.

Not surprisingly, new apprehensions of space and time became common, building on Warhol's insights into what the world was about which had 'changed the meaning of the recognizable' (Indiana, 2010: 149). For example, the network became a standard cultural trope 'as the abstract topological figure which stands for all concrete assemblages of protocols and rules that allow a milieu to be stabilized in such a way that it becomes productive' (Teranova, 2009: 242) Equally, this round of socio-technical practice demanded and produced the recomposition of the urban realm into an urban geography of linked cities, a connected global urban entity where it is impossible to consider any city as separate from any other (Batty, 2011), and each city can pollinate the others.

Now a new round of spatio-temporal practices is under way (Thrift, 2011) in which the manufactory is again being re-apprehended and re-recognized, but this time as if dressed out for a permanent party, which has equally been echoed in and indeed produced by art, and most especially an art in which systematic connections are made between art and space and a kind of blabbermouth talk which was another of Andy Warhol's characteristics

(Caves, 2000).[31] This round is based on systematically growing 'crops' in the new land, made possible by the expressive infrastructure. But the construction of these new kinds of complex collective goods is easier said than done. It is very unclear what a crop is or, indeed, how it can be cultivated in order to yield a profit. Thus, it requires new means of calculation, new business models, new means of aggregating and locating information, and new means of pricing, often based around models of auctions (Easley and Kleinberg, 2010).

So, what might these complex collective goods—crops, if you like—be? I will argue that they are of at least three kinds. First, there is the cultivation of identity. These developments must be instilled into the subject itself, just as happened in earlier times, for example in the ways in which movement produced new demands for settled identities which could be tracked (Groebner, 2007). But now the demand is the other way around. It is for mobile and flattened identities which can be folded into the landscape, whose tracking and tracing is an integral part of who they are, and which can be sold on for profit. It is not surprising that Harney (2010) has argued that what we can now see is the forging of a 'logistical' subject which can continually move on. As newer generations are born, so old models of subjectivity fade away to be replaced by a model in which subjects continually dip into the flow.

In other words, this round of identity formation depends upon the installation of an excessive subject which can inhabit many subject positions as a matter of course and which therefore can generate many more valences. The generation of this excessive meanderer is what capitalism is now trying to get at. If it succeeds, it will have opened up a land of opportunity where not only do extra opportunities to sell lie dormant and ready to be tapped (e.g. through individually tailored advertising) but also means of picking up and boosting invention. The frontier of economic opportunity moves on to integrate physical and psychic infrastructure in the great psychophysical venture of building an expressive infrastructure.

But getting at and generating an excessive subject is difficult. It is easy to get people to connect with each other, but much harder to get them to connect meaningfully. For example, much interaction on the Internet is as blinkered as ever before in its outlook. It does not constitute excess in any form but rather a series of closed networks that are unlikely to generate fresh insight (Ling, 2008). People use the Internet to hide from each other, even as they are connected to more and more people. Getting at the excessive subject is hard work which requires the generation of not only identitarian but also the so-called non-identitarian community in which 'how one thinks of oneself without identity politics, or without individualist politics' (Colebrook, 2010: 145)

---

[31] Warhol's life might be seen as an early version of Facebook or Twitter in his insistence on being continuously in the public eye.

becomes relevant. The idea is to produce forms of collective belonging which go beyond those based on common characteristics such as social, ethnic, or religious categories, which do not presuppose identity. This task demands that location becomes not just a simple identifier but a means of threading these collectives together. There is 'a solidarity of positioning and configurations in space' (Bersani, 2010: 184), of spatial disseminations.

Second, there is inhabitation. Cities cultivate a new kind of inhabitant who can don the city like a cloak. These inhabitants can follow the city's moods, tapping into and amplifying particular emotional keys or tones, and sensing the direction of constant expressive/information flows. That capacity is itself produced by both revealing and cloaking each inhabitant in a selective signature that is a new form of clothing made up out of the textures of information and communications technology (Crewe, 2010; Harper, 2010). Inhabitants start to resemble avatars, at least in the sense that the persona they don can be expressed in more dimensions.

These signatures are expressive in nature. If being in touch is a serious business, then it requires a lot of expressive work which new technologies both aid and constitute as they blur the lines between the living and the non-living through new forms of talk. The result is that mimicry becomes an even more crucial process, understood as an immensely fertile, creative process of gradual variation brought about by attempts at copying which turn into something else. Such processes are much more likely to bite in cities where all kinds of means of comparison and contrast are available all the time than in locations where a thinner information-cum-physical landscape still pertains. City landscapes start to respond, producing spaces which conform to lifestyle.

Third, there are memories. The city becomes a kind of memory palace. More and more of the memories of individuals, their mental images, are being captured and stored, at least as a kind of shorthand, via the machinery of cameras and blogs and social networking sites. The rights to these images are becoming a new kind of property, with certain of them endowed with 'a comparatively high degree of lyrical force/value because their form or content is especially significant' (Caillois, cited in Forbes, 2009: 133). In turn, these images start to become an essential adjunct to what it is to be human and how it can be mapped. A parallel to the human genome project starts to hove into view which maps all of the traces that people leave.

The city now has to deal with the results of these and other developments as both an expressive motor and medium in which increased environmental stimulus becomes a norm. As land has been redefined such that a new layer of territory has been inserted which consists of spaces that can exist at many points in many different combinations, in continual genesis, and that can vary on quite short time scales, so the game changes from brokering one city to brokering many. Cities can sing many songs. Although McDonald's description (2010: 86–7) of a not-so-far-in-the-future Istanbul is figurative, it provides a window into this new world in which cities are explicitly rather than implicitly designed as multiplicities that can allow all kinds of complex collective goods to be collated and constructed:

> The one small window, guarded by a pierced wooden screen, allows glimpses of Adem Dede Square and its stooping apartment buildings. In the white room, the windows open on to other Istanbuls where the streets and buildings are drawn by their inhabitants' supermarket spending or their diseases and medical interventions or the subtle interactions of their geographical, social and religious affiliations. There are the restless Istanbuls of traffics and tracks and tunnels. There are wiry Istanbuls, nervous as a skinned man, of gas and power and data. There are Istanbuls built entirely out of football gossip. For every commodity, for every activity that can be analysed and modelled, there is a city.

Thus, the expressive infrastructure of cities builds and intensifies, producing something that seems like a second nature, both in the way in which it wraps itself around events and the way in which it operates like a natural system of flows and balances. There is, of course, a classic Foucauldian point to be made here: the history of the city can be seen as the successive 'smoothing' of barriers to circulation, by 'organizing circulation, eliminating its dangerous elements, making a distinction between good and bad circulation, and maximizing the good circulation by diminishing the bad' (Foucault, 2008: 18). But there is more to it than this.

First off, the city now becomes something akin to nature in the way that it is apprehended. The dominant urban metaphors move to waves and fields and atmospheres which are natural but anorganic. These metaphors aim to mix what were once considered different entities or orders or oppositions: the natural and the cultural or social, for example, or body and culture. The city is hybrid, governed by a logic of self-organizing complexity, of difference and feedback, rather than generic-specific classificatory difference, and it is apprehended through subsystems of different elements which mean that things can continually emerge and fade. The task of the subsystems is to track and intervene at opportune points, producing niches in which particular tendencies can thrive, often at the expense of others. Thus, the underlying ethos of the new capitalism and the city it spawns is environmental. It is based on making reciprocal environments and so locating a new frontier of and for invention.

Second, the city starts to become 'minded'. The city now contains all kinds of things that think in some way, each wrapped up in their own form of spatial intelligence: human beings and animals, of course, but also software, which, in turn, is producing animate things as well as an 'informed' infrastructure which is gradually being linked up with itself as well as humans. Just as it has been argued that film has a mind of its own—through its function as part of

171

something moving, it can think 'in its own affective way' for itself, so long as we do not assume that all forms of thinking have to be identical to, or consequent on, human thought (Frampton, 2006; Mullarkey, 2009; Shaviro, 2010). The sentient city (Shepard, 2011) starts to become a reality.

Third, the city starts to accumulate what might be called 'undergrowth'. All kinds of events occur which are outside the mainstream and can wander off in directions which are not a part of the overall capitalist project. They may be drawn into it, of course. But, equally, they may exist as a permanently juxta-economic/juxtapolitical zone (Berlant, 2008), orphaned from conventional depictions of the political and the economic but periodically able to define what is regarded as political and economic in the first place (see Benson, 2010). After all, the capitalist project I have outlined is, by its very nature, open-ended and unable to be exactly controlled. Open really does mean open.

Conclusions

In this chapter, I have tried to answer the question 'where is capitalism trying to go next?' Such exercises are inevitably fraught with danger since they often present the world as perfectible when it is always a mess. But one might argue that the world turns up messily is currently to capitalism's advantage in that it provides a sandpit for the kinds of practices I have been trying to describe here, using the fuel of diversity and difference, of competing passions and of clashing ideas and prejudices.

What I have particularly tried to suggest is that the underlying model of what constitutes 'economy' is changing to what might be termed a 'natural' model. This is not a natural economy from which money has been banished. Rather, it is a natural economy because it resembles the process of terraform-ing in that it drives practices of worlding which are concerned with producing environments (or rather, as I have tried to make clear, proto-environments) which do not just provide support for a way of life in the way of infrastructure but are a way of life: infrastructure cannot be separated out since it too has become expressive. In these worlds, every fibre of being is bent to producing landscapes which confirm each and every moment as what will happen. This is an economy which has gone beyond ideology or hegemony in their stricter senses in that it is pre-emptive and makes its moves before the event has completely unfolded.

The main point is that, as we more knowingly construct these worlds, so it became clear that a model of total control can no longer apply. The model changes to a model more like a kind of weather forecasting which itself creates the weather, the aim of which is to harvest the best out of situations. But constructing these kinds of worlds actually produces new kinds of instability.

Three things come to mind. One is the environmental costs—vast injections of electrical power are needed. Another is that, although the model is partially self-organizing, this does not mean that it will just carry right on along. For example, stripping out certain kinds of large bureaucratic control (the big predators, so to speak) might mean producing unbalanced ecosystems. Indeed, part of the strength of the system is that it is continually unbalanced, like fly-by-wire. But that is also its weakness. Equilibrium states can only be local. Variation does not always improve robustness. Systems with too much diversity can just create chaos or randomness (Page, 2011). One more is that this system is devoid of any explicit ideology but its own process of willing itself into being. If it stops delivering the goods, there is nothing there. The analogy that perhaps best fits what I mean is what the Italians called 'trasformismo', an ethos of accommodation without any unity of purpose, without any creed. All procedural activity is a bargain, and without the fulfilment of the bargain, either the system grinds to a halt or something goes missing. Support for a regime based on 'trasformismo' vanishes the moment it can no longer satisfy the demands of its clients.

In other words, there is a political moment here, if only it can be seized. But that is the subject of a forthcoming book (Amin and Thrift, forthcoming 2013).

References

Agamben, G. (1993) *The Coming Community*. Minneapolis: University of Minnesota Press.

Allen, R. C. (2010) *The British Industrial Revolution in Global Perspective*. Cambridge: Cambridge University Press.

Amin, A. and Thrift, N. (forthcoming, 2013) *Arts of the Political: New Openings for the Left*. Durham, NC: Duke University Press.

Ayres, I. (2007) *Super Crunchers: How Anything Can Be Predicted*. London: John Murray.

Battle, L. (2011) 'The Sound of the Future', *Financial Times*, 26 February, p. 1.

Batty, M. (2011) 'When All the World's a City', *Environment and Planning A* 43(4), 765–72.

Batuman, E. (2007) *The Windmill and the Giant: Double-Entry Bookkeeping in the Novel*. Stanford: Stanford University Department of Comparative Literature.

Bender, J. and Marrinan, M. (2010) *The Culture of Diagram*. Stanford, CA: Stanford University Press.

Benson, E. (2010) *Wired Wilderness: Technologies of Tracking and the Making of Modern Wildlife*. Baltimore: Johns Hopkins University Press.

Bersani, L. (2010) *Is the Rectum a Grave? And Other Essays*. Chicago, IL: University of Chicago Press.

Bodenhamer, D. J., Corrigan, J., and Harris, T. M. (eds) (2010) *The Spatial Humanities: GIS and the Future of Humanities Scholarship*. Bloomington: Indiana University Press.

Boltanski, L. and Chiapello, E. (2005) *The New Spirit of Capitalism*. London: Verso.

Boradkar, P. (2010) *Designing Things: A Critical Introduction to the Culture of Objects*. Oxford: Berg.

Bradley, M. (2009) *Colour and Meaning in Ancient Rome*. Cambridge: Cambridge University Press.

Bughin, J. R., Chui, M., and Johnson, B. (2008) *The Next Step in Open Innovation*. London: McKinsey.

Caves, R. (2000) *Creative Industries: Contracts Between Art and Commerce*. Cambridge, MA: Harvard University Press.

Clark, G. (2007) *A Farewell to Alms: A Brief Economic History of the World*. Princeton, NJ: Princeton University Press.

Colebrook, C. (2010) with E. Alliez, P. Hallward, N. Thoburn, and J. Gilbert, 'Deleuzian Politics? A Roundtable Discussion', *New Formations*, 68, 143–87.

Cowen, T. (2011) *The Great Stagnation: How America Ate All the Low-Hanging Fruit of Modern History, Got Sick, and Will (Eventually) Feel Better*. New York: Penguin Dutton e-book.

Crewe, L. (2010) 'Wear-Where? The Convergent Geographies of Architecture and Fashion', *Environment and Planning A*, 42, 2093–108.

Daniels, S., Pearson, M., and Roms, H. (eds.) (2010) 'Fieldworks', Special Issue of *Performance Research*, 15(4).

Danto, A. (2009) *Andy Warhol*. New Haven, CT: Yale University Press.

Davenport, T. L. and Harris, J. C. (2007) *Competing on Analytics: The New Science of Winning*. Boston: Harvard Business School Press.

Davies, E. (2006) *Beyond Dance: Laban's Legacy of Movement Analysis*. London: Routledge.

De Vries, J. (2008) *The Industrious Revolution: Consumer Behavior and the Household Economy, 1650 to the Present*. Berkeley: University of California Press.

Deleuze, G. and Guattari, F. (1987) *A Thousand Plateaus: Capitalism and Schizophrenia*, trans. and foreword by B. Massumi. Minneapolis: University of Minnesota Press.

Dodds, P. S. and Danforth, C. M. (2010) 'Measuring the Happiness of Large-Scale Written Expression: Songs, Blogs, and Presidents', *Journal of Happiness Studies*, 11(4), 441–56.

Dosse, F. (2010) *Gilles Deleuze and Félix Guattari: Intersecting Lives*. New York: Columbia University Press.

Easley, D. and Kleinberg, J. (2010) *Networks, Crowds and Markets: Reasoning About a Highly Connected World*. Cambridge: Cambridge University Press.

Edgworth, F. Y. (1881/2010) *Mathematical Psychics: An Essay on the Application of Mathematics to the Moral Sciences*. Charleston: Bibliolife.

Ferguson, K. (2007) *William James: Politics in the Pluriverse*. Lanham, MD: Rowman & Littlefield.

Flusser, V. (1999) *The Shape of Things: A Philosophy of Design*. London: Reaktion.

Forbes, P. (2009) *Dazzled and Deceived: Mimicry and Camouflage*. New Haven, CT: Yale University Press.

Foucault, M. (2008) *The Birth of Biopolitics: Lectures at the Collège de France 1978–1979*. Basingstoke: Palgrave Macmillan.

Frampton, D. (2006) *Filmosophy*. London: Wallflower Press.

French, S., Leyshon, A., and Thrift, N. (2009) 'A Very Geographical Crisis: The Making and Breaking of the 2007–2008 Financial Crisis', *Cambridge Journal of Regions, Economy and Society*, 2(2), 287–302.

Fung, V., Fung, W., and Wind, Y. (2007) *Competing in a Flat World: Building Enterprises for a Flat World*. Upper Saddle River, NJ: Pearson Education.

Garner, S. (ed.) (2008) *Writing on Drawing: Essays on Drawing Practice and Research*. Bristol: Intellect.

Gibson-Graham, J. K. (2006), *A Postcapitalist Politics*. Minneapolis: University of Minnesota Press.

Govindajaran, V. and Trimble, C. (2010) *The Other Side of Innovation: Solving the Execution Challenge*. Boston: Harvard Business Review Press.

Groebner, V. (2007) *Who Are You? Identification, Deception, and Surveillance in Early Modern Europe*. New York: Zone.

Hagel, J., Brown, J. S., and Davison, L. (2010) *The Power of Pull: How Small Moves, Smartly Made, Can Set Big Things in Motion*. New York: Basic Books.

Harney, S. (2010) 'The Real Knowledge Transfer', *Social Text*. Available at http://www.socialtextjournal.org/periscope/2010/08/the-real-knowledge-transfer.php.

Harper, R. (2010) *Texture: Human Expression in the Age of Communications Overload*. Cambridge, MA: MIT Press.

Harrington, A. (1996) *Re-enchanted Science: Holism in German Culture from Wilhelm II to Hitler*. Princeton, NJ: Princeton University Press.

Hart, K., Laville, J., and Cattani, A. D. (2010) *The Human Economy: A Citizen's Guide*. Cambridge: Polity Press.

Hinderliter, B., Kaizen, W., Maimon, V., Mansoor, J., and McCormick, S. (eds.) (2009) *Communities of Sense: Rethinking Aesthetics and Politics*. Durham, NC: Duke University Press.

Indiana, G. (2010) *Andy Warhol and the Can That Sold the World*. New York: Basic Books.

James, H. (2010) 'The Gospel of Relaxation'. In R. Richardson (ed.), *The Heart of William James*. Cambridge, MA: Harvard University Press, 130–44.

Johnson, S. (2010) *Where Good Ideas Come From: The Natural History of Innovation*. London: Allen Lane.

Jullien, F. (2009) *The Great Image has No Form or on the Nonobject Through Painting*. Chicago: University of Chicago Press.

Kamvar, S. and Harris, J. (2009) *We Feel Fine: An Almanac of Human Emotion*. New York: Scribner.

Knorr Cetina, K. (2010) 'The Epistemics of Information', *Journal of Consumer Culture*, 10, 171–201.

Krauss, R. E. (2010) *Perpetual Inventory*. Cambridge, MA: MIT Press.

Latour, B. and Lepinay, V. A. (2009) *The Science of Passionate Interests: An Introduction to Gabriel Tarde's Economic Anthropology*. Chicago: Prickly Paradigm Press.

Levinson, M. (2008) *The Box: How the Shipping Container Made the World Smaller and the World Economy Bigger*. Princeton, NJ: Princeton University Press.

Lim, B. C. (2009) *Translating Time: Cinema, the Fantastic, and Temporal Critique*. Durham, NC: Duke University Press.

Ling, R. (2008) *New Tech: New Ties: How Mobile Communication is Reshaping Social Cohesion*. Cambridge, MA: MIT Press.

Lukic, B. and Katz, B. M. (2011) *Nonobject*. Cambridge, MA: MIT Press.

McCarthy, A. (2010) *The Citizen Machine: Governing by Television in 1950s America*. New York: Free Press.

McDonald, I. (2010) *The Dervish House*. London: Gollancz.

McNeely, I. F. and Wolverton, L. (2008) *Reinventing Knowledge: From Alexandria to the Internet*. New York: Norton.

Manning, E. (2009) *Relationscapes: Movement, Art, Philosophy*. Cambridge, MA: MIT Press.

Massumi, B. (2009) 'National Enterprise Emergency: Steps Toward an Ecology of Powers', *Theory Culture and Society*, 26, 153–85.

Marx, K. (2005) *Grundrisse: Foundations of the Critique of Political Economy*. Harmondsworth: Penguin.

Mirowski, P. (2011) *Science-Mart: Privatizing American Science*. Cambridge, MA: Harvard University Press.

Mitchell, A. J. (2010) *Heidegger Among the Sculptors: Body, Space, and the Art of Dwelling*. Stanford, CA: Stanford University Press.

Mokyr, J. (2010) *The Enlightened Economy: An Economic History of Britain 1700–1850*. New Haven, CT: Yale University Press.

Mol, A., Moser, I., and Pols, J. (eds.) (2010) Care in Practice: On Tinkering in Clinics, Homes and Farms, Bielefeld: Transcript.

Moulier-Boutang, Y. (2011) *Cognitive Capitalism*. Cambridge: Polity Press.

Mullarkey, J. (2006) *Post-Continental Philosophy: An Outline*. London: Continuum.

—— (2009) *Refractions of Reality: Philosophy and the Moving Image*. Basingstoke: Palgrave Macmillan.

Myers, G. (2001) *William James: His Life and Thought*. New Haven, CT: Yale University Press.

Ober, J. (2008) *Democracy and Knowledge: Innovation and Learning in Classical Athens*. Princeton, NJ: Princeton University Press.

Offer, A. (2006) *The Challenge of Affluence: Self-Control and Well-Being in the United States and Britain since 1980*. Oxford: Oxford University Press.

Page, S. E. (2007) *The Difference: How the Power of Diversity Creates Better Groups, Firms, Schools, and Societies*. Princeton, NJ: Princeton University Press.

—— (2011) *Diversity and Complexity*. Princeton, NJ: Princeton University Press.

Petherbridge, D. (2008) 'Nailing the Liminal: The Difficulties of Defining Drawing'. In S. Garner (ed.), *Writing on Drawing: Essays on Drawing Practice and Research*. Bristol: Intellect, 27–42.

Peuquet, D. J. (2003) *Representations of Space and Time*. New York: Guilford Press.

Prahalad, C. K. and Krishnan, M. S. (2008) *The New Age of Innovation: Driving Co-Created Value through Global Networks*. New York: McGraw-Hill.

Rank, O. (1936/1964) *Truth and Reality*. New York: Norton.

Read, A. (2009) *Theatre, Intimacy and Engagement: The Last Human Venue*. Basingstoke: Palgrave Macmillan.

Richardson, R. D. (2006) *William James: In the Maelstrom of American Modernism*. New York: Houghton Mifflin.

Roberts, A. (2010) *New Model Army*. London: Gollancz.

Rosenberg, D. and Grafton, A. (2010) *Cartographies of Time: A History of the Timeline*. Princeton, NJ: Princeton Architectural Press.

Runciman, D. (2009) 'Bouncebackability' *London Review of Books*, 29 January, 7–10.

Samuel, L. R. (2010) *Freud on Madison Avenue: Motivation Research and Subliminal Advertising in America*. Philadelphia: University of Pennsylvania Press.

Scarpellini, E. (2011) *Material Nation: A Consumer's History of Modern Italy*. Oxford: Oxford University Press.

Sebald, W. G. (2003) *After Nature*. Harmondsworth: Penguin.

Serres, M. (2011) *Malfeasance: Appropriation Through Pollution?* Stanford, CA: Stanford University Press.

Shaviro, S. (2010) *Post Cinematic Affect*. London: Zero Books.

Shepard, M. (ed.) (2011) *Sentient City: Ubiquitous Computing, Architecture, and the Future of Urban Space*. Cambridge, MA: MIT Press.

Stark, D. (2009) *The Sense of Dissonance: Accounts of Worth in Economic Life*. Princeton, NJ: Princeton University Press.

Stengers, I. (2010) *Cosmopolitics I*. Minneapolis: University of Minnesota Press.

Taussig, M. (2009) *What Color is the Sacred?* Chicago: University of Chicago Press.

Teranova, T. (2009) 'Another Life: The Nature of Political Economy in Foucault's Genealogy of Biopolitics', *Theory, Culture & Society*, 26, 234–62.

Thrift, N. J. (2005) *Knowing Capitalism*. London: Sage.

—— (2007) *Non-Representational Theory: Space, Politics, Affect*. London: Routledge.

—— (2009) 'Different Atmospheres: Of Sloterdijk, China and Site', *Environment and Planning D. Society and Space*, 27, 119–38.

—— (2010) 'Halos: Finding Space in the World for New Political Forms'. In B. Braun and S. J. Whatmore (eds.), *Political Matter: Technoscience, Democracy and Public Life*. Minneapolis: University of Minnesota Press, 139–74.

—— (2011) 'Lifeworld Inc. And What to Do About It', *Environment and Planning D. Society and Space*, 29, 5–26.

Toop, D. (1995) *Ocean of Sound: Aether Talk, Ambient Sound and Imaginary Worlds*. London: Serpent's Tail.

Turkle, S. (2011) *Alone Together: Why We Expect More from Technology and Less from Each Other*. New York: Basic Books.

Warhol, A. (1975) *The Philosophy of Andy Warhol*. London: Penguin.

Weiss, B. (1996) *The Making and Unmaking of the Haya Lived World: Consumption, Commoditization, and Everyday Practice*. Durham, NC: Duke University Press.

Section 2

Applications: The Changing Nature of Capitalism, Work, and Organizations in the Public and Private Sectors

8

The Connexionist Nature of Modern Financial Markets: From a Domination to a Justice Order?[1]

Isabelle Huault and Hélène Rainelli-Weiss

Introduction

The financial crisis that began in the summer of 2007, and was accelerated in September 2008 by the failure of Lehman Brothers, has brought fierce and multifaceted criticism down on the financial markets. Some condemn their ability to circulate vast capital sums with no geographical limits and thus their ability to create damaging competition (Arnoldi, 2004; Bryan and Rafferty, 2006; LiPuma and Lee, 2004, 2005; Maurer, 2002; Pryke and Allen, 2000) to the detriment of industrial investment and economic stability. Others are opposed to any regulation that would limit freedom of action. They fear regulation would reduce market activity, prevent the establishment of a fair price in financial deals, and raise the cost of financing businesses and households. This analysis, which is favoured by the promoters of financial innovations, is obviously not free from self-interest. More significantly for our purpose, it relies heavily on a Walrasian concept of purely competitive markets that produce perfect price transparency. This fits poorly with the reality of modern financial markets, which are mostly over-the-counter (OTC) markets involving non-transparent bilateral transactions. In this chapter, we take full account of this mismatch, lift the veil on the nature

[1] The authors would like to thank Glenn Morgan, Marie-Laure Djelic, Sigrid Quack, Vivien Blanchet, Benjamin Taupin, and participants at the EGOS 2010 colloquium in Lisbon, the CRESC February 2010 colloquium in Manchester, the DRM-Most October 2009, and the GREGOR November 2010 workshops in Paris for their advice and constructive comments on earlier drafts of this chapter.

of current financial markets, and think afresh about the challenges posed by the financial system as it stands at present. Our argument is based on the idea that modern OTC financial markets derive from a new capitalist logic—the connexionist logic (Boltanski and Chiapello, 1999/2005). Identifying the values system and characteristics of this logic reveals the distance between the rhetoric of justification used by supporters of the markets and the true mechanisms at stake. It provides paths for solutions to the dysfunctional processes observed on OTC markets.

The promotion of the activity of financial markets refers us back to a theoretical framework known as the efficient-market hypothesis (EMH) (Fama, 1970, 1991). EMH posits that the ability to buy and sell without hindrance allows information on fundamentals held by one party or another to integrate the prices of financial securities quickly and efficiently. Free competition between security issuers and investors thus allows the price to reflect the 'true' and 'fair' value of securities (Carruthers and Stinchombe, 1999) at any given moment. This vision of how financial markets function takes as its ideal the Walrasian model of the perfect market, where the bids and offers of individual agents, each with full access to the available information, are directed to an auctioneer who works out the price and then announces it to traders. It provides theoretical foundations for regulatory options that hinder market activity as little as possible.

Without engaging in the debate about the ability of efficient-market theory to describe the proper functioning of stock markets, we note that most modern financial markets obviously do not fit the Walrasian description. From statistics about world financial markets produced by the Bank for International Settlements (BIS), we can state that in December 2010, derivatives markets were 89 per cent OTC and 11 per cent exchange-traded. As for bond markets, by far the largest segment of financial markets, most sources agree that most trading in bonds occurs in OTC markets. Finally, in recent years, more and more stock trading has become OTC as a result of the deregulation of stock exchanges and the creation of alternative trading platforms. Although no figure seems to be currently available, the current situation is one where OTC markets largely dominate traditional exchanges.[2]

Comprising bilateral transactions between two parties, and determined by the placing of private contracts, these 'markets' allow neither the deal prices nor the volumes exchanged to be placed in the public domain. We are thus faced with a strange situation where, in order to justify largely unrestrictive

---

[2] Assuming 90 per cent of bonds are traded OTC—which probably understates the true figure, taking the gross market value of derivatives to assess the size of the derivatives markets and using the BIS statistics as regards debt and stock securities and derivatives, one obtains a share of 90 per cent for OTC markets versus 10 per cent for exchange markets.

regulations, the supporters of financial markets and financial innovations seem to project the idealized image of the Walrasian market onto the OTC markets, which obviously does not fit the description.

One argument often made to justify this apparent contradiction is that exchange through a private market is a necessary step for financial innovations, which, once widely accepted and used, will be called upon to join more transparent and competitive markets.[3] In any case, regulation should not inhibit business activity because one expected development is progressive homogenization of traded products, resulting in greater liquidity and eventually more efficient competition among those who supply and demand these products. Adopting a historical perspective on developments in modern finance, however, offers very little in favour of the actuality of the process that might lead the OTC markets towards the model of quasi-Walrasian markets. Since the establishment of options and futures markets in their modern form in the 1970s in the EU and the 1980s in Europe, options and futures traded on standardized markets represent a mere 3 per cent of the total of the derivatives market. All the financial innovations that arose on OTC markets have stayed there. The market for interest rate swaps, for example, which constitutes 54 per cent of the entire market in derivative products, is typically an OTC market. The recent crisis experienced by credit derivatives has induced regulators to try to set up clearing houses and to bring their way of functioning closer to that of the organized markets. The apparent slowness with which this change is being accomplished, and the resistance of the parties involved, shows that the process, still very tentative, is neither easy nor natural.

These observations lead us to reject the argument that the OTC model will be only a passing phenomenon on modern financial markets, and to form the hypothesis that OTC markets are different in nature from standardized markets. If participants in financial markets have shown a preference for this kind of market for more than two decades, it is not by chance nor is it likely to be of brief duration. It is more likely that this kind of market fulfils a particular function that needs to be identified and defined. Some elucidation therefore seems necessary to distinguish and re-evaluate the mechanisms that regulate these new-style markets and that might prove to be dysfunctional. This will be a starting point for a renewed and more in-depth criticism of the way the current financial system functions.

---

[3] *The Economist*, for example, in January 2009, advocates: 'Their relationship (that of OTC markets) with exchanges need not be wholly adversarial. Financial innovations may start out in OTC markets and move to exchanges as they mature.' This view was also very often expressed by the credit derivatives promoters we studied in the 1996–2004 period (Huault and Rainelli, 2009).

To contribute to this renewed criticism, we propose to use the theoretical frameworks provided by Boltanski and Thévenot (1991/2006) and Boltanski and Chiapello (1999/2005). We shall try to establish that modern financial markets of the OTC model, far from belonging to the market order described by Boltanski and Thévenot, seem to follow a new capitalist logic—the connexionist logic (Boltanski and Chiapello, 1999/2005). In the first part of this chapter, we endeavour to describe OTC markets from this point of view. This enables us to consider, in the second part, the social critique that may be addressed to modern financial markets and their specific talent for disarming it. The ability of connexionist markets to compromise with their critiques and take up the challenges they present for the financial sphere, the economy as a whole, and society at large, is discussed in part three.

From the Walrasian ideal to modern financial markets

Boltanski and Thévenot (1991/2006) identify and describe six worlds corresponding to six grammars of worth within which individuals move, calling on the scales of one world or another to justify themselves when involved in discord arising from collective action. Each 'world' constitutes a specific justification regime, characterized by a higher common principle, and worlds can be seen as ways of legitimating particular forms of social or economic organization that confer 'worth' on certain activities, processes, and people, through 'tests'. As it is through tests that the value of people or practices can be legitimately assessed, critique of social organization can take either the form of a critique on the fairness of the test within the framework of the world at stake or be more radical and challenge the higher common principle from other justificatory logics.

In Boltanski and Thevenot's conceptualization, three worlds are of some relevance to our work: the first of them being the *domestic world*, which is governed by the principle of place in the ordering of generations, tradition, and hierarchy whereas the dominant value in the *civic world* is the pre-eminence of the collective. In the *industrial world*, the highest principle is efficiency. Finally, the *market world's* higher common principle is competition, where rivalry and competitiveness are seen as positive values. Of these three worlds, the one we are most interested in is the market world, which seems to offer a renewed characterization of the Walrasian ideal of efficient markets. It is of interest to notice that the legitimate test in the market world consists in being able to make more profit than one's competitor, respecting the conditions of free and unbiased competition.

Stock markets, OTC markets, and the 'market order'

The market world described by Boltanski and Thévenot (1991/2006: 252) is characterized by three main traits. The first concerns the nature of relationships between individuals. These are a-temporal, with no past or future and are focused on 'objectivized' objects, in the sense that neither their definition nor their value depends on the persons involved in the transaction. The second characteristic trait concerns the definition of agents, summed up as a client, supplier, buyer, seller, or competitor, roles that individuals can adopt in turn (Aspers, 2009). Individuals in this world are characterized by their detachment from others: they are free and available for all kinds of transactions. The third trait specific to the market world allows the precise identification of its scale, its grammar of worth, and its highest common principle to be found in the predominance of free competition. Although the market world is peopled by individuals who are selfish by nature—they pursue the satisfaction of their desires through their transactions—these inhabitants are bound together by a collective value, a scale of worth that is measured by the degree of free competition operating in this world. Disputes are resolved by establishing the commercial scale of the worth of goods, in other words by price. With Boltanski and Thévenot (1991/2006), we note that the seeming homogeneity of goods exchanged in the market world, as well as the recognition of a price scale, means that each transaction can be compared to other transactions and equivalences can be established. Although the price of a given transaction is the result of negotiations between individuals, there is such a thing as a 'general price', a point of reference, something like a true value, a fair price. The existence of this fair price depends upon the capacity of numerous agents to buy and sell with no hindrance.

These three characteristics of the market world seem to us a fairly precise description of the Walrasian ideal financial market. The single common good recognized by individuals who meet on stock exchanges is the preservation of the conditions for competition between buyers and sellers of stocks, with, as a corollary, the promotion of such exchanges and transparency, which determine the kind of regulation observed on these markets. A question, of course, arises as to whether the rise of electronic trading as opposed to open outcry fundamentally transforms the nature of actual stock exchange markets. The first phase of transformation, typified for example by the replacement of open outcry markets by electronic quotation systems, seems to have had few consequences as regards the view that transparency was the condition for fair competition. However, the recent increase of market fragmentation entailed by the competition of traditional stock exchanges with various kinds of trading platforms might well have blurred the justificatory logics. There are some signs that the competition between market 'places' has reduced the strength of competition mechanisms within markets and overall, so that transparency has lost ground, OTC forms of markets such as dark pools have developed, and the amount of resources invested in by players has become a key determinant in the competitive game of trading faster than anybody else. Fostering practices such as high-frequency and computer-based trading, these developments weaken the view that market activity is still favouring market transparency and fair competition among investors. These two notions, however, remain at the core of the debate financial institutions have with regulators as regards these new practices, evidencing the strength of the market order justification logic when it comes to understanding financial market activity.

In OTC markets, however, the situation is different *by nature*. First and foremost, the question of time scale in derivatives markets is different because contracts can commit parties over several months or years, which implies legal and financial risks. Although derivatives, in contradiction to insurance contracts, specify how contracts are to be settled if the parties agree to terminate in advance, contractors are not detached from OTC transactions once they have been concluded. Disputes between counterparties over settlement issues are not uncommon and de facto account for most of the changes brought to the Master Agreement typically used by derivatives sellers and buyers. Additionally, the objective and homogeneous definition of goods is not as finalized on OTC derivatives markets as it is on stock exchanges. One normally distinguishes relatively standard products, which are sold at competitive prices, from the sort of bespoke products that justify the resort to an OTC market, where sellers can offer their clients products adapted to their needs. In transactions concerning bespoke products, the specification of the product depends, by definition, on the buyer's expectations and the seller's capacity to respond to them.[4]

The question of the interchangeability of agents is also posed in different ways on OTC and stock markets. The BIS statistics show that 39 per cent of all the derivatives market can be attributed to financial institutions committed to revealing the volume and value of their transactions to the central bank in their home country. Fifty per cent of the markets concern 'other financial institutions' and only 11 per cent constitute non-financial agents. Even if the financial institutions concerned alternate playing the roles of buyer and seller, the number of agents on the OTC markets is lower than on exchanges, and we can speculate that not all agents are equal. A study carried out on the market

---

[4] The view the ISDA develops in its contribution to the 2010 MiFID2 consultation organized by the European Commission is that the price of OTC derivatives should be seen as a price for a 'solution', which can 'take weeks, if not months to finalize'. There is 'by definition no benchmark price'.

for credit derivatives (Huault and Rainelli, 2009) showed that 86 per cent of transactions were carried out by the ten biggest international investment banks in 2007. According to the ECB report of April 2009, the situation has worsened with the financial crisis: the disappearance of major players in the market (Lehman Brothers, Merrill Lynch, Bear Sterns) and certain products (monolines, hedge funds) has once more reinforced a concentration that financial authorities judge worrying. Most white papers and recent reports now refer to the G14 or G15 to define the group of dealers who dominate derivatives OTC markets.[5]

Finally, the chief characteristic of OTC markets is that they function opaquely. Comparing the prices of different sellers in these markets is tricky. It is difficult to establish the equivalence of a given transaction because of the heterogeneous nature of OTC contracts and the absence of any publicity about the volume and price of comparable transactions.

These observations provide evidence that, whatever the actual level of competition in OTC markets, their organization principle cannot be said to be revolving around the higher common principle of free and unbiased competition between buyers and sellers. One way to interpret this finding could be to condemn the profits realized on these markets as unfair because financial institutions exchanging in OTC markets do not operate in a proper market. This critical perspective would generate support for a regulatory design aiming at transforming markets for bespoke products into markets for standard products, OTC markets into organized markets. Although interesting, we would like to show in what follows that, in an analytical perspective, we have more to gain in acknowledging the structural specificity of OTC markets and in giving up considering these markets through the Walrasian model lens. But, if OTC markets do not function according to the market order principles described by Boltanski and Thévenot (1999/2006), how can we describe the sphere to which they belong? How can we understand the values that regulate them, the highest common principle to which agents refer to settle the litigation that sets them against each other? What principles do they use to justify market structure when attacked from outside, for example from actors from other worlds (e.g. the civic or the market world in the case of regulators)? In what follows, we attempt to show that OTC markets are governed by the sort of connexionist logic described by Boltanski and Chiapello (1999/2005).

---

[5] This includes the following banks: Bank of America-Merrill Lynch, Barclays Capital, BNP Paribas, Citigroup, Commerzbank AG, Crédit Suisse, Deutsche Bank AG, Goldman, Sachs & Co., HSBC Group, JP Morgan, Chase, Morgan Stanley, The Royal Bank of Scotland Group, Société Générale, UBS AG, Wachovia Bank.

OTC markets as connexionist markets

In their book, Boltanski and Chiapello (1999/2005) describe a reconfiguration of capitalism that turns on the notion of networks. While the observation of reticulation phenomena in economic exchanges is not in itself new (White, 1992), the authors show the extension of connexionist logic in contemporary capitalism, as characterized by multiple meetings and temporary connections that can be set aside and then reactivated at will, over vast geographical distances and between extremely diverse groups. They demonstrate that the development of this logic is not just a factual evolution in methods of economic exchange but is accompanied by the constitution of a veritable 'world'. Within this world, a value system of norms of judgement and principles of equivalence is generated, allowing the definition of internal conditions as 'worthy' and 'unworthy'. More specifically, the notion of project serves as the real pivot of this world, generating a value scale that organizes the relationships between the individuals and things taken up in the connexionist logic.

Thanks to the multiplication of active connections, the project creates a space for production and accumulation in a mainly liquid world (Bauman, 2005) and generates value, justifying the demand to extend the network. For the reticular world, the project constitutes the source of a value system that Boltanski and Chiapello term 'the projective city' and that is driven by a higher principle, the development of a network of connections.

At the heart of this value system is activity, the principle of equivalence by which the dimensions of people and things are measured. Activity in this context does not have the meaning it has in the industrial world, where it is confused with work, or the market world, where it signifies the number of transactions made. Instead, it means the capacity to generate projects or to integrate projects generated by others. For those living in this projective city environment, it is important never to run short of projects, to know how to pass easily from one project to another, and to multiply occasions for making projects. Thus, connexionist beings, the 'worthy person' in the projective city, are both physically and intellectually available, reactive and mobile. Flexible and multi-tasking, they know how to take risks. They can handle ambivalence and are always ready to exploit any opportunities that come their way. They are innovators whose creativity springs rather from recombination (Stark, 1996) than from radical innovation. Their role is to promote collective innovation, to the extent that they would feel awkward about claiming copyright on their ideas. On the other hand, the 'unworthy person' in this city is someone who has difficulty participating in a project and then getting out of it, who does not communicate, who does not seem capable of compromise, and whose ideas appear rigid—someone immobile and inflexible.

In a world where the main activity is establishing connections, connex-ionist beings form particular relationships with the people they work with. They are not usually hierarchical bosses or planners, but 'facilitators', who breathe life and favour self-discipline and innovation. They do not take rare goods for their own profit but redistribute them, especially information. Their role is to favour the mobility of the individuals they work with. Their status as a worthy person requires forms of investment that will lead them to forgo stability and prefer autonomy to security.

The role of innovation on OTC financial markets

In the same way that the general project is the means by which the connexionist world stabilizes forms and generates a system of values, we argue that financial innovation, which drives the growth of modern financial markets, crystallizes their particular connexionist logic. While the financial innovations of the 1970s (options, futures, index derivatives) were created on organized markets (see MacKenzie and Millo, 2003; Millo and MacKenzie, 2009), the great majority of new derivatives invented since the 1980s occurred in OTC markets. There, the main promoters of innovation have been the world's big banks, faced with a major evolution of financial markets in developed countries moving away from the financial model of debt to get closer to a model in which the economy is financed by the markets. When faced with the erosion of their margins in traditional credit activities, banks spotted new sources of income in financial innovation and new product offerings. They also saw the opportunity to main-tain their central position in an environment that was being radically trans-formed. This is how, in developed countries, we ended up with a financial system of markets with new intermediaries, where the banks play a dominant role in the capital markets through OTC markets, rather than a system of direct financing of the economy by the financial markets, which had been the initial aim of the reforms of the 1980s. Temporary zones of accumulation, which create new sources of value for these agents, are made up of complex financial innov-ations that generate different types of ambiguity. The most interesting of these for those promoting new products is the ambiguity surrounding the principles of valuation. In fact, the uncertainty surrounding the pertinent measurement of value brings different models of calculation into competition and potentially generates margins for the inventors of new products (Beunza and Stark, 2005; Lepinay, 2007). The appearance on the markets of products whose definition (see e.g. Huault and Rainelli, 2009; Lepinay, 2007) and valuation generate ambiguities opens up a range of opportunities for inventors, and the possible extension of the network of connections between the agents that handle these complex products (banks, enterprises, energy suppliers, fund managers, small shareholders, etc.). A close view is developed in Engelen et al. (2010: 56), who see financial intermediaries as developing long chains of activity which have 'a multiplicity of points or nodes where well-placed intermediaries are confronted with ever-changing conditions in each new conjuncture'. Financial innovation appears as 'bricolage' where 'the bricoleur is the individual or the group, which turns the nodal possibility into a profitable position by using whatever instruments are to hand to create a business model from product or process' (Engelen et al., 2010: 56). Connecting actors, resources, and risks across time in order to—in theory—resolve uncertainty problems, inventors and promoters of financial innovations that can typically be easily copied generate a system where there is no rest from bringing together different knowledges, expertises, and resources to find new projects, products, customers, etc.

We therefore argue there is a parallel between the role of the project in the reticular markets described by Boltanski and Chiapello (1999/2005) and the role played by innovation in contemporary financial markets. Our thesis is that the creation of new products is not just a given of current financial capitalism but generates an order, a kind of city regulated by a value system whose principle of equivalence is the capacity to generate complex financial innovations.

Beunza and Stark (2005) illuminate the nature of this value system by describing the organization of trading rooms, the places where financial institutions make their connections and where they exchange their products. They point out that these rooms are a heterarchy (Girard and Stark, 2002; Stark, 2009). The relationships between the different members and desks are horizontal, not vertical, and nurture knowledge sharing, as decentralization is the guiding principle. With a flattened organizational hierarchy, no separate offices for hierarchical heads, open space design, and a collegiate atmosphere, the trading rooms where financial products are exchanged these days have a collaborative structure that favours the exchange of information and agents' autonomy. For Beunza and Stark (2005), this kind of organization promotes an entrepreneurial culture that favours innovation. Trading rooms organize the coexistence and adjustment of calculations that result from different measurement systems. Traders therefore appear like entrepreneurs, as Knight (1921) saw it, agents with the capacity to work with coexisting but different evaluation principles. They benefit from the ambiguities that arise from this coexistence (Stark, 2000). The trading room is organized to promote reflexivity, the ability to define and to recombine resources and combinatory innovation (Kogut and Zander, 1992)—in short, to produce new instruments containing ambiguities that guarantee the renewal of competitive appraisals of value and the recurrent appearance of still-undefined opportunities for arbitrage.

Today, since the dematerialization of stock exchanges, the immense majority of financial stocks and products are exchanged through the trading rooms of international financial institutions; however, the heterarchical organization, as described by Beunza and Stark (2005), is clearly linked to the higher common principle specific to OTC markets, that is, the infinite extensions of networks through rather ambiguous financial innovations.[6] Connexionist traders have adapted to this form of market. Their stature is defined by the value system generated on these markets, which gauges their capacity to generate or favour invention, or use complex products that allow the setting up of innovative investment strategies. Their profile shows the characteristic traits that Boltanski and Chiapello attribute to the connexionist being, the 'worthy person' in the projective city. Connexionist traders enjoy autonomy in relation to the institutions that employ them and do not hesitate to play on the competition between potential employers when negotiating a bonus (Godechot, 2007). They are willing to change, relocate, and move easily between the financial centres where the world's market activities are concentrated (Sassen, 2001). They are never short of a project and will readily leave the trading room to set up an entrepreneurial structure or an investment fund, because they are motivated by a logic that MacKenzie (2008: 5) describes: 'So they're going into it [hedge funds] because they want to run something because they're never, ever going to be the guy that sits right at the top [of an investment bank] because they can't be bothered with the politics [i.e. organizational conflicts and jostling for promotion].' Traders are often impatient towards the small people ('unworthy persons') who work in the middle and back office, who are not mobile, and are much less likely to live in an atmosphere of ambivalence, in the ambiguity of definitions or actions or explanations, given that they work in more normalized cognitive frameworks (accounting, deontology, internal controls). However, traders also know how to maintain relationships so that the back office benefits from the results obtained in the trading room (Godechot, 2007). Recognizing the world of traders as a connexionist world, we not only understand their value system but also gain insight into the acceptability of specific social behaviours within this world. A trader claiming some copyright on a product or an arbitrage strategy or refusing to share information within the trading room would be seen as not playing by the rules. In Boltanski and Chiapello's terms, he would be identified less as a networker extender, working for the good of the network, than as a networker, working for himself and adopting behaviours that will be deemed exploitative within the frame of the order of worth. We thus see that the connexionist world, like the other worlds, is equipped with a 'city', however

---

[6] See also Sassen (2005: 22): 'The drive to produce innovations is one of the marking features of the financial era that begins in the 1980s . . . What is perhaps different today is the intensification.'

embryonic it might still appear, which settles the value of the worthy and the unworthy but also defines the acceptability of social behaviours.

The structure of OTC financial markets: connections and networks

If we understand that, in the network world of OTC markets, financial innovations create zones of temporary accumulation of income and enhance the reputation of the institution where they were first developed, then we can grasp the structure of these markets at different levels. The organization of the trading room is a first level, the most micro-economic. A wider approach to the organization set up by the great financial institutions allows the identification of a second circle. In OTC markets, exchanges between trading rooms take place via complex electronic systems, linking rooms that are geographically far apart, in (usually multinational) companies. Trading rooms are carefully separated from the rest of the company's activities, not only physically (it is not unusual for access to be restricted) but also in the way they are governed. This suggests an organization of exchanges that can be described, in Williamson-like terms, as hybrid, network-like, sitting at the frontier between organizations and the market. That it abides neither by the rules of the industrial nor by that of the market world, which are the natural spaces of respectively organizations and markets, but rather by those of the connexionist world does not come as a surprise.

Finally, at a third level that corresponds to a third perspective of OTC markets, there are numerous interconnections between nominally competitive financial institutions. The logic of innovation that permeates OTC markets leads to the flourishing of new products marked, as we have noted, by a certain number of ambiguities. These may be sources of profit but they also put the brakes on market development, causing a creative tension that obliges agents to cooperate even while competing against each other. The extension of the network of agents participating in the new market created around a financial innovation requires setting up joint actions by the principal promoters of these innovations, as has been clearly shown in the case of the credit derivatives market. Here the ISDA (Huault and Rainelli, 2009; Morgan, 2008), an association of investment banks and other OTC market agents, has taken in hand the question of contract definitions, legal qualifications, and revision of standards over a lengthy time span. Certain leaders, such as JP Morgan, are involved in collaborative actions to promote market liquidity. In the construction around the innovations[7] phase of the market, as well

---

[7] Resorting to forms of collaboration between competing organizations to promote an emerging market is not restricted to OTC markets (MacKenzie and Millo, 2003). On the other hand, the need

as in the consolidation phase (which is still incomplete twelve years after the first contracts in the credit derivatives market), cooperation between competing agents seems to be one of the ingredients of the development and functioning of markets. This again speaks for the notion that the game played by actors of the field is not that of pure competition. The polity of the market world seems therefore ill-adapted to understand the value system at stake in this form of market.

We hope to have shown that, in their attempt to show the emergence of a new community—the projective city at the heart of contemporary capitalism—Boltanski and Chiapello supply descriptors that apply most convincingly to OTC financial markets. But beyond highlighting these descriptors and their usefulness in characterizing the difference between OTC markets and organized financial markets (see Table 8.1), the main thing we learn from Boltanski and Chiapello is the revelation of the value system that dominates these markets. At the heart of this value system, we argue, is a particular form of project, financial innovation, which, because it is a source of wealth creation, organizes the relationship between people and objects. The hierarchy that is set up between 'worthy' and 'unworthy' is determined by their capacity to generate, utilize, and recombine financial innovations. This has given the markets a functioning principle that has rarely been seen until now and whose recognition opens what we see as promising avenues for renewing the social critique of financial markets.

In the rest of this chapter, we want to examine the consequences of seeing modern financial markets as connexionist markets. In the next section, we use the connexionist perspective to study the social critique against their flaws and the specific talent they evidence for disarming it.

The social critique of connexionist markets

The value system on which connexionism rests is articulated around the notions of project, network, and permanent change, and has undoubtedly facilitated exponential growth of OTC markets and constant innovation. But behind this success lie major dysfunctions, some of which were laid bare at the time of the financial crisis. These dysfunctions constitute as great a threat for the financial markets themselves as for the wider society. This has generated external critiques from the market and the civic worlds, as well as internal critiques stemming from the connexionist world itself.

---

to perpetuate these collaborations over a lengthy period seems characteristic of markets where the absence of product standardization maintains ambiguities. Promoters of these products have to tackle these ambiguities throughout the market lifetime.

Table 8.1. Principal differences between the market and the connexionist world

	Market world	Connexionist world OTC markets
Time	• Isolated transactions • Brief encounters between sellers and buyers	• Long-term transactions • Long-term cooperation between sellers and buyers
Transparency	• Transparency as the ideal to pursue	• Opacity surrounding the sums concerned and the price of transactions
Agents	• Anonymity • Atomicity • Great number of agents	• Open network, only knowable from one agent to the next • Deterritorialization
Product	• Objective definition • Homogeneity	• Tailor-made solutions

External and internal critiques of OTC markets

Given the deep instability of the international financial system, and more recently the jolt of the financial crisis, the discrepancy between the 'market order' value system promoted by financial actors and the very reality of its functioning is revealed. The disjuncture between discourse and action opens up the space for critique on the part of the actors involved in the system. As Boltanski notes (2009: 29), it became apparent that the order referred to in the discourse of agents of OTC markets did not 'conform in fact to the values which have been adopted in principle'. For example, the highly mobile and immediately negotiable character of sophisticated derivative products, which are likely to be sold on as soon as they have been launched, is seen as favouring opportunism and, in a purely speculative logic, as creating major financial crises.

From a market order viewpoint, this situation can be considered as a market failure, where financial institutions have been able to make massive profits in a context where the conditions for free competition were not met. Not operating in a proper market, they can be seen to have failed the 'test' of the market order of worth. It thus appears that the connexionist logic might give rise to a form of specific dysfunction, where opportunism founded on the ability to take advantage of information asymmetries can destabilize markets and threaten their very existence. This makes it clear that fostering market activity does not guarantee in itself the efficiency of the financial system. Through the financial innovation of credit derivatives, for example, banks transferred risks towards investors who, on the whole, trusted the optimistic opinions of credit rating agencies. When the issued securities proved to be toxic, an extraordinary breakdown of confidence followed, resulting in a brutal drying up of the market and general collapse. The almost total disappearance of entire segments of the market, like collateralized debt obligations (CDOs), threatened the survival of markets characterized by opaque transactions centred on very ambiguous products (Huault and Rainelli, 2009).

From a civic order perspective, the race to innovate in OTC derivatives provokes strong criticism (Arnoldi, 2004; LiPuma and Lee, 2004, 2005; Maurer, 2002; Pryke and Allen, 2000), with derivatives accused of radically transforming capitalism and increasing unlimited competition everywhere (Bryan and Rafferty, 2006). Bryan and Rafferty in particular see the continual invention of derivative products as an unprecedented way of linking markets, making it possible to compare and contrast formerly disparate and hetero-geneous securities, leading to a *commodified nightmare* (Fourcade and Healy, 2007). Some worry about the neo-capitalism thus created, which is by nature essentially financial and speculative, free-floating in relation to the real econ-omy. Neo-capitalism takes advantage of the mobility of capital, preferring immediate maximum profit through ever more sophisticated financial innov-ations. It has the know-how to profit from the worldwide networking of the financial world by placing resources in competitive situations, and to impose itself as a hyperpower to the detriment of industries and states. Because of the recurrence, violence, and spillovers of recent financial crises, the notions of the common good, general interest, and responsibility come to front-stage. The crisis leads to a focus on the inequalities that emerge and on the destabil-izing effects of the power of finance that impact state budgets and, through this, the provision of goods more generally. This is all the more the case as big banks had to ask for government rescue, which weakens their position when trying to protect their interest vis-à-vis regulatory reforms in progress (see e.g. the debate about the Dodd Frank Act in the United States and a new version of the MiFID[8] in Europe).

In terms of internal critics, the network mechanisms are seen as encour-aging the development of a form of exploitation specific to the connexionist logic, 'where the success and strength of some actors are *in fact* attributable, at least in part, to the intervention of others whose activity is neither acknow-ledged nor valued' (Boltanski and Chiapello, 2005: 360). In the connexionist world, this exploitation is rooted in the mobile/immobile differential, the dominant taking advantage of the immobility of the dominated, 'which is the source of their poverty' (Boltanski and Chiapello, 2005: 363). From this point of view, the distribution of jobs between front and back office in big investment banks reveals the power that flexible and very innovative individuals have over those who are immobile. Thus, the social capital that employees in the front office enjoy, their technical knowledge, their ability to innovate continuously, and the prestige of their position give them the status

---

[8] Market in Financial Instruments Directive.

of 'worthy' players in the connexionist world, allowing them to impose their own logic and game rules. Conversely, back-office employees give support and back up work in an environment where routine and ordinary tasks are the order of the day, rather than innovation and the making of extraordinary profits. Innovators have the capacity to strike up relationships, enter networks, engage in winning transactions, and play on the ambivalence of accounting, risk-taking, and moral frameworks. The counterpart to this is the immobility of back-office employees, who are not paid a great deal and who get little respect for their tasks of control, registration, and compensation (Godechot, 2006). By remaining *in situ*, little people secure the presence of the strong. Traders on OTC markets incarnate this logic perfectly. They are flexible, mobile, and likely to defect if dissatisfied, threatening to accept golden handshake packages and move to competing institutions, taking their skills, market share, or client portfolios with them—in other words, a sum of resources that is greater than the resources linked to their own personal productivity (Godechot, 2006). It is the threat to move that leads senior management to provide more and more generous packages of returns, increasing the inequality between those who are part of these projects and networks and those who are outside of them. Overall, the good fortune of the one side depends on the misfortune of the others, immobile people contributing to the value-creating process without being recognized as they should be (Boltanski and Chiapello, 2005: 360–1).

The connexionist logic specificity is inherent to its foundation on open networks, marked by geographical distances between agents for whom interpersonal links are replaced by hypermobility and fluidity (Knorr Cetina and Bruegger, 2002), all of which act as facilitators of opportunism. As Bauman pointed out (2005), those who benefit from the system need freedom of movement, non-commitment, and liquidity, unlike those whose feet are firmly on the ground (see also Clegg and Baumeler, 2010).

The specific talent of the connexionist world to disarm the critique

However strong the criticism, the connexionist logic seems to have a specific ability to disarm it and avoid responding to it. We argue this ability relies not only on strong deterritorialization, which makes accountability ineffective, but also on the extreme technicality of financial products, which makes external control and public debate difficult.

Firstly, as Boltanski and Chiapello (1999/2005) underline, it seems that the 'ontology of the network has been largely established in such a way to liberate human beings from the constraints of justification (...) The network is presented as a plane of immanence—to use Gilles Deleuze's expression (...). This dispenses with the loops of reflexivity that take the form of moral judgement'

(Boltanski and Chiapello, 1999/2005: 106–7). It is therefore tricky to identify references to justice specific to the connexionist logic, which is characterized by constant deterritorialization, where very mobile individuals have a disinclination for accountability. As the network is open, it continuously modifies itself, making it difficult to determine where participants are. 'Fairness' in the distribution of status, according to people's contributions, presupposes closing the list of relevant parties at any given moment. In a completely networked world, no such closure is possible. The network is continually extended and altered, with the result that 'there exists no opposite principles for finalizing at a given point in time, the list of those between whom scales of justice may be established' (Boltanski and Chiapello, 1999/2005: 106). For example, there is no equivalent here to the solutions for opportunism formulated by Abolafia (1996) who studied Wall Street markets ethnographically in the early 1980s and 1990s. Any recourse to domestic logic—relying on group culture, trust, strength of community norms, fear of reprisals—seems to have become inoperable on modern financial markets because the network remains open and individuals are constantly on the move. The networked world belongs to an ephemeral aggregate of experiences and interests, not to a charter of rights and obligations (Castells, 2000: 264) and the situation provides little hope for improvement. Any attempt to fix a position in the network according to a cultural code would condemn the network to obsolescence: it would become too rigid and disappear.

Regarding 'voices' stemming from other worlds—and particularly the civic world—their difficulties arise from permanent displacements in capitalism, dismantling the critique that struggles to make sense of all these transformations (Boltanski and Chiapello, 1999/2005). The creation of permanently innovative derivative products renders accounting frameworks and control procedures ineffective, even before they can be used (Boltanski and Chiapello, 1999/2005: 509). Extreme mobility and continuous innovation destabilize the critique, which is prey to great inertia, deeply disoriented and disarmed when it comes to stabilizing forms of justice. Normalization and control are institutionalized and codified and as such are characterized by deep immobility, which immediately disqualifies them when they are faced with the permanent evolution and sophistication of the activities they are supposed to regulate. Thus, the moral constraints and internal rules intended to limit the movements of members in the front office have little effect on traders who play on the ambiguities of products and markets. Innovators are miles ahead of their immobile colleagues, who remain in fear of being disconnected, are out of the game, and have been abandoned by their more mobile colleagues (Boltanski and Chiapello, 1999/2005). All in all, the mechanisms for controlling opportunism are fatally weakened because of their status as 'unworthy' players in the connexionist world.

Besides, the hyper-instrumentalization and the ultra-technicality of the products financial actors invent give them the opportunity to set game rules that only they understand. This complexity prevents external actors, from other worlds, intervening, criticizing, and debating. The increasing technicality of derivative products pushes the financially uninitiated further and further from any democratic decision-making. As Boltanski said (2009: 200), 'the often technical character of statements and the measures taken makes it difficult or even useless to transmit them to the public at large'. This sophistication, intended to create pockets of profit, disarms critics in that it relates to an unquestionable technical reality. Financial structures become the exclusive preserve of experts who base their legitimacy on the authority of science, models, and technology. No public debate is possible in a context where the social world is foreclosed and neutralized by hyper-instrumentalization.

Connexionist markets and the civic world: urge to compromise or capacity to maintain the conditions for domination?

The situation we depict raises one question: What values can be promoted and what practices deployed to bring out a sense of justice in the financial system? One of the ways in which this could be done would be by building the projective city, that is to say, by formulating principles of fairness adjusted to the logic of the real functioning of the financial world. Another way would be to resolve discord with the market and the civic world through coercion.

Forms of justice in the connexionist world: building the projective city?

To counteract loss of trust, which might threaten the very existence of the networked market, some degree of long-term commitment and reciprocal control is required. This might provide foundations for the building of a 'projective city' (Boltanski and Chiapello, 1999/2005). The project constrains the network to submit itself to a form of justice (Boltanski and Chiapello, 1999/2005: 107) in at least one direction: the redistribution of connections and sharing of information, which will allow network extension and so benefit everybody.

Concrete devices are needed to make this principle enforceable. One of these is a mechanism of identification and traceability of people and products. In the case of financial markets, this supposes the existence or setting up of supranational bodies. The extraterritorial space towards which the capital markets have tended puts them out of the reach of the nation-states, which up to now were the only ones capable of supervising them (Bauman, 2005: 190). The reform of OTC markets demands the presence of powerful public agents on a worldwide scale and a true supranational coordination to build a new form of legal structure. Some authors see the drawing up of an official legal status as a way of restraining the different forms of exploitation carried out by networks (Boltanski and Chiapello, 1999/2005: 383). The creation of new laws for hybrid forms, like the great interbank networks, could generate special norms for protection specific to the network, with the setting up of supranational balancing powers that would have legal means of control. This proposition could take the form of state-run independent centres, of a 'super-intendent' or institutions for arbitration whose mandate would be to preserve the common good (Boltanski and Chiapello, 1999/2005: 304–84). The network would need to be included in the legal world, 'to define the role and responsibilities of the constituent units, to establish the rules by which they conduct their transactions and to resolve their disputes' (Boltanski and Chiapello, 1999/2005: 384).

Yet, if we look closely at current developments in the international financial system, it does not seem that agents are resolutely committing to this path of action. Nor does it seem that states have succeeded in convincing them of the need for such arrangements. It seems there is little chance that the connexionist world will self-regulate spontaneously or lend itself to this kind of regulation, a position that will lead unavoidably to a much more confrontational way of handling the discord with the market and the civic worlds, as the proposed reforms on both sides of the Atlantic suggest.

Solving the dispute through coercion?

A first solution would be to turn to the market world, and to impose its logic onto the connexionist sphere. The idea here is to combat the imperfections inherent in OTC markets by bringing in more standardization. The recent reforms sketched in the Dodd Frank Act for the United States and in the MiFID2 for Europe consist in favouring the displacement of as many OTC transactions as possible onto organized markets. The higher principles of the market world—competition and transparency—are indeed seen by most regulators as weapons with which to tackle the dysfunctions related to connexionism. For example, the proposal to move the trading of OTC derivatives onto exchanges or electronic platforms and to set up clearing houses reflects the desire to combat the opacity and bilateralism of OTC contracts. Clearing houses, in particular, incarnate the will to reduce the ability of certain actors to capture 'super-profits' and to reduce risks by making hedging and collateral more prominent and more significant. According to Morgan (2010: 16), the main parties in favour 'argued that the OTC markets had become highly complex and what was needed was a mechanism whereby trades between parties could be netted out so that the real exposure (and therefore the real risks being held) would be visible'. The challenge could be to encourage standardized markets by establishing trading platforms equipped with clearing houses that would be effectively regulated and supervised.

The efforts made by various governments to save the world's financial system seemed at first to subscribe to this way of thinking: their main aim was to fight the crisis in market liquidity, in particular that of the credit derivatives market and the subprimes. The notion of liquidity is a reflection of the idea of the perfect market, with no asymmetries of information and opportunism. Carruthers and Stinchombe (1999: 353) base their analysis on the definition of economists: 'By liquidity of a market, economists mean that standardised products can be bought and sold continuously at a price that everyone in the market can know, and that products are not normally sold at a price that diverges substantially from the market price. The idea is that every-one can know at all times what the price is, and only one price obtains in the market. Liquidity, like efficiency, is considered one of the great virtues of perfectly competitive markets.' Liquidity is the sign of an efficient market, peopled with numerous investors and buyers who are in a position to exchange their stocks at transparent prices. In financial theory, they describe market offers as the ability to sell stocks easily, with no institutional interven-tion, in a laissez-faire context. 'Liquid markets being good, unliquid markets are bad' (Langley, 2009: 12).

However, to work in this way, financial markets need different types of specific guarantee (Graham and Richardson, 1997; Picciotto and Mayne, 1999; Sassen, 2005: 31) and an enormous amount of work from governments. Carruthers and Stinchcombe (1999) point out their reliance on the reduction of transaction costs and the standardization of securities to enable liquidity. In this logic, which is far removed from laissez-faire, as Foucault notes (2004: 124), state action encourages competition.

But what becomes of this quest for transparency and competition if we accept that the very particular nature of OTC financial markets, driven by permanent innovation, makes it difficult if not impossible for them to func-tion according to Walrasian criteria? If we accept our hypothesis that OTC markets are not a transitory form of modern financial markets, they do not seem destined to join the ranks of the most transparent and competitive. They seem to belong to a different species of organized markets, a different logic, a different value system and to respond to specific problems. The recourse to the principles of the market world presupposes a transformation of OTC markets so radical that it is highly unlikely it would ever happen. Some financial operators within ISDA already struggle against current attempts at reform because their ultimate interests (in terms of profitability) do not lie in greater transparency, increased standardization, or a total removal of ambiguity. The chief lobbyist of the ISDA, for example, judges that excessive standardization might encourage speculation, and it does not really contribute anything, while custom-made products answer the needs of enterprises and investors. To wit, opponents to the reforms have developed a conceptual line of reasoning showing that the traditionally desired feature of exchanges such as product standardization, liquidity, or price transparency are unwanted on up-to-now OTC markets.

The limits of the power of the market world to help remedy the dysfunctions of connexionist logic have been well identified by Boltanski and Chiapello (1999/2005). 'Connexionist opportunism cannot, for one thing, be checked by the commercial city (...). Part of the interest of connections stems in fact from the inspection of resources that were not regarded as commodifiable or amenable to contracts (...). It is this incompleteness that explains the relative inoperability of the constraints that the commercial order rests on' (1999/2005: 378).

Faced with this difficulty, another solution could be to solve the discord between the connexionist and the civic worlds, in the very heart of the civic city. It would then take the form of a more radical restructuring of the financial system, based on sanctions. As Bauman (2005: 195) stated, 'the journeying of economic initiatives to every corner of the planet would not be extravagant nor would they be guided only by temporary profit with no heed paid to collateral victims'. Partitioning off financial markets might hold back the destructive effects of generalized connexionism (Orléan, 2008: 40): the disconnection that follows might prevent savings banks from intervening on financial markets and taking risks with the money of small savers. Partitioning and legal barriers effectively raise the costs of doing deals, and create additional expense for those managing to overcome these obstacles.

There are some who recommend a much more drastic limit to the risks taken by banks, forbidding the most toxic of financial innovations such as derivative products, 'because these markets and these products are based on the principle of an incredible accumulation of counterpart risks' (Lordon, 2008: 179).

Finally, financial innovations, which are the motor of modern finance, lead to the formation of ultra-technical markets where only the inventors really understand the rules of the game. Getting beyond this stage of extreme technicality would be a means of containing the 'domination regime' based on the increasing value of change (Boltanski, 2009: 203) and the exploitation of innovations. One aspect to be addressed urgently would be how to put a brake on 'the uncontrollable dynamic of financial innovation, which multiplies products of an incredible complexity and where it is impossible to measure the risk' (Lordon, 2008: 171), so that the fight against hyper-instrumentalization denounced by Thrift (2006: 298) can preserve the common good and the affirmation of the civic world.

Overall, the question remains as to whether the connexionist logic of OTC markets is currently committed in trying to solve the discord with the civic world. Does it not aim on the contrary at escaping from the constraints of justification in a pure regime of domination, where domination refers to a capacity to 'restrict critical space or what ultimately amounts to the same, to deprive criticism of any leverage on reality' (Boltanski, 2009: 176)?

Conclusion

In our analysis, we have tried to lift the veil on the singular nature of modern financial markets. Our analysis in connexionist terms has allowed us to reconsider the challenges posed by the financial system and to identify the dysfunctions whose underlying mechanisms were hitherto difficult to perceive. We have shown that the permanent innovation that drives the financial worlds allows dominant agents to create profitable instruments and to capture a large part of the value produced. Their opportunism is difficult to contain in the open, globalized networks where the usual regulations (Abolafia, 1996) and normalization are considerably weakened. The structural dualism we have highlighted between those who draw up the norms—the immobile or 'small' players, unworthy persons in the connexionist world—and those who play on the ambiguity move around and get around the rules, condemns control devices to uselessness. To this difficulty must be added the absence of product traceability and increasing sophistication, which makes the chain of responsibility more and more diffuse in opaque networks. Overall, our analysis emphasizes the specific ability of the connexionist world to disarm the critique. By exposing the dysfunctions created by the connexionist logic, we have finally been able to suggest some paths for thought and action to tackle these problems. Should we build a 'projective city' by rethinking, for example, international regulation and building new laws? Current developments lead us to doubt that there will be enough awakening of conscience among the actors in the connexionist world to perform this solution which would require their being able to spontaneously commit into the structuring of the novel regulation. Should we return, in a somewhat coercive manner, to the 'market world', despite the cost of raising a radical contradiction to the intrinsic dynamics of modern financial markets—and is this way practicable? Our analysis shows that there are reasons to doubt.

A last solution remains, which amounts to resolving disputes in the heart of the civic world by encouraging the partitioning of financial markets, banning certain products, and promoting desophistication (Lordon, 2008). Indeed, the growing complexity of modern financial products blocks out reality and stifles the emergence of a public debate. It seems then important to reject the appropriation that expert knowledge implies (Rancière, 1998). In this context, Castells speaks of developing a society based on values rather than the technico-economic deployment that characterizes the domination of a networked society. Repoliticizing the world of finance (De Goede, 2004) would free the civic world from its subordination to experts and allow it to reaffirm itself.

Identifying the connexionist nature of modern financial markets finally appears as a step forward in undermining the notion that more exchanges of more products on financial markets is beneficial overall for society. Grounded in a market-order justificatory logic, this view, which has been widely used to foster the deregulation of the financial industry and the promotion of financial innovation, is substantially weakened by the adoption of a connexionist representation of markets. One temporary conclusion could be that there would be advantages in displacing the burden of the proof of financial innovation advantages or at least harmlessness from regulators to financial innovation promoters. More fundamentally, recognizing the connexionist nature of OTC markets enlightens the ambiguity of the new form of capitalism embodied in OTC markets. The connexionist polity can simultaneously be seen as a justificatory device in charge of legitimating a new world and therefore new forms of inequalities and exploitation *and* as an enterprise aiming at making this new world fairer. The question remains as to its capacity to durably disarm the critique and escape, for the most part, to constraints of justification, as opposed to working out some kind of compromise with the civic world. Part of the answer depends on the strength but also on the relevance of the social critique towards the connexionist polity, to which we hope to have contributed in this chapter.

References

Abolafia, M. (1996) *Making Markets: Opportunism and Restraint on Wall Street*. Cambridge, MA: Harvard University Press.

Arnoldi, J. (2004) 'Derivatives: Virtual Values and Real Risks', *Theory, Culture & Society*, 21, 23–42.

Aspers, P. (2009) 'Knowledge and Valuation in Markets', *Theory and Society*, 38(2), 111–31.

Bauman, Z. (2005) *Liquid Life*. Oxford: Blackwell Publishing.

Beunza, D. and Stark, D. (2005) 'How to Recognize Opportunities: Heterarchical Search in a Trading Room'. In K. Knorr Cetina and A. Preda (eds.), *The Sociology of Financial Markets*. Oxford: Oxford University Press, 84–101.

Boltanski, L. (2009) *De la critique: Précis de sociologie l'émancipation*. Paris: Gallimard.

——Chiapello, E. (2005) *The New Spirit of Capitalism*. London: Verso (originally 1999, *Le nouvel esprit du capitalisme*. Paris: Gallimard).

——Thévenot, L. (2006) *On Justification: Economies of Worth*. Princeton, NJ: Princeton University Press (originally 1991, *De la justification, Les économies de la grandeur*. Paris: Gallimard).

Bryan, D. and Rafferty, M. (2006) *Capitalism with Derivatives: A Political Economy of Financial Derivatives*. Basingstoke: Palgrave Macmillan.

Carruthers, B. and Stinchcombe, A. (1999) 'The Social Structure of Liquidity: Flexibility, Markets and States', *Theory and Society*, 28, 353–82.

Castells, M. (2000) *The Rise of the Network Society. The Information Age: Economy, Society and Culture Vol. I* (2nd edn.). Oxford: Blackwell.

Clegg, S. and Baumeler, C. (2010) 'From Iron Cages to Liquid Modernity in Organization Analysis', *Organization Studies*, December, 31(12), 1713–33.

De Goede, M. (2004) 'Repoliticizing Financial Risk', *Economy and Society*, 33, 197–217.

Engelen, E., Erturk, I., Froud, J., Leaver, A., and Williams, K. (2010) 'Reconceptualizing Financial Innovation: Frame, Conjuncture and Bricolage', *Economy And Society*, 39(1), 33–63.

Fama, E. F. (1970) 'Efficient Capital Markets: A Review of Theory and Empirical Work', *Journal of Finance*, 25, 383–417.

——(1991) 'Efficient Capital Markets: II', *Journal of Finance*, 46, 1575–617.

Foucault, M. (2004) *Naissance de la biopolitique*. Paris: Gallimard.

Fourcade, M. and Healy, K. (2007) 'Moral Views of Market Society', *Annual Review of Sociology*, 33, 285–311.

Girard, M. and Stark, D. (2002) 'Distributing Intelligence and Organizing Diversity in New Media Projects', *Environment and Planning, A*, 34(11): 1927–49.

Godechot, O. (2006) 'Hold-up en finance: Les conditions de possibilité des bonus élevés dans l'industrie financière', *Revue française de sociologie*, 47, 341–71.

——(2007) *Working rich: Salaires, bonus et appropriation du profit dans l'industrie financière*. Paris: La Découverte.

Graham, E. and Richardson, J. D. (1997) *Global Competition Policy*. Washington, DC: Institute for International Economics.

Huault, I. and Rainelli, H. (2009) 'Market Shaping as an Answer to Ambiguities: The Case of Credit Derivatives', *Organization Studies*, 30, 549–75.

Knight, F. (1921) *Risk, Uncertainty and Profit*. New York: Houghton Mifflin.

Knorr Cetina, K. and Bruegger, U. (2002) 'The Virtual Societies of Financial Markets', *American Journal of Sociology*, 107, 905–51.

Kogut, B. and Zander, U. (1992) 'Knowledge of the Firm: Combinative Capabilities and the Replication of Technology', *Organization Science*, 3(3): 383–98.

Langley, P. (2009) 'The Performance of Liquidity in the Sub-Prime Mortgage Crisis'. In *Proceedings of Securitisation, Risk and Governance Conference*, City University London, 6–7 May.

Lepinay, V. A. (2007) 'Decoding Finance: Articulation and Liquidity Around a Trading Room'. In D. MacKenzie, F. Muniesa, and L. Siu (eds.), *Do Economists Make Markets?* Princeton, NJ: Princeton University Press.

LiPuma, E. and Lee, B. (2004) *Financial Derivatives and the Globalization of Risk*. Durham, NC: Public Planet Books, Duke University Press.

——(2005) 'Financial Derivatives and the Rise of Circulation', *Economy and Sociology*, 34, 404–27.

Lordon, F. (2008) *Jusqu'à quand? Pour en finir avec les crises financières*. Paris: Raisons d'Agir.

MacKenzie, D. (2008) 'Hedge Funds', *Essay for London Review of Books*, 30(23), 9–12 November.

——Millo, Y. (2003) 'Constructing a Market, Performing Theory: The Historical Sociology of a Financial Derivatives Exchange', *American Journal of Sociology*, 109, 107–45.

Maurer, B. (2002) 'Repressed Futures: Financial Derivatives' Theological Unconscious', *Economy and Society*, 3, 15–36.

Millo, Y. and MacKenzie, D. (2009) 'The Usefulness of Inaccurate Models: Towards an Understanding of the Emergence of Financial Risk Management', *Accounting, Organization and Society*, 34(5), 638–53.

Morgan, G. (2008) 'Market Formation and Governance in International Financial Markets: The Case of OTC Derivatives', *Human Relations*, 61, 637–60.

——(2010) 'Legitimacy in Financial Markets: Credit Default Swaps in the Current Crisis', *Socio-Economic Review*, 8(1), 17–45.

Orléan, A. (2008) 'Au-delà de la transparence de l'information, contrôler la liquidité', *Esprit*, 11, November, 38–42.

Picciotto, S. and Mayne, R. (1999) *Regulating International Business: Beyond Liberalization*. Basingstoke: Macmillan.

Pryke, M. and Allen, J. (2000) 'Monetized Time-Space: Derivatives—Money's "New Imaginary"?' *Economy and Society*, 29, 264–84.

Rancière, J. (1998) *Aux bords du politique*. Paris: La Fabrique.

Sassen, S. (2001) *The Global City: New York, London, Tokyo*. Princeton, NJ: Princeton University Press.

——(2005) 'The Embeddedness of Electronic Markets: The Case of Global Capital Markets'. In K. Knorr Cetina and A. Preda (eds.), *The Sociology of Financial Markets*. Oxford: Oxford University Press, 17–38.

Stark, D. (1996) 'Recombinant Property in EastEuropean Capitalism', *American Journal of Sociology*, 101, 993–1027.

——(2000) 'For a Sociology of Worth'. Paper presented at the workshop on *Heterarchy: Distributed Intelligence and the Organization of Diversity*, Santa Fe Institute, October.

——(2009) *The Sense of Dissonance: Accounts of Worth in Economic Life*. Princeton, NJ: Princeton University Press.

Thrift, N. (1997) 'The Rise of Soft Capitalism', *Cultural Values*, 1(1), 29–57.

——(2006) 'Re-inventing Invention: New Tendencies in Capitalist Commodification', *Economy and Society*, 35, 279–306.

White, H. (1992) *Identity and Control: A Structural Theory of Social Action*. Princeton, NJ: Princeton University Press.

9

The Distinctiveness of Nordic Welfare States in the Transformation to the Projective City and the New Spirits of Capitalism[1]

Peer Hull Kristensen

Introduction

The transition to experimentalist economies, and new forms of work organization, has, in many of the advanced industrial societies been painful for most social classes. In the United States, for example, it has led to a growing inequality in which the ever-expanding number of new projects offers those in the financial sector (or closely connected to it, such as lawyers and accountants) and participants in high-tech industries great opportunities for high income and wealth gains. On the other hand, it has meant stagnating incomes for most lower middle-class families and factory workers, together with a growing pool of migrant workers, often illegal, who are poorly paid for long and arduous hours of work in the service sector and agriculture (Reich, 1991).

In contrast to many analyses but consistent with their general approach, Boltanski and Chiapello (2005) seek to understand how these new patterns of work and inequality are constructed, justified, and changed in response to critique. In their view, the most recent period of capitalism involves a shift from bureaucratized and Taylorized modes of working into a system based on projects and networks. They focus in particular on the relationship between

[1] This chapter builds on parts of the first chapter in Kristensen and Lilja (2011). I am grateful to Oxford University Press for allowing me to make use of the material for this purpose, to the colleagues from whose comments I benefited (especially Marko Jaklic, Kari Lilja, Glenn Morgan, Eli Moen, Charles Sabel, and Jonathan Zeitlin) and for the research grant from the Danish Social Science Research Council, the EU FP7 Translearn project, and the SONIC World Class Initiative at CBS that made it possible.

mobility within networks and the way in which this relates to the ability to access and extract value in terms of high salaries and other rewards. They argue that the level and depth of inequality which appears to be associated with this has to be seen in terms of politics and power, not as an inevitability. It is this idea that motivates this chapter.

The chapter consists of, firstly, a brief discussion of Boltanski and Chiapello's framework and in particular their analysis of the 'projective city'. The second section provides a discussion of how the welfare state impacts on the form that the projective city takes in different contexts and focuses in particular on welfare states in the Nordic countries. It relates the development of active labour markets to the analysis of the projective city. The final section shows how in the Nordic countries compared to elsewhere this contributes to a broader more negotiated form of economy in which the positive aspects of mobility and the projective city are delivered and the more negative consequences in terms of inequality are reduced in significance.

The projective city

Boltanski and Chiapello (2005) see the emergence of the 'projective city' as one that puts a premium on those who are highly mobile in networks. Projects and networks consist of temporary relationships in which expertise is brought together to create new value for ever more demanding consumers. It reflects an economy in which the application of knowledge and skills to old and new problems becomes the key to growth. Extending market share requires innovation, novelty, finding new products, and launching them quickly into price-sensitive markets. Bureaucratic, Fordist models of organization are too inflexible to compete in this environment. The emphasis shifts to smaller, more flexible forms of work organization where skills and knowledge circulate rapidly around networks searching for appropriate projects in which to invest time and energy.

What Boltanski and Chiapello term the 'projective city' is therefore characterized by high levels of mobility and movement across economic and geographical spaces, between firms as well as between and within networks. The 'projective city' promises fulfilment for the individual in terms of the application of brain power to exciting new frontiers of innovation and change. It offers the opportunity to participate in new ventures where not only risk and uncertainty are high but also rewards, both financial and psychological, can be high. Participating in this world, being a valued player in this game, requires not only that the individual possesses skills and knowledge but also that the individual participates in various sorts of networks that transmit information about opportunities, reputations, and rewards for moving around this system. Participating in one project gives rise to the possibility of admission into a new one. Projects become extensions of the self; this form of capitalism 'invades' the self more directly than Fordism. It puts pressure on the individual to identify strongly with work as a creative outlet, as an 'authentic' expression of the self. This level of commitment spills over into questions about the degree to which family and other social relationships can be maintained in the face of such demands from the workplace.

In Boltanski and Chiapello's schema, drawing on Boltanski and Thévenot (1991), forms of capitalism require systems of justification that exist not just as ideologies, that is, sets of values that lack material anchoring, but as what they term 'tests'. So the projective city justifies itself in terms of the ability of individuals to realize their potential and engage in meaningful work through the use of their skills and knowledge. The 'test' for any particular society is whether this is what actually happens.

As Boltanski and Chiapello show in relation to French society, the projective city favours certain mobile elites of French society; these are the ones who have the chance to develop the skills and knowledge and the networks. Many other members of French society are left out of this often because they are bound to a single place and lack such networks, for example, because of age, spatial location, educational attainment, and family circumstance. They also are more likely either to possess few or no skills or to possess the sort of skills that are limited in their value to traditional manufacturing occupations which are in turn a declining part of the economy. Thus, French society fails the test—the vision of the new capitalism may be strong but it is not open to all. Many are excluded outright from entering the projective city. Instead, they are exploited by the new economy, as the jobs for which they can apply are generally low paid, unstable, and unrewarding. This creates a dualism in which core jobs are well paid with good work conditions, high welfare benefits, and security, whilst there is an ever-growing secondary labour market composed of part-time, temporary workers with insecure employment, low wages, and poor welfare benefits (Palier and Thelen, 2010). Boltanski and Chiapello are keen to emphasize that those benefiting from the projective city can only do so because they can call on the cheap labour of the immobile—to provide them with services, for example, in the domestic and state spheres, looking after and educating children or taking care of elderly relatives; in the market sphere by the provision of cheap personal services, etc. Therefore, this is not dualism in the sense of two disconnected parts of a society. Rather, in the terms of Boltanski and Chiapello, in some societies networkers, the immobile, and the excluded may co-create a complementary dynamic between 'great men' and 'small people': The 'small people' 'are exploited in the sense that the role they play as a factor in production does not receive the acknowledgement it merits; and that their contribution to the creation of value added is not remunerated at the requisite level for its distribution to be deemed fair' (2005: 363).

Mobility in Boltanski and Chiapello's universe is foremost a question of being able to move among projects—physically or mentally. It is a question of not being tied to existing routines, loyalties, habits of life, or possessions of property. But seen from this perspective, most people from 'humble stations' (Smith, 1969) do indeed seem quite immobile. They are simultaneously inscribed within a narrow or low education, tied to family obligations—both children and parents—dependent for the little they have achieved in terms of incomes on loyalty to a single employer, and risk a lot if they neglect their space-bound obligations.

On the other hand, if we imagine a family, in which both husband and wife want to live a mobile working life, engaging themselves in shifting projects with shifting working hours, where they temporarily have to be away from their house, their children, and their normal jobs, taking new courses or new educations, perhaps going abroad to set up a new plant or join an international project team, the challenge seems clear. Everything else being equal, such a working life seems possible only for people with incomes high enough to pay for the services of others, who can help them look after children, parents, garden, etc. For that reason, it seems very difficult, in France as well as in the United States, to transform from the ranks of the immobile to the ranks of the mobile.

Welfare states and the projective city

The question is whether this degree of inequality has to be the outcome of the transition towards the 'projective city' model of capitalism. Can the welfare state, using this term in its broadest sense to include state provision of services in the fields of education, labour markets, health, and social care, make a difference? Could it be that particular forms of welfare state enable firms and employees on a broader scale to engage in the mobile life of learning organizations and the projective city? The answer in this chapter is that there are some societies that may be said to pass this test or at least get closer to passing this test than others. In this section of the chapter, the way in which the welfare state has been modified in the Nordic countries is discussed as an example of how actors can transform institutions in order to make the 'projective city' more than just failed rhetoric.

Certainly, it appears that at the level of work organization, the degree of transition from more Fordist models towards more networked models differs across countries as might be expected from the findings of the societal effects school (Maurice et al., 1986). Whereas Anglophone countries have developed lean types of organizations, many continental European countries have been content to preserve existing organizational forms, while the Nordic welfare states have developed towards 'learning organizations' (Lorenz and Valeyre, 2003: 13). The findings of the Third Working Condition Survey from Eurofound reported that in Denmark, for example, 60 per cent of those surveyed said that they worked in learning organizations, whilst the number was only 38 per cent for France and 44.3 per cent for Germany—and extremely low for Portugal (26.1 per cent) and Greece (18.7 per cent). This picture was repeated in the Fourth European Working Condition Survey (European Foundation for the Improvement of Living and Working Conditions, 2007: 60), which grouped all the Nordic countries as having active working organizations with high degrees of employee autonomy, where employees both engage in using own ideas and face a steady stream of learning challenges from the organization. Detailed case studies of firms representing such organizational forms in Denmark (see Kristensen and Lotz, 2011; Kristensen et al., 2011) showed that firms in manufacturing themselves were spaces for mobility as employees moved between operative, ad hoc developmental and monitoring teams. Employees were in direct contact with customers and suppliers, while also being highly mobile on the external market. In many ways, this seems to suggest that in the Nordic countries much broader sections of the workforce have made the transition to become mobile. In doing so, the proportion of the population left immobile is much less than in other societies and the gap between the two is reduced, leading to more egalitarian outcomes.

Many observers have held the view that high taxes and income redistribution explain why the Nordic countries are more egalitarian than other societies. This might have been the explanation in the past, but the argument here is that today this egalitarianism may be much more related to features that enable a higher proportion of the population to become mobile citizens of the 'projective city' and to reduce the numbers that are immobile, with consequent effects on the overall economic competitiveness of the society.

André Sapir (2005) suggests that the Nordic model combines high efficiency (because it provides sufficient incentive to work and therefore relative high employment rates) with high equity (as the risk of poverty is relatively low). The Nordic model shares high efficiency with the Anglo-Saxon model, which is, however, low on equity. It shares high equity with the continental (European) model, which is, however, low on efficiency. The Mediterranean model is low on both equity and efficiency. Efficiency in employment rates seems to be easier to achieve by unemployment insurance (as in the Nordic countries) than by employment protection legislation (as in the continental and Mediterranean countries). According to Sapir, redistribution (via taxes and transfers) can explain equity and the avoidance of poverty risk only to a limited extent. However, 'the correlation coefficient between the index of poverty and the measure of educational attainment' is very significant. 'The proportion of the population aged 25–64 with at least upper secondary education is highest in the Nordic (75 per cent of a cohort) and Continental (67 per cent) countries and lowest in Anglo-Saxon (60 per cent) and Mediterranean (39 per cent) countries, a ranking that matches perfectly the position of country groups in terms of poverty risk' (Sapir, 2005: 8).[2] Perhaps, there is no guarantee that education gives access to the projective city, but it seems quite evident that it provides individuals with an armoury to become more flexible and to obtain access to the means that make it possible to redefine one's role more easily.

Hacker (2006) offers another clue to the difference. In his detailed discussion of retrenchment in American welfare, he shows that such retrenchment has not taken place simply by cutting existing benefits. Rather, it has come about in the United States because of an increase in risks derived from globalization and changed family structures and the shouldering of those risks primarily by individuals and their families with little sharing of the risks with firms or the state. State and political actors have abstained from recalibrating social programmes to this new risk profile. Hacker summarizes the new risks and their consequences for American society in this way:

> The constellation of risk that citizens face has changed significantly in the past three decades due to linked changes in work and family (Esping-Andersen, 1999; Skocpol, 2000). In the employment sector, the shifts include rising levels of earning inequality, growing instability of income over time, increased employment in services and in part-time and contingent work, and increased structural (rather than cyclical) unemployment. In the realm of family relations, the changes include rising rates of divorce and separation, declining fertility (a root cause of population ageing), and the increasing prevalence of lone parent, female-headed families. Connecting the two domains is perhaps the most fundamental shift in the worlds of work and family—the dramatic movement of women into paid employment. (2006: 20)

Increasing inequality and a tripling of instability (between 1970 and 1990) of incomes follow in the wake of these new social risks in the United States. Framed in the language of Boltanski and Chiapello, many try or are forced to be mobile in the American economy, but fail and are faced temporarily or permanently with drops in family incomes. In such a system, the threat of ending up in poverty, divorce, and social exclusion is huge—at least for the lower strata.

However, the American or French outcome (see Boltanski and Chiapello, 2007: xxxv–xxxvii) is not unavoidable. In principle, US social policy could have

---

[2] In the Nordic countries, less than 10 per cent (and for Norway only 5 per cent) leave school without a qualification in one or another form, and this is matched by very few other countries (OECD, 2006b).

adapted to changing social realities. As the path-breaking feminist writings on the welfare state show (e.g. Orloff, 1993; Stetson and Mazur, 1995), some nations—most strikingly, the Scandinavian welfare states—have dramatically expanded public protections that help women enter the labour force and balance work and child-rearing. Many of these same nations have also tackled the new realities of the labour market with active employment and training policies (Levy, 1999). Putting aside some modest exceptions, however, the United States did not follow this path (Hacker, 2006: 24–5).

As Wheelock and Mariussen (1997) argue, the core characteristics of welfare states may influence, to a high degree, the dynamics in families and their relationship to the labour market. For instance, in means-tested systems, such as that in the United Kingdom, there might be economic incentives for a male breadwinner becoming unemployed to ask his wife to withdraw from a part-time job in order to obtain the maximum social benefits, while in a universalistic welfare state, where the social benefits follow the individual, an unemployed breadwinner might undertake household work in order for his wife to expand her labour market activities. In the first case, bad luck may be compounded by the form of welfare provision and the poverty trap; in the second, it may be exploited as an offensive opportunity.

What sort of system avoids these consequences of growing inequality between the mobile and the immobile in the projective city? Certainly, Nordic countries appear to differ dramatically from most countries in how they reshaped the welfare system in the 1990s in order to meet the sorts of challenges described and to maintain their broad commitment to organizing capitalism in a more social democratic way than most other countries. In this respect, they have sought to pass the test set by the 'projective city' and to turn it into a reality for a broader proportion of the population than is the case elsewhere.

What are the reasons why the Nordic countries may differ from most other Western countries in the transition phase towards the projective city? First, by offering their citizens much more equal educational opportunities they equip a larger proportion of the population with the educational background for handling risks, shifts, and changes.[3] Second, by sharing these (family and working life) risks with their citizens, the states help citizens to move from one job to another, from one life-phase to another, from a high- to a low-income situation, etc., so that citizens can be continuously more economically active than in other types of societies. Third, by providing social services that make it possible to live a work life where there is unpredictability and risk, for example, about the time that work will take or the mobility requirements

---

[3] This does not imply that they have solved the educational problems. Compared to Finland, Norway and Denmark, and to a lesser degree Sweden, perform poorly in PISA tests.

that work will make or the skills required to participate in new forms of work for both men and women, it becomes easier for individuals and families to take on these risks. This, in turn, means that more people can enter the experimentalist, projective economy.

The institutions that support such risk-sharing and servicing have been reformed and grown in importance, sophistication, and significance with globalization and an increasing participation rate in the labour market in the Nordic countries. In most other social models, we might expect that many risks have become privatized, no longer the responsibility of the state but of the individual and the family. The cost of insuring against such risks for the individual is prohibitive for many; only the richest are able to do so. As a result, differences increase between the included and the excluded, and it is close to impossible to move from being excluded to being included, whereas moving in the other direction (i.e. from being included to being excluded) is a permanent risk in a globally competitive economy.

According to Streeck (2009), the German way of handling these challenges has been very different from that of the Nordic states. In Germany, the federal state has supported the cost of keeping a major part of the population out of employment by subsidizing the social contributions from firms towards its pensioners and its apprentices. This in turn, however, has created a huge divide between the included and excluded, to the detriment of public finance (see also Palier and Thelen, 2010).

The Nordic way, on the other hand, shows that the state can share risks with families in two ways. First, there is the transferring of cash benefits to compensate for lost or missing incomes in times of problems, temporary unemployment, etc., which enables citizens to concentrate on getting a new job by improving their skills and training and not just jumping in to the first job offered because of fear of poverty coming from the state of being unemployed. Second, by providing services the state creates an infrastructure, making it possible for families to live under the hectic pressure resulting from the new forms of work organizations or, if in trouble, help the individual back on their feet. The National Economic and Social Council (NESC, 2005: table 2.4) shows that the great differences between high- and low-performing countries in terms of employment to population ratios are their abilities to engage older people, women, and persons with low levels of education into active employment. Not only are these groups exposed to greater risks than others, but they 'exhibit significant heterogeneity with specific constraints potentially facing—for example—lone parents, people with disabilities, members of ethnic minorities' (ibid.). Building a welfare state that can bring these groups into employment in good jobs, that is, making them part of the projective city, significantly reduces inequality in a society.

In terms of public services, Sweden and Denmark were ranked first and second, respectively, among EU countries in both 1993 and 2001, while Finland moved from third to seventh (ibid.: table 4.1). The generosity of the Nordic countries is particularly significant when it comes to expenditures on disability and unemployment services (where Denmark is the number one spender) (ibid.: table 4.7). But public spending on childcare, probably the most urgent for maintaining a family in the projective city, was also highest in the Nordic countries. As a result of the system of comprehensive public financial support for childcare, enrolment rates for very young children under 3 years of age are around 40 per cent or above in Finland, Norway, and Sweden. Enrolment rates are even higher in Denmark and Iceland. On average, across the OECD (Organisation for Economic Co-operation and Development) countries, 23 per cent of 0–3-year-olds use formal childcare; in Austria, the Czech Republic, Italy, Greece, Germany, Mexico, and Poland, it was less than 10 per cent in 2004 (OECD, 2007a: 135). Child-to-staff ratios in childcare institutions in the Nordic countries are fairly low (lowest in Denmark and highest in Finland) (ibid.) and staff are generally better educated in the Nordic countries (ibid.). In Denmark and Sweden, similar services are provided for out-of-school hours for schoolchildren. In all Nordic countries, the percentage of salary that parents pay for these services is among the lowest of the OECD countries.

The effects of these policies are significant. Fertility rates are comparatively high, 1.77 in Sweden, 1.80 in Denmark and Finland, and 1.84 in Norway, against the OECD average of 1.63. The general participation of women in the labour market is comparatively very high, and extremely high for mothers and sole parents compared to other OECD countries, while child poverty rates are very low (2.4 per cent in Denmark, 3.4 per cent in Finland, and 3.6 per cent in Norway and Sweden) (OECD, 2007a: table 1.1). In 1980, data suggested that fertility rates were lowest in countries with the highest employment rates for women (as expected), but surprisingly, in 2005, OECD (ibid.) found that fertility rates are highest where female employment rates are also the highest. However, without the influence of the Nordic countries on the slope of the curve, this latter relationship could hardly be established.

This is all the more interesting, as the tendency for women to work full time in double-income families is also highest in the Nordic countries (ibid.; Lewis and Plomien, 2009). Yet, there are large differences among the Nordic countries concerning whether those women that take part-time jobs do so voluntarily or because of the need to fit around family care. Whereas approximately 60 per cent of the part-time working women in Finland and Sweden do so for this reason, it is only a little more than 30 per cent in Denmark (OECD 2007a).

Table 9.1. Public spending as percentage of GDP on families and on elderly, 1998[a]

	Public spending on families	Of which services	Public spending on elderly	Of which services
Denmark	3.77	2.23	9.77	2.95
Finland	3.36	1.44	8.53	1.54
Sweden	3.31	1.68	11.17	3.71
United Kingdom	2.22	0.49	10.58	0.81
United States	0.51	0.29	5.20	0.05

[a]Cash amount for a two-earner family with two children as a percentage of GDP.
Source: OECD (2007*b*: 66).

In Norway, the percentage of part-time working women is currently 41 per cent, most of which is involuntary.[4]

This situation does not necessarily mean that Nordic families generally find that they are in an ideal situation. An OECD (2007*b*) study showed that Nordic families—in contrast to individuals (Calmfors et al., 2007)—are indeed working many hours per week. Double-income families (aged 20–50 and with a child under 6) are typically well off, and both these and those who 'just manage' have a high preference for reduced working hours. Stress is rapidly spreading in the Nordic countries, indicating that people face the turmoil of the projective city. Without the support of an enabling welfare state, this degree of inclusion would hardly be possible. Table 9.1 gives an overview of the extent to which the Nordic countries provide support for families (including the elderly) compared to the Anglo-Saxon liberal market economies, and it is obvious that herein lies a major explanation for their diverse constitution as societies.

Not surprisingly, the difference in the level of spending is huge compared to the United States in all respects, but compared to the United Kingdom the levels are not very different; rather here it is the kind of spending that differs because the proportion spent on services is much higher in the Nordic countries. As seen from Table 9.2 the same differences are repeated when the Nordic countries are compared with the EU-15 countries. Total spending is only a bit higher, but the difference for benefits in kind (services) is enormous. The table also shows that among the Nordic countries there are important differences in how public services and transfer incomes are distributed for different activities, and it is obvious that the different Nordic countries act as enablers for very different behavioural patterns.

One of the most striking differences in patterns is discovered when comparing figures for paid sick leave with amounts spent on vocational training for

---

[4] Information from the Norwegian Central Bureau for Statistics (SSB).

Table 9.2. Expenditure on chosen benefits in PPP per inhabitant, 2005

Category/country		DK	SE	FI	NOR	EU-15	EU-27	Nordic vs. EU-15 (%)
Sickness/health care	Paid sick leave	265	485	302	940	227	197	154
	Inpatient care	990	610	592	1301	937	810	78
	Outpatient care	449	873	806	689	725	631	98
Disability	Disability pension	503	700	523	1020	287	255	200
	Accommodation	**169**	**154**	**27**	**15**	**67**	**57**	**174**
	Home help	**101**	**217**	**50**	**69**	**22**	**19**	**558**
Old age	Old-age pension	2055	2256	1787	1991	2404	2096	85
	Anticipated old-age pension	529	198	147	52	100	98	291
	Accommodation	**34**	**473**	**103**	**380**	**60**	**51**	**339**
	Assistance with daily tasks	**455**	**191**	**71**	**261**	**38**	**32**	**629**
Survivors	Survivors pension	0	179	233	109	287	245	48
Family/children	Maternity allowance	152	181	113	195	40	35	372
	Parental leave benefit	–	–	58	60	17	16	341
	Family or child allowance	273	214	232	294	306	263	78
	Child day care	**440**	**241**	**240**	**309**	**73**	**63**	**421**
	Accommodation	**139**	**83**	**52**	**60**	**18**	**15**	**507**
Unemployment	Unemployment benefit	371	330	393	205	254	215	144
	Early retirement for LM reasons	–	0	112	8	25	22	224
	Vocational training	–	**36**	**39**	**6**	**19**	**16**	**197**
Housing	Rent benefits	199	147	69	15	147	127	94
Social exclusion	Income support	178	86	71	114	41	37	272
Total		7302	7654	6020	8093	6094	5300	119
Total other benefits in kind		**1338**	**1395**	**582**	**1100**	**297**	**253**	**372**
Total in-cash benefits + health care		5964	6259	5438	6993	5797	5047	106

Source: Eurostat (2008); calculations produced by Marko Jaklic and Aljaz Hribernik.
Highlighted texts indicate other benefits in kind (services).

Table 9.3. Social protection as share of GDP and share of other in-kind benefits within it

Country	Social protection as % of GDP (2000–5)	Share of other in-kind benefits
Italy	24.7–26.4	3
Greece	23.5–24.2	11
United Kingdom	26.9–26.8	12
Denmark	28.9–30.1	21
Sweden	30.7–32.0	23
Norway	24.4–23.9	18
Finland	25.1–26.7	16
EU-15	27.0–27.8	9

Source: Eurostat (2008: 3, 6).

the unemployed.[5] Where the former is comparatively low for Denmark and Finland, the latter is comparatively low for Sweden, and extremely low for Norway. This indicates that in Norway and Sweden a higher proportion of the population is parked on passive social support than in Denmark and Finland (see also Calmfors et al., 2007). Nordic differences, however, are small when compared to the larger landscape of the EU. The share of gross domestic product (GDP) spent on social protection is not that different within the EU, but the share of services within the number differs a lot among the countries. Apparently, Sweden comes first, closely followed by Denmark, but then there is a jump to Norway and Finland in the share of services (Table 9.3).

Comparing the structure of social benefits, two things are noticeable. First, Nordic countries generally spend less on pensions and health care but more on other cash benefits and other in-kind benefits. Second, focusing on in-kind benefits only, an interesting pattern appears: Nordic countries tend to spend a lower share on health care and a higher share on other in-kind services. It is the other way round with most other countries.

This pattern could mean two mutually exclusive things. One explanation could be a simple difference in the treatment of certain expenses in Nordic countries that would underestimate the health care expenditure and overestimate other in-kind benefits. Another, and possibly a more plausible, explanation would, however, be that Nordic countries have, in fact, taken an 'enabling' approach to social protection resulting in replacing hospital care with domestic care and assistance. Data from Table 9.4 support this reasoning. While expenditure for inpatient and outpatient care in Nordic countries is below the EU-15 average, at 22 per cent and 2 per cent, respectively, Nordic countries spend 74 per cent more on accommodation and 458 per cent more on home help for disabled persons, and 239 per cent more for accommodation and 529 per cent more on assistance with daily tasks for old people, than the EU-15 average.

---

[5] We know from other sources that Denmark is the number one spender on vocational training—see below.

Table 9.4. Structure of social benefits for selected countries (%)

Country	Cash—pensions	Cash—others	Kind—health care	Kind—others
Italy	59	13	25	3
Greece	50	13	26	11
United Kingdom	42	17	29	12
Denmark	38	23	18	21
Sweden	41	18	18	23
Norway	34	25	23	18
Finland	43	20	21	16
EU-15	47	20	24	9

Source: Eurostat (2008: 6).

The political economy of mass-mobilized societies

Having built up such complicated systems of active service provisions, the Nordic countries have transformed as political economies as the state–economy relation has become different from most other countries. There is hardly a choice for the Nordic welfare states with regard to including people in the new regime of mobility. Given the structure of their social spending, they cannot afford long-term or high levels of structural unemployment; they need to increase participation rates on the labour market. For example, the OECD (2006a) has calculated how a 1 per cent reduction in unemployment affects potential GDP growth and cyclically adjusted public budget balances in different countries. While the effect on potential GDP only varies between 1.1 and 1.6 per cent in all OECD countries, the Nordic countries consistently achieve the largest effects (1.5–1.6 per cent compared to an average within the EU of 1.3 per cent). Variations, however, are very considerable on public budget balances. Whereas countries such as the United States and Japan are only affected by 0.3 per cent, and the Euro area with an average of 0.6 per cent from a 1 per cent increase in unemployment rates, the effect is 1.2 per cent for Denmark, 0.9 per cent for Finland, and 1.0 per cent each for Norway and Sweden. When Nordic countries run into periods of high unemployment, they risk jeopardizing both growth and state finances very rapidly. Therefore, they have good reasons for investing more readily in institutions and services that may assist their populations more quickly to find employment.

As a result, Denmark, Sweden, and Norway have initiated a number of instruments to activate the unemployed by providing social services and introducing controls to ensure that the unemployed actively seek employment. Measured in terms of expenditures per unemployed as a percentage of GDP per capita in 2000/1—following just after the Netherlands and Ireland—are three Nordic countries, Denmark spending 60 per cent, Sweden 50 per cent, and Norway 40 per cent. Only Finland seems to have embarked on a different route, spending only around 20 per cent.[6] Comparing the level of activation services with unemployment figures (see e.g. Madsen, 2006: 341), there seems to be very convincing covariation: the higher the activation expenditure the lower the unemployment figure, and the higher the employment frequency of the population.

In Denmark, for example, the transformation to an activation regime happened as a 'silent revolution' during the 1990s (Torfing, 2007). Explaining the high and increasing unemployment rates of the 1980s as a result of wages being too high compared to the skills and productivity of the unemployed, the right-wing government opted for wage reductions as a solution. But wages could be reduced only if unemployment compensation rates were reduced—and this was met by resistance by a majority of parties. Realizing that the skill gap between the employed and the unemployed could be brought down only by upgrading the skills of the unemployed, the Social Democratic led government from 1994 opted for a solution where the unemployed were offered further training and individualized activation counselling. With this step, a transformation of welfare institutions occurred. They moved from being passive compensators for bad luck on the labour market towards becoming active co-constructors of new professional identities, thus better fitting the country for the connexionist, project-led economy.

Especially in Denmark, the Active Labour Market Policies (ALMPs) are seen to constitute a third pillar of the 'golden triangle of flexicurity', the other two being a generous welfare system and a flexible labour market (Madsen, 2006). Flexible labour markets have initially been seen as systems that avoid restrictive practices regarding employers' rights to hire and fire employees, while rigid labour markets may be institutionalized through Employment Protective Legislation (EPL). While EPL has been seen as protective of workers' rights, it also makes a sharp distinction between the excluded and those included on the labour market to the effect that the large excluded proportion of society never comes close to taking up roles in the core of well-paid, highly mobile jobs which is characteristic of the projective city. Consistently, the Anglo-Saxon countries have the least restrictive EPL, which is expected to give the employers the freest hand in hiring and firing workers. But this has also implied that a large proportion of the labour force work under very bad conditions and receive low salaries, as argued by Boltanski and Chiapello.

Interestingly, Denmark stands out in terms of flexibility among both the Nordic and the continental welfare states. Thus, in an aggregated index of

---

[6] A similar pattern—although with some deviation especially concerning the Netherlands—is found in Salais (2003: figure 12.3: 339).

OECD countries Denmark is 10th, Finland 14th, Norway 21st, and Sweden 22nd in terms of flexibility (Økonomi- og Erhvervsministeriet, 2006). Mobility analyses confirm this picture, showing that in Denmark more than 20 per cent of the employed change workplace during a year (1998), while the figure is 19 per cent for Finland, 17 per cent for Norway, and 12 per cent for Sweden. In 2001 the average seniority in the same job in Denmark was less than eight years, close to nine in Norway, and close to ten in Finland, while Sweden topped at a level of eleven years (ibid.). Ironically, Norway and Denmark were the countries in which employees felt the highest degree of job security (ibid.). This greatly contrasts with Spain, where the proportion of yearly job shifts is higher than even Denmark, but in Spain employees feel very insecure in their jobs (ibid.; see also Arnal et al., 2001).

Another dimension of labour market flexibility in the Nordic countries is the high participation rate in vocational training courses. Typically (in 2003), in the Nordic countries around 60 per cent of employees with higher education participated in such training, 40 per cent with craft skills and 30 per cent of the (so-called) unskilled workers. While the level in the United States was similar for the two former groups, the difference was pointed with respect to the unskilled, only 13 per cent of whom were in vocational training (ibid.). Denmark spends the most public resources on adult education and further training (0.85 per cent of GNP), primarily on the unemployed and marginalized groups (0.67 per cent) but is also the largest spender in relation to the employed. Finland comes lower, spending only 0.2 per cent of GNP, primarily on the unemployed (Økonomi- og Erhversminis-teriet, 2006: figure 11.6).

One of the most surprising lessons from Denmark is that mobility in the labour market is not primarily caused by employees being fired by employers. Universal welfare states give rights and privileges to workers not associated with an employment contract as tends to be the case in both Anglophone and conservative welfare states. Therefore, workers have more freedom to search for new jobs if dissatisfied with current employers, because they do not risk simultaneously jeopardizing their pensions, health insurance, etc. (Morgan, 1997). In Denmark, most employees leave a job in exchange for a new one (Eriksson et al., 2006: 104). Even during periods of high unemployment, for example in 1980, this number amounted to 200,000, whereas only 80,000 were dismissed and became unemployed. In periods of low unemployment, for example in 2000, approximately 260,000 left a job because they had found a new one, while only 40,000 became unemployed for a time between jobs. Thus, Danish flexicurity is, to a great extent, characterized by employees looking for new challenges in other places.[7] Consequently, employees are as active as employers in creating the dynamic of the system, because they deselect employers not offering opportunities to improve skills.

These issues all have repercussions on the so-called 'transitional labour markets' (Schmid and Gazier, 2002), emphasizing that during a life course individuals run through a number of transitions (from education to employment, between family life and employment, between employment and unemployment and back, and between employment and retirement). In general, the Nordic countries seem to master such transitions most effectively with the result that they also prolong the lifetime period of employment up to retirement the longest, particularly Norway, Sweden, and Denmark (Huldt and Edlund, 2008; OECD, 2007b).

In the United Kingdom, Ireland, Denmark, the United States, and Australia, employment rates are high for all age groups. In Belgium, Greece, France, Italy, Germany, and Luxembourg, employment is heavily concentrated on the middle of the life cycle, with low employment rates for both youths and seniors. Observations available for two further country groups show asymmetric situations: Austria and the Netherlands have relatively high employment rates for youths but low rates for seniors; by contrast in Sweden, Finland, Portugal, and Japan, employment rates are relatively low for youths and high for seniors.

In the so-called 'liberal' countries, the relatively low level of social protection and the more limited role of education and training create incentives to work throughout a lifetime, while the Nordic countries favour better equilibrium between training (education and in-career training) and employment. Note that the case of Denmark is special in this respect: youth employment rates are high in the country but this mainly reflects the employment of students, compatible with continuing education (ibid.).

This means that, in continental and Southern European countries, careers become compressed to the median age group (age 25–54), which is also a period of child-rearing. This gives the less well paid and those in insecure jobs the worst conditions for cultivating the skills and capabilities that it takes to live in learning organizations and in the projective society, and to progress along its emerging career routes of frequent role and project shifts. Another interesting aspect that emerges by studying the Nordic model from a life course perspective is that interpersonal redistribution is much less than the intrapersonal redistribution of incomes. In essence, the system can be seen as a way for the individual during periods of high earning to pay through their taxes for periods of trouble (unemployment, education, retirement) or transition (OECD, 2007a: ch.8).

---

[7] This tendency is widespread in the Nordic countries, but the temptation to seek a new job to get new challenges or if one disagrees with the current boss is much higher in Denmark, where the temptation to shift job to get a higher wage is also lowest (17 per cent) (Politiken 26.01.2005).

The Nordic countries as situational negotiated economies

The argument in this chapter has been that Nordic welfare states have developed ways of working that facilitate individuals becoming part of the projective city. We have shown that part of the explanation for this phenomenon lies in how public institutions have learned to combine in networks to supply services in personalized ways so that they help enable individuals deal with their distinct problems, rather than providing standardized forms of social protection, as found in the more bureaucratic welfare states of the past.[8]

A major reason for this may reside in the way in which Nordic countries tend to hand over major responsibilities to local levels both through the division of labour among state, regions, and municipalities and among the local and central levels of unions and employers' associations. It is a generally held view among those studying local autonomy (see e.g. Demokrati-udvalget, 2004; Rattsø, 2004) that it is a distinctive characteristic for Nordic countries that they decentralize spending and administration of larger welfare schemes more widely to local levels that hold taxation rights. Sellers and Lidström (2007) have constructed a comparative index that systematically proves this. They also show that in Denmark, Sweden, and to some extent Norway, the social democratic welfare state was pre-conditioned by high degrees of local autonomy:

> Both functionally and politically, local empowerment of this kind helped make the construction of the Social Democratic welfare state possible. First, the resulting infrastructure gave local governments the administrative, legal, and fiscal capacities to pursue the universalistic, egalitarian aspirations of the welfare state. Second, in conjunction with the strong national system of local parties that had emerged across the country, empowered local government provided a vehicle to mobilize local support for the welfare state. National legislators in the coalitions of Social Democratic and Agrarian parties that passed welfare legislation could trust the political leadership in the local governments to carry out new welfare-related policies. (ibid.: 624)

The effect of local autonomy is that institutions and their users are much more closely connected in tight networks. As Sabel (2005) emphasizes, this makes situational co-design of public services possible, which may be recombined in many different ways, dependent on how institutional actors, private citizens, and enterprises form 'polyarchies' of cooperation to solve novel problems in

---

[8] This approach calls for studies along trajectories that have been suggested by Dorf and Sabel (1998), and Liebmann and Sabel (undated). For a condensed argument, see Sabel (2005). For an extensive argument focused on a comparison of Denmark and Finland, see Sabel et al. (2011).

experimental ways. Through such initiatives, experimental ways of organizing may diffuse between the private and the public sector. The projective economy may embrace the entire economy, not only the private and the R&D-oriented part of the public sector.

The Nordic countries are also known for their elaborated form of corporatism, based on a high rate of unionization. By maintaining unionization rates at the level of 70–80 per cent (Norway being at the level of 55 per cent) compared to 20–40 per cent in other EU countries, they stand out concerning the nature of their corporatism (European Commission, 2004). During the heyday of Keynesianism, this provided the basis for a strong system of centralized negotiations in which wages, working conditions, etc. could be effectively negotiated and coordinated with state spending on welfare schemes. Finland and Norway seem to have stuck to this centralized pattern, whereas Sweden and Denmark have moved to sector levels and, in Denmark in particular, to local enterprise bargaining and agreements (ibid.).

Probably this is the explanation why the Nordic countries have been able to reduce nominal wage increases to a reasonable level and combine it with modest, but quite steady, growth in real wages, while at the same time reducing unemployment significantly (ibid.; Madsen, 2006). The strength of unions and employers now seems to be used to modify wage drift in tune with macro-economic policies of the state, so that the business sector is better able to exploit, in a competitive way, international cyclical upturns. With respect to municipalities, the state has both delegated the implementation and administration of welfare services and established negotiations and control of budgets that limit spending levels and public deficits, despite an unlimited demand for free social services (Demokratiudvalget, 2004: ch. 2). With the growing implementation of the welfare state at local levels, corporatism has increasingly moved from state to localities or regions, has broadened its scope, and included increasing numbers of associations (NGOs in environment, housing, culture) that try to influence the local specification of how services should be designed and developed.

In Denmark, for instance, this movement has, in particular, led to the involvement of users in the governance of welfare services (patient groups to hospitals; parents on school boards, etc.). As most of these services have been run under continuously reduced budgets, institutions have been forced to innovate and collaborate across boundaries in order to deliver individualized services in novel ways and at reduced costs. This has led to what Bogason (2001) terms 'fragmentation' of the public sector as decisions are, apart from the budget, increasingly taken by the individual institution.

The result is a local system of institutions interacting in a network that has lost its former rule-bound, routinized, and predictable way of functioning. In many, but diverging, ways, the public sector may itself have become part of the experimentalist networked 'projective city', where services can be innovated, combined, and recombined, according to changing circumstances and needs. The participation of users, interest groups, and social movements may mobilize a much larger segment of the population to determine the social use of institutions, and the public sector may be used for the highly shifting ways of co-constructing complementarities. In this way, the public sector itself may serve as a gateway for inclusion into the high-mobility mode of the new experimentalist economy. The propensity to make use of possibilities for participation and influence in the Nordic countries is at a significantly higher level than the EU average, especially in working life, where the indicator for Denmark is 69, for Norway is 66, and for Sweden is 61, while it is 44 for Europe as a whole. This may be another reason why learning organizations have evolved more quickly and consequently in the Nordic countries.

Conclusions

Given the evolution described in this chapter, it is no wonder then that the public attitude towards globalization was rather positive in the Nordic countries up to the time of the financial crisis. A survey showed 'that the proportion of those considering that globalization either represents a threat to employment or has a rather negative effect on employment is far greater in continental (52 per cent), and Mediterranean (45 per cent) countries, than in Anglo-Saxon (36 per cent), and Nordic (37 per cent) countries' (Sapir, 2005).

The Nordic countries seemed, thus, to have found templates for development under globalization, before the financial crisis. They had begun to construct the projective city in ways that met the tests such a mode of organizing set for itself—in terms of providing opportunities for all groups to participate on a relatively equal basis and resisting the effort to exclude a substantial section of society and to exploit this group in order to maximize the gains of the mobile. Nordic countries in different and diverse ways had been able to increase the abilities of men and women, young and old, ablebodied and disabled, to participate in this new economy. As Roberto Unger suggests, the task involves 'the development of political, economic, and social institutions that both equip the individual and multiply his chances of changing pieces of the established setting of his work and life as he goes about his ordinary activities. Diminishing the dependence of change on calamity they raise him up; they make him godlike. The specific answer to all these questions is that the state should help the individual not to be little' (Unger, 2007: 206).

Obviously the Nordic countries offer windows of opportunities for a radically more benevolent variety of the new spirit of capitalism, where the division between the mobile and the immobile, the included and the excluded, is much less pronounced than in other countries progressing along the same basic path. The big question is whether the less fortunate in these transitions can learn from the Nordic countries to rejuvenate the path towards the projective city.

The leading country of the coordinated market economies, Germany, and the leading country among the liberal market economies, the United States, are both in trouble. Streeck (2009) in the case of Germany (see also Palier and Thelen, 2010 on Germany and France) and Davis (2009) and Friedman (2007) in the case of the United States account for historical processes in which actors exploit their host institutions in unintended ways and exhaust them, with the consequence that disorganizing takes place in one institutional sector after another. Such a diagnostic endeavour seems to be a good choice for explaining why these societies are in trouble, and what these troubles are all about. In many ways, we could have made a similar analysis of the Nordic countries. Neo-liberal-inspired reforms of the welfare state have, in many ways, hardened the situation for the unemployed; unions have become weakened and their position in tripartite and central negotiations is less important; the labour market is less regulated and social policy more restrictive; banks and financial institutions have followed in the wake of globalization and adapted entirely new codes of conduct. What Streeck calls 'liberalization' has certainly also taken place in the Nordic countries.[9] However, instead of just expecting liberalization to take place as a form of disorganization, our contention is that a constructive organizing process has also taken place by which old and new institutions take on new roles, are recombined to constitute new complementarities, and changes the 'rules of the game'. Looking closer into these societies will reveal much more than simply playing out the forces of markets; a complex pattern of new interactions—new ways of integrating action within and across institutional sectors—was, and is, in the making.

We have limited ourselves to understanding how the Nordic countries evolved, broadly speaking from 1995 to 2005, and are thus studying a very distinctive period in Nordic history—the period between two financial crises. Of course, the prosperity of the Nordic countries is not limited to this period, but the current financial crisis might seriously question the model of the Nordic economies. Numerous analysts (Haugh et al., 2009) have compared the repercussions that followed in the wake of the bursting of the bubble

---

[9] Whereas Hall and Soskice (2001) saw the Nordic countries as varieties of coordinated market economies, others have been less certain. Hotho (2009), for example, through a quantitative cluster analysis, groups Denmark and Finland together with the Netherlands, Luxembourg, and Switzerland (small open economies), whereas Sweden and Norway are grouped with Austria, Belgium, and Germany (collaborative economies). Paunescu and Schneider (2004) show how some of the Nordic countries transformed towards the LME type between 1990 and 2005.

economy in Japan in the early 1990s which left it with highly indebted banking, corporate, and personal sectors to those that followed from the Nordic bank crisis of the late 1980s and early 1990s. Liberalization of quite closed and heavily regulated bank-based systems led in both cases to a boom–bust pattern ending in financial crises, deep recession, and negative growth rates, especially in Finland and Sweden. Also in the other Nordic countries, the immediate effects were serious. The fiscal costs of the crisis were enormous, as budget deficits and public debt soared when tax revenues declined and government expenditures increased, largely due to the working of automatic stabilizers. Government support for the financial system ballooned in the short run. The private sector—in particular holders of stocks in banks and other financial institutions—was hit by huge wealth losses (Chen et al., 2009).

This is a description of the situation in the early 1990s, but it also describes the financial crisis that began in 2008 and has now reached new levels with the crisis of sovereign debt and the Eurozone equally well. Public budgets are already showing deficits, because of both unemployment benefits and the extensive use of employment services. Whereas Japan adopted a wait-and-see policy during its lost decade in the 1990s, causing very low growth rates and a sense of stagnation in the economy and the society as a whole (Haugh et al., 2009), the Nordic countries were forced to take action rapidly. As Chen et al. (2009) point out, the Nordic countries changed a number of practices, thus in monetary policy from pegged targeting to inflation targeting, towards rule-based policies in public finance, liberalized foreign ownership, reduced taxation of income and wealth, and redesigned corporate governance laws. The defects of liberalization were combated with more liberalization in many sectors questioning the egalitarian tradition. But then again, the ALMP and public sector innovation—as we have seen—led to a resurgence of a new inclusive pattern more accommodating to globalization—and the Nordic countries could be pulled out of stagnation by export-led growth. Most observers see the Nordic countries as having come to terms with open financial systems after the 1990 crisis, but there are also sceptics that maintain that the pace of capital accumulation slowed down, in particular in Finland and Sweden, to the effect that unemployment rates more persistently became higher (Karanassou et al., 2008). From this perspective, financial crises may have lasting negative effects on prosperity, which seems to be the case in Japan where, although growth rates recovered somewhat in the 2000s, overall economic confidence and growth rates remain fragile.

It is too early to assess how the current financial crisis will affect the Nordic countries and the evolution of inclusive projective cities by creating enabling welfare states. There is no doubt that this architecture creates a different system for risk-sharing than the financial-market-driven system prevalent in the Anglo-Saxon world and eagerly imitated in both France and Germany.

This could indicate that the Nordic countries are better able to continue to develop towards projective cities than those that only depend on financial risk-sharing. On the other hand, the speed of globalization of the Nordic countries during the 1990s, both in terms of FDI and exports as a percentage of GDP (Chen et al., 2009: fig. 10), where the latter has grown almost at the same pace as that of China, makes the Nordic countries very dependent on how the global system will react to the financial crisis. A cumulative reduction in exports and imports, as in the 1930s, would be much more challenging to them than most other countries due to their extreme open economies. For Horn et al. (2009), the general tendency to increase inequality has serious repercussions on global demand. Whereas low-income groups in the United States compensated for this by borrowing more money, households in Germany reacted by increasing their savings ratio. Consequently, the mechanisms that could secure global demand have been undermined with the collapse of the financial system—and have made countries increasingly dependent on the projective capabilities of their new capitalisms.

References

Andersen, T. M., Holmström, B., Honkapohja, S., Korkman, S., Söderström, H. T., and Vartiainen, J. (2007) *The Nordic Model: Embracing Globalization and Sharing Risks*. Helsinki: ETLA.

Arnal, E., Ok, W., and Torres, R. (2001) 'Knowledge, Work Organization and Economic Growth', *Labour Market and Social Policy Occasional Papers, No 5*. Paris: OECD.

Bogason, P. (2001) *Fragmenteret Forvaltning. Demokrati og netværksstyring i decentraliseret lokalstyre*. Århus: Systime.

Boltanski, L. and Chiapello, E. (2005) *The New Spirit of Capitalism*. London: Verso.

——Thévenot, L. (1991) *On Justification: Economies of Worth*. Princeton, NJ: Princeton University Press.

Calmfors, L., Corsetti, G., Devereux, M. P., Honkapohja, S., Saint-Paul, G., Sinn, H.-W., Sturm, J.-E., and Vives, X. (2007) 'Scandinavia Today: An Economic Miracle?' *EEAG Report on the European Economy*, http://ideas.repec.org/a/ces/eeagre/vy2007ip82-120.html.

Casper, S. (2000) 'Institutional Adaptiveness, Technology Policy, and the Diffusion of New Business Models: The Case of German Biotechnology', *Organization Studies*, 21, 887–914.

——(2008) 'Social Structure and Market Place Information within California Biotechnology'. In E. Moen (ed.), *Science and Society in the Age of Globalization: Past Reforms and Future Challenges*. Oslo: The Research Council of Norway.

——Lehrer, M., and Soskice, D. (1999) 'Can High-technology Industries Prosper in Germany: Institutional Frameworks and the Evolution of the German Software and Biotechnology Industries', *Industry and Innovation*, 6, 6–23.

——Vitols, S. (1997) 'The German Model in the 1990s: Problems and Prospects', *Industry and Innovation*, 4, 3–12.

Chen, H., Jonung, L., and Unteroberdoerster, O. (2009) 'Lessons for China from Financial Liberalization in Scandinavia', *HKIMR Working Paper No. 26*.

Davis, G. F. (2009) *Managed by the Markets: How Finance Re-shaped America*. Oxford: Oxford University Press.

Demokratiudvalget (2004) *Demokrati i Norden*. Copenhagen: Nordisk Ministerråd (ANP 2005: 701).

Dorf, M. C. and Sabel, C. F. (1998) 'A Constitution of Democratic Experimentalism', *Columbia Law Review*, 98, 267–473.

Eriksson, T., Ibsen, R., Li, J., and Westergård-Nielsen, N. (2006) *Globalisering og det danske arbejdsmarked*. Copenhagen: Jurist- og Økonomforbundets Forlag.

Esping-Andersen, G. (1999) *Social Foundation of Postindustrial Economies*. Oxford: Oxford University Press.

European Commission (2004) *Industrial Relations in Europe*. Brussels: Directorate-General for Employment and Social Affairs, Unit D.1.

European Foundation for the Improvement of living and Working Conditions (2007) *Fourth European Working Conditions Survey*, Dublin (http://www.eurofound.europa. eu).

Friedman, T. L. (2007) *The World is Flat: A Brief History of the Twenty-First Century*. New York: Picador.

Hacker, J. S. (2006) 'Policy Drift: The Hidden Politics of US Welfare State Retrenchment', paper presented at a workshop in the International Centre of Business and Politics, Copenhagen Business School, June.

Hall, P. A. and Soskice, D. (eds.) (2001) *Varieties of Capitalism: The Institutional Foundations of Comparative Advantage*. Oxford: Oxford University Press.

Haugh, D., Ollivaud, P., and Turner, D. (2009) 'The Macroeconomic Consequences of Banking Crises in OECD Countries', *OECD Economic Department Working Paper, No. 683*. Paris: OECD Publishing.

Horn, G., Dröge, K., Sturn, S., van Treeck, T., and Zwiener, R. (2009) 'From the Financial Crisis to the World Economic Crisis', *Policy Brief October—English translation of IMK Report No. 41*. Düsseldorf: Hans Böckler Stiftung.

Hotho, J. (2009) 'A Measure of Comparative Institutional Distance', *Center for Strategic Management and Globalization, Copenhagen Business School, SMG Working Paper No 7*.

Huldt, C. and Edlund, J. (2008) 'Age and Labour Market Commitment in Germany, Denmark, Norway and Sweden', *Work, Employment and Society*, 22, 109–28.

Karanassou, M., Sala, H., and Salvador, P. F. (2008) 'Capital Accumulation and Unemployment: New Insights on the Nordic Experience', *Cambridge Journal of Economics*, 32(6), 977–1001.

Kristensen, P. H. and Lilja, K. (eds.) (2011) *Nordic Capitalisms and Globalization: New Forms of Economic Organization and Welfare Institutions*. Oxford: Oxford University Press.

——Lotz, M. (2011) 'Taking Teams Seriously in the Co-creation of Firms as Economic Agency', *Organization Studies*, 32(11), 1465–89.

————Rocha, R. (2011) 'Denmark: Tailoring Flexicurity for Changing Roles in Global Games'. In P. H. Kristensen and K. Lilja (eds.), *Nordic Capitalisms and Globalization: New Forms of Economic Organization and Welfare Institutions*. Oxford: Oxford University Press, 86–140.

Levy, J. (1999) 'Vice into Virtue? Progressive Politics and Welfare Reform in Continental Europe', *Politics and Society*, 27(2), 239–73.

Lewis, J. and Plomien, A. (2009) 'Flexicurity as a Policy Strategy: The Implications for Gender Equality', *Economy and Society*, 38(3), 433–59.

Liebmann, J. and Sabel, C. F. (2003) 'A Public Laboratory Dewey Barely Imagined: The Emerging Model of School Governance and Legal Reform', *NYU Journal of Law and Social Change*, 23(2), 183–304.

Lorenz, E. and Valeyre, A. (2003) 'Organizational Change in Europe: National Models or the Diffusion of a New "One Best Way"?' Paper prepared for the 15th Annual Meeting on Socio-Economics LEST, Aix-en-Provence, 26–28 June.

Madsen, P. K. (2006) 'How Can it Possibly Fly? The Paradox of a Dynamic Labour Market in a Scandinavian Welfare State'. In J. L. Campbell, J. A. Hall, and O. K. Pedersen (eds.), *National Identity and the Varieties of Capitalism: The Danish Experience*. Montreal: McGill-Queen's University Press, 321–55.

Maurice, M., Sellier, F. and Silvestre J.-J. (1986) *The Social Foundation of Industrial Power*. Cambridge, MA: MIT Press.

Morgan, G. (1997) 'Financial Security, Welfare Regimes, and the Governance of Work System'. In R. Whitley and P. H. Kristensen (eds.), *Governance at Work: The Social Regulation of Economic Relations*. Oxford: Oxford University Press, 104–22.

NESC (National Economic Social Council) (2005) *The Developmental Welfare State*, No. 113, May. Dublin: National Economic & Social Development Office.

OECD (2006a) *OECD Employment Outlook: Boosting Jobs and Incomes*. Paris: OECD Publishing.

————(2006b) *Education at a Glance: OECD Indicators 2006*. Paris: OECD Publishing.

————(2007a) *Babies and Bosses: Reconciling Work and Family Life. A Synthesis of Findings for OECD Countries*. Paris: OECD Publishing.

————(2007b) *Modernising Social Policy for the New Life Course*. Paris: OECD Publishing.

Økonomi- og Erhvervsministeriet (2006) *Danmark i den globale økonomi, Konkurrencer-edegørelsen 2006*. Copenhagen: Schultz.

Orloff, A. S. (1993) *The Politics of Pensions: A Comparative Analysis of Britain, Canada and the United States 1880–1940*. Madison: University of Wisconsin Press.

Palier, B. and Thelen, K. (2010) 'Institutionalizing Dualism: Complementarities and Change in France and Germany', *Politics and Society*, 38(1), 119–48.

Paunescu, M. and Schneider, M. (2004) 'Wettbewerbsfähigkeit und Dynamik Institutioneller Standortbedingungen: Ein empirischer test des "Varieties-of-Capitalism" ansatzes', *Schmoller Jahrbuch*, 124(1), 31–59.

Rattsø, J. (2004) 'Local Tax Financing in the Nordic Countries'. In *Economic General Report for the 2004 Nordic Tax Research Council Meeting in Oslo*.

Reich, R. B. (1991) *The Work of Nations: Preparing Ourselves for the 21st Century Capitalism*. New York: Alfred A. Knopf.

Sabel, C. F. (2005) 'Globalization, New Public Services, Local Democracy: What's the Connection?'. In OECD, *Local Governance and the Drivers of Growth*. Paris: OECD Publishing, 111–31.

——Saxenian, A, Mittinen, R., Kristensen, P. H., and Hautamäki, J. (2011) *Individualized Service Provision in the New Welfare State: Lessons from Special Education in Finland*. Helsinki: Sitra Studies 62.

Salais, R. (2003) 'Work and Welfare: Towards a Capability Approach'. In J. Zeitlin and D. M. Trubek (eds.), *Governing Work and Welfare in a New Economy: European and American Experiments*. New York: Oxford University Press, 317–44.

Sapir, A. (2005) 'Globalisation and the Reform of European Social Models', In Background document for the presentation at ECOFIN Informal Meeting in Manchester, September 9.

Schmid, G. and Gazier, B. (eds.) (2002) *The Dynamic of Full Employment: Social Integration by Transitional Labour Markets*. Cheltenham: Edward Elgar.

Sellers, J. M. and Lidström, A. (2007) 'Decentralization, Local Government, and the Welfare State', *Governance*, 20(4), 609–63.

Skocpol, T. (2000) *The Missing Middle: Working Families and the Future of American Social Policy*. New York: W. W. Norton & Co.

Smith, A. (1969) *The Theory of Moral Sentiments*. Indianapolis: Liberty Classics.

Stetson, D. M. and Mazur, A. G. (eds.) (1995) *Comparative State Feminism*. Thousand Oaks, CA: Sage.

Streeck, W. (2009) *Re-forming Capitalism: Institutional Change in the German Political Economy*. Oxford: Oxford University Press.

Torfing, J. (2007) *Det Stille Sporskifte i Velfærdsstaten. En diskursteoretisk beslutningsprocesanalyse*. Aarhus: Aarhus Universitetsforlag.

Unger, R. (2007) *The Self Awakened: Pragmatism Unbound*. Cambridge, MA: Harvard University Press.

Wheelock, J. and Mariussen, Å. (1997) *Households, Work and Economic Change: A Comparative Institutional Perspective*. Boston: Kluwer Academic Publishers.

Whitley, R. (2000) 'The Institutional Structuring of Innovation Strategies: Business Systems, Firm Types and Pattern of Technical Change in Different Market Economies', *Organization Studies*, 21, 855–86.

Zeitlin, J. and Trubek, D. M. (eds.) (2003) *Governing Work and Welfare in a New Economy: European and American Experiments*. New York: Oxford University Press.

Zysman, J. and Schulze-Cleven, T. (2006) 'How do Wealthy Nations Stay Wealthy? Creating Value in the Digital Era'. Paper presented at the BRIE Conference, Berkeley, USA, May.

10

From 'New Spirit' to New Steel-Hard Casing? Civil Society Actors, Capitalism, and Crisis: The Case of Attac in Europe

Silke Ötsch, Pier Paolo Pasqualoni, and Alan Scott

Introduction: capitalist spirits, old and new[1]

In good time for the centenary of *The Protestant Ethic and the Spirit of Capitalism*, *Le nouvel esprit du capitalisme* (1999—English translation 2005a) offered us an account of capitalism's putative new spirit. In many respects, the picture the authors draw of modern capitalism is a familiar one within contemporary social theory and sociology: one repeated by proponents and critics of neo-liberalism and globalization alike and popularized by Richard Sennett in his best selling *The Corrosion of Character* (1998). But what is distinctive about Boltanski's and Chiapello's analysis is the prominence given to changes in the conduct of life associated with this new spirit. It is this, rather than the shared term 'spirit' alone, that invites a comparison between their analysis and that offered by Weber at the turn of an earlier *fin de siècle*.

Wilhelm Hennis has long argued that a—perhaps *the*—key concept in Weber's 'science of man' (*Wissenschaft vom Menschen*) is *Lebensführung*, the conduct of life. And so, it is Hennis (2000a: 27) who draws our attention to the following passage:

> We want to investigate, on the one hand, the types of 'selection processes' that large-scale
> industry carries out—according to its immanent requirements—on that part of the popu-
> lation bound to it via its professional fate; on the other hand, the type of 'adaptation' of

---

[1] The introduction to this chapter and the later discussion of professions reworks some material from Pasqualoni and Scott, 'Capitalism and the Spirit of Critique: Activism and Professional Fate in a Contemporary Social Movement/NGO', *Max Weber Studies*, 6(1), 2006, 147–70.

'manual' or 'mental' labour in large-scale industry to the life conditions that this industry offers them.

In this way, the question should gradually be addressed: *what kind of men [was für Menschen]* does modern large-scale industry, by virtue of its immanent characteristics, *fashion [prägen]*, and what *professional* (and thus, indirectly also *extraprofessional) fate* does it hold in store for him? (Weber, 1908: 37—original emphasis)[2]

By replacing 'large-scale industry' with 'project-oriented regime' (*cité*), we get a strikingly close approximation to Boltanski's and Chiapello's research problem. Similarly, if we accept Hennis's view that Weber's central problem is 'the "cultural meaning" of the economic form which has come to dominate modernity' (2000*a*: 164), then the parallels become even more apparent. On this account, the starting point—the given—is the life *orders* and the *powers* associated with them; each with their 'given regularity' and 'organized form of rationality': '*each* of these orders makes a demand, forms, characterizes a variety of "impositions" or perhaps opens up possibilities for future conduct, involves a formative tendency for the "personality"'' (Hennis, 2000*b*: 65). Here the Weberian notion of life orders appears more or less identical to Boltanski and Chiapello's *cité*. Hennis goes on to ask: 'what becomes of the person who enters such an order, or is caught in the "power" of one...?' Under capitalism—*the* modern economic form—this question becomes translated into one of professional fate (*Berufsschicksal*), which is so central to the above Weber quotation.

However, whereas Weber's Protestant subjects sought a (potentially lifelong) calling, for the project subject old-fashioned qualities of reliability, stability, and solidity give way to activity, process, and future orientation. Agents are led into an action trap in which they are propelled, or dragged, into an infinite, though poorly defined, future:

In the project-oriented *Cité*, a 'great one' must be adaptable and flexible. He or she is polyvalent, able to move from one activity, or the use of one tool, to another. A 'great one' is also active and autonomous. He or she will take risks, make contact with new people, open up new possibilities, seek out useful sources of information, and, thus, avoid repetition. (Boltanski and Chiapello, 2005*b*: 169)

The emphasis upon risk-taking, interpersonal skills, and trust-building and networking abilities, plus the capacity to move between—and act effectively within—a variety of contexts or subsystems, is central to their account. In return for success, the project subject must be willing to make an investment that may entail sacrificing 'all that could curtail one's availability, giving up lifelong plans' (Boltanski and Chiapello, 2005*b*: 169; Chiapello and Fairclough, 2002: 191). The ethic of the project regime is the precise opposite of Martin Luther's 'Here I stand. I can do no other'.

---

[2] Where the reference given is to a German-language text, the translations are our own.

232

On this account, project workers and their managers have to develop a set of complementary skills quite different from those of, say, the traditional bureaucratic subject (cf. Du Gay, 2000). The successful actor is no longer rewarded with a stable career, but with an increase in *employability* (cf. Pongratz and Voß, 2003). They must prove themselves in order to be better placed to garner future contracts. Entrepreneurialism comes to replace loyalty as the personal quality that is recognized and rewarded, and, to switch back to Weber's language, selected for. The oft-proclaimed 'long march through the institutions' has made a significant contribution to capitalism's contemporary form. In the project-oriented regime, this march is transformed from a *collective* effort to capture key social positions synchronically (via a division of labour) with subversive intent, into a *private* undertaking in which individuals *sequentially* progress through a number of institutions in the course of their *individual* careers.

Most of the considerable attention that *The New Spirit of Capitalism* has drawn has focused upon these central themes: new work forms and regimes of justification. However, Part III of the book has a more political focus: on the potential for a renewal of capitalism critique emerging out of—or in reaction against—the project *cité*. It is this theme that we want to follow up here. This entails a shift from the level of the individual career to that of collective actors, in our case an SMO (social movement organization). Thus, our question is not Weber's in its original form—*Was für Menschen?*—but a variation: what kind of organization is selected for and fashioned in the current environment? This emphasis upon selection at the collective level, while distinct from Boltanski and Chiapello's focus on individual careers, is consistent with Weber's view of politics as a selection mechanism (*Auslese*—see Breiner, 2004). However, we shall retain Boltanski and Chiapello's focus on employability, applying the notion not to individuals but to a collective actor. Employability at the level of the individual actor has its equivalents at the level of institutions and, as in our case, organized civil society actors where it translates into campaign impact, effectiveness, media profile, etc. Volker Heins (2002) has made explicit the parallel we have in mind between the individual as an entrepreneur of the self (cf. Boltanski and Chiapello's project workers) and new political forces (in his case, NGOs) as entrepreneurial collective actors by characterizing the latter as the 'neue Selbständige der Politik' (lit. the new self-employed of politics). Just as individuals must seek to increase their employability—must 'prove themselves'—in competition with others doing the same, so SMOs vie for attention, for recognition, and for influence within the social movement sector and media landscape.

The case study upon which we draw is part of a research project that focused on one contemporary SMO—Attac (*Association pour une Taxation des Transactions financières pour l'Aide aux Citoyens*)—and was conducted periodically from

2003 to 2011.[3] This globalization-critical—or alter-globalization—SMO was founded after the publication of an article, written as an immediate response to the Asian crisis, by Ignacio Ramonet in *Le Monde diplomatique* (December 1997) entitled 'Désarmer le marchés' (disarming the markets). This piece unleashed an unexpectedly broad public response. Attac grew out of that response with great rapidity in terms of both membership and geographical spread. Today, it is the most resonant single organizational label of the globalization-critical scene, at least in continental Europe.[4]

For Boltanski and Chiapello 'la relance de la critique' in the 1990s grew out of a development in which activists in the mid-1980s became increasingly occupied with humanitarian aid. This reorientation brought with it the accusation that they were apolitical, opportunistic, and conformist. However, the milieu that emerged out of this 'depoliticization', while 'very diverse, heterogeneous even', nevertheless 'forms a continuous web where contracts can be established, opportunities developed, and partial agreements concluded for selective operations on specific points' (Boltanski and Chiapello, 2005a: 351). Attac—an SMO started in France—may appear to be the exemplary case of such a 'continuous web'. Our concern is with the subsequent fate of one such 'web' and with it current chances for 'employability' in the wake of the 2008 financial crisis.

Activism and engagement in an SMO/NGO

In this section, we give an account of Attac in Europe. We examine first its work and campaign methods, and then seek to identify points of similarity and difference between its practices and those Boltanski and Chiapello gather under the label 'project *cité*'. Second, we ask what kind of organization is selected for within a given environment, and examine how Attac seeks to maintain and improve its 'employability' in our extended sense.

Work forms and modus vivendi

Attac's common goal is to 'oppose neo-liberal globalization and develop social, ecological, and democratic alternatives so as to guarantee fundamental

---

[3] The analysis presented here is based upon (*a*) ethnographic and action research into, and in cooperation with, one national Attac group: Attac-Austria (2003–6, see Pasqualoni and Treichl, 2004, for further detail); (*b*) key actor interviews with activists in the European Attac Network (2006–8); (*c*) further key actor interviews in 2011 undertaken in order to deepen and update the analysis.

[4] See Cassen (2003) for an insider's account of Attac in France and its early spread. For a first-rate analysis of Attac's emergence in Germany (and particularly its relation to the media), see Kolb (2004).

rights for all' (Attac, 2011). The democratic control of financial markets was from the outset, and remains, a key demand. Besides a broad agreement on the main goals—usually fixed in the statutes or a founding declaration—each national network within Attac may choose its own structure and political focus. Nevertheless, the structures in most national branches are similar. There is a strong base of local and regional groups composed of activists who decide autonomously on their activities. Local activists may take up suggestions for activities that have been agreed upon at the supra-regional level and may in turn propose activities to other levels. National Attac networks are usually coordinated by a board. There are further structures such as working groups at the national or European level specializing in issues such as financial markets and taxes, social questions, the European Union (EU), world trade, agriculture, privatization, etc. There has been an understanding that political work should be undertaken by activists on an exclusively voluntary basis in order to maintain the SMO character. However, both routine administrative work and press relations are dealt with by employees. Finally, some Attac networks have among their membership organizations that support and work with them. Particularly at nation level, Attac is engaged in alliances with other actors such as unions, NGOs, and other SMOs. Educational work in the field of the (international) economy and finance (*alphabétisation économique*), mobilizing citizens, and exceeding political pressure are the strategies adopted in pursuing its aims.

Within the SMO, there is a variety of work forms. Semi-professionalized project-like work forms can be found in campaigns addressed to government agencies or to private companies. This type of activity, however, forms only a small part of Attac's work but has a high public profile. Beyond campaigning, there is a further work form: the use of 'windows of opportunity'. Here, activists who have been working continuously within their field of activity mobilize when a political opportunity arises, for example when there is a high level of political and/or media attention on an issue. Attac used this strategy in the case of the referendum on the European Constitution (2005), in the process of introducing international taxes ('Lula Initiative'),[5] and in other less high-profile cases. There are also combinations of the two strategies mentioned so far. One aim of such agenda-shifting, surfing, and cutting strategies—which do appear to conform to the demands of project-oriented *cité*—and of Attac's network structure is to involve as many actors and as diverse a group of actors as possible. This applies to both strategies. Thus,

---

[5] An initiative launched by French President Jacques Chirac and Brazilian President Luiz Inacio 'Lula' da Silva to introduce global taxes (e.g. an air ticket levy and/or Financial Transaction Tax) on those who profit from globalization to fund the Millennium Development Goals (MDGs) of the United Nations.

there are shifting alliances in different political fields. As noted above, there are tendencies of differentiation within Attac such that actors specialize in specific areas. Compared to more established actors, it is possible to rise quickly within the SMO but, unlike a traditional career, there is little institutionalized support.

Against the background of the shift Boltanski and Chiapello ascribe in an ideal-typical fashion to the intellectual/spiritual consequences of capitalism, Attac may appear an exemplary form of contemporary protest. It differs from the classical Weber–Michels model of the political party or movement as a disciplined hierarchy insofar as its organizational form approximates that of a 'network of networks' (Gerhards and Rucht, 1992): a 'light' organization of an almost 'franchising' character. For advocates of resource mobilization theory (RMT), Attac would appear to be very close to a movement acting within a movement sector much as a firm acts within its business sector: through product diversification, tailoring to local markets, franchise, an emphasis upon brand recognition, and so on.[6] Both internationally and nationally, Attac continues to adopt a variety of roles, which change from time to time according to the political requirements of the moment; these come to the fore for the entire organization or remain focused upon particular niches. In these niche environments, different actors are present who, according to requirement, represent potential partners who are regularly mobilized when the opportunity arises, particularly one promising success (in terms of media attention, etc.).

In sum, in many respects, and mainly due of its diversity, Attac is a highly flexible organization and in this sense resembles the networker of the project *cité*. It is present in different regions, engages a broad range of activists who address distinct issues, and have diverse competences. In contrast to less tightly organized social movements, Attac mobilizes, lobbies, and has an office and a press officer. On the other hand, the SMO is less flexible than smaller actors with hierarchical structures because key decisions must be taken by consensus (particularly in Attac-Germany, Austria, and Italy). While the SMO addresses a wide variety of issues beyond financial markets (generally perceived as its key focus), it must adhere to its key demands, which again limits its flexibility. Thus, in comparison to other actors (e.g. unions or political parties), Attac seems to incorporate many of the features of Boltanski's and Chiapello's project *cité*. However, it would be misleading to press all Attac's modes of operation into this mould. A great deal of its activity takes place within more stable and continuous forms. In local groups, there is often a core team of local coordinators and individuals who do educational

---

[6] McCarthy and Zald (1977) is the *locus classicus*.

work on a continual basis and local campaigning, or participate in supra-regional and sometimes also thematic work. Even if thematic working groups or scientific councils participate partially in projects or campaigns, there is other continuous work—that is, building up knowledge in specific fields. In brief, types of work of the project-oriented *cité* coexist with types of work and legitimation patterns of others, notably the industrial *cité* (with its emphasis on efficiency) and the civic *cité* (Boltanski and Thévenot, 1999).

What kind of organization?

It is tempting to interpret the particularities of Attac in terms of the kind of general diagnosis of contemporary capitalism the *New Spirit* argument offers. However, a more middle-range option remains available: one focusing on the logic and developmental phases of an SMO and on organizational impera-tives. In Attac's case, the first phase lasted from 1998 to the financial crisis of 2008. Since 2008, Attac's critique has become a common political good and it has continued to articulate a critique of neo-liberalism with the aim of contrib-uting to its delegitimation.[7] This new context poses different organizational dilemmas: ones that may have to be addressed through a shift away from the earlier work forms which demanded much of the activists in terms of time and engagement and towards more professionalized forms.

We can start with the ways in which the SMO articulates these issues and dilemmas for itself:

> In a sense Attac is an innovative project that cannot simply be fitted into the category of network, international institution, NGO, or movements. It crosses over all these forms and seeks to combine the advantages of each while avoiding their disadvantages: the flexibility and openness of a network structure but with-out their looseness; the power of social movements without their instability; the competence, stability and tight organization of NGOs and associations without their dependencies and bureaucratic tendencies. [...] If Attac understands how to combine these aspects appropriately in different situations, a dynamic stability may emerge that secures a successful political future for the project. What you call such an organizational form is secondary (no doubt someday something will occur to organizational sociologists). (Attac, 2006 [2001])

These kinds of dilemmas are indeed much discussed by organizational soci-ologists and within social movement analysts (e.g. Tarrow, 2011). But, from a

---

[7] This poses a new set of organizational challenges (further discussed later). These issues are in part being met by a consolidation process in terms of membership. As activists get more experienced and specialized in some areas, this project modus vivendi becomes less common than in the first phase. Particularly in thematic working groups, there was a 'brain drain' as activists found more stable work in other organizations, parties, NGOs, and universities.

broadly Weberian perspective, they have deeper roots. They are not merely problems for collective actors but existential questions for any agent within a particular social location, caught within any set of 'powers and orders' whether out of necessity or (as with Attac activists) volition. The point has been well made by Constans Seyfarth, who argues that for Weber all professions can be characterized in terms of the basic tensions and incompatible demands in which they are caught. These differ from case to case:

> With the progress of disenchantment, intellectualization, and rationalization, the elemental tension between the exceptional and the ordinary [Außeralltäglichkeit und Alltag] becomes transformed and differentiated without ever vanishing [...] Formal and substantive rationality is especially important for lawyers; the tension between an ethic of responsibility and of conviction for the politician; one of irrationality and rationality—in countless variations—for science; the tension between personal and impersonal factors is particularly evident in his occasional observations on nurses. The distinction between the exceptional and the ordinary forms the common frame for all these differentiating tensions. (Seyfarth, 1989: 394)

None of these predicaments can be simply overcome; rather, 'they must be dealt with constantly, and in ever new ways, within practical professional action. Due to the irrational conditions for, and the provisional nature of, each solution, the practical coping [Bewältigung] drives (clearly not as the only factor!) the development onwards' (ibid.: 394). Seyfarth traces the origins of these provisional solutions to the charismatic interventions of exceptional individuals the routinization (Veralltäglichung) of which constitutes professionalization: 'professional action is characterized by a continuous practice of "substantive" or "internal" routinization of exceptional achievements [Leistungen]' (ibid.: 393).

The specific form of such challenges differs from case to case. On Weber's account, for the professional politician the challenge is to balance 'passion' with 'a sense of proportion' ('Leidenschaft und Augenmaß zugleich', 1988 [1919]: 560); an ethic of conviction (politics as cause) with the ethic of responsibility (politics as technical skill and as judgement). It is the balance between the contrasting demands of legitimacy and efficiency (often articulated in terms of the question: 'SMO or NGO?') that characterizes the central tension within social movements. A basic characteristic of an SMO is its search for legitimacy: members seek a new legitimacy in the face of hegemonic power by standing up for what they see as the interests of the society as a whole, and linking these back to everyday experience. In the case of NGOs, the weight lies more towards efficiency: the effective pursuit of specific aims (e.g. via lobbying), that is, seeking to influence specific political or market processes with the aim of achieving concrete changes.

Joachim Raschke, one of the most influential social movement analysts in Germany, in an observation on the German Greens made before they 'resolved' rather than coped with these conflicting demands by becoming a political party, makes this efficiency versus legitimacy dilemma explicit. In the phase of transition, the Greens liked to characterize themselves as a 'movement-party'. Raschke, however, brands them a 'party against their own will':

> The Greens have a basic problem: they fail to unify *legitimacy and efficiency*. Other parties have to struggle with the same problem, but in the case of the Greens the chasm is enormous: what is legitimate is not efficient; what is efficient is not legitimate. (Raschke, 1993: 33—emphasis added).

Tension between efficiency and legitimacy can be viewed as the equivalent for new political actors to that between politics as technical skill and politics as cause (*Sache*) for the professional politician that Weber famously described in 'Politik als Beruf' (1988 [1919]; English 1994 [1919]). *Efficiency*, which happens to be the main source of legitimation within the industrial *cité*, here might also be translated into the equivalent at the collective level of Boltanski and Chiapello's *employability* at the level of the individual career.

In the case of Attac, the tension between legitimate and effective action (measured in part in terms of impact) takes—as we have already indicated—the specific form of the social movement versus NGO dilemma (the option of becoming a party is off the agenda, not least in the light of the Greens' example). This is a tension that both movements and activists—like Weber's professionals—must deal with on a routine basis. And here, too, we find an ambivalent response. On one hand, campaign methods are typically chosen less according to a single ideological criterion than because they appear likely to succeed (or at least have impact), and campaign themes are chosen that have not yet been claimed by other NGOs with a specific profile and expertise in the field. In terms of Weber's classical typology (1972 [1922]: 12–13), such an instrumental orientation takes priority over the value-rational aspects of Attac's protest repertoire. On the other hand, Attac does not carry through its campaigns in the same way as an NGO would, not least because it is dependent upon its activists' freely given time. These activists bring with them their own concerns, thus broadening the campaign's focus to value-rational issues beyond narrowly conceived instrumental campaign aims. Campaigns are also often accompanied by wide educational initiatives that reach well beyond the clearly defined initial and/or core aim of the campaign. Activists also display some resistance to the soft pressure placed upon successful movements to shift from SMO to NGO, with all the changes in action repertoire and organizational form that it entails. An oppositional role remains attractive to most activists who continue to demand and defend it. This demonstrates reservations vis-à-vis the natural extension of activity onto the stage of representative democracy (Holland-Cunz, 2003): reservations that are reinforced by the stories of 'unacceptable conditions' in which 'consultation' takes place and actors are played off against each other.

While the focus of mainstream political actors points to an imperative of impact, Attac's political role and significance lies in effectively questioning the latter's legitimacy, both raising questions of social justice and confronting mainstream politics with tentative solutions for 'another world'. Because one of the distinctive characteristics of SMOs and NGOs (in contrast to, say, motor clubs or indeed unions) is that they must represent interests beyond those of their membership (cf. Heins, 2002), Attac has to retain its value-rational elements. Thus, rather than interpret Attac as an unambiguous example of the shift 'from membership to management' (Skocpol, 2003), it is probably more useful to see it as dealing on a day-to-day basis with the issue of legitimacy *and* efficiency with their persisting and perceived tensions: between internal participation *and* external political impact; between value rational orientation *and* instrumentality; between the requirements of both flexibility/speed *and* stability. To resolve these tensions definitively would entail a shift of identity and merely generate other tensions in their place. In this sense, Attac can indeed be viewed as 'arranging relatively durable compromises between different worlds [...that] differ with respect to the kinds of worlds they largely rely on, and the kind of compromises which support them' (Boltanski and Thévenot, 1999: 376).

This legitimacy versus efficiency question has been posed anew, and in a sharper form, since the financial crisis of 2008. It is to this new context that we now turn.

Organized civil society and the challenge of the 2008 crash

In the current context, Attac and similar alter-globalization SMOs must address two types of challenge. The first is conjunctural: how to position themselves in the context of the financial crisis of 2008 and its aftermath. The other is more structural and political: how to adapt their action repertoires to changes in the nature of governance associated with the increasing reliance upon '*new* public policy instruments' (Lascomes and Le Galès, 2007), 'soft law' (particularly within the EU, see Kassim and Le Galès, 2010), 'expert groups' (Gornitzka and Sverdrup, 2011), the participation of experts in core commissions (Froud et al., 2010), and the presence of 'econocrats' in key positions (Engelen et al., 2011: 198);[8] and upon non-government agencies such as

---

[8] Engelen et al. (2011: 198) define the econocrat as 'a particular kind of technocrat, one whose background is in (mainstream) economics. [...] Although the specific field of expertise is different, like other technocrats, the econocrat has an underlying belief in finding technical solutions to

international institutions, central banks, credit rating agencies, and the rest. All this makes it more difficult to regain democratic control over banks and financial institutions, even if the political will were there. This second development can be interpreted as part of a wider remodelling of political steering mechanisms along market and 'market-friendly' lines (cf. Marquand, 2004) and the breakdown of the 'institutional pillarization' between the state and the market (Crouch, 2000) and the emergence of financial markets as a 'second sovereign' alongside and competing with citizens (*Staatsvölkern*— Beckert and Streeck, 2012: 10). We shall conclude by discussing these two challenges and by linking the current circumstances back to those analysed by Boltanski and Chiapello in the 1990s.

The current conjuncture

In order to understand the kinds of new threats, challenges, and opportunities alter-globalization face 'post'-financial crisis, we shall suggest—in a rather polarized and ideal type fashion—two possible scenarios with contrasting implications for civil society actors. The first envisages a restabilization of the neo-liberal regime and the second continued crisis.

Scenario 1: The first scenario is a restabilized regime that closely resembles the 'neo-liberal' regime that it replaced. We might call this the *'Crouch scenario'*. Crouch (2011) argues that the seeming demise—the 'strange non-death'—of neo-liberalism (or of what he generally prefers to call 'privatized Keynesianism') will see the installation of a regime that only slightly modifies the parameters of the preceding order. The main thrust of policy has been to re-establish the old order—or a close approximation—through austerity measures in the desperate attempt to lessen the public debt incurred by the necessity of nationalizing the debts of financial institutions, and occasionally of those institutions themselves, and, under the pressure of financial markets and speculators, the costs of interest on state deficits. While the crisis— according to Crouch—has delegitimized the neo-liberal ideal of the *un*regulated market, we will not see anything like a return to Keynesianism, but rather the promotion of the *self*-regulating market in which corporations are charged with the task of policing themselves. This regime will, he argues, seek its new legitimation in Corporate Social Responsibility (CSR).

often complex policy problems. Given their specific expertise, econocrats can be found both in places where economic policy is debated, developed, and implemented (such as the Treasury or Bank of England) and also at other policy sites where an economist's toolkit might assist with decision-making.' They go on to note that 'increasingly, authority lay with networks of individuals who rested those authority claims on the "scientific" status of the knowledge which they derived from sub-disciplines such as financial economics, which are closely linked to the practice of finance.'

Scenario 2: The above account assumes that the replacement of neo-liberalism with a closely related regime *may* be successful, or at least successful enough. But we cannot know that yet. The alternative scenario is one of continuing instability. This is the prognosis made by two leading German economic sociologists: Jens Beckert and Wolfgang Streeck (2011, 2012), so let us call this the *Beckert–Streeck scenario*.[9] In their analysis, the 2008 financial crisis was not a single crisis, but merely the start or result of a series of crises, or—the same idea expressed differently—a single crisis of long duration consisting of a series of distinct phases. Their core argument is that the crisis will be sustained for an indeterminate period because potential solutions are either potentially effective but, given the effects of a sustained period of neo-liberalism, politically unacceptable (e.g. increases in taxation) or politically acceptable (e.g. further draconian cuts in public expenditure) but ineffective because they will produce further destabilization ushering in the next crisis phase.

These two—again we stress ideal-typical—scenarios pose alter-globalization movements with differing threats and opportunities. While Crouch himself is far from pessimistic about the role of civil society actors in challenging the legitimacy of the current and emerging order (Crouch, 2011: 178), were the new regime he postulates successfully installed a series of dilemmas would be posed for SMOs such as Attac.

The 2008 financial crisis made many of Attac's demands, as they say in German, *salonfähig* (fit for decent company). The post-2008 crisis period saw a brief moment in which calls for much tighter state regulation of markets (and particularly, of course, financial markets) and the reining in of financial practices—not least bonus schemes for CEOs and financial managers—became common across a wide spectrum of politics. What we have since seen, however, is politicians' reform pronouncements and reform initiatives buckling under lobby and other pressures. If what we have labelled the Crouch scenario turns out to be correct, then, from the perspective of an SMO such as Attac, the whole post-crisis context *may* come to be seen as a lost opportunity: if our demands cannot be realized in the course of exactly the kind of crisis that our analysis predicted, then when? They may find themselves witnesses to the closing of a unique window of opportunity.[10] This, in turn, may

---

[9] As noted, our contrast between these two scenarios is also somewhat ideal typical. Crouch is careful to avoid implying that the installation of the CSR regime will be fully successful; he merely wishes to eschew the view that the crisis will induce a new statism—a return to genuine Keynesianism. Read in this light, the two prognoses are not as mutually exclusive as our presentation of them implies.

[10] Crouch in fact suggest a different, and more optimistic, scenario for SMOs or—in a broader sense—for civil society than the one we suggest here. In his view citizens' movements, journalists, and academics are increasingly challenging powerful corporate actors. They also have new tools of communication via the Internet and are able to confront corporations to a degree that parties are not. Irrespective of the fate of neo-liberalism, a tension will remain between four field powers: the state, the market, corporations, and civil society (Crouch, 2011: 179).

produce the kind of disappointment that sparks a 'shifting involvement' as understood by Albert Hirschman (1982), the dedicatee of *Le nouvel esprit*. The experience of such disappointment[11] would pose new dilemmas both for SMOs and, in the form of personal dilemmas, for their activists. Some activists may respond in the way that Hirschman predicts: the frustrations of public engagement driving them back into the private realm. Such a response, if widespread, would herald the decline of globalization-critical or anti-neoliberal movements and, perhaps, the end of the social movement cycle that we have seen since the late 1990s/2000s. But there is another possibility, one that Hirschman does not consider, namely the further radicalization of such movements and of (some of) the individuals involved in them: the abandonment of the search for a balance between those methods that are efficient and those that are legitimate. Such a response would herald not the absolute decline of such movements, but their transformation into something else: neither into SMO nor NGO, but into 'enclaves' (cf. Douglas and Mars, 2003). Substantively, this would mean shifting from an incremental critique of capitalism in its neo-liberal guise to a more fundamental critique of capitalism itself. Neither of these possibilities would be 'good news' for globalization-critical SMOs. The crisis could then become a crisis for the SMO itself: one that may at some point see the emergence of a 'successor movement' (Raschke, 1987) but in the medium term would mean either decline or transformation; or, since these are not mutually exclusive possibilities (indeed they may be mutually reinforcing), both.

While Beckert and Streeck are not—any more than Crouch is—predicting capitalism's demise, their analysis suggests a quite different set of possible futures for alter-globalization and globalization-critical movements. The unfolding crisis/crises could continue to supply opportunities for campaigns with impact and would thus sustain the strategy of maintaining a balance between the imperatives of legitimation and efficiency by strengthening the hand of those committed to what, up to now, has been the dominant strategy: a pragmatic and reform-oriented position which, while radical, fell short of a traditional capitalism critique and sought to address decision-makers, governments, and the EU as well as its own 'public'. This may be combined with a proliferation of such movements and collective action within or beyond Attac's geographical area (Europe), and with the emergence of new protest movements and repertoires. The rapid geographical spread of Occupy movements—from Wall Street to CBDs across the world—in 2011 suggests this, even though it is not clear at the time of writing whether these movements will maintain their level of mobilization, or whether their concerns will

---

[11] As Hirschman (1982: 13) notes, the full significance of the experience of 'disappointment' is more evident in German: *Enttäuschung*, lit. dis-deception.

translate into government-led reforms, or indeed whether they will dissipate and/or, as has already happened in several prominent cases, be successfully removed by police action.

We can see these possible alternative futures for the SMO in Attac's debates since 2008. There have been two main positions: (*a*) Attac should radicalize (critiquing capitalism as such rather than merely its neo-liberalism form and oppose growth in principle) or (*b*) provide more expertise and further professionalize. The first option recalls the times when its demands were perceived as more radical, but now in a context in which (at least briefly and on a discursive and general level) there seem to be few enemies left, at least in public opinion. Attac should thus revive its tradition (and save its reputation) as a social movement and become what it was initially—for example, adopt a more critical position and developing radical utopias. The second option points to the virtues of NGO strategies: of grasping the opportunity the crisis offers and seeking to exercise greater influence on decision-makers to achieve pragmatic but real reforms, which may later open the way to more radical demands. Both options represent a search of 'employability' in the new context, though reaching out to different actors and audiences.

But the continual effectiveness and legitimacy of civil society actors depends, too, on the strategies, and the success of the strategies, of the two 'sides'—market actors and their critics (whether governments or civil society actors)—under conditions in which changes of governance style have altered the rules of game for both governments and civil society actors.

Addressing the crisis under conditions of altered political steering

> Souverän ist, wer über den Ausnahmezustand entscheidet. (Carl Schmitt, 1996 [1922]: 13)

As Carl Schmitt's (in)famous formulation—'sovereign is he who decides on (determines) the state of exception'—reminds us, a crisis is not a natural fact. It is a construct. It becomes the object of struggle both over its nature and origin (the power of definition or 'framing') and, in part depending on who frames the crisis most effectively, over the measures appropriate to address it. In that struggle, in the early stages of the current crisis, it was the nation-state that appeared to be sovereign in Schmitt's sense. As time has gone by, sovereignty appears to have shifted towards market actors—particularly financial market actors—who seem able to call up the state of exception at will and have turned what was a failure of markets into an apparent failure of states. As Wolfgang Streeck (2011: 26) put it: 'the same Manhattan-based ratings agencies that were instrumental in bringing about the disaster of the global money industry are now threatening to downgrade the bonds of states that accepted a previously unimaginable level of new debt to rescue that industry and the capitalist economy as a whole'. Things have moved fast since Streeck wrote that, but in such a way as to support what he was suggesting even more strongly. Both governments and civil society actors appear to be among the losers of this shift in the initiative: the former being caught between the demands and pressures of the financial markets and those of citizens affected by the austerity measures demanded by markets (see Beckert and Streeck, 2012 for the EU case).

Thus, paradoxically, while many of Attac's basic positions are now shared by a wide political spectrum, the initiative has shifted in favour of finance and economic elites—in favour of those who profited before the crisis and who now find themselves again able to pile on the pressure by deploying *Sachzwangargumente*: argument to the effect that the facts—the economic and financial realities—demand a particular course of action; that, in other words, there is no alternative (TINA) to austerity and to the bail-out of states, where possible with public money, in order to avoid a chain reaction in case one or several systemic financial companies fail, or a state is unable to pay its debts thus driving up the costs of refinancing for other states. The interests of elites appear to trump the (initial) reform intent. Elite actors dominate new legislative moves on the bases of their specific interests, know-how, resources (human and financial), and their discursive strength in specialized discourses. A banking crisis has been transformed into a crisis of sovereign debt, and the interests of economic elites are represented as national interests. The result is a sharpened 'shock therapy' (cf. Klein, 2007), most dramatically of the kind being instituted within the Eurozone with the help of technical instruments such as balanced budget amendments or budgetary rules enforced by debt ceilings (*Schuldenbremsen*), which effectively constrain political decisions, or are used to impose and legitimate the interests of the most powerful players.[12] Citizens are overwhelmed by these developments and recognize their implications, if at all, only retrospectively.[13]

---

[12] This is a theme that dramatically entered the French presidential election when, in a widely reported comment, the socialist candidate, François Hollande, declared in his first major campaign speech that his true adversary—the world of finance—was faceless, nameless, without party, would never stand for election but nonetheless ruled ('[...] mon véritable adversaire n'a pas de nom, pas de visage, pas de parti, il ne présentera jamais sa candidature et pourtant il gouverne. Cet adversaire c'est le monde de la finance', quoted in *Le Monde*, 23 January 2012).

[13] Various bank rescue funds represent a particularly striking example of this self-imposed disenfranchisement of politics to the advantage of financial markets. The German Soffin and Soffin II funds, which are provided with €400 billion for loans and €480 billion for guarantees the distribution of which is not decided by the federal parliament (the Bundestag) but by a commission which is barred from providing information on the use of the funds to either the public or the government, is a case in point (Bundestag, 2012; Schumann, 2009). This removal of discretionary powers over the budget from political decision and scrutiny is justified in terms of sustaining the competitiveness of national banks.

The rapidity of this shift of initiative away from states and towards markets can (perhaps can only) be explained in terms of changes—over circa the last quarter of a century—in the ways in which states govern: changes in turn deeply associated with neo-liberalism. In an analysis that deserves more attention than it has received, at least in the Anglophone world, Bétrice Hibou (2004) has argued that policies that support the interest of economic elites strengthen rather than weaken the position of political elites. She was specifically writing about the privatization of state assets, but the argument may apply equally to a later stage of neo-liberalization: to the kinds of market-inspired steering described in the non-functionalist version of the policy instruments literature where the emphasis is upon the shift from the legal and regulatory instruments of 'command and control' to the public policy instrument of 'negotiated governance' (see Lascomes and Le Galès, 2007: 13). A public policy instrument is a *'device that is both technical and social, that organizes specific relations between the state and those it is addressed to, according to the representation of meanings it carries'* (ibid.: 4—original emphasis). Crucially, these devices are not neutral 'tools', but instruments of power that reorder the relationship between governing and the governed by partially determining 'the way in which actors are going to behave', and creating 'uncertainties about the effects of the balance of power' so as to 'eventually privilege certain actors and exclude others'. In this way, new public instruments are said to 'constrain the actors while offering them possibilities' and 'drive forward a certain representation of problems' (ibid.: 9). The resulting (partial) shifting of politics out of the realm of (parliamentary or public) debate and law onto that of technical instruments and soft law is a significant change in the nature of the political.

This partial 'instrumentalization' of governance has implications for organized civil society actors too. First, it alters the political opportunity structures in such a way that traditional social movement repertoires, such as mass mobilization, appear to be increasingly ineffectual: to whom should such rallies and demonstrations be addressed when the most obvious addressee—government—can claim its own subordination to instruments that are reified in the old Marxist sense? Secondly, and likewise linked to declining relevance of both public debate and mass mobilization, the issues that SMOs have to address are becoming increasingly technical in nature and more complex, not least due to the international scale and involvement of diverse legal systems. Not only are financial markets highly complex, but the increasing reliance of governments on new public policy instruments is a further moment in the evolution of a technocratic mode of politics that requires ever greater expertise to grasp, let alone to challenge.

Correspondingly, the influence of SMOs comes increasingly to depend not on how many people they can get on the streets, but how much technical expertise they can muster in order to position themselves as potential—interesting and legitimate—interlocutors for both the media and policy makers.[14] With these changes in governance mechanisms, the aim of political struggle appears to have shifted from that described by Weber—regaining access to the means of legitimate coercion—to one in which the aim is (or is first) that of gaining understanding and control of the technical instruments of governance.[15]

In sum, in the 'post'-crisis context, more and more of Attac's demands have been taken up within mainstream politics and by other actors but to less and less effect. At points of crisis, politicians look, sometimes in desperation, for responses. At such times, the influence of SMOs and NGOs, who have long been critical of the system in crisis and have sought to articulate alternatives, can increase, if only briefly. In the post (or continuing) crisis context, what we are seeing is ambiguous some of Attac's original demands, in particular the Tobin Tax (witness the conversion of a majority of EU states to a tax on financial transactions), have been adopted or proposed for legislation, but the crisis has also been effectively used as an opportunity to introduce further neo-liberal policies in a dramatically radicalized form, and to reinstate the business model and technocratic solutions (cf. Engelen et al., 2011). What has counted more in this new context than mobilization and over-arching ethical and political argument has been the high and growing expectation of Attac's expertise on a range of problems in finance and economics.

Conclusion: a new spirit or a new *stahlhartes Gehäuse?*

The world in which we now live is significantly different from that analysed in *Le nouvel esprit du capitalisme*. We now have a 'regime' that is only weakly legitimized—if not delegitimized—and yet able to exercise effective pressure upon democratically elected governments. In this sense, Boltanski and Chiapello's concern with legitimation, justification, and justice appears to have been overtaken by events, and is perhaps no longer as pertinent as it was. We seem to be in a situation in which political legitimacy—insofar as it is relevant at all—might be more plausibly understood in James C. Scott's terms: not as

---

[14] There is thus, unsurprisingly, a concern that SMOs that focus on finance have difficulties in imposing their demands because there are too few people to act as watchdogs, for example in financial reforms, and to provide coherent alternative solutions for issues such as the restructuring of banks.

[15] This is a situation similar to the one Naomi Klein describes in the case of Mandela's government in South Africa in the 1990s, which she suggests failed to solve the economic gap between white elites and the majority of the black population because the movement and new government, focused as it was on symbolic issues, failed to deal with apparently technical questions on finance such as monetary policy. See Klein (2007).

positive support for a regime but as the simple belief that little can be done in the face of power (Scott, 1990), or as stories that elites tell to each other and about themselves (cf. Barker, 2001).[16] This shift is not a matter of evil markets versus virtuous governments, but is a reflection of a longer term and fundamental change in state steering mechanisms. In this sense, the crisis that we have been witnessing since 2007/8 is as much a political as an economic one. It was governments that implemented the regime, instruments, and mechanisms that we now see at work, thus engineering their own subordination, and that of their citizens, to market actors and pressures at key moments. If, in the 1990s, it was still appropriate to speak about a new 'spirit' of capitalism, it may now be more urgent to be thinking about a new *'stahlhartes Gehäuse'*—a new steel-hard casing, better known as the 'iron cage'.

References

Attac (2011) *About Attac.* Available at http://www.Attac.org/en/overview (accessed 28 January 2012).

Attac Deutschland (2006 [2001]) *Zwischen Netzwerk, NGO und Bewegung. Das Selbstverständnis von Attac. 8 Thesen.* Available at http://www.Attac-netzwerk.de/fileadmin/user_upload/bundesebene/Attac-strukturen/Attac_Selbstverstaendnis.pdf (accessed 28 January 2012).

—— (2008a) *Declaration, Das Casino schließen!* Available at http://www.casino-schliessen.de/forderungen/ (accessed 28 January 2012).

—— (2008b) *Das Finanz-Casino schließen! Erklärung des Attac-Ratschlags am 12. Oktober 2008,* 28ff. Available at http://www.Attac-netzwerk.de/fileadmin/user_upload/Gremien/Ratschlag/Protokolle/2008_Protokoll_Herbstratschlag%20D%C3%BCsseldorf.pdf (accessed 28 January 2012).

Barker, R. (2001) *Legitimating Identities: The Self-Legitimation of Rulers and Their Subjects.* Cambridge: Cambridge University Press.

Beckert, J. and Streeck, W. (2011) 'Eine Verteilungsfrage. Die nächste Stufe der Finanzkrise'. *Frankfurter Allgemeine Zeitung,* Feuilleton, 20 August 2011. Available at http://www.faz.net/aktuell/feuilleton/debatten/kapitalismus/eine-verteilungsfrage-die-naechste-stufe-der-finanzkrise-11111142.html (accessed 28 January 2012).

—— —— (2012) 'Die Fiskalkrise und die Einheit Europas', *Aus Politik und Zeitgeschichte,* 62(4), 7–17.

Boltanski, L. and Chiapello, E. (2005a) *The New Spirit of Capitalism,* trans. Gregory Elliott. London: Verso. First published as *Le nouvel esprit du capitalisme.* Paris: Gallimard, 1999.

—— —— (2005b) 'The New Spirit of Capitalism', *International Journal of Politics, Culture and Society,* 18, 161–88.

[16] This may indeed apply to the management texts that provide the data for Boltanski and Chiapello's analysis.

—— Thévenot, L. (1999) 'The Sociology of Critical Capacity', *European Journal of Social Theory*, 2(3), 359–77.

Breiner, P. (2004) ' "Unnatural Selection": Max Weber's Concept of *Auslese* and his Criticisms of the Reduction of Political Conflict to Economics', *International Relations*, 18, 289–307.

Bundestag (2012) *Entwurf eines Zweiten Gesetzes zur Umsetzung eines Maßnahmenpakets zur Stabilisierung des Finanzmarktes*, Drucksache 17/8343, 17 January 2012. Available at http://dipbt.bundestag.de/dip21/btd/17/083/1708343.pdf (accessed 28 January 2012).

Cassen, B. (2003) 'Inventing Attac', *New Left Review*, 19, 41–60.

Chiapello, E. and Fairclough, N. (2002) 'Understanding the New Management Ideology: A Transdisciplinary Contribution from Critical Discourse Analysis and New Sociology of Capitalism', *Discourse & Society*, 13(2), 185–208.

Crouch, C. (2000) 'Markets and States'. In K. Nash and A. Scott (eds.), *The Blackwell Companion to Political Sociology*. Oxford: Blackwell.

—— (2011) *The Strange Non-Death of Neo-Liberalism*. Cambridge: Polity Press.

Douglas, M. and Mars, D. (2003) 'Terrorism: A Positive Feedback Game', *Human Relations*, 56(7): 763–86.

du Gay, P. (2000) *In Praise of Bureaucracy*. London: Sage.

Engelen, E., Ertürk, I., Froud, J., Johal, S., Leaver, A., Moran, M., Nilsson, A., and Williams, K. (2011) *After the Great Complacence: Financial Crisis and the Politics of Reform*. Oxford: Oxford University Press.

Froud, J., Moran, M., Nilsson, A., and Williams, K. (2010) 'Wasting a Crisis? Democracy and Markets in Britain after 2007', *Political Quarterly*, 81(1), 25–38.

Gerhards, J. and Rucht, D. (1992) 'Mesomobilization Contexts: Organizing and Framing in Two Protest Campaigns in West Germany', *American Journal of Sociology*, 98(3), 555–96.

Gornitzka, A. and Sverdrup, U. (2011) 'Access of Experts: Information and EU Decision-Making', *West European Politics*, 34(1), 48–70.

Heins, V. (2002) *Weltbürger und Lokalpatrioten: Eine Einführung in das Thema Nichtregierungsorganisationen*. Leverkusen: Leske & Budrich.

Hennis, W. (2000a) *Max Weber's Science of Man*, trans. K. Tribe. London: Threshold Press.

—— (2000b) *Max Weber's Central Question* (2nd edn.), trans. K. Tribe. London: Threshold Press.

Hibou, B. (2004) 'From Privatising the Economy to Privatising the State: An Analysis of the Continual Formation of the State'. In B. Hibou (ed.), *Privatising the State*. London: Hurst & Co, 1–46.

Hirschman, A. O. (1982) *Shifting Involvements*. Oxford: Basil Blackwell.

Holland-Cunz, B. (2003) *Die alte neue Frauenfrage*. Frankfurt am Main: Suhrkamp Verlag.

Kassim, H. and Le Galès, P. (2010) 'Exploring Governance in a Multi-level Polity: A Political Instruments Approach', *West European Politics*, 33(1), 1–21.

Klein, N. (2007) *The Shock Doctrine: The Rise of Disaster Capitalism*. New York: Metropolitan Books.

Kolb, F. (2004) 'The Impact of Transnational Protest on Social Movement Organisations: Mass Media and the Making of Attac Germany'. In D. Della Porta and S. Tarrow (eds.), *Transnational Movements and Global Activism*. Lanham: Rowman & Littlefield, 95–120.

Lascomes, P. and Le Galès, P. (2007) 'Understanding Public Policy Through Its Instruments', *Governance*, 20(1), 1–21.

McCarthy, J. D. and Zald, M. (1977) 'Resource Mobilization and Social Movements: A Partial Theory', *American Journal of Sociology*, 82(6), 1212–41.

Marquand, D. (2004) *Decline of the Public*. Cambridge: Polity Press.

Pasqualoni, P. P. and Treichl, H. M. (2004) *Aktivismus als Beruf? Zum Selbstverständnisprozess von Attac Österreich*. Innsbruck: Studienverlag.

Pongratz, H. J. and Voß, G. G. (2003) *Arbeitskraftunternehmer: Erwerbsorientierungen in entgrenzten Arbeitsformen*. Berlin: Edition Sigma.

Raschke, J. (1987) 'Zum Begriffe der sozialen Bewegung'. In R. Roth and D. Rucht (eds.), *Neue soziale Bewegungen in der Bundesrepublik Deutschland*. Bonn: Bundeszentrale für politische Bildung, 19–29.

—— (1993) *Die Grünen: Wie sie wurden, was sie sind*. Cologne: Bund-Verlag.

Schmitt, C. (1996) [1922] *Politische Theologie. Vier Kapitel zur Lehre der Souveränität* (7th edn.). Berlin: Duncker & Humblot.

Schumann, H. (2009) 'Der Bundestag und die Krise. Ein Parlament entmachtet sich selbst'. *Der Tagesspiegel*, 27 March 2009. Available at http://www.tagesspiegel.de/politik/deutschland/der-bundestag-und-die-krise-ein-parlament-entmachtet-sich-selbst/1484248.html (accessed 28 January 2012).

Scott, J.C. (1990) *Domination and the Arts of Resistance*. New Haven, CT: Yale University Press.

Sennett, R. (1998) *The Corrosion of Character*. New York: W. W. Norton.

Seyfarth, C. (1989) 'Über Max Webers Beitrag zur Theorie professionellen beruflichen Handelns, zugleich eine Vorstudie zum Verständnis seiner Soziologie als Praxis'. In J. Weiß (ed.), *Max Weber heute: Erträge und Probleme der Forschung*. Frankfurt am Main: Suhrkamp Verlag, 371–405.

Skocpol, T. (2003) *Diminishing Democracy: From Membership to Management in American Civil Life*. Norman, OK: University of Oklahoma Press.

Streeck, W. (2011) 'The Crisis of Democratic Capitalism', *New Left Review*, 71, 5–29.

Tarrow, S. (2011) *Power in Movement: Social Movements and Contentious Politics* (3rd edn.). Cambridge: Cambridge University Press.

Weber, M. (1908) 'Methodologische Einleitung für die Erhebung des Vereins für Sozialpolitik über Auslese und Anpassung Berufswahlen und Berufsschicksal der Arbeiterschaft der geschlossenen Großindustrie'. In Marianne Weber (ed.), *Gesammelte Aufsätze zur Soziologie und Sozialpolitik*. Tübingen: J. C. B. Mohr, 1988 [1924].

—— (1972) [1922] *Wirtschaft und Gesellschaft* (5th edn.). Tübingen: J. C. B. Mohr.

—— (1988) [1918] 'Politk als Beruf'. In J. Winkelmann (ed.), *Gesammelte politische Schriften*. Tübingen: J. C. B. Mohr. English translation: 'The Profession and Vocation of Politics'. In P. Lassman and R. Speirs (eds.), *Weber Political Writings*. Cambridge: Cambridge University Press, 1994, 309–69.

—— (2002) *The Protestant Ethic and the Spirit of Capitalism*, trans. S. Kalberg. Oxford: Blackwell.

11

Benchmarking for the Greater Good? The 'New Investment Paradigm' in European Higher Education

Kathia Serrano-Velarde

Introduction

This chapter addresses the reframing of universities in European Union (EU) policy discourse since the launch of the Lisbon strategy in 2000. It shows how and why universities came to be understood as investment objects for private investors in EU policy discourse. Hence, the study tackles two interrelated issues: (*a*) the institutionalization of a new policy activity at the European level and (*b*) the development of an argumentative arsenal aimed at justifying and legitimizing private investments for a 'common good'.[1] At the centre of our theoretical approach to this complex form of institutionalization lie the concepts of 'test' and 'critique' as developed by Boltanski and Chiapello in *The New Spirit of Capitalism* (2005). However contested their analytical approach to capitalist dynamics might have been in the past among the French and international research community, we propose to take the premises of this work as a starting point to shed light on a complex political phenomenon: the ideological shift in higher education policy-making. We therefore work with EU policy documents spanning a five-year period, from 2003 to 2008, and analyse how the discursive construction of higher education investments went hand in hand with the institutionalization of a specific European benchmark. By including higher education investments in the

---

[1] In economic terms, common goods are defined by accessibility and non-rival consumption.

regular benchmarking exercise, the EU imposes a new 'idea of university' (Jaspers, 1980) that serves both public and private interests. EU higher education policy therewith enters an accumulation process which is essential to the logic of capitalism. Our analysis thus focuses on an evolutionary stage of capitalism that precedes the dynamics described in *The New Spirit of Capitalism*. In essence, we try to capture the fleeting moment when the fluidity of boundaries between the 'just' and the 'unjust', the 'legitimate' and the 'unacceptable', becomes visible and tangible in the European discourse on higher education.

Expanding capitalist activities to a public institution

The New Spirit of Capitalism is a milestone in the long-standing research programme of the French sociology of critique. When Boltanski and Thévenot started to work on the theme of justification as structuring the momentum of social order in the 1980s, their aim was to develop a new type of agency (Boltanski and Thévenot, 1982, 1991). By proposing a discursive approach for understanding social action and change as result of a non-deterministic type of agency, the authors offered an alternative to Bourdieu's all-encompassing paradigm of social reproduction (Bénatouil, 1999; Nachi, 2006). The conceptual framework of the sociology of critique takes seriously what people have to say about themselves and the way they act (Celikates, 2006; Turner, 2007). It looks for the reasons, the motives which inform human action, and locates them in a socially constructed notion of 'justice' and 'morality' (i.e. a normative framework to distinguish the 'just' from the 'unjust'). The analytical focus of this interactive type of sociology has thus always been on situations that bring these underlying motives out in the open: moments of confrontation and conflict or, in the words of Boltanski and his co-authors, 'disputes'. In a dispute, the parties involved need to explain their reasons for acting in a way that they can legitimately claim to be right. Disputes thus confront justifications that refer to common frameworks of justice, shared understandings of worth and greatness, and by doing so, transcend the mere rhetorical dimension. They call on individuals, collectives, 'things' to evaluate the stakes involved and to find a settlement as to who has the strongest argument. Whereas the interactive dimension has been central to Boltanski and Thévenot's work since their first publications, the notion of dispute has been revised and enriched over the years (Wagner, 1999). One of the most important contributions of *The New Spirits of Capitalism* has been to specify the two central aspects related to the notion of dispute—'test' and 'critique'—and to elaborate on their dynamic components.

The working principles of capitalism

Before delving into the theoretical argument, let us dwell on the bigger picture presented in *The New Spirit of Capitalism* and the three main theses it addresses. In fact, the opening statement of Boltanski and Chiapello is revealing: 'the subject of this book is the ideological changes that have accompanied recent transformations in capitalism' (Boltanski and Chiapello, 2005: 3). From the outset, the authors establish a connection between the changing nature of capitalism and the so-called 'ideological' changes.[2] This connection is what the authors call the 'spirit' of capitalism, after Max Weber's seminal study on the ethics of Protestantism (Weber, 2009). In a sense, Boltanski and Chiapello take the same starting point as their German precursor: a minimalist definition of capitalism as 'imperative to unlimited accumulation of capital by formally peaceful means' (Boltanski and Chiapello, 2005: 4) in conjunction with a genuine curiosity as to why such an 'absurd system' (Chiapello and Fairclough, 2002) succeeded in captivating and mobilizing the efforts of the masses. On one hand, capitalism must ensure that people engage in the accumulation process, but on the other it does not possess an endogenous sense of morality (or even a deeper meaning), nor do its systemic constraints suffice to motivate continual public support. Thus, Boltanski and Chiapello agree with Weber that individuals need a legitimate (or moral) reason to engage in capitalist activities, a reason that can only be external to capitalism. While Weber identifies the locus of morality (and modernity) in the religious lifestyle of Protestants, *The New Spirit of Capitalism* identifies a plurality of motives that drive people to play their part in the capitalist production process. This is as far as the comparison of Weber's 'spirit' and Boltanski and Chiapello's 'new spirit of capitalism' carries us. Indeed, Weber concentrated his historically rooted analysis on the emergence of capitalism. *The New Spirit of Capitalism* goes one step further by widening the focus and taking into account the evolution of capitalism.

Thesis 1: Individuals need moral reasons to engage in capitalist activities. These reasons are external to capitalism. They legitimize and constrain capitalist action.

---

[2] The term 'ideology' is defined as 'a set of shared beliefs inscribed in institutions bound up with actions, and hence anchored in reality' (Boltanski and Chiapello, 2005: 3). It is important to note that Boltanski and Chiapello dissociate themselves from the classic, Marxian notion of ideology. Rather, they work with an understanding of ideology that bears close similarities with the Foucauldian-inspired definition of 'discourse' proposed by critical discourse analysis (Chiapello and Fairclough, 2002; Laclau, 1989; Norval, 2000). In this perspective, the terms 'ideology' and 'discourse' can be used interchangeably. Discourses are defined as 'a relational ensemble of signifying sequences that weaves together semantic aspects of language and pragmatic aspects of action' (Torfing, 2005: 14).

Boltanski and Chiapello identify a number of moral frameworks that refer to distinct concepts of justice and repertories of action the authors somewhat misleadingly call 'cities'.[3] The concept of cities is of crucial importance to understand the social dynamics in capitalist societies, as it serves as a discursive resource for both capitalism and its critics. Both sides of the argument refer to a moral framework when expressing or answering critique in a given situation. The question, whether the opponents refer to the same moral framework or different ones, is what constitutes the evolutionary component of capitalism. In a dispute, the two sides either (*a*) refer to the same notion of justice but feel insecure about the relative worth of their argument, in which case they proceed to the systematic evaluation of their respective positions according to a common frame of reference (as proposed by the city of reference) or (*b*) they refer to different spheres of justice (i.e. different cities), in which case each party will need to justify its actions so as to render them plausible and legitimate in the eyes of the other. In the first case, Boltanski and Chiapello talk about 'testing', in the second, about 'critique'. We will see that both aspects are highly correlated. For the moment, however, let us concentrate on the dynamism implied by this dichotomist use of cities in the critique of capitalism. In the critique of capitalism, the 'agents' of capitalism such as executives, business firms, etc. are confronted with a claim of injustice that is legitimate and morally grounded, yet it is formulated in another city. In order to ensure the sustainability of capitalist enterprise, these agents thus need to develop justifications that take into account and partially internalize the critiques issued from the opposite side. They thereby develop the discursive resources of capitalist action and become immune to the original critique. This process of readjustment can have larger repercussions and even bring about a transformation of capitalism.

Thesis 2: Capitalist agents and critics refer to the same frameworks of justification. By responding to a given critique, capitalist agents internalize the moral repertoire of their opponents, thereby contributing to the evolution and consolidation of the power base of capitalism.

In essence, critique is systematically integrated into the capitalist repertoire of justification and testing, thereby strengthening its moral base. Capitalism thus continues to engage people and secures its present and future existence. The accumulation process remains untroubled, though its ideological framework has been altered so as to accommodate claims of injustice.

---

[3] Boltanski and Thévenot identify six cities (inspirational, domestic, reputational, civic, commercial, and industrial) in their work *On Justification* (1991). In *The New Spirit of Capitalism*, Boltanski and Chiapello discovered a seventh moral order (the projective city). In this study, we will not go into details on the cities. Rather, we propose to concentrate on the analytical dimension of Boltanski and Chiapello's *oeuvre*.

Thesis 3: Capitalism does not change its content (i.e. the accumulation process), but adjusts its form in order to ensure continuous engagement.

Reviewing these basic assumptions, we can state that engagement, justification, and critique are the central aspects of capitalist evolution. They all come together in the design and implementation of a 'test'. 'Tests of strength' are institutionalized devices to evaluate and rank legitimate claims and arguments according to a common frame of reference. As such, they 'enact' (Giddens, 1984) the discursive resources of capitalism.

A grammar of disputes for academic capitalism? [4]

We are interested in the discursive construction of universities as public institutions as well as objects for private investments. Thus, the focus lies on an aspect that has been neglected in the research of the evolutionary dynamics of capitalism implied by Boltanski and Chiapello: the expansion of capitalism (i.e. its inherent logic and the ideologies it works with) into societal sectors that previously belonged to the public realm. Indeed, we wonder how European universities became involved in the accumulation process of modern societies. In order to retrace this development, we centre our analysis on the discursive construction of a European benchmark for public and private investments in higher education. Using the terminology of Boltanski and Chiapello, this type of benchmark constitutes a 'testing device', a common frame of reference for the investment community allowing not only for the institutionalization of a new notion of justice in higher education governance but also for the systematic comparison of its agents according to a pre-defined metric.

We already mentioned that test is the key component for understanding the extension of capitalist activities into new fields. Tests play a boundary-spanning role and have an ordering function. First of all, a 'test' binds actors to a common frame of justice. By connecting agents and ideologies, the test excludes all notions of justice and repertoires of action (i.e. cities) that have no relevance in a specific situation. Hence, a test stipulates what is legitimate and what is not in a given context and among a given set of actors. By mobilizing agents, discursive resources, and 'things', it enforces the reverberation and acceptance of what it stands for (i.e. a specific sense of morality and system of justice). Second, according to Boltanski and Chiapello, tests are systems of equivalences in a Simmelian sense (Simmel, 2009) and have a powerful ordering function. They foreclose insecurity concerning the relative

---

[4] The title refers to the prominent monograph by Slaughter and Leslie *Academic Capitalism: Politics, Policies and the Entrepreneurial University* (1997).

worth of agents and causes at stake by proposing a common measure of justice and establishing equivalences. This form of evaluation presupposes, however, a reference to a social order that is considered to be just and legitimate by all parties. As the locus of legitimacy lies outside capitalism, so does the ideology that structures and informs the test. The order of worth and the system of equivalences it proposes are thus contingent on the moral agenda/the city that informs the test and lends legitimacy to the procedure. Tests are thus a way of involving actors within a shared understanding of justice and worth in a given context by excluding alternative interpretations and value judgements. In the case of private investments in higher education, the European benchmark has a two-fold function. First, it institutes an order of worth, a common measure for both the investor and investee, who find themselves included in a continuous benchmarking exercise. Second, the discursive framing of this benchmark—that is to say its justification and illustration in policy documentation—provides an ideological grounding for private investments in higher education.

The introduction and institutionalization of a 'test of strength' is what is at stake in the analysis we propose to carry out. We argue that the extension of capitalism to new fields, such as higher education, is dependent on the institutionalization of testing devices, such as benchmarks, which mobilize agents and confer on them a sense of justice regarding the capitalist principles they are to apply and defend.

The new investment paradigm in European higher education

The 'new investment paradigm' and the odyssey of the 2 per cent GDP benchmark

Although they have been discussed by European ministers and EU representatives since the early stages of European integration as being a central target for European action, universities never really managed to become an EU priority (Corbett, 2005). Instead, the categorization of higher education as social policy hindered its establishment as a full-fledged policy field, as 'European integration has created a constitutional asymmetry between policies promoting market efficiencies and policies promoting social protection and equality' (Scharpf, 2002: 645)—meaning that the economic project to create a single market took precedence over the social protection of European citizens and workers. Consequently, social policy remains a national matter. The redistributive nature of social policy and the subsidiary character of national education and research were particularly a problem for the establishment of EU executive power in the realm of higher education (Bache, 2006; Banchoff, 2002; Ertl and Phillips, 2006). In fact, universities did not find their place on the European agenda until the 2000 Lisbon council of European ministers. The declaration of the introduction of the Lisbon agenda urged the EU to revisit its priorities, as the agenda highlighted the economic value of know-ledge and innovation. In their ambitious declaration, European ministers called on Europe to become 'the most competitive and dynamic knowledge based economy in the world, capable of sustainable economic growth with more and better jobs and greater social cohesion' (European Council, 2000). Universities thus find themselves in the position to realize the longstanding, yet complicated goal of a single Europe: to combine an economic agenda with a social policy framework for all European citizens. Certainly, the year 2000 was a turning point for higher education and research policies, which sud-denly attracted increased political attention. The omnipresent notion of economic competitiveness has changed the formulation of EU policies in education and training in favour of educational benchmarks and quality control in the framework of the Open Method of Coordination (De Ruiter, 2010; Ertl, 2006), hereafter OMC. Universities were thus propelled into a new policy era, wherein they have to activate their economic and social potential and measure their progress by referring to a set of comparable benchmarks and standards. The phenomenon we are interested in is the creation of a European benchmark for higher education investments in the framework of the OMC, which is a policy instrument devised by the European Commission to over-come the reticence of member states (Héritier, 2002; Kohl and Vahlpahl, 2004) with regard to the Europeanization of social policy issues, including education and research. It is characterized by a 'soft law' approach (Trubek and Trubek, 2005) insofar as the guidelines and the regular benchmarking exercise proposed in this voluntary framework are not attached to particular con-straints or sanctions. The benchmarks and guidelines are prepared by the European Commission in collaboration with expert organizations and subse-quently implemented by the European Council. Since the Lisbon Council in 2000, the European Commission has worked towards the ratification of a new benchmark for higher education: increasing public and private 'investments' for higher education to 2 per cent of GDP.

However original this thought may seem at first sight, let us keep in mind that the idea of 'private investments' in education is far from new. Since the 1960s, research has revealed that the so-called educational investments lead to improvements in marginal productivity and, hence, to economic growth (Heyneman, 2001). Nobel Prize winning economist Gary Becker dedicated his early work to investment in skills and the evolution of one's lifetime earning capacity (Becker, 1962), thereby contributing to the development of life-cycle economics and human capital theory. Nowadays, rates of return estimates based on Becker's work are widely used for assessing current public training and related assistance programmes (Rosen, 1993). Nevertheless, it is

257

important to point out that these approaches mostly focus on the individual level. In this particular equation, students, workers, and researchers constitute investment 'objects' for private investors. Individual assets (i.e. individual skills, private financial resources) and expectations (i.e. better career prospects) form the basis for calculating the profit margins of educational investments. What is important to note about EU investment discourses in education is its focus on the organizational level. EU policy discourse on private investment for higher education concentrates primarily on private investments to higher education and research institutions. By framing universities as investment objects, the locus of investment shifts from the educated individual to research and education infrastructure. Universities are thus integrated into a unique productive relationship where they figure as a profitable business opportunity capable of generating tangible added value for those who dare to invest. By concentrating our analysis on the discursive constitution of an investment object, we want to draw attention to the underlying, value-laden process that precedes and accompanies the introduction of benchmarks. Analysing the institutionalization of a benchmark thus means to observe the discursive construction of parameters of justice and morality that work for all parties involved in this capitalist enterprise. Going back to Boltanski and Chiapello's terminology, we can state that the 'test of strength' attached to the new EU investment paradigm includes more than the current 2 per cent GDP benchmark. Rather, it also comprises the underlying moral framework and the justification it provides for private investments in higher education. This leaves us with the following question: How did the European university become a legitimate object for private investments? Or, in Boltanski and Chiapello's words: What are the 'ideological resources' that make it possible to think about universities as a place for capitalistic activities and to subsequently institutionalize this ideological shift in the form of a benchmark? Are there limits to a capitalistic perception of universities? What aspects of higher education are excluded from the continuous accumulation process capitalism embodies?

Method and data

In order to examine this discursive process, we proceeded in three steps. First of all, we executed a template analysis (Crabtree and Miller, 1999; King, 2004) of thirty EU policy documents dealing with private and public 'investments' in higher education. The documents are all official and publicly available through the platform of the European Register. Our theoretical sample (Keller, 2008) contains council conclusions, communications, parliamentary documents, speeches, commissioned work, green papers, working papers, and memos. Hence, we deal with a broad spectrum of texts from different institutions of the EU political apparatus. Despite the fact that we included texts from different policy fields (i.e. research and education), all of these documents quote each other, thereby confirming (*a*) the idea of a strong link between research and training policies and (*b*) the overall cohesiveness of the investment discourse for higher education at the European level. The corpus encompasses texts from the years 2003 to 2008 and retraces the discursive trajectory of the 2 per cent GDP benchmark for higher education investments. The length of the selected texts varies from 10 to 150 pages. We worked with the analytical software Atlas.ti to code and analyse the corpus according to a set of nine broad thematic categories (actors, context, investment, constraints, information asymmetry, organization and governance, social issues, themes of change, economic themes). These nine categories were subsequently subdivided into 140 codes. We employed an open coding procedure to generate subcodes and code families. In the second step, we proceeded with a sequential analysis of the main transversal categories (or 'integrative themes', King, 2004) of 'investments', 'constraints', and 'information asymmetry'. Finally, the analysis was complemented by a series of interviews with actors and stakeholders who were involved in the drafting process and the discussion of the selected documents. We thereby wanted to include the contextual dimension (Phillips and Hardy, 2002) in the discursive analysis and check for potential incoherencies in data interpretation.

Analysis

'Expenditure' versus 'investment': understanding the paradigm shift

The discursive construction of the so-called 'new investment paradigm' for higher education began with the confrontation of the terms 'expenditure' and 'investment', and the diagnosis of a 'funding gap'. From 2003 onwards, public spending or 'expenditure' was seen in negative terms (i.e. 'deficit spending', 'shortfalls'). The state had failed to provide European universities with 'the critical mass' necessary to become active in global competition. Throughout the documents, public expenditure is circumscribed with terminology that suggests stagnation, even regression. Where progress is noted, it is framed in euphemisms ('slight increase') and clashes with the omnipresent picture of the accelerating pace of globalization.[5] Public spending was thus claimed to be 'insufficient' for ensuring appropriate levels of performance in higher education. This gap widens further with regard to 'competing' or 'comparable'

---

[5] By the word 'framing', we refer to procedures of discursive framing as described in Benford and Snow (2000). Frames are interpretative schemata that enable participants to locate, perceive, and label occurrences.

higher education systems such as those in the United States, Canada, and Japan, the omnipresent reference countries. Consequently, European universities are declared to be in danger of lagging behind global developments and 'modernity'. It is noteworthy that none of these notions (be it 'competition' or 'modernity') is developed in much detail. Rather, they confer a generic and abstract framing of the situation which evokes a diffuse sense of urgency: an urgency to re-establish European authority as the cradle of modernity and leadership among global competitors, that is, an urgency to invest more in higher education.

The question that is central to all these documents is 'how to fill the funding gap'? Since public expenditure is considered inadequate for providing universities with the means to compete, attention turns to alternative, non-public resources. This shift raises different yet interrelated questions: Where should these resources come from, if not from the public purse? To what extent should these resources complement/substitute public funding? What are the terms of this new funding pact? By raising these questions, the European Commission self-imposes an explorative mission to discover 'untapped resources' in the European higher education area. European policy documents from 2003 to 2008 contribute to this objective by identifying non-public financial resources and, most importantly, defining the conditions under which they can legitimately be mobilized for and by universities. This exercise was punctuated by a series of commissioned reports and studies that aimed at '[Supporting] the development of a comprehensive mapping of research foundations to document the overall financial contribution to the field, but also [identifying] and [reviewing] best practice examples and [facilitating] cross fertilisation and exchange of experience' (Report by an Expert Group, 2005: 29). Hence, EU policy aims at achieving visibility of actors and interests in a field (i.e. higher education finance) that has long been overshadowed by state intervention. It is our understanding that by 'mapping' this interactive framework, European political institutions reframe the notion of higher education finance in a way that legitimizes the accumulation of (private) capital. They do so by identifying non-public 'investors', anticipating their interests as well as their expectations and providing rules and norms for interaction (i.e. separating legitimate profit claims from the illegitimate). EU policy discourse thereby works with a broad definition of the private sector that encompasses for-profit as well as non-profit organizations. Both types of private contributions are referred to as 'investments'.[6]

---

[6] Interviews with EU officials revealed that the switching from a funding terminology that revolved around the word 'expenditure' to the terminology of 'investment' was a conscious choice of policy-makers and, as such, needs to be understood as a reference to the Lisbon agenda. Since Lisbon referred to knowledge creation and dissemination as economic processes, research and training institutions (especially universities) are considered part of the production/

This simple reference to added value is what constitutes the core principle of the European 'paradigm shift' in higher education policy. Whereas higher education 'expenditure' referred to a tightly framed distributional order suggesting net costs only (the state funds universities to fulfil their public duty), making use of the 'investment' repertoire opens the field to innovative actor constellations, therewith suggesting a new type of synergetic outcome, a return on investment for all parties involved. The declaration of the former commissioner of education Janez Potočnik, 'University is an opportunity let's seize it!' (Potočnik, 2008: 69), illustrates this discursive turn in a concise way. Regarding this statement, let us first take note of the homogenizing singular notion of the 'university' and the plurality of actors (the community of 'us') involved in this particular evidence. All universities become targets for the interests of an indefinite number of private investors ('us'). The singular of 'opportunity' thereby reflects the singular of 'university', implying that the university as a whole becomes a business opportunity. As opposed to the 'expenditure' framework, where private entities (i.e. individuals, enterprises, philanthropic organizations) primarily funded individual research projects, the investment focus lies on the organizational structure, the academic institution as a whole. Second, the choice of the pronoun 'us' indicates the inclusion of the reader (in this case, the political audience) in the field of investors. 'We' adheres to all potential investors that might consider giving to universities. Third, the exclamation mark in the second half of the sentence suggests an urgency to act and thereby reflects the overall spirit of the discourse as illustrated by the 'funding gap' trope.

In appealing for private investments, European policy discourse opens up a new field for capitalist action: higher education. It is our theoretical understanding that the EU thereby gives a moral backdrop for capitalist activities in higher education and provides justification for certain aspects of capitalist behaviour while rejecting others. Discussing the potential of private investments for a common good thus raises questions: Under what conditions can private contributions to higher education be considered legitimate and just?

We identified three steps leading to the institutionalization of a legitimate investment claim:

1. The establishment of an investment 'case';
2. The definition of legitimate and illegitimate action in different types of investment cases; and
3. The reframing of a common good as an open and multifaceted concept allowing for private gains.

---

productivity cycle. The 'contribution of universities to the knowledge economy' is to generate economically added value and contribute to the accumulation of capital.

We believe that European policy discourses describe rules of engagement mobilizing certain repertoires of justification and thereby contributing to capitalist expansion into new policy fields.

Step 1. 'Make your case'

The first step of the institutionalization process consists of creating the exclusivity of the investment case. While public expenditure mostly deals with anonymous entities (taxpayers, the state, universities) in an indefinite timeframe, 'investments' require the commitment of individual actors as well as the construction of an investment case, that is, an investment project with a beginning and an end, visible costs and assets, and—most of all—the promise of an investment reward at the end of the engagement period. Compared to public expenditure, investments refer to lucrative, individual projects of limited duration. The 'case' metaphor has entered European discourses at an early stage and emphasizes the selective and limited nature of higher education investments as highlighted by the following quote:

> Having done the research, consultants can help universities make their case. This can involve: the preparation of a one-page description of the project in plain language, explaining 'how it will change the world'; the preparation of a financial plan (. . .); and even the identification of 'naming' opportunities for the funder. The case needs to be solid, stable and reliable. (. . .) It is also important to spell out the social return on Investment (. . .). This puts a monetary value on social impact. And finally, it is also important to tailor the case, i.e. to specify how the project fits the donor's objectives, priorities and interests. (European Commission, 2008c: 286)

The quote highlights the necessity of 'tailoring' the case according to context-specific factors (i.e. the interests and expectations of investment partners) so as to make the rules of engagement such as duration, assets, costs, and return visible to all stakeholders. Circumscribing the case and establishing its exclusivity with regard to public spending (which is by definition non-lucrative and anonymous) is what creates visibility and—most importantly—'credibility' (i.e. the justification to invest) among potential investees. Both concepts are discussed in the second part of our analysis. For the moment, let us look at the fact that the case metaphor ensures (a) actor exclusivity and (b) input/output visibility. The interesting part—with regard to Boltanski and Chiapello's theory of testing—is that an exclusive set of actors shares the basic premises of interaction. Establishing a case creates visibility of actors' constituencies, resources, and costs. It allows for the distribution of responsibilities and tasks and thereby ensures the possibility of 'sharing' (meaning) and 'negotiating' (rules and interests) among investor and investees. Indeed, both terms are used with great profusion in policy discourse and indicate the necessity of establishing common rules of behaviour, norms of conduct, and stable expectations in the investment community. The clarity of these rules and norms is constitutive for the creation of stable expectations and therefore central to the investment decision. Hence EU policy texts put a special emphasis on the discussion of measures and procedures allowing for clarity and avoiding 'disputes' and 'misunderstandings' among actors, especially with regard to the fairness of the redistributive procedure and the soundness of the scientific output.

Having discussed the procedure of constructing case exclusivity and the selection of actors involved in the frame of investments, let us now turn to the question of how this exclusive interactive arrangement is given meaning and legitimacy. What are the justifications provided for private investments or, most importantly, what critiques does the European investment discourse address?

Step 2. Legitimate and illegitimate investment cases in higher education

Before delving into the analysis, it is important to note that the discursive constructions of non-profit and for-profit investments differ significantly with regard to the norms and justifications they provide for capitalist activities. We will thus offer separate accounts of these investment cases.

THE PRIVATE EXPLOITATION OF A COMMON GOOD

For-profit investment in universities refers to situations in which businesses transfer money to universities in the framework of a research contract or collaboration. To start with, it is important to note that business investments are discussed in the ontological framework of classic economic theory. Investments turn out to be biased and thus critical from the moment the balance of net costs becomes asymmetric and blurs the perfect market equity of the transaction. 'Exploitation' is a central concept for the justification and critique of for-profit investments in universities. The term has thus different value connotations. For one, exploitation is a central aspect of business transactions. It is based on the operationalization of a resource in the most effective and efficient way so as to generate value. The exploitation of research thereby refers to the commercialization process of a research finding and thus to the generation of tangible added value for the business. The exploitation of universities is unproblematic if the costs of exploitation are equally distributed among the production partners and public access to research data is guaranteed. Exploitation becomes a problem once these conditions become biased. European policy discourse addresses these two points in its critique of exploitation.

The first critique addressed with regard to exploitation is one of cost and risk asymmetry. Cost asymmetry can be detected on both sides of the investment. For the investor, cost asymmetry is equivalent to information asymmetry. The business does not have sufficient information on the investment object (most especially on the tangible and intangible assets) to judge the quality of the investments and expected returns. Not being able to estimate the costs of investments becomes a major 'risk' to the business community and thus a reason not to invest. On the investee side, cost asymmetry is seen as an abuse. The investment deal is conceived in a way that systematically disadvantages universities and does not cover the real-time research costs of the institutions (e.g. overheads). In this case, the public nature of universities (i.e. public funding of the research infrastructure) is exploited to private ends: 'When the research field is precisely defined, it is easier to negotiate rights at an earlier stage and to avoid misunderstandings/disputes. (. . .) In case of collaboration, the publicly funded research institution must ensure that, looking at the rights and obligations of all partners, the contract is balanced, in order to exclude the possibility of passing any indirect State aid through too favourable conditions from the research institution to the industrial partner(s). In the case of contract research, research institutions should expect to recover full direct and indirect costs of all research activities undertaken unless they obtain rights to (some of) the outputs of the research' (European Commission, 2007b: 172). Overcoming cost asymmetry thus requires cost transparency and enforceable formalization procedures (i.e. intellectual property rights, research contracts, and exploitation agreements) that are examined in great detail and confer additional political legitimacy to EU policy initiatives in this field. The ideal exploitation situation for universities is one that produces 'mutual benefit', a term we investigate in step 3 of the present analysis.

The second critique regarding exploitation concerns public access to research findings. Investors aim at producing an exclusive exploitation agreement. By financing the creation of new insights with commercial impact, the so-called 'innovations', the investor establishes a competitive advantage. Knowledge represents a central asset to the existence and success of a business. Consequently, sharing knowledge about innovation would decrease the economic value of the business product. However, by restraining or closing public access to academically produced research findings and data, business priorities undermine the public mission of universities. European policy discourses address this problem of injustice in a surprisingly direct manner: 'How far can [universities] move in the direction of commercial exploitation and at the same time further research for the public good?' (Report by an Expert Group 2005: 276). Nevertheless, this claim of injustice has not yet evolved into concrete solution finding/ policy recommendations. The discussion from 2003 to 2008 hints at a reframing of innovation with the aim of transcending the mere financial/economic priority attached to it and proposing a number of discursive means to integrate the public dimension into the R&D framework, for instance by referring to a so-called 'public domain or open innovation approach' (European Commission, 2008*e*: 45). Compared to the discursive register which underlies for-profit investments, non-profit cases are constructed via a different set of concepts. This shall be presented in the following section.

'HOW TO MAKE A DIFFERENCE'—THE CASE OF NON-PROFIT
INVESTMENTS IN HIGHER EDUCATION
Although it may seem surprising that non-profit investments constitute a form of capitalist activity, the argumentation and terminology clearly link this type of private contribution with a specific accumulation strategy. Even though economic value does not seem to be a priority of non-profit organizations, the discourse engenders a different notion of return on investment to the fore: foundations or trusts aim at 'making a difference'. This recurring phrasing highlights the non-profit mission of promoting social change in a way that is apparent and visible to the wider public. The return on investment non-profits strive for is a normative impact on societal evolutions. This approach thereby clashes with the traditional discursive representation of the 'public good' (i.e. public/open access to a certain type of resource) by postulating a personalized, punctual, and traceable impact of individual institutions on the outlook of society. The terminology applied to this dynamic of change is a 'visionary' one. The investment case (i.e. the exploitation agreement in the profit scenario) becomes a 'vision', a 'cause' that 'convinces' potential investors, generates identification potential, and inspires philanthropic commitment. The 'vision' represents the essence of the organization, its relation to society and change (i.e. what it stands for). By identifying with and financing a vision, the investor becomes part of it. Non-profits thus inscribe themselves in a normative project, a transaction of limited duration, comparable to the business case that generates tangible added value in the form of impact visibility or change. 'To attract more funding, universities first need to convince stakeholders— governments, companies, households that existing resources are efficiently used and fresh ones would produce an added value for them' (European Commission, 2005*c*: 62). The vision thereby furthers the goals of the university as well as the founding mission of the non-profit.

There are two types of critiques expressed with regard to philanthropic investments. For one, the investment situation is judged unfair or unjust, when private money (i.e. the money of the non-profit organization) is used to substitute public expenditure. From the perspective of the non-profit, being instrumentalized for the funding of operational tasks and thereby taking over the role of the state as principal financier of public institutions is against their organizational (or private) mission. This type of funding does not complement, but rather acts as a substitute for, public expenditure. Hence, it does not ensure outcome visibility for the funded institution or for the non-profits mobilizing the funds. Non-profit investments would have to finance day-to-day operations (i.e. reproduction and stability) instead of promoting a change project. Second, from the perspective of higher education institutions, this critique concerns the illegitimate influence of non-profits on the public mission of higher education institutions. But what constitutes illegitimate influence? The most spectacular example of open dispute and 'resistance' to non-profit influence involves academic freedom. Academic leadership and fundraising teams thus need to ensure that their activities 'will not compromise academic freedom' (European Commission, 2008c: 262). This critique focuses on the scientific legitimacy of the academic institution, which must not comply with the objectives of wealthy individuals, thereby losing its impartiality.

Step 3. 'Mutual' and 'public benefits'

Discussing the possibility of promoting private investments for a common good (i.e. higher education) requires a discursive commitment to find a common ground that justifies both sides of the investment. In addition to clarifying the expectations of private investors and public investees, the investment discourse needs to embed them in a common frame of reference, a shared 'ideological' grounding. In the realm of European higher education, this discursive rapprochement is marked by the political ambition to balance the two core principles of the Lisbon strategy 'promoting economic competi-tiveness' and 'achieving social cohesion'. The inherent complexity of this task results in a discursive hybridization that advocates both sides of the invest-ment for a common good, that is, the economic and the social side. The European investment discourse is thus filled with hybrid constructions such as 'socio-economic benefits', 'social efficiency', or 'social value of the invest-ment'. An educational investment has to be both 'efficient and equitable', thereby embracing the inherent paradox of the political mission, instead of clarifying it. The central concepts of this discursive hybridization are the notions of 'mutual' and 'public benefit'. They frame the positive return of private investments for the public institution in particular and the common good in general. Although they cannot be seen as neologisms, the terms 'mutual benefit' and 'public benefit' need to be understood as figures of compromise in the discursive effort to legitimize capitalist activities in higher education.

In the business setting, return on investment is framed as 'mutual benefit'. The mutuality of benefits thereby indicates a situation where both parties experience tangible returns on investment while avoiding cost asymmetry. Hence, this 'win-win situation' is characterized by complete cost transparency and symmetry. Especially, the mutual character of the existing bonds and long-term commitments among business parties and universities is emphasized in this regard. Indeed, business investments in higher education are not understood as short-term, one-time transactions. Rather, they are embedded in a transaction framework that promotes successive and repeated exchanges. Borrowing from network theory, we might suggest that the above-mentioned relation is akin to a 'strong tie' (Granovetter, 1973). Business investments thus build on a reciprocal trust relationship of long duration. The words 'mutual', 'sustainable', and 'trust' become characteristic of this type of situation where the mutuality of benefits is ensured, among others, through clear (or institutionalized) rules of engagement for all parties involved. 'Mutual benefits' have a public dimension insofar as they guarantee an optimal trade-off for both the business and the public institutions. The term is thus distinct (*a*) from the notion of 'profit', which does not include the idea of mutual or symmetric benefit-sharing and (*b*) from the notion of 'public benefit' used in the non-profit context. With regard to non-profit investment, it is necessary to take into account the discursive construction of the social responsibility of non-profits. Philanthropy, it is argued, has its roots in charitable giving or 'the redistribution of primarily economic resources from higher to lower income groups' (Report by an Expert Group, 2005: 125). We have already discussed the fact that philanthropic giving to universities is linked to the non-profit claim of furthering social change. However, let us be more precise with regard to the 'public' impact non-profits aim at by providing funds to public institutions. To start with, it is necessary to point out that the omnipresent notion of public benefit is not clearly defined and loosely refers to all organizations that fulfil a public aim or claim non-profit status (i.e. all those organizations that do not work for profit). 'Public benefit' can be understood as the (least) common denominator of both public and non-profit organizations. Indeed, both types of organizations—public and non-profit—transcend the mere profit-seeking exercise and contribute to social welfare. They serve a public mission, though the scope of this mission varies according to the type of organization. While public organizations serve the general public and are thus inclusive by nature, non-profit organizations fulfil one or more social purposes, thereby promoting social change among/through a limited constituency (i.e. schoolchildren, young artists, the elderly). It is the social nature of non-profit enterprises that qualifies them for the 'public' label. Yet the public addressed by non-profit action is inherently limited and exclusive. Private contributions can contribute to the provision of a common good, yet with some limitations: for-profit investments serve the interest of an individual public institution while non-profits fulfil public purposes by providing punctual support to selected social initiatives.

Conclusion

However relevant our fascination with Boltanski and Chiapello's evolutionary model of capitalism might be, it poses manifold problems with regard to further operationalization. Thus, it remains unclear whether we are actually dealing with a full-bodied research programme à la Parsons or a pragmatic tool box à la Foucault. This chapter proposed an empirical investigation of one explanatory model: the constitution of a 'test of strength'. By focusing on the sedimentation of social orders through the creation and reform of testing devices, the authors develop a discursive notion of institutionalization that combines path-dependent and evolutionary explanations.

Since the development of a test is considered a precondition for capitalist activity, we focused on an aspect of Boltanski and Chiapello's work that has garnered comparatively little attention: the expansion of capitalism to decom-modified spheres of activity. In essence, we tried to sharpen our understanding of the antecedents or moral premises of capitalism and the subsequent constitution of an interface to critique. This chapter has shown how the spirit of capitalism unfolded in the university, a public institution once dominated by a primarily social discourse and scientific ethos (Merton, 1973). We therefore gathered evidence regarding European policy and its increasing focus on raising the level of private investments in higher education. We have seen that the new EU investment paradigm aims for continuous, if not long-term, engagement of private parties in the funding and provision of higher education services. The political discourse maintains that private investments merely complement public funding. Nevertheless, by opening up the field of higher education to private actors and by hinting at the existence of added value, a return on investment for all parties involved, the private 'investment' discourse questions the distributional (and social) order of the public 'expenditure' framework. It is our understanding that, by exploring the possibilities of private contributions to higher education, European policy is reframing the notion of higher education finance in a way that legitimizes the accumulation of (private) capital in the realm of public higher education. Policy-makers do this by identifying non-public 'investors', anticipating their interests as well as their expectations, and providing rules and norms for capitalist activities in higher education. The formalization of the 2 per cent GDP benchmark certainly needs to be understood as an effort to increase the visibility of private investments and create, at the same time, a reliable and shared 'testing device' to measure the level of capitalist activities in higher education. The introduction of a legitimate and common standard of capitalist behaviour thus paves the way for further capitalist action in the academic world.

This account of the institutionalization of a new discursive regime in higher education opens up two main research avenues. First, the current debate on 'standardization' as a policy instrument (Brunsson and Jacobsson, 2000) mainly focuses on issues of market coordination and soft coercion. The analytical perspective of Boltanski and Chiapello thus introduces an interpretative dimension that considers standardization as the institutionalization of interpretative schemes and norms of behaviour which constrain future choices and thereby promotes the continuity and adaptability of the policy path. Second, our analysis pointed to the constructive and creative effects of hybridization as a means to introduce capitalist working mechanisms into formerly decommodified settings. Since capitalist logics need to penetrate a social order in order to become functional, the ensuing discourse is likely to promote inherently hybrid patterns of justification. Further research is needed to explore the idea of hybridization as a means to institutionalize and alter capitalist logics. Yet, this research perspective presupposes an open concept of moral order that is neither absolute nor finite, as postulated in the analysis of Boltanski and Thévenot (1991). Instead, the moral order of a polis should be considered a malleable interpretative framework permeable to negotiation. Only if we consider the possibility of transcending the inherent social order of the 'polis' through agency and interaction do we fully take into account the creative dynamic of capitalism and its agents.

References

Bache, I. (2006) 'The Europeanization of Higher Education: Markets, Politics or Learning?', *Journal of Common Market Studies*, 44, 231–48.

Banchoff, T. (2002) 'Institutions, Inertia and European Union Research Policy', *Journal of Common Market Studies*, 40, 1–21.

Becker, G. (1962) 'Investment in Human Capital: A Theoretical Analysis', *Journal of Political Economy*, 70, 9–49.

Bénatouil, T. (1999) 'A Tale of Two Sociologies: The Critical and the Pragmatic Stance in Contemporary French Sociology', *European Journal of Social Theory*, 2, 379–96.

Benford, R. and Snow, D. (2000) 'Framing Processes and Social Movements: An Overview and Assessment', *Annual Review of Sociology*, 26, 611–39.

Boltanski, L. and Chiapello, E. (1999) *Le nouvel esprit du capitalisme*. Paris: Gallimard.

————(2005) *The New Spirit of Capitalism*. London: Verso.

——Thévenot, L. (1982) *Les cadres. La formation d'un groupe social*. Paris: Éditions de Minuit.

————(1991) *De la justification. Les économies de la grandeur*. Paris: Gallimard.

Brunsson, N. and Jacobsson, B. (2000) *A World of Standards*. Oxford: Oxford University Press.

Celikates, R. (2006) 'From Critical Social Theory to a Social Theory of Critique: On the Critique of Ideology After the Pragmatic Turn', *Constellations*, 13, 21–40.

Chiapello, E. (2003) 'Reconciling the Two Principal Meanings of the Notion of Ideology: The Example of the Concept of the "Spirit of Capitalism"', *European Journal of Social Theory*, 6, 155–71.

——Fairclough, N. (2002) 'Understanding the New Management Ideology. A Transdisciplinary Contribution from Critical Discourse Analysis and New Sociology of Capitalism', *Discourse & Society*, 13, 185–208.

Corbett, A. (2005) *Universities and the Europe of Knowledge: Ideas, Institutions and Policy Entrepreneurship in European Union Higher Education Policy, 1955–2005*. Basingstoke: Palgrave Macmillan.

Crabtree, B. and Miller, W. (1999) 'Using Codes and Code Manuals: A Template Organizing Style of Interpretation'. In W. Miller and B. Crabtree (eds.) *Doing Qualitative Research*. Newbury Park: Sage, 163–79.

de Ruiter, R. (2010) 'Variations on a Theme: Governing the Knowledge-based Society in the EU Through Methods of Open Coordination in Education and R&D', *Journal of European Integration*, 32, 157–73.

Ertl, H. (2006) 'European Union Politics in Education and Training: The Lisbon Agenda as a Turning Point?', *Comparative Education*, 42, 5–27.

——Phillips, D. (2006) 'Standardization in EU Education and Training Policy: Findings from a European Research Network', *Comparative Education*, 42, 77–91.

European Commission (2008) *Communication from the Commission to the European Parliament, the Council, the European Economic and Social Committee and the Committee of the Regions: An Updated Strategic Framework for European Cooperation in Education and Training*. Brussels: European Council.

European Council (2000) *Conclusions of the Lisbon European Council, 23–24 March 2000*. Brussels: European Council.

——(2006) *Investing More in Knowledge and Innovation: Presidency Conclusions*. Brussels: European Council, 25–26 March 2006.

Giddens, A. (1984) *The Constitution of Society: Outlien of the Theory of Structuration*. Cambridge: Polity Press.

Granovetter, M. (1973) 'The Strength of Weak Ties', *American Journal of Sociology*, 78, 1360–80.

Héritier, A. (2002) 'New Modes of Governance in Europe: Policy Making without Legislating?' In A. Héritier (ed.), *Common Goods: Reinventing European and International Governance* Lanham, MD: Rowman & Littlefield, 185–207.

Heyneman, S. (2001) 'General Introduction: Global Issues in Education', *Peabody Journal of Education*, 76, 1–6.

Jaspers, K. (1980) *Die Idee der Universität*. Berlin: Springer.

Kaiser, R. and Prange, H. (2006) 'Missing the Lisbon Target? Multi-level Innovation and EU Policy Coordination', *Journal of Public Policy*, 25, 241–63.

Keller, R. (2008) *Wissenssoziologische Diskursanalyse—Grundlegung eines Forschungsprogramms*. 2. Aufl. Wiesbaden: VS Verlag.

King, N. (2004) 'Using Templates in the Thematic Analysis of Text'. In C. Cassel and G. Symon (eds.), *Essential Guide to Qualitative Methods in Organizational Research*. London: Sage, 256–70.

Kohl, J. and Vahlpahl, T. (2004) 'The "Open Method of Co-ordination" as an Instrument for Implementing the Principle of Subsidiarity?', *European Journal of Social Security*, 6, 363–90.

Laclau, E. (1989) 'Politics and the Limits of Modernity', *Social Text*, 21, 63–82.

Merton, R. (1973) *The Sociology of Science: Theoretical and Empirical Investigations*. Chicago: University of Chicago Press.

Nachi, M. (2006) *Introduction à la sociologie pragmatique*. Paris: Armand Colin.

Norval, A. (2000) 'The Things We Do with Words. Contemporary Approaches to the Analysis of Ideology', *British Journal of Political Sciences*, 30, 313–46.

Phillips, N. and Hardy, C. (2002) *Discourse Analysis: Investigating Processes of Social Construction*. Thousand Oaks, CA: Sage.

Rosen, S. (1993) 'Risks and Rewards: Gary Becker's Contributions to Economics', *Scandinavian Journal of Economics*, 95, 25–36.

Scharpf, F. (2002) 'The European Social Model. Coping with the Challenges of Diversity', *Journal of Common Market Studies*, 40, 645–70.

Simmel, G. (2009) *Philosophie des Geldes*. Köln: Anaconda.

Slaughter, S. and Leslie, L. (1997) *Academic Capitalism: Politics, Policies and the Entrepreneurial University*. Baltimore: Johns Hopkins University Press.

Torfing, J. (2005) 'Introduction. Discourse Theory: Achievements, Arguments and Challenges'. In J. Torfing and D. Howarth (eds.), *Discourse Theory in European Politics*. Basingstoke: Palgrave Macmillam, 1–33.

Trubek, D. and Trubek, L. (2005) 'Hard and Soft Law in the Construction of Social Europe: The Open Method of Coordination', *European Law Journal*, 11, 343–64.

Turner, B. (2007) 'Justification, the City and Late Capitalism' *Sociological Review*, 55, 410–15.

Wagner, P. (1999) 'After Justification: Repertoires of Evaluation and the Sociology of Modernity', *European Journal of Social Theory*, 2, 341–57.

Weber, M. (2009) *Die protestantische Ethik*. Köln: Anaconda.

Primary sources

Centre for the Study of Higher Education Management (CEGES) (2007) *Rates to Return and Funding Models in Europe: Final Report to the Directorate-General for Education and Culture of the European Commission*. Valencia: Valencia University of Technology.

Committee on Industry, Research and Energy/Rapporteur: Pilar del Castillo Vera, Rr. (2006) *Report on Implementing the Community Lisbon Programme: More Research and Innovation—Investing for Growth and Employment: A Common Approach*. Strasbourg: European Parliament.

Coreper (Part 1). (2008) *Draft 2008 Joint Progress Report of the Council and the Commission on the Implementation of the 'Education & Training 2010' Work Program 'Delivering Lifelong Learning for Knowledge, Creativity and Innovation'—Adoption*. Brussels: Council of the European Union.

European Commission (2003a) *Investing Efficiently in Education and Training: An Imperative for Europe*. Brussels: European Commission.

——(2003b) *Investing in Research: An Action Plan for Europe*. Brussels: European Commission.

European Commission (2003c) *The Role of the Universities in the Europe of Knowledge*. Brussels: European Commission.

——(2005a) *Communication from the Commission: Consultation Document on State Aid for Innovation*. Brussels: European Commission.

——(2005b) *Council Decision Concerning the Specific Programme: 'Ideas' Implementing the 7th Framework Programme (2007–2013) of the European Community for Research, Technological Development and Demonstration Activities*. Brussels: European Commission.

——(2005c) *Mobilising the Brainpower of Europe: Enabling Universities to Make their Full Contribution to the Lisbon Strategy*. Brussels: European Commission.

——(2005d) *More Research and Innovation—Investing for Growth and Employment: A Common Approach*. Brussels: European Commission.

——(2006a) *Delivering on the Modernisation Agenda for Universities: Education, Research and Innovation*. Brussels: European Commission.

——(2006b) *Frequently Asked Questions: Why European Higher Education Systems Must be Modernised?* Brussels: European Commission.

——(2006c) *Implementing the Renewed Partnership for Growth and Jobs. Developing a Knowledge Flagship: The European Institute of Technology*. Brussels: European Commission.

——(2007a) *The European Research Area: New Perspectives*. Brussels: European Commission.

European Commission, (2007b) *Improving Knowledge Transfer between Research Institutions and Industry Across Europe: Embracing Open Innovation. Implementing the Lisbon Agenda*. Luxembourg: Office for Official Publications of the European Communities: European Communities.

——(2008a) *An Updated Strategic Framework for European Cooperation in Education and Training*. Brussels: European Commission.

——(2008b) *Commission Staff Working Paper (Accompanying Document to the Report from the Commission to the Council)*. Brussels: European Commission.

——(2008c) *Engaging Philanthropy for University Research—Fundraising by Universities from Philanthropic Sources: Developing Partnerships between Universities and Private Donors*. Luxembourg: Office for Official Publications of the European Communities: European Commission.

——(2008d) *Report from the Commission to the Council on the Council Resolution of 23 November 2007 on Modernising Universities for Europe's Competitiveness in a Global Knowledge Economy*. Brussels: European Commission.

——(2008e) *Commission Recommendation on the Management of Intellectual Property in Knowledge Transfer Activities and Code of Practice for Universities and other Public Research Organisations*. Luxembourg: Office for Official Publications of the European Communities: European Commission.

European Parliament (2003) *Report on Investing in Research: An Action Plan for Europe*. Strasbourg: European Parliament.

Expert Group on R&D and Innovation (2006) *Creating an Innovative Europe*. Luxembourg: Office for Official Publications of the European Communities: European Commission.

Figel', J. (2004) *Reforming Higher Education*. Communication on 6 December 2004 at Charles University Prague. Brussels: European Commission.

—— (2006) *European Institute of Technology (EIT)*. Communication on 16 March 2006 at the Informal Education Council in Vienna. Brussels: European Commission.

—— (2007) *Modernising Universities in Europe*. Communication at the high level meeting organized by the Portuguese presidency of the European Union on 6 November 2007 in Lisbon. Brussels: European Commission.

General Secretariat (2007) *Council Resolution on Modernising Universities for Europe's Competitiveness in a Global Knowledge Economy—Adoption of Council Resolution*. Brussels: Council of the European Union.

Potočnik, J. (2006) *Europe's Universities in the Lisbon Strategy: Potential and Challenges*. Communication at the Danube Rector's Conference on 22 September 2006 in Maribor. Brussels: European Commission.

—— (2007a) *High Level Meeting on the Modernisation of Universities*. Communication at the high level meeting organized by the Portuguese presidency of the European Union on 6 November 2007 in Lisbon. Brussels: European Commission.

—— (2007b) *Philanthropy in the European Research Area*. Communication at the European Forum on Philanthropy and Research Funding on 4 December 2007 in Brussels. Brussels: European Commission.

—— (2008) *Europe's University Sector: Unleashing the Untapped Potential*. Communication at the colloquium of the French Conference of University Presidents on 4 April 2008 in Brussels. Brussels: European Commission.

—— (2009) *The European Spirit*. Acceptance of honorary degree from Ghent University on 20 March 2009 in Ghent. Brussels: European Commission.

Report by an Expert Group (2005) *Giving More for Research in Europe: The Role of Foundations and the Non-profit Sector in Boosting R&D Investment*. Brussels: European Commission.

——(2006) *Ricardis: Reporting Intellectual Capital to Augment Research, Development and Innovation in SMEs*. Luxembourg: Office for Official Publications of the European Communities: European Commission.

The Council of the European Union (2009) *Council Conclusions of 12 May 2009 on Strategic Framework for European Cooperation in Education and Training*. Official Journal of the European Union.

12

New Spirits of Public Management . . . 'Post-Bureaucracy'

Paul du Gay

It used to be reasonably easy to outline the contours of the administrative state, to distinguish public administration from other forms of organized activity, and to identify the professional role of state bureaucrats, public administrators, or career civil servants in the conduct of government. No longer. Over the last three decades, public administration, particularly but not exclusively its Anglo-Saxon variant, has been subject to extraordinary degrees of turbulence. As the American scholar of public management Gerald Caiden (2006: 515) has argued, there have been periods in the past when public administration as an institution of government 'has undergone considerable upheavals . . . but rarely . . . at so fast and furious a pace, rarely so radical and revolutionary'. For another American scholar, Michael Lind (2005: 37), this continuous reform of the public administration is best seen as a vast political and managerial experiment 'as audacious in its own way, as that of Soviet Collectivism'. Among its most significant consequences has been what Alan Supiot (2006: 2) terms the *'délitement'* or 'unbedding' of public institutions. He points in particular to the role of political elites themselves in this process of deinstitutionalization, not least in their enthusiastic desire to be unencumbered by existing norms and machineries of government that might in some way abrogate their freedom to experiment (see also Quinlan, 2004). He argues that one significant casualty of this *délitement* has been a prized achievement of Western political and juridical practice—the distinction between a public office and the person who occupies it. 'Initially intended to characterise the office of sovereign, this distinction signifies that the office does not die, that it has a dignity transcending the human being who provisionally occupies it and who must respect it. When that respect is erased, public office from the highest to the most modest, is perceived as the private property of the present holder who can use it as he sees fit' (Supiot, 2006: 3).

This chapter explores some of the reforms of public administration as a bureaucratic institution of government that have contributed to this process of *délitement*, and examines their consequences for the relationship between 'person' and 'office' in the practice of governmental administration. In so doing, it seeks to make connections, and draw some distinctions, too, with the analysis of the *New Spirit of Capitalism* proffered by Luc Boltanski and Eve Chiapello.

I begin by highlighting certain key criticisms of the bureaucratic form that have circulated over the last three decades or so within sociology, social theory, and organization studies, on one hand, and those proposed in the management discourse analysed by Boltanski and Chiapello, on the other. I indicate how each trades upon a particular representation of the work of the premier theorist of bureaucracy, Max Weber, in the course of mounting what turn out to be remarkably similar romantic critiques. I then proceed to indicate how these sorts of criticisms feed into, and indeed help frame, the changing ethical template that programmes of 'post-bureaucratic', 'entrepreneurial', and 'responsive' managerial reform are held to require of public administrators. In so doing, I have cause to highlight certain political and administrative dangers that attend this ethical shift. In particular, I show how, among many other consequences for conduct, the latter can generate a subtle and insidious emphasis upon particular forms of loyalty and commitment to the current governing party ('the all on one team' approach), or of policy enthusiasm ('owning' the policy and championing its 'delivery'), and indicate the ways in which these pose serious problems for the maintenance of what we might term the 'conservation standards' appropriate for enhancing the capacities of public administrators as 'constitutors' of responsible democratic governments.

One of the main arguments of the chapter is that many of the political and administrative virtues associated with the development and reproduction of an ethic of bureaucratic office in public administration—in particular the capacity to act with what Weber (1994*a*) famously termed a 'spirit of formalistic impersonality' hence 'without affection or enthusiasm, and without anger or prejudice'—are either unappreciated or simply ignored in contemporary programmes designed to inculcate the requisite 'responsiveness' and 'enthusiasm'. This carries with it certain dangers that earlier analysts of bureaucracy were more than aware of. In particular, the work of Max Weber, and especially his theorization of bureaucracy as *officium* and politics as a vocation, provides a continuing source of inspiration for those who seek to hold onto an 'ethics of office' in an increasingly alien environment.

275

Max Weber and the bureaucratic form: critic, celebrant, or historical anthropologist?

Much of what passes for criticism of the bureaucratic form within sociology, social theory, and organization studies, and indeed, within what Boltanski and Chiapello (2007: 57–102) term neo-management discourse, does so with reference to the work of Max Weber. For each, Weber is seen as the premier theorist of bureaucracy. However, their interpretations of Weber's views on bureaucracy differ significantly. In certain forms of sociology, for example, Weber is represented as one of the chief critics of bureaucracy, and his work is referenced with respect to what is considered to be his perceptive, even prophetic, analysis of this organizational form's inherent 'dark side'. Here is a critic of modernity, Bauman (1989), for instance, argues, who highlights the instrumentalizing, rationalizing logic of bureaucratic action, and points to its role in undermining substantive forms of morality (see also Ritzer, 2004). Within contemporary managerial discourse, on the other hand, a rather different picture of Weber emerges. Here, we find a celebrant of bureaucracy as the most efficient form of organization known to humanity. This Weber is something akin to a paradigmatic adherent of the—discredited—'closed system-rational actor' school of organizational analysis. As two of his more populist critics make clear, Weber got it all wrong because 'he pooh-poohed charismatic leadership and doted on bureaucracy; its rule driven, impersonal form, he said, was the only way to ensure long term survival' (Peters and Waterman, 1982: 5). In this reading, Weber is positioned as a basically well-intentioned but ultimately misguided celebrant of bureaucracy: misguided because he pays too much attention to formal rationality and not enough to its inherent dysfunctions. The latter ultimately matter more than the former, for the managerialists, precisely because they eventually begin to paralyse the organization, making it unable to fulfil its instituted purposes except at tremendous cost—socially and emotionally, for instance—particularly to those working within what is conceived of as its hyperrational 'frame'. Here, as Boltanski and Chiapello (2007: 85, 98; see also Du Gay, 1991, 1994, 1996) point out in their discussion of neo-managerial discourse, bureaucracy

> connotes authoritarianism and arbitrariness, the impersonal blind violence of cold monsters, but also inefficiency and squandering of resources. Not only are bureaucracies inhuman, they are also unviable . . . [T]he discrediting of bureaucracy and its project of eliminating everything that is not 'rational'—that is formalizable and calculable—should we are told, facilitate a return to a 'more human' modus operandi, in which people can give full vent to their emotions, intuition and creativity.

For both critical sociologists and the neo-managerialists, Weber's concerns with bureaucracy ultimately cohere around questions of rationalism and rationalization The former locate Weber as a key critic of Western rationalism and its 'instrumental' logics, who views with horror the ethical and emotional disfigurements that the primary institutional carrier of this form of rationalization—bureaucracy—is producing. The latter locate Weber as a leading advocate of rational management, and, hence, as an unconscious promoter of bureaucracy's inherent tendency to displace 'morality', 'emotion', and, indeed, all forms of substantive human value from organizational existence. What both approaches share, therefore, is first, the assumption that rationalization is Weber's key theme, and second, that, when we come to analyse the consequences of bureaucratic action, most especially the advances in efficiency and economy it registers, we can see that increasing instrumental rationalization comes at too high a price for those immediately subject to its dictates, and also for the societies it helps to bring into being. In this way, both the image of Weber as critic, and that of Weber as celebrant, of bureaucracy point towards a similar conclusion: the importance of constructing a post-bureaucratic future where the human and social ends of organizing and managing are once again invested with more value than are their means, and the negative human consequences of hierarchy, instrumental rationality, and impersonality can be addressed and remedied (Hecksher and Donnellon, 1994).

However, as two of the most impressive scholars of Weber's work, Mommsen (1987) and Hennis (1988), for instance, have argued, it does not take much familiarity with Weber's *oeuvre* to see that Max Weber is innocent of the so-called Weberianism that adopts a uniform, monolithic conception of the historical phenomena of rationalization. As Weber argued, on a number of occasions, rationalism can mean many different things. In *The Protestant Ethic and the Spirit of Capitalism*, for instance, he warns that

> The history of rationalism shows a development which by no means follows parallel lines in the various departments of life . . . In fact, one may—this simple proposition should be placed at the beginning of every study which essays to deal with rationalism—rationalise life from fundamentally different basic points of view and in very different directions. Rationalism is a historical concept which covers a whole world of different things. (Weber, 1930: 77–8)

Many sociologists and management gurus who comment on his work often appear to imagine that the distinctions suggested by Weber are, so far as Weber's own studies are concerned, flattened out by the modern advance of that dead hand of instrumental rationality—bureaucracy (Bauman, 1989; Ritzer, 2004). However, it is relatively easy to point to the vital importance that Weber attaches to the lasting and intrinsic differences between, for instance, the style of rationality appropriate to the bureaucrat and those of the entrepreneur and the politician, for example (Du Gay, 2000; Gordon, 1987). As I hope to show, there is still much to be gained from focusing upon these differences.

However, and to return to the matter at hand, this continues to leave open the question as to whether and in what ways rationalization determines the overall themes and purposes of Weber's *oeuvre*. One response to this question has been provided by Wolfgang Schluchter (1981), who sees the varieties of rationalization that Weber's studies deal with as ultimately staging posts on the road to a complete theory of rationalization. However, perhaps one of the most problematic aspects of this proposal is Weber's own stated doubts concerning the extent to which the different historical 'problem-spaces within which questions about rationalisation come to be posed can usefully be merged together under the auspices of a single overarching theory' (Gordon, 1987: 294).

If, as Weber argued, we need 'to remind ourselves that rationalism may mean very different things', then to represent Weber as involved in a project of tracing 'a universal-historical process of rationalization' is somewhat misleading, if not misplaced. The problematic of rationalization is more diverse and context-specific than such a grand narrative allows for or appreciates. Rather, Weber's work points to the ways in which different 'orders of life' (*Lebensordungen*) exhibit their own distinctive and non-reducible forms of 'organized rationality'. These have to be described and understood in their own terms, rather than being 'coordinated' into a meta-theory of rationalization (Mommsen, 1987: 42–3). As Wilhelm Hennis (1988: 94) puts it, the process of rationalization for Weber has 'to be related to each life order if we are to perceive the significance it has in his work'. Not only this, the tensions between these forms of organized rationality need to be outlined and appreciated. They do not necessarily follow the same path, towards the same end. Rather, they often have non-uniform trajectories, not entirely unrelated to their rather differing purposes and the ethos framing them. Here, then, there are in principle a plurality of competing rationalizations, each of which 'is dependent upon a different value position, and these value positions are, in their turn, in constant conflict with one another' (Mommsen, 1987: 44). As Weber (1994b: 357) famously asked, 'is it in fact true that any ethic in the world could establish substantively identical commandments applicable to all relationships, whether erotic, business, family or official, to one's relations with one's wife, greengrocer, son, competitor, with a friend or an accused man?'

In contrast to those commentators seeking to find in Weber's work, or more likely, imprint upon that work, the tracing of a uniform, unilinear, and monolithic process of rationalization, other interpretations of the Weberian *oeuvre* have stressed the importance of a more contextually specific focus on the organized forms of rationality that must be confronted by all those who become involved in particular 'life orders'. Here the central focus is upon *Lebensführungen*: the conducts of life, and the various forms of their rationalization in specific life orders (Hennis, 1988, 2000; Minson, 1993, 1998; Saunders, 1997; Turner, 1992).

The claim, most notably advanced by Wilhelm Hennis, that a focus on *Lebensführung* constitutes a, if not the, key object of Weber's work, involves three interlinked propositions. First, Hennis argues that most of Weber's work is centrally concerned with the conduct of life as its first and most pressing topic. Among the texts that Hennis refers to in order to back up this claim is, unsurprisingly, Weber's most famous essay *The Protestant Ethic and the Spirit of Capitalism*, with its focus upon the methodical conduct of life instilled by the Calvinist sects. Second, Hennis argues that the concern with *Lebensführung* inspires and illuminates the methodology of Weber's major works, pointing in particular to *Economy & Society*, where the 'arena of normative and de facto powers' is imagined and assessed in terms of the influence of collective forces upon individual life-conduct (1988: 84).

> The point of departure is that of external given conditions. The life-orders, how-ever, do possess an inner regularity, . . . each of these orders makes a demand, forms, characterises, a variety of 'impositions' or perhaps opens up possibilities for future conduct, involves a formative tendency for the 'personality' . . . What fate do these orders dictate, open up to or withhold from the persons placed in their power by conditions of time and place? Is this Weber's theme? (Hennis, 1988: 65)

That this is indeed Weber's main theme is, as far as Hennis is concerned, evidenced by his third claim: For Weber, no ultimate moral or philosoph-ical justification for a given form of life is possible in modern societies, 'because the different value systems of the world stand in conflict with one another' (1988: 22). Between these different life-orders, there is frequently a battle of different gods of different religions: '[D]estiny not science pre-vails over these gods and their struggles. One can only understand what the divine is for one system or another, or in one system or another' (Weber, 1989: 22). In *Science as a Vocation*, Weber encourages his audience to be 'polytheistic', and to take on the persona specific to the life-order within which they are engaged. In the absence of a universal moral norm, or a conclusive victory for one form of organized rationality over all others, Weber asks, how are individuals to develop 'character' or 'personality' (*Persönlichkeit*)? In considering the future of modern societies, and the individuals existing within them, Weber's deepest concern, Hennis argues, is the cultivation of individuals with 'personality': those willing and able to live up to the ethical demands placed upon them by their location within particular life-orders, whose life-conduct within those distinctive orders and powers—the public bureau, the firm, the parliament—can combine practical rationality with ethical seriousness.

In *Science as a Vocation*, Weber's answer to this problem is clear and direct: 'Ladies and gentlemen: Personality is possessed in science by the man (*sic*) who serves only the needs of his subject, and this is true not only in science' (1989: 11). The individual with 'personality' is one who is capable of personal dedication to a cause (*Sache*), or the instituted purposes of a given life-order, in a manner that 'transcends individuality' (Hennis, 1988: 88). It is in this sense that it is possible, for example, for bureaucrats to be 'personally' committed to the ethos and purposes of their distinctive office even though that ethos lies outside of their own personal (i.e. individual) moral predilections or principles. The possibility of different categories and practices of personhood requiring and expressing distinctive ethical comportments, irreducible to common underlying principles, appears quite foreign to those for whom a common or universal form of moral judgement is held to reside in the figure and capacities of the self-reflective person or individual agent (e.g. Habermas) or indeed, that of the 'networker' or 'the businessed person' (Peters, 1989). This context-specific, and thus 'limited', conception of 'personality' cautions against the siren-calls of those political romantics—socialists, anarchists, the *littérateurs* (we know their contemporary counterparts only too well)—seeking to hold onto, or re-establish, the idea of the 'complete' human being: an ultimate, supraregional persona that could function as the normative benchmark for all others.

Hennis argues passionately, and with a wealth of documentary evidence, that at the heart of Weber's work lies a moral anthropology at profound variance with both the positivistic tendencies and Kantian philosophical assumptions of the human sciences in the present and previous century. He argues that for both a positivistic and high theoretical social science, which, in Weber's own words, sought to 'shift its location and change its conceptual apparatus so that it might regard the stream of events from the heights of reflective thought' (Weber, quoted in Hennis, 1988: 104), questions of *Lebensführung*, of 'personality' and life-orders, would have little interest. However, if we managed to descend from such heights, they might once again become very important indeed. For Hennis (1988: 104), Max Weber's work finds a place in the pre-history of this sort of social science only once his central problems, questions, and concerns are neglected. In Hennis's view, Weber's work belongs, rather, to the late history of a rather different practical science of mankind (*Menschentum*) and, we might add, to a distinctive ethical tradition: the ethics of office. Seen in this light, Max Weber's work provides a classic account of the ways in which a distinctive and important role for an ethics of office can be maintained in an increasingly alien environment, through, for example, his theorization of bureaucracy as *officium* and politics as a vocation (Condren, 2006: 347; Hennis, 1988: 104, 2000: 156).

Office as a vocation: Weber and the moral economy of bureaucracy

If, as I have suggested, Weber is approached first and foremost as a historical anthropologist of *Lebensführung*, then it becomes clear that his work on bureaucracy is neither unequivocally celebratory nor overtly critical. Indeed, it becomes apparent that Weber was not simply or exclusively interested in offering a formal organizational theory of 'bureaucracy' at all, for good or ill, but rather, as Wilhelm Hennis (1988, 2000) has suggested, with specifying the ethical-cultural attributes of bureaucratic conduct. In order to approach Weber's work in this way—as a historical anthropologist of *Lebensführung* or 'conduct of life'—it is first necessary to dispense with the detritus of the Parsonian inheritance in Weberian scholarship, and to focus instead upon Weber as a somewhat eccentric and isolated moral theorist in a tradition of the ethics of office (Condren, 2006: 24). To put it in its most general propositional form: a presupposition of office was the expectation that people are educated (in the widest sense of that term) to live up to the demands and requirements of their respective offices. An office (*Lebensordnung*) was an

> 'identifiable and discriminate constellation of responsibilities and subordinate rights and liberties asserted to be necessary for their fulfilment' and manifested not in an individual, represented as a distinctive, reflective and autonomous 'self' but rather in a persona. In other words, individual identity was specific to office, referring only to bodies considered as personae, as instituted statuses or conditions. (Condren, 2006: 29)

For Weber, bureaucracy was a historically contingent and variable 'life-order' (*Lebensführung*) constituting a distinctive ethical milieu in its own right, one whose practices of formalistic impersonality gave rise to certain substantive ethical goals. Thus, in his classic account of the 'persona' of the bureaucrat, for instance, Weber (1978, II: 978ff.) treats the impersonal, expert, procedural, and hierarchical character of bureaucratic conduct as elements of a distinctive ethos. Here, office itself constitutes a 'vocation', a focus of ethical commitment and duty, autonomous of and superior to the bureaucrat's extraofficial ties to kith, kin, class, or conscience. The ethical attributes of the 'good' bureaucrat— strict adherence to procedure, commitment to the purposes of the office, abnegation of personal moral enthusiasms, and so on—represent a remarkable achievement (Hunter, 1994: 157). In particular, Weber (1978, II: 983ff.) stresses the ways in which the ethos of bureaucratic office-holding constitutes an important political resource because it serves to divorce the administration of public life from private moral absolutisms. Without the historical emergence of the ethos and persona of bureaucratic office-holding, Weber argues, the construction of a buffer between civic comportment and personal principles—a crucial feature of liberal government—would never have been possible.

Indeed, without the 'art of separation' (Walzer, 1984) that the state bureau effected and continues to effect, many of the qualitative features of government that are regularly taken for granted—for instance, formal equality, reliability, and procedural fairness in the treatment of cases—would not exist.

As Weber makes clear, the crucial point of honour for bureaucrats is not to allow extraofficial commitments to determine the manner in which they perform the duties associated with their office. 'On the contrary', the bureaucrat 'takes pride in preserving his impartiality, overcoming his own inclinations and opinions, so as to execute in a conscientious and meaningful way what is required of him by the general definition of his duties or by some particular instruction, even—and particularly—when they do not coincide with his own political views' (Weber, 1994a: 160). 'The official has to sacrifice his own convictions to his duty of obedience' (1994a: 204). This does not mean that officials only do the boring, routine work of public or state administration.

> Independent decision-making and imaginative organizational capabilities are usually also demanded of the bureaucrat, and very often expected even in large matters. The idea that the bureaucrat is absorbed in subaltern routine and that only the 'director' performs the interesting, intellectually demanding tasks is a preconceived notion of the literati and only possible in a country that has no insight into the manner in which its affairs are conducted. (Weber, 1994a: 160)

The key to understanding the ethos of bureaucratic office, Weber argues, resides in 'the kind of responsibility' associated with it. It is this, and not simple divisions between task complexity and simplicity or between policy making and routine administration, that distinguishes the 'demands addressed' to this 'position'. As Weber (1994b: 330) puts it,

> An official who receives a directive which he considers wrong can and is supposed to object to it. If his superior insists on its execution, it is his duty, even his honour to carry it out as if it corresponded to his innermost conviction, and to demonstrate in this fashion that his sense of duty stands above his personal preference ... This is the ethos of office.

Without this 'supremely ethical discipline and self-denial', Weber (1994b: 331) continued, the whole apparatus of the state would disintegrate, and thus all the political benefits deriving from it, would too.

Similarly, Weber (1978, I: 225–6) argued that it was odd for the *literati* to criticize bureaucratic conduct as antithetical to the realization of substantive ends; that is, as simply the organizational vehicle by which instrumental values supersede and/or eliminate all substantive values. Rather, as he made clear on a number of occasions, the 'formalism' of bureaucratic conduct—its instituted blindness to inherited differences of standing and prestige—produces the very substantive effects—enhancing democracy and equality, for example—that the literati claimed bureaucratic conduct would destroy (Weber, 1978, I and II; 1994*b*).

> The dominance of a spirit of formalistic impersonality: 'Sine ira et studio', without hatred or passion, and hence without affection or enthusiasm. The dominant norms are concepts of straightforward duty without regard to personal considerations. Everyone is subject to formal equality of treatment; that is, everyone in the same empirical situation. This is the spirit in which the ideal official conducts his office. The development of bureaucracy greatly favours the levelling of status, and this can be shown historically to be the normal tendency. Conversely, every social levelling creates a favourable situation for the development of bureaucracy by eliminating the office-holder who rules by virtue of status privileges and the appropriation of the means and powers of administration; in the interests of 'equality', it also eliminates those who can hold office on an honorary basis or as an avocation by virtue of their wealth. Everywhere, bureaucracy foreshadows mass democracy . . . (Weber, 1978, I: 225–6).

In other words, the exclusion of extraofficial considerations from the conduct of official business, and the strictly formalistic impersonality with which that business was conducted, was a prerequisite not only of impartial and efficient administration, but also crucial to the production of mass democracy and increased social equality. This idea that the 'formal' rationality of bureaucratic conduct itself gives rise to substantive ethical goals and effects, and is rooted in its own *Lebensordnung* or ethical life-order: that of the bureau, has been largely ignored by critics keen to 'rehumanize' official life through 'post-bureaucratic' means. Like the literati chided by Weber in his own day, contemporary anti-bureaucrats in the arena of public or governmental administration, as in private sector management, focus much of their attention upon the presumed negative consequences of the bureaucrat's formalistically impersonal obligations of office, and demand a shift in the relationship between these obligations and what they conceive of as the official's principal duties—to deliver the policies that their political governors demand of them with maximum enthusiasm and enterprise. It is to the work of these critics that I now turn.

Enthusiasm, responsiveness, and 'post-bureaucracy'

It would be difficult to underestimate the importance allocated to qualities of enthusiasm and enterprise in recent discourses of organizational reform in both private and public sector management. From the hyperbolic commandments of Tom Peters (1989) to 'develop a public and passionate hatred of bureaucracy' through to Gary Hamel's demands (2000) for 'revolutionary management', the emphasis has been on breaking with bureaucratic norms and forms of conduct in the name of innovation, risk-taking, and organizational and personal liberation (Armbrüster, 2005; Du Gay, 2005). While, in the aftermath of the corporate scandals at Enron, Worldcom, and others, the shine was somewhat taken off the tropes of revolutionary rule-breaking, nonetheless the equation of entrepreneurial enthusiasm with getting things done or delivering results, as the current wisdom has it, has far from disappeared from programmes of organizational reform. In discussions of public sector performance, for instance, governments of many different political hues have come to the conclusion that Weberian bureaucracy is not a solution but rather a barrier to 'delivery'. In their search for responsive, entrepreneurial forms of public management, party political governments rail against the obstruction and inertia of conservative bureaucrats, and seek instead to surround themselves with enthusiastic, committed champions of their policies. The testimony of the former head of (former) Prime Minister Blair's Public Service Delivery Unit offers a taster of precisely such an attitude.

> Most of all there is the danger of underestimating the extraordinary deadweight of institutional inertia. Senior civil servants generally recognised the need for change, but found it hard to bring about—the deadweight of the culture held them back... Bold sustained leadership is a pre-requisite for transformation, professions left to themselves rarely advocate more than incremental change... (Barber, 2007: 72, 124–5, 144).

Here, the demand is for a break with bureaucracy in the name of transformation, performance, passion, and much else besides. There is, from this perspective, no recognition, and thus no respect, for the possible political and governmental positivities of attention to precedent, for institutionalized caution, and for consultation and cross-checking. As the former Senior Civil Servant Sir Michael Quinlan (2004: 128) notes, such a focus on 'delivery' and 'performance' as part and parcel of a sustained focus on the achievement of practical results can

> slide into a sense that outcome is the only true reality and that process is flummery. But the two are not antithetical, still less inimical to one another. Process is care and thoroughness; it is consultation, involvement, and co-ownership; it is (as we were reminded by the failure of international process in the run-up to the Iraq war) legitimacy and acceptance; it is also record, auditability, and clear accountability. It is accordingly a significant component of outcome itself; and the more awkward and demanding the issue—especially amid the special gravity of peace and war—the more it may come to matter.

In this sense, bureaucratic practices are less the epitome of inefficiency and anachronism as post-bureaucratic enthusiasts would have it than crucial material means through which responsible democratic governance is

practically achieved. As John Uhr (1993: xvii) puts it, the bureaucratic vocation therefore helps furnish many of the 'conservation standards' appropriate
to the political management of the state, including the ordered management
of 'change' between governments of differing political hues.

In recent years, as Boltanski and Chiapello, for example, indicate, the issue
of 'transformational leadership' has emerged as a hot topic within the field of
management—both public and private. Like the critics of 'entrepreneurial
governance' who preceded them (Dean, 1999; Du Gay, 1991, 1996; Rose,
1990, 1992, 1999), Boltanski and Chiapello indicate that recourse to visions
and leadership emerges where the self-optimizing, creative beings located at
the heart of the new managerial discourse are deemed in need of governance,
but not of the sort associated with hierarchical, formalized bureaucratic
administration. Rather, controlled decontrol and government at a distance—
with its double shuffle of autonomization and responsibilization—are
the order of the day, where managers communicate vision to employees,
making meaning for them and thus helping them to own 'change' and take
responsibility for 'delivery' and 'outcomes'. In Britain, the New Labour Government's White Paper, *Modernising Government* (CM4310, 1999) and its
related policy documents (Cabinet Office, 1999*a*, 1999*b*) placed considerable
emphasis upon the capacity of transformational leadership—outlined by
Barber, above—to help change the culture of 'risk aversion' that it considered
endemic to the British Civil Service. Thus, the White Paper stated that officials
must 'move away from the risk-averse culture inherent in government' and
that this was to be achieved through removing 'unnecessary bureaucracy
which prevents public servants from experimenting, innovating and delivering a better product'. As with a previous attempt to inculcate 'real qualities of
leadership' amongst senior civil servants, the *Next Steps* report (Cabinet Office,
1988: para 35), quite what this meant in the British constitutional context,
where ministerial accountability was still assumed to be a crucial constitutional convention, was not at all clear. At one level, encouraging all senior civil
servants to become leaders and to take individual personal responsibility for
their decision-making would make the accountability trail more, not less,
complicated. With so many leaders among politicians and civil servants,
where would the buck stop, exactly? Indeed, would not the distinction
between these categories of person become somewhat blurred—and their
respective 'responsibilities of office' compromised—if everyone is equally
assumed to be a leader? Throughout the Anglo-American world, governments
have been busy preaching the virtues of entrepreneurial enthusiasm as part of
a search for more 'responsive' forms of public management. In Britain, the
former Labour government's obsession with 'delivery', combined with non-
too-subtle distaste for the traditions of the Civil Service as the 'other governing
profession', led it quickly to demand changes in the 'ethos' governing the

conduct of public administrators (Newman, 2005). As the former British Home Secretary, Charles Clarke, put it, 'what I think we'd benefit from is a more effective managerial quality at the top, and I'd say put the "just do it" ethic in, is the change that's needed' (*BBC Radio 4*: 25.07.2002). Once again, the civil servant as part of an institutional 'gyroscope of state' and bulwark against what Walt Whitman once described as 'the never ending audacity of elected persons' was to be reconfigured as a something akin to an enthusiastic, energetic, and entrepreneurial 'yes-person'. The consequences of such a shift in style and emphasis for the British Civil Service as a constitutional bureaucracy have become increasingly clear. The last three decades have witnessed a concerted attempt by governing parties in many different political contexts to strengthen their control over state bureaux. One aspect of this particular trend has been the erosion of the powers of centralized staffing agencies that safeguarded public service recruitment and promotions from political or official interference; strengthening ministerial control of top departmental appointments by removing the need to consult an independent staffing agency; substituting short-term contracts for security of tenure in top official posts; and generating the general attitude that party-political governments should not have to tolerate obstruction or inertia from conservative bureaucrats, and should instead insist they were supported by enthusiastic advocates of their policies who would ensure that the latter were 'delivered' (Chapman, 2004). In attempting to achieve these ends, however, politicians and their advisers have arguably weakened the legitimate role of officials in government by undermining the Weberian ethos of bureaucratic office (Chapman, 2004; Du Gay, 2000; Parker, 1993). In particular, the tactic of increasing the use of external appointments to senior civil service positions, and, especially, the appointment of those with known prior policy enthusiasms, has given rise to two particular problems. The first is that of ensuring that standards in state service are maintained—that the obligations of office are lived up to; the second is that distinctions between office and self are not so blurred that the state service becomes a politically partisan institution. In the United Kingdom, for instance, the political neutrality, or party political impartiality, of the British Civil Service, has flowed in no small part from its career basis (Bogdanor, 2001; Chapman, 2004). Career civil servants are expected to serve successive governments of differing party political hues. The key to being able to do this, as Weber indicated, is to cultivate a degree of indifference to the enthusiasms of all political parties. Traditionally, at least, civil servants have been trained to conduct themselves in such a manner. Indeed, in Britain, as elsewhere, people with strong party political or single issue interests have—until relatively recently—been unlikely to be appointed to senior civil service positions, or to present themselves for consideration as candidates in the first place (Chapman, 1988). As a result, civil servants have been likely to greet the panaceas of all political parties with caution. Inevitably, this leads them to embrace party political programmes with less fervour than party political enthusiasts would like. But this is part of their job, one assigned to them by the constitution. And in fulfilling this role they may be seen as servants of the state. It is precisely this statist/constitutional role—an obligation of office—that is being affected by political demands for displays of 'enthusiasm' amongst civil servants, and which is evident in the growing number of partisan appointments to the senior echelons of the service. New recruits coming from outside—whether from commercial organizations or social enterprises—will generally lack the traditional patterns of experience, such as those gained by being a private secretary to a minister, which help inculcate in civil servants those very conducts of impartiality described by Weber. Moreover, someone recruited from outside the service by virtue of relevant knowledge and approved commitments is likely to arrive with all sorts of partisan baggage derived from their previous situation. That is almost inevitable, if 'new' enthusiastic civil servants are expected to be cheerleaders for government, and act as committed champions for specific policies. It is not easy, however, for those same people to both fulfil such a role and at the same time to conform to traditional practices of subordination and lack of constitutional personality, their views being those of their minister, and not their own (Bogdanor, 2001).

As Bogdanor (2001: 296) has suggested, it is not clear, therefore, how far outside recruitment to senior policy positions in the civil service can avoid the dangers of politicization, or at least a degree of prior policy commitment, incompatible with traditional notions of 'political impartiality'. The problem here, in effect, is that office and self become blurred, with committed champions coming to see the office as an extension of themselves, thereby effecting a confusion of public and private interests and identities. The American scholar Patrick Dobel (1999: 131) calls this 'zealous sleaze', a process whereby individuals come to view public office as an extension of their own will and ideological commitments—their enthusiasms. The introduction into state bureaux of too many people with prior policy commitments and enthusiasms sympathetic to the government of the day could therefore easily undermine the traditional obligations of office framing the conduct of the Civil Service as an institution of government. Similar objections can be made concerning the increased use of special advisers, especially when, as in some well-known cases in the United Kingdom, this category of actors has been allotted extraordinary powers to issue orders to civil servants, or has, through its gatekeeper role with ministers, effectively been able to negate the influence of civil servants in the area of advising on policy issues (Daintith, 2002; Jones, 2002; Oliver, 2003; O'Toole, 2006).

Well before the latest manifestations of the ethics of enthusiasm and enterprise in government and public administration, the problems attendant upon the promotion of such capacities among officials was considered and foreseen by the Secretary to the Fulton Committee—perhaps the best known of the post-Second World War official parliamentary inquiries into the role and function of the British Civil Service. As a result of his career in the British Civil Service, and his reflections upon its constitutional role and purposes, R.W. Wilding had some interesting things to say about the place of enthusiasm and enterprise in the professional ethic of the career public administrator. He argued that it was necessary for bureaucrats to 'distinguish energy from commitment; it is absolutely necessary to pursue today's policy with energy; it is almost equally necessary, in order to survive, to withhold from it the last ounce of commitment' (quoted in Chapman, 2006: 6). For Wilding, as for Weber, enthusiasm for particular policies is dangerous for public administrators precisely because it means that bureaucrats become increasingly indistinguishable from politicians (or entrepreneurs) in that they too are encouraged to engage in 'partisanship, fighting, passion—*ira et studium*' (Weber, 1994b: 330). If they act outside of the limits of their office, or if the office itself becomes indistinguishable from another department of existence, bureaucrats will have ceased being bureaucrats and have become something else altogether. This is probably just what the critical sociologists and neo-managerialists would wish, given their commitments. But this raises another question. How then, can public administrators continue to live up to the obligations of their office? The abiding problem of 'enthusiasm' in administrative life is precisely the ways in which it can effectively undermine what Weber and Wilding see as the political and governmental virtues of the non-sectarian comportment of the bureaucratic person. In so doing, the ethics of enthusiasm run the risk of returning the administration of public life to the pursuit of private moral absolutisms, rather than, as Weber noted in his discussion of the moral economy of bureaucratic ethics, divorcing it from them.

Concluding comments

The development of the bureaucratic ethos, that non-sectarian comportment of the person outlined by Weber, furnishes the state with an important tool. The political and social positivities flowing from this bureaucratic ethos derive in large part from its own imperviousness to particular sorts of enthusiasm. This does not preclude bureaucrats from pursuing their instituted purposes with energy, demonstrating rigorous dispassionateness, integrity, and propriety, including appropriate attention to criteria of efficiency, effectiveness, and economy (as understood in a governmental sense) in the conduct of official business, for example. This commitment, though—one for behaving constitutionally, within the confines of their office, as servants of the state—

precisely excludes enthusiasm for particular policies themselves. As recent events in the United Kingdom have demonstrated, most notably, perhaps, those surrounding the decision to go to war in Iraq, enthusiasm for a particular course of action, combined with impatience with due process considerations and the minutiae of bureaucratic record-keeping, can lead to all sorts of problems. After all, it is a matter of considerable public interest/statist concern if the mediating or 'buffering' role performed by bureaucratic ethos is bypassed or transcended, and enthusiasm, for an ideal of democratization, say, and hunch, about the presence of weapons of mass destruction, for instance, play a greater role in governmental decision-making than a comprehensive and frank assessment of available evidence and as full and fair a consideration of the likely effects of those decisions as is practically feasible. Particularly so, when what is delivered as a result is the very opposite of that claimed and expected. Perhaps, such an untutored appeal to 'enthusiasm' is a mechanism for returning us, in however oblique a sense, to the sorts of conditions—uncertainty, insecurity, and so forth—the development of the state and the bureaucratic ethos were designed to prevent. In other words, such enthusiasms can produce that institutional *délitement* described and condemned by Supiot (2006) as well as Boltanski and Chiapello (2007).

The antipathy towards enthusiasm inherent in the bureaucratic ethos has its own *raison d'être*. While it is easy to see how such an ethos can be viewed by politicians, for example, as a licence to obstruct, it was, until comparatively recently, generally considered indispensable to the achievement of responsible (as opposed to merely 'responsive') government, because it was seen to balance and even complement political will, making governance more effective in the long run.

As John Rohr has suggested, the bureaucratic ethos is in important respects necessarily *unresponsive*. The role accorded to governmental bureaux in many polities has been deliberately devised to isolate officials from the electoral process, or from the demands of 'special interests', for example, thus institutionalizing the very 'unresponsiveness' which so many enthusiasts decry. And, it has been so organized to serve a positive political purpose—to help preserve a modicum of stability, consistency, and continuity, in the face of the vagaries and experimental enthusiasms of partisan politicians, for instance. In this specific and limited sense, the bureaucratic ethos is a conservative one, or better, perhaps, a *conservational* one. The bureaucratic comportment of the person embodies an acceptance, which no moral zealot really can abide, of the irreconcilable diversity of human goods, and an awareness of the possible costs, moral and otherwise, of pursuing one end to the detriment of another. In this way, the bureaucrat tends to see in every controversial change to existing social arrangements the possibility of important losses as well as the opportunity for certain gains (Larmore, 1987: xiv). Like the ethos of the

Lawyer/Statesman described so eloquently by Anthony Kronman (1993: 161), the good bureaucrat (contra Bauman) 'is unlikely to be moved by that passion for purity which motivates the adherents of every great political simplification' and to approach programmes of radical change with a degree of caution unlikely to appeal to the party political enthusiast. In this way, though, rather than being soulless, uncaring 'pen pushers', unelected policy wreckers, or unentrepreneurial 'automata of the paragraphs', as the *literati* (old and new) would have it, the bureaucrat's antipathy to enthusiasm can be seen to provide an important service to the state, and to make a crucial contribution to the long-range effectiveness of government.

The main argument of this chapter has been that, when applied to the office-based commitments of professional civil servants, contemporary political and managerial demands for increased 'responsiveness' and 'enthusiasm' associated with a 'New Spirit of Public Management' and its siren call for a 'post-bureaucratic' departure from the features of the bureaucratic ethos outlined by Weber, should be treated with considerable scepticism. As we have seen, the demand for greater levels of 'personal' involvement on the part of career civil servants in championing and delivering policies, and related demands upon them for increased levels of personal attachment to those policies, has been a hallmark of a number of recent political and managerial initiatives in government. In the United Kingdom, for instance, as I indicated earlier, one area where this has become more evident is in the practice of appointing to Civil Service positions people with known policy commitments who governing politicians regard as 'one of us' in a way that they do not so regard career civil servants. This does not imply that these enthusiasts are necessarily members of the same political party as their recruiting sergeants, but simply that they are advocates of particular policy programmes or solutions favoured by the governing party, and are committed to seeing them delivered. At the same time, and not unrelatedly, there has also been a substantial increase in the number of so-called 'special advisers' operating in government, some charged with executive responsibilities, and once again exhibiting a more partisan approach to policy making and delivery than career civil servants would be expected to manifest (O'Toole, 2006).

The consequences for the institutional and ethical integrity of governmental machinery of this embedding of enthusiasm or 'partisanship' within the organs of the state need careful consideration. Both historical evidence concerning the part played by zealous moral or spiritual enthusiasms in stirring up civil sedition and disobedience in the name of obedience to divine revelation, and contemporary problems attendant upon the creation of a new breed of civil servants 'more entrepreneurial ... more adventurous like their private sector counterparts', individuals keen to take risks in their passionate desire to 'deliver' (Cabinet Office, 2004), suggest that the contemporary passion for the 'ethics of enthusiasm' may be dangerously misplaced. In their search for greater control over the state bureaucracy and for a more committed approach from it to delivering what they want, politicians may well have weakened or undermined the important role played by the bureaucratic ethos—with its spirit of formalistic impersonality—in the responsible operation of a state and in the effective running of a constitution. When advocates of the ethics of enthusiasm characterize governmental administration as an unreconstructed Weberian world of 'formal rationality', they forget that for Weber such an ethic of *Zweckrationalität* was not merely 'instrumental' or dependent upon arbitrarily given ends. Rather an ethos of formalistic impersonality—'without affection or enthusiasm'—was premised upon the cultivation of indifference to certain ultimate moral ends. This indifference was a remarkable, if ultimately fragile, achievement, requiring those subject to its demands to learn to take cognizance of the incompatibility between a plurality of enthusiastically held convictions about rival moral ends, and hence the possibly disastrous consequences of pursuing one of them at the expense of the others. Seen in this light, formal rationality is not predicated upon an amoral instrumentalism, a wilful obstructionism, or incapacity to 'deliver', but on what we might term a positive, statist, 'ethics of responsibility'. To the extent that the 'New Spirit' that Boltanski and Chiapello (2007) describe and analyse now frames the conduct of state institutions, some of the consequences of this development may be quite profound, as Crouch (2004), among others, has indicated. Such consequences include a redefinition of the boundary between the state and private interests, such that public authority is eroded—a diminution of office-based competence—in a number of key areas of governance, and the scope for patronage, private influence, and opportunities for corruption are considerably enhanced—the blurring of office and self, and the re-emergence in suitably contemporary guise of office as a tradable good.

References

Armbrüster, T. (2005) 'Bureaucracy and the Controversy between Liberal Interventionism and Non-Interventionism'. In P. du Gay (ed.), *The Values of Bureaucracy*. Oxford: Oxford University Press, 63–86.

Barber, M. (2007) *Instruction to Deliver: Tony Blair, Public Services and the Challenge of Achieving Targets*. London: Politico's.

Bauman, Z. (1989) *Modernity and the Holocaust*. Cambridge: Polity Press.

BBC Radio 4 'Analysis'. 'Miraculous Mandarins' Broadcast date: 25.07.2002.

Blumenberg, H. (1985) *The Legitimacy of the Modern Age*. Boston, MA: MIT Press.

Bogdanor, V. (2001) 'Civil Service Reform: A Critique', *The Political Quarterly*, 291–9.

Boltanski, L. and Chiapello, E. (2005) *The New Spirit of Capitalism*. London: Verso.

Cabinet Office (1988) *Improving Management in Government: The Next Steps*. London: HMSO.

—— (1999*a*) *Vision and Values*. London: Cabinet Office.

—— (1999*b*) *Civil Service Reform*. London: Cabinet Office.

Cabinet Office (2004) *The Civil Service Commission 1855–1991: A Bureau Biography*. London: Taylor & Francis/Routledge.

—— (2006) 'The Ethics of Enthusiasm', *Public Money & Management*, January 5–7.

Caiden, G. (2006) 'The Administrative State in a Globalizing World: Trends and Challenges'. In N. S. Lind and E. Otenyo (eds.), *Comparative Public Administration: The Essential Reading*. New York: Elsevier, 515–42.

Chapman, R. A. (1988) *Ethics in the British Civil Service*. London: Routledge.

CM4310 (1999) *Modernising Government*. London: HMSO.

Condren, C. (2006) *Argument and Authority in Early Modern England: The Presupposition of Oaths and Offices*. Cambridge: Cambridge University Press.

Crouch, C. (2004) *Post-Democracy*. Cambridge: Polity Press.

Daintith, T. (2002) 'A Very Good Day to Get Anything Out We Want to Bury', *Public Law*, Spring, 13–21.

Dean, M. (1999) *Governmentality*. London: Sage.

Dobel, P. (1999) *Public Integrity*. Baltimore: Johns Hopkins University Press.

du Gay, P. (1991) 'Enterprise Culture and the Ideology of Excellence', *New Formations*, 13, 45–61.

—— (1994) 'Making up Managers: Bureaucracy, Enterprise and the Liberal Art of Separation', *British Journal of Sociology*, 45(4), 655–74.

—— (1996) *Consumption and Identity at Work*. London: Sage.

—— (2000) *In Praise of Bureaucracy*. London: Sage.

—— (ed.) (2005) *The values of Bureaucracy*. Oxford: Oxford University Press.

Gordon, C. (1987) 'The Soul of the Citizen: Max Weber and Michel Foucault on Rationality and Government'. In S. Whimster and S. Lash (eds.), *Max Weber: Rationality and Modernity*. London: Allen & Unwin, 293–316.

Hamel, G. (2000) *Leading the Revolution*. Boston, MA: Harvard Business School Press.

Heckscher, C. and Donnellon, A. (1994) *The Post-Bureaucratic Organization: New Perspectives on Organizational Change*. London: Sage.

Hennis, W. (1988) *Max Weber: Essays in Reconstruction*. London: Allen & Unwin.

—— (2000) *Max Weber's Science of Man*. Newbury, Berks: Threshold Press.

Hunter, I. (1994) *Re-thinking the School*. Sydney: Allen & Unwin.

Jones, N. (2002) *The Control Freaks*. London: Poltico's.

Kronman, A. (1993) *The Lost Lawyer*. Cambridge, MA: Harvard University Press.

Larmore, C. (1987) *Patterns of Moral Complexity*. Cambridge: Cambridge University Press.

Lind, M. (2005) 'In Defence of Mandarins', *Prospect*, October, 34–7.

Minson, J. (1993) *Questions of Conduct*. Basingstoke: Macmillan.

—— (1998) 'Ethics in the Service of the State'. In M. Dean and B. Hindess (eds.), *Governing Australia: Studies in Contemporary Rationalities of Government*. Sydney: Cambridge University Press, 47–69.

Mommsen, W. (1987) 'Personal Conduct and Societal Change'. In S. Whimster and S. Lash (eds.), *Max Weber: Rationality and Modernity*. London: Allen & Unwin, 35–51.

Newman, J. (2005) 'Bending Bureaucracy: Leadership and Multi-Level Governance'. In P. du Gay (ed.), *The Values of Bureaucracy*. Oxford: Oxford University Press, 191–210.

Oliver, D. (2003) *Constitutional Reform in the UK*. Oxford: Oxford University Press.

O'Toole, B. (2006) *The Ideal of Public Service*. London: Routledge.

Parker, R. (1993) *The Administrative Vocation*. Sydney: Hale and Iremonger.

Peters, T. (1989) *Thriving on Chaos*. Basingstoke: Macmillan.

——Waterman, R. (1982) *In Search of Excellence*. New York: Harper & Row.

Quinlan, M. (2004) 'Lessons for Governmental Process'. In W. G. Runciman (ed.), *Hutton and Butler: Lifting the Lid on the Workings of Power*. Oxford: British Academy/Oxford University Press, 112–30.

Ritzer, G. (2004) *The McDonaldization of Society*. Thousand Oaks, CA: Pine Forge Press.

Rohr, J. (1998) *Public Service, Ethics, and Constitutional Practice*. Lawrence, KS: University of Kansas Press.

Rose, N. (1990) *Governing the Soul: The Shaping of Private Self*. London: Routledge.

——(1992) 'Governing the Enterprising Self'. In P. Heelas and P. Morris (eds.), *The Values of the Enterprise Culture: The Moral Debate*. London: Routledge, 141–64.

——(1999) *The Powers of Freedom*. Cambridge: Cambridge University Press.

Saunders, D. (1997) *The Anti-Lawyers*. London: Routledge.

Schluchter, W. (1981) *The Rise of Western Rationalism*. Berkeley: University of California Press.

Supiot, A. (2006) 'The Condition of France', *London Review of Books*, 28(11), 1–9.

Turner, C. (1992) *Modernity and Politics in the Work of Max Weber*. London: Routledge.

Uhr, J. (1993) 'Administrative Responsibility and Responsible Administrators: An Introduction'. In R. S. Parker (ed.), *The Administrative Vocation*. Sydney: Hale and Iremonger, xiii–xxiii.

Walzer, M. (1984) 'Liberalism and the Art of Separation', *Political Theory*, 12(3), 315–30.

Weber, M. (1930) *The Protestant Ethic and the Spirit of Capitalism*. London: HarperCollins.

——(1978) *Economy & Society* (2 vols.). Los Angeles: University of California Press.

——(1989) 'Science as a Vocation'. In P. Lassman and I. Velody (eds.), *Max Weber's Science as a Vocation*. London: Unwin Hyman, 3–31.

——(1994*a*) 'Parliament and Government in Germany under a New Political Order'. In P. Lassman and R. Speirs (eds.), *Weber: Political Writings*. Cambridge: Cambridge University Press, 130–271.

——(1994*b*) 'The Profession and Vocation of Politics'. In P. Lassman and R. Speirs (eds.), *Weber: Political Writings*. Cambridge: Cambridge University Press, 309–69.

13

Authenticity at Work: Questioning the New Spirit of Capitalism from a Micro-sociological Perspective

Susanne Ekman

Introduction

Western working life and labour markets have experienced significant changes during the last decades, particularly in the so-called knowledge work sector: lifelong employment is rare, flexibility is celebrated, and the focus on authenticity, originality, and networking is increased (see e.g. Bonner and Du Gay, 1992; Garsten, 1999; Gill and Pratt, 2008). There is a great deal of disagreement, however, as to the moral and sociological nature of these changes. Has society finally found a way to combine capitalism and authentic meaning, as certain branches of management literature claim (e.g. Allen et al, 1982; Deal and Kennedy, 1982; Kotter and Heskett, 1992)? Or is it rather more refined profit maximization based on the colonization of employee souls, as critical voices claim (e.g. Barker, 2002; Casey, 1995; Fleming, 2009; Kunda, 1992; Ray, 1986; Sennett, 2006)? In *The New Spirit of Capitalism* (2005), Luc Boltanski and Eve Chiapello make an important contribution to the analysis of recent changes in capitalism and their moral aspects, amongst other things the celebration of authenticity in working life. The purpose of this chapter is to present and discuss Boltanski and Chiapello's analysis of current-day capitalism by using my two empirical case stories from the creative industries as empirical backdrop. The main contribution of the chapter is to show how micro-level empirical data may offer important nuances to the macro-level diagnosis made in *The New Spirit of Capitalism*. These moderations primarily concern the *contradictory* role of authenticity ideals in creative knowledge work, as they play out in micro-sociological interactions. The chapter will argue that discourses about authenticity do indeed contribute to increased worker vulnerability, contradictory managerial demands, and anxiety-provoking tension between instrumentality and authenticity, as Boltanski and Chiapello argue. However, the very same discourses are also used by workers to refuse tedious or mundane tasks, to demand high levels of personal attention and 'catering' from the managers, and to display contradictory and opportunistic behaviour. This produces numerous instances of managerial and organizational vulnerability as they try to accommodate key employees on whom their competitive advantage depends to a large degree. In other words, the chapter argues that, once we delve into ethnographic details, we learn that vulnerability and exploitation do not follow the neat division between managers and employees—or even between organizations and their actors. Rather, the authenticity discourse and its paradoxical relation to increased control are mobilized by all parties in an attempt to improve their own conditions. In this complex game, there are certainly losers, but they are not all employees! So my argument is that we need to establish an analytical gaze that can handle the *contradictory* consequences for *both* managers and employees of the increased focus on authenticity and flexibility at work.

The chapter starts by summarizing the primary argument in *The New Spirit of Capitalism*, focusing on the *connexionist* logic which is characterized by a celebration of authenticity and flexibility. It then moves on, briefly, to place the book in a larger context of organizational theory similarly grappling with the consequences of increased focus on authenticity and flexibility in late capitalism. Here, I mainly concentrate on discussions about affective labour, corporate culture, and post-bureaucracy. After this, the empirical cases are introduced and then discussed from two different angles. The first angle corroborates the macro-analysis made by Boltanski and Chiapello and supported by numerous critical researchers. The second angle, however, highlights the contradictory consequences of the authenticity discourse at work, seen from a micro-level perspective of daily interactions between managers and employees.

The New Spirit of Capitalism

The New Spirit of Capitalism is an ambitious sociological project with the intention of studying the practices of and conditions for critique of capitalism in modern society. For this purpose, Boltanski and Chiapello challenge the classical Marxist split between base and ideology and instead suggest the concept of 'spirit', which is inspired by Weber's notion of the Protestant ethic. Boltanski and Chiapello use this term to describe how the fundamentally absurd activity of profit accumulation can gain massive popular support.[1] Through 'morale' or 'spirit', capitalism makes itself attractive to the participants whom it must recruit in order to survive—that is, the owners, managers, and employees. It is precisely the split between the basic principle of profit-maximizing on one hand and an ever-changeable morale or spirit on the other that gives capitalism its remarkable immunity to radical critique, Boltanski and Chiapello argue. They offer a detailed analysis of the three successive spirits of capitalism, each being the result of capitalism incorporating the most vehement criticism into a new version of its morale. Not only can the morphing spirit neutralize critique, it can in fact turn it into enhanced productivity and accumulation.

According to Boltanski and Chiapello, the current *connexionist* logic is the latest example of how a vehement critique has been absorbed into the capitalist morale and thus turned into an asset for profit-maximizing. The critique was voiced in the 1960s when Leftists protested against capitalism's suppression of authenticity, creativity, freedom, and individuality. In the following decades, working life came to be characterized by flexible and temporary contracts, a focus on the authenticity and emotional life of employees as an asset to the organization, the spread of self-directed work, and similar now-familiar developments. Aspects which were originally lacking in the capitalist spirit are now turned into central drivers. Authenticity ideals, in the sense of focusing on the private and emotional realm and looking for self-realization, were no longer excluded from working life, but instead served as momentum for more accumulation. The absorption of this critique into the capitalist spirit resulted in the formation of the so-called *connexionist* logic which idealizes the following kind of persona: enthusiastic, involved, flexible, adaptable, versatile, employable, autonomous, not prescriptive, in touch, tolerant, knows how to engage others, and has potential (Boltanski and Chiapello, 2005: 112). Conversely, people should refrain from displaying characteristics such as being intolerant, authoritarian, local, rooted, attached, or preferring security. In the *connexionist* logic, high status depends on the ability to mediate, to undertake projects, and to create and maintain networks: 'Life is conceived as a *succession* of projects; and the more they differ from one another, the more valuable they are' (ibid.: 110).

As a remedy to Taylorist woes, the *connexionist* dynamic with its focus on mobility and authenticity has indeed had an effect, Boltanski and Chiapello concede. But they proceed to claim that this very remedy has now turned into

---

[1] Profit accumulation is absurd for both the employee and the capitalist, they claim. It is absurd for the employee because he does not reap the fruits of his own hard labour, and because he has to accept a long life of submission to rules and regulations decreed by others. Likewise, profit accumulation is absurd for the capitalist, because it catches him in an ever-accelerating and ever-more closed repetition of optimization, which in many ways is decoupled from the basic pleasures in life.

new forms of oppression which themselves need to be remedied. They list a number of conditions that enhance worker vulnerability in a context of authenticity. In the scope of this chapter, I will only focus on two of them. First, according to Boltanski and Chiapello, the rise in autonomy has been accompanied by a paradoxical rise in control mechanisms exerted via new information technology, group pressure, standardization procedures, etc. (ibid.: 430, 432). Often, workers find themselves faced with dual, semi-contradictory demands as a result of this. Second, an additional vulnerability is brought about by the paradox inherent in the attempts to commodify authenticity (ibid.: 445–7). The paradox consists in the fact that authenticity is largely defined precisely by its absence of strategic or monetary concerns. Normally, we understand authenticity as a matter of being true to one's 'inner Self' and acting in accordance with existential values rather than instrumental concerns. Nevertheless, the market has become a primary context for narratives and promises about authenticity, both in the sense of 'experience economy' and in the sense of increased focus on human emotion and 'sincerity' in working contexts. This fundamental paradox generates high levels of anxiety and frequent cycles of enchantment and disillusionment, Boltanski and Chiapello argue. These are the two points about increased worker vulnerability that I will put to a micro-sociological test in this chapter.

Boltanski and Chiapello's work has become seminal in discussions on capitalism, management discourse, and working life, and even now, ten years after its appearance, it can still give rise to heated discussions amongst sociologists, economists, and management researchers. The book has been exposed to many forms of criticism: The authors are criticized for using an exclusively French context to make rather sweeping claims about capitalism in general (Parker, 2008: 611). Others argue that their focus on moral justifications and discourse downplays the importance of political developments and the impact of the public sector on the dynamics of capitalism (Kemple, 2007: 158). From a more Marxist angle, their focus on discourse or 'spirit' has been claimed to downplay or ignore the 'physical neutralization' of critical voices in capitalism. Such physical neutralization could be attempts to break up trade union organization in the workplace or public scapegoating of the unemployed (Wolfreys, 2008). It has also been pointed out that they ignore the many factors apart from ideological criticism that affect how capitalism develops, such as globalization, natural disasters, technological developments, etc. (see Parker, 2008: 613). Most persistently, they have been exposed to a number of methodological criticisms revolving around the fact that their work is based on readings of management literature. As data material, Boltanski and Chiapello use two volumes of management texts dating from the 1960s and the 1990s, respectively. They consider these texts an expression of the existing ideals about participation in working life, and thus as informative about how the capitalist enterprise is legitimized in different periods. Critics ask them whether management literature is sufficient to support their claims, or if they should not have included financial literature (Gadrey in Leca and Naccache, 2008: 615). They also ask whether focusing on the 1960s and 1990s does not skew the analysis of how organizational and managerial trends have developed (Hatchuel in Leca and Naccache, 2008: 616). And finally, many critics question the lack of methodological interplay between management texts and ethnographic data. The gist of this criticism is that a study of managerial texts may tell us something about how a certain segment of people (writers of management literature—and in fact only a specific group of such writers) think about management, but does it tell us anything about capitalism per se? Do we not need to pursue the reception of these texts in the everyday practices, and do we not also need to look for other discursive trends than simply those of a certain line of management texts? (Leca and Naccache, 2008: 616). This chapter picks up this latter line of criticism by showing what a macro-level study may miss in the absence of supplementary ethnographic material.

Flexibility and authenticity in late capitalism

Boltanski and Chiapello are not the only writers concerned with the nature of the intensified focus on flexibility and authenticity in our current era. In fact, one could argue that interest in the fate of workers' emotional life when faced with the instrumental demands of their workplaces has been present in organization studies since the neo-humanist school of Mayo (1945) and Maslow (1954). Another important development occurred during the 1980s with the surge of 'corporate culture' in Western companies. The theories behind this surge drew on a similar concern with the marriage of emotional and instrumental spheres, arguing that a strong common goal and distinct organizational values were able to dissolve the tension between authentic self-realization and instrumental pursuit of profit (e.g. Ashby, 1999; Carlzon, 1993; Handsfield and Ghosh, 1994; Peters and Waterman, 1982; Shrednick et al., 1992). In popular management literature, the vision of the workplace as the optimal stage for personal development and authenticity has also been pervasive throughout the last decades. It can be gauged in titles such as: *Your Authentic Self: Be Yourself at Work* (Giardina, 2002) and *The Art of Waking People Up: Cultivating Awareness and Authenticity at Work* (Cloak and Goldsmith, 2003). For management and leadership similar titles abound, for example: *Self-Confrontation, Self-Discovery, Self-Authenticity and Leadership: Discover Who You Are and Transform the Leader in You* (Okafor, 2009). What all the above-mentioned writers have in common is the belief that work can and should be a place for authentic existential projects undertaken by both managers and employees, and that the presence and encouragement of such authenticity will at the same time benefit the organization's pursuit of profit.

In a reaction against these suggestions, a whole body of critical literature dissects the oppressive, exploitative, and pathological aspects of flexibility and authenticity in working life. A number of researchers drawing on Marxism and critical theory problematize the commodification of subjectivities in new capitalism. For example, the sociologist Arlie Hochschild coined the term 'emotional labour' (1983) in order to describe a growing tendency towards attaching exchange value to human feelings. Her work has inspired a number of similar studies with the same focus, namely how the ability to display sincerity, emotional presence, and authenticity has become central to the definition of the good worker in many lines of business (see e.g. Theodosius, 2008; Totterdell and Holman, 2003; Van Maanen, 1991). The key argument is that the attachment of exchange value to emotions engenders severe conditions of alienation for the workers, who are no longer in possession of a private sphere protected from instrumentalization.

Marxist critique of authenticity and emotional labour has also gained massive momentum in an Italian context, most famously voiced by Michael Hardt and Antonio Negri (2000). Like Hochschild—and like Boltanski and Chiapello—they worry about the consequences of increasingly blurry lines between working life and private life. Through the spread of what they call 'immaterial labour', which deals in social interaction, communication, creativity, ideas, and affect, exchange value now colonizes new terrain by commodifying subjectivities. Hardt and Negri speak of 'the social factory' in order to indicate that society as a whole has become a territory for productivity and profit accumulation, feeding on the most intimate realms of people's existence. In a CMS context, Hardt and Negri's theory has been adopted by Peter Fleming who expands on it in his book about 'authenticating techniques' in modern working life (2009). A similar concern is voiced by Richard Sennett who focuses on the moral consequences of increased flexibility, temporary work, and short-term projects. According to Sennett, this endangers professional ethics about craftsmanship and loyalty, creating instead a superficial and 'zapping' workforce that is easily exploited and, in addition, lacks robust moral values.

Other researchers have focused on how therapeutic and emotional language has become increasingly mandatory and normalized in public space (e.g. Illouz, 2007; Rose, 1999). In this context, the individual is expected to desire freedom and self-realization and to master 'sincere' and 'authentic' communication about themselves. These values, deriving from humanistic psychology, have been appropriated by modern management in order to sustain entrepreneurial activity and increased productivity, they claim. In other words, the so-called 'psy-sciences' form a perfect alliance with neo-liberal ideals about private enterprise and individual initiative free from state intervention, so the argument goes (Du Gay and Salaman, 1996).

In a CMS context, the matter of authenticity has attracted critical attention in studies of 'post-bureaucracy' and 'corporate culture'. Both terms refer to a set of managerial techniques that tone down hierarchical structures in favour of team work, self-management, and high involvement in collective organizational values (Barker, 2002; Casey, 1995; Kunda, 1992; Ray, 1986; Willmott, 1993). Many CMS studies consider post-bureaucratic techniques as a symptom of new capitalism whose demand for innovation, multi-tasking, and originality cannot be met by traditional Taylorist-minded workers. As a remedy for this, the organizations encourage passion, dedication, and 'personal touch' in their employees. The scholars argue that the purported emancipation and authenticity offered by such managerial techniques serve only to disguise a more thorough and subtle control, exercised through the colonization of emotional life and identities (see e.g. Casey, 1995; Fleming and Sturdy, 2009; Knights and Willmott, 1989; Kunda, 1992; Sennett, 1998).

As we can see, the critical debates on authenticity are largely in line with Boltanski and Chiapello's arguments, namely that autonomy has increased, but so has control; and that personal feelings and quests for authenticity are targeted by commodification, resulting in anxiety and disorientation for the employees. It is worth noticing that the overall debate about authenticity at work seems split into two slightly overcoherent positions: one that regards workers as powerful winners in a perfect marriage between profit and meaning, and another that regards them as fairly powerless victims of a sophisticated normative control. In other words, there seems to be very little research that strikes a third and more contradictory position from whence both phenomena might be considered true at the same time. The discourse about authenticity at work may generate worker vulnerability in some respects, and worker opportunities in others—and similarly so for managers. The purpose of this chapter is to make an attempt at establishing such a third position in which both managers and employees are seen as experiencing contradictory effects of a given cultural trend—in this case the rise of authenticity discourses at work. My claim is that such a third position depends on careful empirical studies of daily practices and interactions, which cannot be captured by a purely textual analysis like the one undertaken by Boltanski and Chiapello.

Below, I will move on to present my two empirical cases and the methodological approach behind them.

Constructing cases and avoiding the usual suspects

My fieldwork was conducted in what one could call the heart of the *connexionist* dynamic. I spent three months in a large media company and another three months in a large publishing house. These two sites were picked on the assumption that they housed a considerable number of employees who come very close to the ideal-typical person in a *connexionist* society (as mentioned above): enthusiastic, involved, flexible, adaptable, versatile, employable, autonomous, not prescriptive, in touch, tolerant, knows how to engage others, and has potential (Boltanski and Chiapello, 2005: 112). My agenda was to study the degree to which this *connexionist* discourse dominated, and how it affected manager–employee interaction, working identities, and working ethics.

Media[2] is a large media company. During the last decades it has expanded from producing one TV channel and one radio channel to offering a range of channels and an expansive website with multimedia content. Media employs around 3,000 employees, and around 25 per cent of these are hired on temporary contracts. In addition to this, there is a fairly high turnover, which makes the organization largely dominated by project-based work. The employees are a mixture of academics, journalists, self-taught creative, and then a group of administrative staff with backgrounds such as law, economics, business administration, etc. In my study, I only focused on the producing staff, not the administrative staff. The recent changes in media are similar to those described by Georgina Born (2004): increased casualization of employees, increased subcontracting, and establishment of internal market mechanisms in the organization. As such, Media was the ideal site for exploring the various facets of *connexionist* dynamics.

After my fieldwork in Media, I spent another three months in the large publishing house Booker. Booker is about 10 per cent the size of Media, but still a fairly large company with several departments and a considerable layer of management. During my fieldwork, I focused on two editorial departments: children's books and modern fiction. I also followed top management plus the interactions between Sales and the editorial departments. In Booker, the staff is mainly composed of academics, although it does include a few self-taught 'aficionados'. Like Media, Booker has undergone a process of increased commercialization with higher rates of efficiency, more focus on market dynamics, and investment in highly commercial 'concept books'. 'Old-fashioned' staff has been sifted out in favour of young, dynamic, and commercially talented editors.

---

[2] Both 'Media' and 'Booker' are pseudonyms meant to ensure the anonymity of the organizations.

While on fieldwork, I was given my own office space, PC, mail account, and working desk. I was present on a nearly daily basis, participating in meetings, lunches, seminars, parties, and daily routines. Contrary to a regular employee, I travelled around the organizational hierarchy in a way which only an outsider could have access to. This liminal position of being both 'more inside' and 'more outside' than the 'natives' is the classical anthropological tool for collecting data (see e.g. Cook, 2010). It allows the researcher to compare practices and issues from contexts that do not have access to each other. The same conflict about, say, performance appraisal technologies, could be observed as it was framed during informal employee lunches, during top management meetings, and during collective weekly meetings. This provides a rare opportunity to understand how the same issue looks from different perspectives, and how the various actors make sense of each other.

In addition to observations, I conducted twenty-five in-depth interviews, lasting around two hours each. These interviews were equally distributed on the two organizations and on managers and employees. Furthermore, I studied a number of organizational documents such as strategy plans, stress programmes, annual appraisal interview forms, job advertisements, etc. During my interviews, I attempted to follow a line that would allow unex-pected plots and steer clear of 'the usual suspects'. I did this by approaching the same issues from a number of different angles: normative questions, experiential questions, factual questions, negatively phrased questions, and positively phrased questions. By pursuing the question of, say, 'good manage-ment' from all these angles, I could compare how the framing of the issue affected the answers. This multiple-venue form of saturating my data reduced the risk of constructing habitual or one-dimensional analytical narratives. In addition to this, I used certain therapeutic models of interaction as inspiration for the interview form. Drawing on techniques developed to engage quarrel-ling spouses with one another (Hendrix et al., 2005), I sought to increase my tolerance for 'dissonance' and 'difference', instead of jumping to my own preferred conclusions. Put very briefly, these techniques consist in substantial 'mirroring' which invites the counterpart to relate more and more details in a safe ambience, combined with prolonged 'asking for more' practices. Together, these techniques help lifting both parties out of habitual, biased, or overly implicit interactions.

When conducting observations, I used a similar principle. Here, I drew on the fieldwork techniques developed by George Marcus, called 'multi-sited ethnography'. Multi-sited ethnography is inspired by the anti-essentialist approach in ANT, which challenges the notion of 'bounded sites' as a relevant way to construct the locus of study. Instead, it suggests following 'chains of relevance' which often cross borders between departments, groups, organiza-tions, and even nations. Rather than 'mapping' a bounded site, one 'tracks' a phenomenon through its travels across territories (Marcus, 1995). Although I did operate with two bounded sites, namely Media and Booker, I pursued my observations inside those two sites according to the multi-sited principles. In constructing the criteria for relevance, I chose to focus on intensity. When there was intense debate, intense conflict, intense joy, or intense normativity, I would follow this. Concretely, I analysed who or what were the parties to this intensity, and then I investigated the intense phenomenon from their perspectives. An example could be the disagreement over how to treat celebrity writers in Booker: should they be pampered, or should they be treated as the familiar old clients, which they often were. This was a source of much conflictual intensity, and I would pursue it from as many angles as possible: top management, middle management, senior editors, junior staff, Sales, etc. Analysing this conflict from numerous perspectives gave me an insight into not only this particular issue but also structural tendencies in how the various parties related to each other, and the differences in their stakes.

Altogether, these methodological techniques were employed in an attempt to generate multi-layered material with a high sensitivity to contradictions, paradoxes, and tensions in daily interactions. It is this sensitivity that may add important micro-level nuances to the large-scale analysis made in studies such as *The New Spirit of Capitalism*. Below, I will describe some of these contradictory interactions.

Authenticity, commodification, and control

As mentioned above, the key concern voiced by both Boltanski and Chiapello and by critical researchers on authenticity in general is the vulnerability that this discourse engenders for the workers. This chapter focuses on two of these purported vulnerabilities: first, the coexistence of discourses about authenticity and flexibility with increased control via performance measures, documentation demands, standardization, etc.; second, the anxiety-provoking contradiction between the quest for authenticity and the commercial agendas for which it is mobilized in an organizational context.

Below, I pursue these two concerns into the empirical details from my cases. In the first section, I will corroborate the relevance of the critiques by presenting ethnographic data that back them up. However, in the second section, I will show that the very same ethnographic data can be 'turned around' and used to illustrate how employees mobilize the ambiguities for their own agendas, thus often rendering management vulnerable and even hampering strategic profit optimization. The point of this exercise is to show the validity of Boltanski and Chiapello's textual study while at the same time illustrating the complex details from daily practice which it misses. It also serves as an important commentary on critical research about authenticity in a broader context. The chapter claims that, even if there might be good cause for analyses that point out the exploitative and vulnerability-enhancing aspects of authenticating capitalist techniques, there is *as* good cause for ethnographic studies pointing out how workers operate strategically in the same techniques, thus creating small pockets where the capitalist principles are delayed, hampered, or challenged. As I will return to later, this is important not least because the workers often resist offers of more realistic, yet less spectacular work conditions, precisely due to the possibilities they associate with a highly intense, ambiguous, and contradictory setting. In other words, my empirical data suggest that the 'exploitation' of authenticity discourses at work is practised by employees just as much as by management and organizations, and that the ensuing vulnerability is distributed across the manager–employee distinction, rather than along it.

Increased worker vulnerability as a consequence of authenticating techniques

Both Media and Booker depend on high-involvement employees with a considerable creative drive and a willingness to invest personally in their work task. In both organizations, there was an explicit celebration of the innovative and entrepreneurial employees who looked beyond the mere contractual framework of their assignments. Managers in both organizations criticized 'old-fashioned' employees who allegedly had the tendency to rely on rules, regulations, standards, and habits. In contrast, they were looking to recruit flexible, enthusiastic, and open-minded employees who were able to 'assume responsibility' and 'think out of the box'. For example, the manager John compares two of his employees: Luke, who is competent and conscientious, versus Camilla who is talented and extroverted. Although Luke meets all the professional requirements of a good editor, the manager still prefers Camilla, despite her lack of experience. The main point, according to John, is that Camilla 'challenges' him and 'develops him personally', whereas Luke just 'goes to work and then goes home'. In other words, at the end of the day, personal or 'authentic' traits were more important than strictly professional skills, according to this manager.

However, the celebration of authenticity and autonomy was frequently combined with relatively tight control and regulation vis-à-vis the employees. They should be authentic, but in a systematic and controllable way, one could say. This paradox is commented upon by the Media employee Peter:

Of course we have to invest in developing personally. And our manager wants to systematize that, which is fine. But it's also a little tough to be forced to do like this, and this, and this in order to develop personally!

On one hand, employees are met with a self-actualization discourse that emphasizes the value of personal development and authenticity. On the other, at the same time, they are met with the requirements to fit this personal development into specific organizational needs dictated by the manager. As Peter explains, there is an inherent tension in this, which can be 'a little tough'. As Boltanski and Chiapello noted, the focus on authenticity in work settings introduces an anxiety-provoking paradox between instrumental and non-instrumental dynamics, which the employee is left to struggle with individually.

A similar tension can be seen in the way managers handle their position of authority. Often, they send double messages about the nature of the vertical interaction. Below, the employee Nathan describes his experience of this:

In our department we have a 'flat structure'. Gordon keeps saying he isn't our boss. [...] But you need someone with the final responsibility who will say: 'Did you get this done today?' And it's weird, because Gordon often delegates assignments and says: 'Can't you be in charge of that?' He doesn't want to be the only one in charge of things. But if you make a decision about the thing he has put you in charge of, then he will often come two weeks later and say: 'It shouldn't be like that. It should be like that and that.' So he delegates responsibility, and then he takes it back. He wants to control everything.

Again, we see a situation where employee autonomy is encouraged, but only as long as the manager is 'in the mood for it', so to speak. Since both control- and autonomy-based practices are in play in the organization, the manager simply moves back and forth between them at his own discretion. This leaves the employee in a vulnerable position where he only faces the burden of both practices, but never gets to reap the benefits.

Precisely because there are two practices and discourses at play at once (one emphasizing control and hierarchy, another emphasizing autonomy and authenticity), resistance from subordinates can be eclipsed by managerial shifts in discourse. This happened in a case involving a top manager and a middle manager in Booker. The top manager informed the middle manager that a timely delivery of the department strategy plan was 'absolute top priority'. He let the middle manager know, in no uncertain terms, that all else should be put aside for the sake of finishing the strategy plan in time. The middle manager proceeded as instructed, and to his surprise was faced with a highly displeased top manager at the end of the week. *'Did you not know that our competitor has failed to renew the contracts with some of their authors?!'*, he demanded to know. The middle manager agreed that he did.

'*Well, why haven't you been out there trying to catch these authors?!*', the infuriated top manager asked. To this, the puzzled middle manager replied that he had tended to the strategy plan as instructed. '*But you should KNOW that this company depends on good authors! How else will we make our income?!*', the top manager retorted. During this interaction, the top manager shifted discourse without clarifying it to his subordinate. When insisting on the timely strategy plan, he deployed a hierarchical discourse of giving orders. However, as he learned about the authors, he shifted to an autonomy discourse of expecting independent subordinates capable of making personal assessments. Again, the subordinate is faced solely with the demands from both discourses, without reaping any of the rights or benefits. If he insists on the hierarchical discourse, he can be labelled 'too old-fashioned', and if he insists on the autonomy discourse, he can be labelled 'too irresponsible'. Below we can see an example of a manager labelling regulation-oriented employees as 'old-fashioned':

> There are still a few employees left in Media who are from the 'old school'—[...] who focus more on rules about working hours and all sorts of professional subtleties. That bothers me and provokes me; mostly because I find it puzzling, since they're actually the ones who will end up losing to others.

As we can see from this quote, there are potential sanctions towards the so-called 'old-fashioned' employees, expressed somewhat opaquely as a prediction that they will 'end up losing to others'. However, at the same time employees were faced with this kind of managerial approach:

> I just make sure that there is a fundamental spirit of: 'Of course you should deliver something!' [...] Nobody should say 'What about blah blah blah?'. It's an official order that they should deliver this. If they don't, then they've sort of fired themselves.

In this quote, the implication is that, if employees do not follow orders without asking critical questions, then they are irresponsible or uncooperative, which might cost them their job. So the employee who insists on regulations is old-fashioned and risks facing sanctions. But the employee who questions regulations is irresponsible and also risks facing sanctions.

As we can see in the section above, the critique voiced by Boltanski and Chiapello and several organizational scholars is highly relevant. Worker vulnerability is indeed heightened as a result of project-based work which celebrates autonomy and authenticity while at the same time enforcing increased control and regulation. Not only are workers faced with contradictory demands but they also have to struggle with the anxiety of their existential involvement being put to instrumental use in the organization.

However, as I shall illustrate below, the very same contradictory dynamics were mobilized by employees in their interaction with the organization and its managers, often resulting in managerial and organizational vulnerability.

Increased organizational and managerial vulnerability as a consequence of authenticating techniques

In the hands of employees, the somewhat ambiguous relation between authenticity, control, and instrumental action was also deployed for personal agendas. One could say that employees generated the same kind of cross-pressure and contradictory demands towards their workplace and their managers as the other way around. This created considerable challenges for daily management, and sometimes forced the organizations to make decisions that were not immediately beneficial for profit maximization.

While managers emphasized that employees should provide personal authenticity to serve commercial concerns, the employees emphasized, in turn, that they would *only* pursue commercial concerns in a context of authenticity. In practice, this was expressed in two ways: employees would be loyal and motivated only if they were offered continuous, personalized, and detailed validation from their managers. In the absence of such existential mirroring of their 'authentic' work contribution, employees would cause strife, work less, absent themselves on grounds of 'stress', or join the competition. Similarly, employees considered it a prerogative to have stimulating, challenging, and ever-developing work tasks. In the event that they were given too many administrative or routine-like assignments, sanctioning behaviours such as the ones mentioned above would occur. These employee demands put considerable pressure on managers in the daily interactions. Below, we can see the kinds of expectations about authenticity and validation that employees had towards their managers. The employee is describing to me how a good manager should be:

> He should be insightful about people. He should find it easy to talk to people. He should be trust-inspiring. There are some people you simply trust, and to whom you would tell everything, even if you don't quite know why. So: You should trust that you could come to him and say anything. But it also requires that he is present and knows people, and that we know him. It should be a person who gives feedback—a LOT of feedback: pats on the back or the opposite. Someone who constantly asks questions and invites you to confide in him about your dreams for the future.

This employee quote is in fact the perfect parallel to the earlier examples of authenticity norms expressed by managers. In both cases, there is the expectation that the organizational counterpart should offer existential 'services' in the sphere of work in order to meet the norm of 'good employee' or 'good manager'. Obviously, it is not enough for the manager to provide clear instructions or perform skilled coordination and planning. Rather, he should be the ideal image of an embracing and validating mentor. One should be able to 'simply trust' him, because he has that certain something which makes him a perfect mirror for the recognition-hungering employee. In other words, the manager's task is to provide the employee with a sense of being special and unique. If these 'validation services' are not delivered, the employees have strong reactions. Below, I am interviewing a worker who has just explained that if she does not receive regular feedback, her ambitions dwindle. Then she goes on:

> Yeah, I just don't wanna do it, you know. I don't wanna be there. I mean, if nobody can give me a medal for what I do, or say: 'This is great or this is bad', then I just can't bother to stay.

These quotes show that the employees are as fierce in their coupling of work and authenticity as are the managers. They expect 'a medal' for what they do, and if they do not get it, they simply 'can't bother to stay'. As one can imagine, managers were often at a loss about how to satisfy these encompassing demands for validation. Several of them told me that they had the feeling of being in a kind of 'recognition regime' where the employees' need for personal attention was almost bottomless.

Next to the request for attention and validation was the expectation to be offered highly stimulating and personally challenging assignments. Employees seemed to think that self-actualization was part of the job contract, and if the organization failed to deliver this opportunity, they were in their right to look for another job. As such, there was a relatively low sense of duty if the self-actualization prospect was not sufficiently promising.[3] Words such as 'routine', 'administration', 'fixed assignments', 'boring', or 'water carrier' were used to describe reasons why one might be intensely unhappy with work or be looking for a new position. Below, an employee describes to me what she needs in order to feel satisfied with her job:

> It's really important that you get to...how shall I put it...: play a little. Some people might call it getting responsibility. That you get some of the bigger projects and are put in charge of them. [...] I think it's really important to be challenged all the time. And that's part of the reason why I was looking for a new job, when I was

---

[3] This is very similar to Anthony Giddens's point about love and marriage in late modernity. It hinges on both parties' feeling that the self-actualizing prospects are larger than the 'costs' at any given moment. Consequently, their mutual 'commitment' is the object of permanent re-evaluation and possible discontinuation (Giddens, 1992).

offered this one. I was actually already on my way out [of the previous one]. Because the moment I'm not challenged anymore, then I have to leave. Then I have to move on. If the managers won't help me being challenged, then I have to challenge myself and move on.

The employees quoted above were all valuable workers who would be a significant loss for the organization if they resigned. In some cases, their resignation could have dramatic consequences, if they joined the competition and took with them a number of important clients. As a result of this, managers often fretted over how best to plan and present the assignments in a manner which would leave all employees feeling that they were special, autonomous, and self-actualizing.

Interestingly, the employee demands for influence, challenges, and responsibility were combined with demands for the opposite, namely instructions, authority, and protection. As such, the employees displayed precisely the same contradictory expectations towards their organizational counterpart as did the managers. They often complained that they were left too alone with their assignments without getting detailed standards for quality. These complaints were made even if they had spent much energy fighting for this kind of responsibility and personal influence. So on one hand, the good manager should provide working conditions such as autonomy, influence, and responsibility. If he failed to do so, he was 'old-fashioned' or 'control-fixated'. However, on the other hand, the good manager should provide working conditions such as authoritative instructions, limits, and validation. If he failed to do so, he was 'negligent' or 'absent'.

Below is an example of an employee who resorted to sanctions when she felt insufficiently validated and accommodated in her self-actualization demands. The story is told by one of her colleagues:

Melanie is just pissed off and has called in sick with stress. But as I see it, it's pure defiance. She didn't get to continue her book project, and then she just called in sick. [. . .] Of course, I understand that she feels frustrated about not getting the validation she wants for the work she has done. And that our new manager is just telling her what to do. [. . .] But I still think it's pretty crappy of her. I talked to her last Friday, and she certainly wasn't stressed then. She was frustrated and wanted to look for other jobs, but there were no signs of stress. And it fit perfectly that when she finished her project and had to move into our team, she called in sick. I think that our manager has the same interpretation, but he can't get away with saying that. People can use stress for anything.

Melanie's story is just one example of employees resorting to relatively resource-demanding sanctions when they did not feel accommodated in their (contradictory) demands. There were numerous cases of highly dramatic conflicts between managers and employees when it came to determining the nature of the assignments. As already mentioned, a great deal of managerial effort was spent considering how such conflicts or employee sanctions could be minimized. These efforts included making decisions that were contrary to immediate concerns about profit and logistics. For example, top management in Booker discussed the financial benefits of rationalizing editorial work so that the more 'old-fashioned' workers were responsible for basic editing, whereas the 'extroverted' workers were responsible for entrepreneurial tasks such as networking and inventing new concepts. Making this rationalization would allow the organization to increase efficiency in both types of activity, because there would be a better fit between worker profile and assignment. However, this idea was abandoned, because top management anticipated a virtual uproar from staff if such a thing was suggested. It would become a fight about 'emotions', as they said, when it should in fact be about 'production'.

Discussion: critical research on authenticity

As we can see above, the matter of increased employee vulnerability in work contexts celebrating authenticity and flexibility is fairly complex. Based on my empirical material, I would claim that neither the mainstream nor the critical approach quite finds a formula for handling this complexity. Below, I will try to discuss the complexity in more detail.

First, it is complex, because there is evidence that both managers and employees use the authenticity discourse and contradictory expectations to pressure each other. This means that, on one hand, the critical points about increased worker vulnerability and the muddling of instrumental and 'authentic' management practices are to the point. On the other, management's techniques and discourses of authenticity are constituted in synergy with similar discourses and techniques practised by the employees. This results in situations where the organizations and managers are placed in vulnerable positions as a result of employee pressure. In other words, the vulnerability caused by *connexionist* logics seems to be distributed across the manager–employee division, rather than along it.

Second, the question of vulnerability is complex, because there is evidence that many employees are highly reluctant to reduce the focus on authenticity and flexibility, even though it generates a number of pains and burdens. As such, there seems to be a significant synchronicity between the desire of *connexionist* organizations and the desire of *connexionist* employees. If one were to distil this synchronicity into a single term, it could be called 'limitless growth'. While the organization desires limitless growth in a financial sense, the employee desires limitless growth in an existential sense. Precisely this synchronized desire for limitlessness generates a form of *connexionist* logic which cannot merely be labelled 'normative control' exercised by management (as argued by, e.g. Knights and Willmott, 1987; Kunda, 1992; Wilmott, 1993). The employee desire is a vital ingredient in the continuation and intensification of authenticated work. In fact, I have witnessed numerous occasions where managers offered their over-intense employees possibilities for 'downsizing' or moderating their commitment. However, these suggestions were met with refusal and even anger by the employees who considered limitless existential growth of their prerogative in a work setting. Being offered more 'realistic', yet less existentially spectacular working conditions did not correspond with their vision of a desirable career. They were aware of the vulnerability connected to such an approach, but nevertheless insisted on their 'right' to a borderline health-threatening intensity. As one employee said at the prospect of a manager intervening with protective measures: *'Hands off! It's my program. I decide if I want to walk the plank'*. This kind of employee dedication often represents a liability to the organization, because it risks being accompanied by breakdowns and long periods of (employer financed) illness. Also, it makes it difficult for the manager to distribute the menial, tedious, or repetitive assignments which must be handled in every organization. Notably, there were inverted situations in which the employee asked for downsizing and protective routines while the manager refused due to efficiency requirements. Once again, we can see that the matter of vulnerability and exploitation seems to be contextual rather than associated with structural positions such as manager or employee.

This complexity is corroborated by a number of unions for knowledge or affective work. I have talked to unions for journalists, academics, social workers, teachers, and lawyers. All of them tell me the same story: it is increasingly difficult to formulate a labour struggle that the workers can identify with. When they frame it as a matter of remuneration, the knowledge workers say that they do not get motivated by money. When they frame it as a matter of protective regulations, the workers say that they work in order to be free. But at the same time, the workers speak with great nostalgia about traditional and predictable work settings. And all along, more and more workers decide to leave unions altogether, because they do 'recognize themselves' in the union struggles.

Finally, the matter of vulnerability is complex, because vulnerability and external success very often seem to go hand in hand in *connexionist* settings. By this I mean that some of the most successful employees in my ethnographic material, if measured by external parameters like career, status, and opportunities, were at the same time the most emotionally vulnerable ones. Obviously, one should be careful how far to push this claim, and how boldly to claim insight into emotional vulnerability. But with those reservations in mind, I would still argue that there was a significant correlation between fitting the ideal typical *connexionist* persona (as described above) and display-ing characteristics such as intense need for validation, restlessness, self-criticism, oscillations between self-deprecation and megalomania, and lack of realistic boundary drawing. These kinds of employees could, given that they were endowed with a certain talent, make steep career climbs in the creative knowledge work environment. Apparently the cocktail of intense attention-seeking and fluid boundaries generate promising, albeit demanding, workers. But where does this mixture between success and vulnerability leave us in our attempt to formulate critically engaged analyses of authenticity at work? Are these workers victims who need to be protected? As we heard above, they adamantly oppose such protection, because they prefer the pursuit of intense validation through limitless work. Are they the winners then, as Boltanski and Chiapello suggest, because they match the ideal typical *connexionist* persona who is rewarded with success and opportunities at work? Or are they lost winners, maybe? The point of these questions is to emphasize that this is yet another manner in which the question of vulnerability becomes complex and contradictory in the *connexionist* setting.

It seems that the focus on authenticity and flexibility at work calls for fairly 'messy' analytical plots with a high tolerance for paradoxes and tensions. Traditional analytical guidelines, such as the distinction between manager and employee, come under pressure. Instead, there is a need for perspectives that capture surprising simultaneities: that managers become both more influ-ential and more vulnerable in this setting—and so do employees; that the most successful employees are also the most vulnerable ones, seen from another angle; and that the most exploitative work conditions are sometimes the most coveted ones by employees.

Conclusion

In this chapter, I have used two ethnographic case stories from the creative knowledge work sector to discuss Boltanski and Chiapello's work *The New Spirit of Capitalism*. I have focused primarily on their notion of the *connexionist* logic, which is characterized by a celebration of authenticity and flexibility at work. Through a reading of their study, alongside more general academic debates about affective labour and post-bureaucracy, I have identified a wide-spread concern with the increase of worker vulnerability as a consequence of these developments. Two sources of such worker vulnerability are highlighted throughout the critical academic debates: first, the fact that managerial demands for authenticity are frequently combined with increased standard-ization and control, thus establishing contradictory expectations; second, the fact that there is an anxiety-provoking tension between the quest for sincere authenticity and the instrumentalization of this attitude for commercial purposes. These were the two concerns that I decided to pursue into my ethnographic material.

The data from my two fieldworks suggested the need for a slightly messier plot about vulnerability in *connexionist* work settings. While there was plenty of material that corroborated the two critical concerns, there was also plenty of material that indicated contradictory phenomena. Simplifying somewhat, these contradictions could be categorized into three points. First, it soon became evident that not only worker vulnerability was enhanced in the *connexionist* setting, but also managerial and organizational vulnerability. This was because the *connexionist* workers utilized the same kinds of contradictory expectations towards their organizations as the other way around. They wanted authenticity and meaning, but they also wanted protective authority. Furthermore, they would often refuse to work unless the assignments were sufficiently promising in a self-actualization perspective. Certainly, not every employee could get away with a successful counter pressure in this form. Factors such as 'cultural capital', network, clients, timing, and personality determined whether an employee could force management into 'catering' behaviour which was sometimes decidedly contrary to immediate instrumental interests. But a significant amount of managerial resources went towards struggling with such employee demands and minimizing the associated costs.

Second, a large number of the employees seemed to be specifically attracted to the kinds of intense and ambiguous work settings which critical research labels as vulnerability-enhancing. In fact, they often actively resisted offers to reorganize their work into a more 'realistic', but less 'intense', form. So while organizations were pursuing limitless growth in a financial sense, employees were using these very same organizations as a stage for pursuing limitless personal growth. In such a dynamic, it became difficult to determine who was 'taking advantage' of whom. Rather, there seemed to be a mutual fantasmatic quest which made both organizations and employees willing to endure very high risks, even if they sometimes degenerated into mutual accusations.

Finally, the ethnographic data suggested that there was a fairly high coincidence between external success and personal vulnerability. Many of the most spectacular careers were made by employees who on one hand embodied the *connexionist* persona, yet on the other showed fairly low robustness in self-esteem and realistic boundary-drawing. This generated a significant group of highly successful workers who were at the same time, from another perspective, the greatest victims of the *connexionist* dynamic. Their personal vulnerability entered a highly risky, yet highly productive and addictive, synergy with the *connexionist* ideals about being enthusiastic, versatile, and flexible.

Put differently, their success became the most important source of exacerbating their vulnerability.

This leads me to suggest that there are at least three issues that are relevant to pursue in future research on authenticity and flexibility at work. First, it would be fruitful to study vulnerability not only along the manager–employee distinction but also across it. It would be highly relevant to explore empirically *who* in both groups becomes vulnerable or powerful *when* and *in which contexts* as a consequence of authenticated work.

Second, in certain branches of knowledge work and affective labour it would be interesting to consider whether a new understanding of the concept of exploitation is called for. The kind of work that qualifies as exploitative according to traditional definitions (e.g. because it consists of contradictory and intensified expectations without concomitant rise in financial remuneration) is at the same time the kind of work that counts as the most desirable for a large number of *connexionist* employees. In this case, does the traditional definition of exploitation still apply? And if not, then how could a new form of labour struggle be defined in this context?

Thirdly, and this is maybe the most important point, what happens to the notion of realistic responsibility when both organizations and employees share a fantasy about limitless growth facilitated through authenticity? Maybe this should be our greatest concern: how vulnerable we become, both managers and employees, when we use work as a means to escape the sometimes tedious and humbling aspects of responsibility and instead flee into a fantasy about limitless development.

References

Allen, R. F. et al. (1982) *The Organizational Unconscious: How to Create the Corporate Culture You Want and Need*. Atglen: Schiffer.

Ashby, F. C. (1999) *Revitalize Your Corporate Culture: Powerful Ways to Transform Your Company into a High-Performance Organization*. Houston: Cashman Dudley.

Barker, J. (2002) 'Tightening the Iron Cage: Concertive Control in Self-Managing Teams'. In S. Clegg (ed.), *Central Currents in Organization Studies: Contemporary Trends*. London: Sage, 180–210.

Blackledge, P. (2007) 'The New Spirit of Capitalism: Review', *Capital & Class*, 92, 198–201.

Boltanski, L. and Chiapello, E. (2005) *The New Spirit of Capitalism*. New York: Verso.

Bonner, F. and du Gay, P. (1992) 'Representing the Enterprising Self: Thirtysomething and Contemporary Consumer Culture', *Theory, Culture & Society*, 9, 67–92.

Born, G. (2004) *Birt, Dyke and the Reinvention of the BBC*. London: Secker & Warburg.

Budgen, S. (2000) 'A New "Spirit of Capitalism"', *New Left Review*, 1, 149–56.

Carlzon, J. (1993) 'Moments of Truth: New Strategies for Today's Customer-Driven Economy'. In J. L. Pierce and J. W. Newstrom (eds.), *The Manager's Bookshelf: A Mosaic of Contemporary Views*. New York: HarperCollins.

Casey, C. (1995) *Work, Self and Society*. London: Routledge.

Cloak, K. and Goldsmith, J. (2003) *The Art of Waking People Up: Cultivating Awareness and Authenticity at Work*. San Francisco: John Wiley & Sons.

Cook, J. (2010) 'Ascetic Practice and Participant Observation, or, the Gift of Doubt in Field Experience'. In J. Davies and D. Spencer (eds.), *Emotions in the Field: The Psychology and Anthropology of Fieldwork Experience*. Stanford: Stanford University Press, 239–66.

Deal, T. E. and Kennedy, A. A. (1982) *Corporate Cultures: The Rites and Rituals of Corporate Life*. Harmondsworth: Penguin Books.

du Gay, P. and Salaman, G. (1996) 'The Conduct of Management and the Management of Conduct: Contemporary Managerial Discourse and the Constitution of the "Competent" Manager', *Journal of Management Studies*, 33(3), 263–82.

Fleming, P. (2009) *Authenticity and the Cultural Politics of Work: New Forms of Informal Control*. Oxford: Oxford University Press.

——Spicer, A. (2007) *Contesting the Corporation*. Cambridge: Cambridge University Press.

——Sturdy, A. (2009) ' "Just Be Yourself!": Towards Neo-normative Control in Organisations?', *Employee Relations*, 31(6), 569–83.

Foucault, M. (1988) 'Technologies of the Self'. In L. Martin, H. Gutman, and P. H. Hutton (eds.), *Technologies of the Self: A Seminar with Michel Foucault*. Amherst: The University of Massachusetts Press, 16–49.

——(1997) *The Politics of Truth*. Los Angeles: Semiotext(e).

Garsten, C. (1999) 'Betwixt and Between: Temporary Employees as Liminal Subjects in Flexible Organizations', *Organization Studies*, 20(4), 601–17.

Giardina, R. (2002) *Your Authentic Self: Be Yourself at Work*. Hillsboro: Beyond Words Publishing.

Giddens, A. (1992) *The Transformation of Intimacy: Sexuality, Love and Eroticism in Modern Societies*. Stanford: Stanford University Press.

Gill, R. and Pratt, A. (2008) 'In the Social Factory? Immaterial Labour, Precariousness and Cultural Work', *Theory, Culture & Society*, 25(7–8), 1–30.

Handsfield, R. and Ghosh, S. (1994) 'Creating a Quality Culture through Organizational Change: A Case Analysis', *Journal of International Marketing*, 3, 7–36.

Hendrix, H. et al. (2005) *Imago Relationship Therapy: Perspectives on Theory*. San Francisco: Wiley.

Illouz, E. (2007) *Cold Intimacies: The Making of Emotional Capitalism*. Cambridge: Polity Press.

Katz, W. (2007) 'Democracy and the New Capitalism', *New Labor Forum*, 16(2), 126–30.

Kemple, T. M. (2007) 'Spirits of Late Capitalism', *Theory, Culture & Society*, 24(3), 147–59.

Knights, D. and Willmott, H. (1987) 'Organizational Culture as Management Strategy', *International Studies of Management and Organisation*, 17(3), 40–63.

————(1989) 'Power and Subjectivity at Work: From Degradation to Subjugation in Social Relations', *Sociology*, 23(4), 535–58.

Kotter, J. P. and Heskett, J. L. (1992) *Corporate Culture and Performance*. New York: Free Press.

Kunda, G. (1992) *Engineering Culture*. Philadelphia. Temple University Press.

Laclau, E. (1996) *Emancipation(s)*. New York: Verso.

Leca, B. and Naccache, P. (2008) 'Book Review: *Le Nouvel Esprit du Capitalisme*: Some Reflections from France', *Organization*, 15(4), 614–20.

Marcus, G. E. (1995) 'Ethnography in/of the World System: The Emergence of Multi-sited Ethnography', *Annual Review of Anthropology*, 24, 95–117.

Maslow, A. H. (1954) *Motivation and Personality*. New York: Harper.

Mayo, E. (1945) *The Social Problems of an Industrial Civilization*. North Stratford, NH: Ayer.

Okafor, P. C. (2009) *Self-Confrontation, Self-Discovery, Self-Authenticity and Leadership: Discover Who You Are and Transform the Leader in You*. Bloomington: Authorhouse.

Parker, M. (2008) 'Book Review: The Seventh City: *The New Spirit of Capitalism* by Luc Boltanski and Eve Chiapello'. *Organization*, 15, 610–14.

Peters, T. J. and Waterman, R. H. (1982) *In Search of Excellence*. New York: Harper Row.

Ray, C. A. (1986) 'Corporate Culture: The Last Frontier of Control?' *Journal of Management Studies*, 23(3), 287–97.

Rose, N. (1999) *Governing the Soul: The Shaping of the Private Self*. New York: FAB.

Sennett, R. (1998) *The Corrosion of Character*. London: W.W. Norton.

——(2006) *The Culture of the New Capitalism*. London: Yale University Press.

Shrednick, H. R., Shutt, R. J. and Weiss, M. (1992) 'Empowerment: Key to IS World-Class Quality', *MIS Quarterly*, 16(4), 491–505.

Theodosius, C. (2008) *Emotional Labour in Health Care: The Unmanaged Heart of Nursing*. New York: Routledge.

Totterdell, P. and Holman, D. (2003) 'Emotional Regulation in Call Centres: Testing a Model of Emotional Labour', *Journal of Occupational Health Psychology*, 8, 55–73.

Turner, B. S. (2007) 'Extended Review: *Justification, the City and Late Capitalism*', *The Sociological Review*, 55(2), 410–15.

Van Maanen, J. (1991) 'The Smile Factory: Work at Disneyland'. In P. Frost et al. (eds.), *Reframing Organizational Culture*. London: Sage, 58–76.

Willmott, H. (1993) 'Strength is Ignorance, Slavery is Freedom: Managing Culture in Modern Organizations', *Journal of Management Studies*, 30(4), 515–52.

Wolfreys, J. (2008) 'Won't Get Fooled Again? The New Spirit of Capitalism', *International Socialism*, 118, 217–21.

Index

Note: Bold entries refer to figures and tables.